Cartmel Fell

A Patchwork History

Jennifer Forsyth

with illustrations by the author
sections, plans and elevations by Alan Forsyth

HAYLOFT

First published 2007

Hayloft Publishing Ltd, Kirkby Stephen,
Cumbria, CA17 4DJ

tel: + 44 (0) 17683) 42300
fax. + 44 (0) 17683) 41568
e-mail: books@hayloft.eu
web: www.hayloft.eu

Copyright © Jennifer Forsyth 2007

ISBN 1 904524 46 X

A catalogue record for this book is available
from the British Library

The right of Jennifer Forsyth to be identified as the author of this work has been asserted by her in accordance
with the British Copyright Design and Patents Act, 1988.

Apart from any fair dealing for the purposes of research or private study or criticism or review, as permitted under the Copyright Designs and Patents Act 1988 this publication may only be reproduced, stored or transmitted in any form or by any means with the prior permission in writing of the publishers, or in the case of reprographic reproduction in accordance with the terms of the licences issued by the Copyright Licensing Agency.

Printed and bound in the EU

Papers used by Hayloft are natural, recyclable products made from wood grown in sustainable forests.
The manufacturing processes conform to the environmental regulations of the country of origin.

Contents

Acknowledgements 5
Foreword 7
Introduction 8
Parish Government 12

Map 1   Height   17
          Height Quaker Meeting House   25
          Heightside   32
          Hare Hill   34
          Low Tarn Green   38

Map 2   Thorphinsty Hall   41
          High Tarn Green   50
          Foxfield   55
          Pattison How   59
          Simpson Ground   64
          Little Thorphinsty   69
          Ashes   76

Map 3   Gateside   81
          Ravensbarrow Lodge   82
          Swallowmire   85
          Hodge Hill   91
          Chapel House   98
          Bridge House   101
          Cowmire Hall   103
          The School   111
          St Anthony's Church   119
          Danes Court or The Parsonage   130
          Pool Garth   134
          Pool Garth Nook   137
          Jumping Down or Low Green   139
          Blewthwaite   141
          Thornythwaite   145
          School House   147
          Sow How   148

Map 4   Greenthorn   153
          Burblethwaite Hall   155
          Burblethwaite Mill   161
          Collinfield   165
          Bowland Bridge   170
          Goswick Hall   178
          Mason's Arms or Strawberry Bank   180
          Lightwood   183
          Hollins   186
          Addyfield   189
          Bryan Beck   192
          The Lound   199

Map 5   Haycote   202
          Haycote Cottage   205
          Borderside   206
          Barkbooth   210

Map 6   Hartbarrow   214
          Oaks   222
          Ludderburn   228
          Moor How   234
          The Wood   240

Map 7   Old House Beck/Low House Beck   245
          Birket Houses   248
          Rosthwaite   256
          Rulbutts   258

Map 8   Gill Head   259
          Spooner Close   264

Map 9   Tower Wood   268

Map 10   Blakeholme   272
          Blakeholme Wray   275

Appendices and index of family names   277

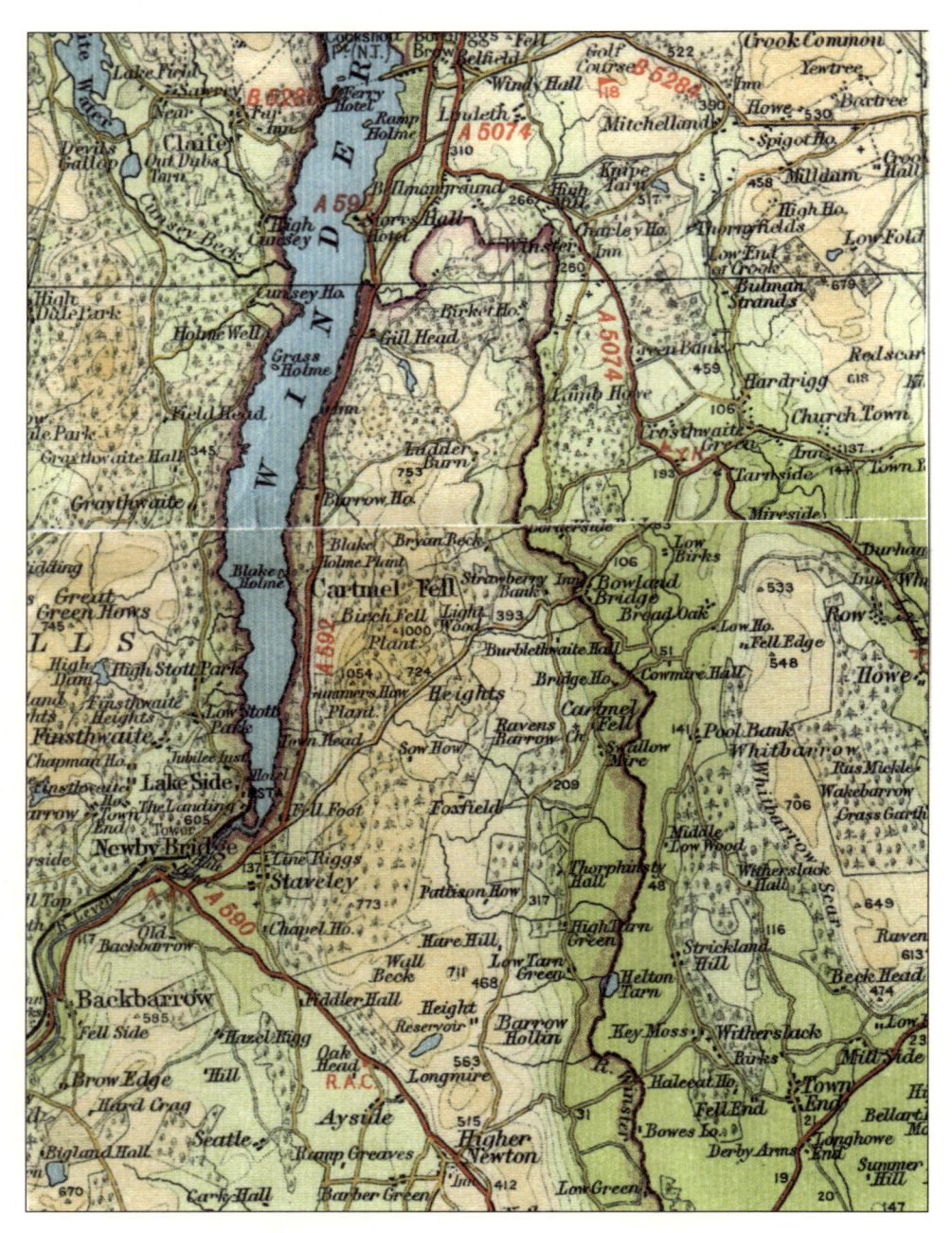

Cartmell Fell in the 1930s. Old Lancashire boundary in purple.

Acknowledgements

THIS list is compiled with great anxiety, because of the fear of forgetting someone who has been helpful. I apologise now for any omissions.

First, I thank my husband, who collaborated in hatching the Cartmel Fell and District Local History Society. He has patiently read drafts and suggested improvements, taken photographs and made plans and drawings of some of the farmsteads. He has also nagged me into completing this compilation of notes and tried to stop me from getting side-tracked.

Next, I should like to thank jointly, all the members of our Society, past and present. They have been enthusiastic in exploring our territory, recording and passing on information of all kinds, not to mention co-opting help from non-members.

The Centre for North West Regional Studies at Lancaster University has provided many a guiding hand, and I would like to thank in particular Dr Jean Turnbull, Dr David Shotter and Professor John Marshall. John was kind enough to read a very early draft and suggest ways of tackling the subject. He also passed on to me some research of his colleague, the late professor G. P. Jones, including many local wills and inventories.

The staff of Kendal and Barrow Record Offices have been unfailingly helpful, and I have had the benefit of Richard Hall's prodigious memory. He remembers his clients' interests and can suggest contacts other than the Record Office sources.

Amongst those who have lent me documents and photographs are Hazel Archer, Helen Caldwell, the Clarke family, Mrs E. Cleasby, Robert James Cockerton, Phyl and Phil Edwards, Claude and Audrey Harrison, David and Pat Hodgson, Ben Holme, Gladys Lishman, Janet Martin, William Matthews, John and Beryl Offley, Mrs. Margaret Pannikkar, the late Les Park, John and Ivy Pearson, Jim Smith, the late Minnie Walker, Geoffrey Wightman and Lucy Woof.

Trevor and Sheila Holland invited me to see and record all the stages of archaeology uncovered at Thorphinsty Hall when it was renovated in 2002.

Correspondence with people doing family research has been copious and includes Jackie Bailey, Paul Baker, R. E. Bell, Jane Boney, Colin and Marion Brackpool, Claire Brockbank, R. and L. M. Copland, Pauline Cowen, Joan Duke, Phil Edwards, Julia Galbraith, Sue Graham, Sydney Graveson, Kath Hayhurst, Ben High, the late Lucy Holmes, Beryl and John Holt, Jane Hughes, David Kinsman, Bill and Marty Lancaster, Andrew Lowe, Ailna and Douglas Martin, John Moore, Michael Newton, Annie Park, Peter Park, Henry Poole, R. W. Poole, the late Joe Scott, Fred Sedgwick, Barry Skinner, Ian Sykes, Walter Tatlock, Suzanne Tiplady and David Watson.

Michael Berry extended to me the freedom of his extensive library, which contains many unusual sources. Jim Wilson has helped me many times with my various computer problems and has always solved them.

Finally, I owe a great debt to Janet Martin. She had just completed the complex task of editing the late Angus Taylor's work *The Websters of Kendal,* and offered to do the same for me. Her knowledge and expertise as an historian has saved me from many a blunder.

Foreword

I have called this book *A Patchwork History* because it is constructed from a rag-bag of information. Some of this is from already published work, some is from documents still in private hands and a good deal is taken from the parish records. Fortunately, those were deposited in Kendal Record Office in 1965, before the parish chest (in which they were kept) was stolen from the church in the 1980s. Wills of local farmers are mostly in Preston Record Office, and these give great insight into pedigrees, and lifestyle too if inventories are attached. More recent history comes from *Voices of Cumbria*, in which Cartmel Fell Local History Society participated for the county Millennium Oral History project, and of course, some is legend or hearsay. I hope I have clearly differentiated between the sources.

The Cartmel Fell Local History Society was founded in 1983 with the express purpose of photographing and researching the farmsteads of the parish, though it now has a much wider remit. Without this cloak of respectability, it seemed impertinent to take photographs, pry into private documents, or even to enquire if any originals were still in the owners' possession. My husband Alan and I tried to photograph all the farms within the year 1993-1994, and whilst we were there asked questions about what the owners knew about their own properties. We asked about date-stones, carved cupboards, water sources, documentation and legends, and also what they themselves considered to be of interest. One of the recurring features we noted was that of ancient farmhouses being guarded by even more ancient yew trees. Once people understood our mission, if anything new came to light, we would get a telephone call or a message via the post office at Bowland Bridge. If a property changed hands, some of the vendors allowed us access to the title deeds in advance, and when alterations uncovered archaeological details we would have a 'phone call: 'Come and have a look at this!'

It is sad that so many solicitors have cleared their cellars of the original parchments and replaced them with typed abstracts of title, but there are still many documents on the fell which go back to the seventeenth and eighteenth centuries and the owners have been exceedingly generous in lending them to me, so I cannot thank them enough. Nearly all these people have given permission to have their documents copied for deposit in the Kendal Record Office, so anyone wishing to follow up the detail can now do so.

The amount of documentation for any given farm is extremely variable. The more important families tend to have had more written about them and produced more paper work, but even paupers get mentioned in parish documents, with disbursements from the parish chest, and these vary from apprenticeship fees to a pair of corsets. A few farms have old estate maps with field names, and these can be useful in locating 'lost' farmsteads, those that have disappeared or changed their names.

After any publication of this kind, people inevitably ask: 'Why didn't you get in touch with me? I know the real story.' If I had known <u>who</u> to ask, I would have done so, but even after these words are printed, the Cartmel Fell Local History Society would like to receive any contradictions or amendments, and I apologise in advance for any mis-representation as it will be my fault entirely.

Jennifer Forsyth, 2007

Introduction

IF Cartmel Fell was inhabited in Neolithic times, no evidence has been found. Part of a stone hammer was discovered near Simpson Ground, but this was in hardcore which had been brought in to make a forestry road, the origin of which was unknown. This artefact is now in the Ruskin Museum at Coniston.

The anonymous biographer of St. Cuthbert wrote of 'the Saint of Cartmel,' who had a donation from King Ecgfrith of Northumberland 'and all the Britons in it.' This king died in AD685, but how far the land of Cartmel extended at that time is not known. The term 'Britons' usually meant those western people who spoke a form of Welsh, and place-names of old Welsh extend up to the Scottish borders in the north-western corner of England.

The Vikings came to the western Lake District from Ireland and the Isle of Man before the Norman Conquest, and many of the place-names on Cartmel Fell reflect a Norse origin, including the very word 'Fell'. '*Thwaite*s', which abound, pinpoint the clearance of scrub or woodland, and we surmise that the Norseman Thorfin must have been a man of property, as his pass or *sty* winds up the lower slopes of the fell, passing Thorphinsty Hall. One of the earliest recorded surnames on the fell is that of the Swainson tribe, or Svenson as it must originally have been. Perhaps Sven came with Thorfin and his descendants had a few centuries to consolidate their holdings, as by the sixteenth and seventeenth centuries they were wealthy and had status and considerable property.

Cartmel Fell was once held by the Priory at Cartmel, and it is assumed to have been the pasture for the priors' flocks. The Priory was saved from total destruction at the dissolution of the monasteries because it was the parish church for the people of the town. It was also the mother church for the surrounding townships, of which Cartmel Fell was one of seven. These divisions were to a large extent self-governing, each having its own rotating officials to take care of the parish management. The chapel warden was the accountant and manager for church affairs, the petty constable was responsible for law and order, perhaps travelling to quarter or petty sessions, and to help him there was a grave. The overseer of the poor had the task of finding homes for the orphans and destitute of his area and apportioning money for food and clothing, but also to apprentice children so that they might not be a burden on the parish, which was not a wealthy one. These officials were all yeomen, owning their estates, and in Cartmel Fell, there was an ordered progression of parish officers from one farm to the next, repeated cyclically over perhaps 30 to 40 years, but each man serving for one year. The method of appointment changed over the centuries, but after the dissolution of the monasteries until the end of the seventeenth century, these men were officially appointed at Cartmel Church on Easter Monday. After that, the system gradually fragmented and the chapelries made their own appointments. It seems that deputies could serve, for whatever reason, and the account books in Kendal Record Office attest to this. There were variations in the way in which parishes divided these tasks, with some sub-divisions of the officers' duties, but throughout Cumbria a similar system pertained. It was quite usual for a 'surveyor of the highways' to be appointed in a parish, but Cartmel Fell does not seem ever to have had such an official. The roads might have been described as by-ways or mere tracks, so perhaps drainage and surfacing were left to individuals, but tarmac was not laid on the lesser roads across the fell until the mid-twentieth century, and public spirited locals still clear the drains today.

Cartmel Fell was originally in the county of Lancashire 'North of the Sands' until it became part of Cumbria in 1974. This northern part of the county was always somewhat isolated by geography, as the road around the northern part of Morecambe Bay via Milnthorpe was not only circuitous, but up to 30 miles longer than the intrinsically more dangerous, but far more direct routes across the sands at low tide. The ever-changing channels of the rivers empty into the funnel of Morecambe Bay, thus creating quick-sands. The bay is wide and flat, so the tide recedes for miles, but when it begins to flow, it races across the empty sands at the speed of a galloping horse, so wise travellers used to put themselves into the care of the guide. This service had been performed since monastic times, the priors appointing the guide. After the Reformation, the office was for generations an hereditary one of the Carter family. Today, the bay crossing is usually undertaken to raise money for charities, and the guide still stakes out the safe route, using 'brobs', which are small branches of evergreen, but in former times, travellers across the sands needed a real purpose to embark upon the journey.

The area of Cartmel Fell was described in the 1851 Mannex directory as being 'an extensive alpine region,' and this fairly describes the parish. The fell extends for about eight miles along the eastern shore of Windermere, and whereas today the lake fringe has many large houses, built by industrialists and merchants in the nineteenth and twentieth centuries, in earlier times the dwellings here were few, and the road was nearer to the lake. The upper reaches of the western fell are steep and craggy, rising to the 321 metre summit of Gummers How, so there were no settlements here. The eastern side is gentler, and this is where most of the earliest farmsteads can be found. The river Winster winds through the valley bottom and this was not only the parish boundary, but also that between Lancashire and Westmorland, until the county of Cumbria was created in 1974.

More land was taken into private ownership during the enclosures of the late eighteenth and early nineteenth century. Until then, the uplands of Cartmel Fell had been common grazing for the parishioners, but the Napoleonic Wars had caused great inflation and anxiety about food supplies. Further south, much of England's common land had already been enclosed by various Acts of Parliament, often with great loss to the cottagers who kept a few geese or sheep. The surveyor's report for this parish was completed in 1797, but the implementation of the work must have taken many years. The huge hand-written tome describing and mapping the individual enclosures, and listing their ownership, is in Kendal Record Office with another in Preston Record Office. The schedule includes stipulations as to the depth and width of drainage ditches and maps show where new walls were to divide up the heathland. Today, one might wonder if all the expense was justified, as rough peaty upland is fairly intractable, even with huge doses of lime. The land was allotted to the yeomen, according to the acreage owned at the time, so therefore known as 'ments,' often shortened to 'lots.' All over land, hundreds of miles of walls were thrown over the fells, the construction of which may have provided a temporary income for dispossessed commoners. The local commentator of the area was William Pearson of Borderside in Crosthwaite and he remarked that enclosures in Cartmel Fell only affected one man, a horse-dealer who kept his animals on the common land.

The mode of life on the fell must have changed very little between 1537 when Cartmel Priory was dissolved, and the end of the nineteenth century, but the industries were far more numerous than today. Even the smaller becks had mills using water-power. These were mostly for fulling woven woolen cloth, but every parish had at least one corn mill which was owned by the lord of the manor. By the nineteenth century, water-power was being used for saw-mills, such as at Gill Head, and for bobbin-turning for the Lancashire cotton mills. There was a small amount of iron industry on the fell in the seventeenth century, at Burblethwaite, Smithy Hill and Thorphinsty, and charcoal burning and other woodland industries kept much of the woodland in coppiced form. Today, these coppice woods have grown to straggling heights, as they are no longer cut every fifteen or so years, but their form can be identified by their multiple trunks. Another important woodland industry was that of bark-stripping for tanning. This task was performed in early summer and was usually the bark of young oak trees, but after larches were introduced in the eighteenth century, their bark was used too. The farm Barkbooth is in the Winster valley bottom and can be dated back the sixteenth century. The name indicates where the bark was stored before use, as it had to be kept dry.

It would seem that the population of our parish is today much the same as it was in the seventeenth century, if one accepts that families averaged two adults and two and a half children, but the make-up of those numbers is very different. Farming and the woodland industries were once the bread-and-butter of the fell-folk, but today there are many retired couples, few children and an increasing number of holiday homes, though in Cartmel Fell these are mostly new conversions of farm buildings. There was a population bulge in the nineteenth and early twentieth centuries when the school became very full, necessitating a new wing to be built, but the growth was short-lived. Evacuees in the Second World War created another temporary increase in schoolchildren, but these numbers subsided when the war was over.

A visitor from the past might have trouble in identifying the ancient farmsteads, as so many alterations and additions have taken place over a thousand years or more, but quite often there is a core of an ancient building hidden behind an eighteenth century exterior. In some cases, the original house was demolished and the usable materials recycled in a nearby dwelling such as at Barkbooth. In other instances, like Bryan Beck or Borderside, the old house was relegated to barn status when the new house was built. Timbers were valuable and re-used, and an example can be seen in the eighteenth century barn at Little Thorphinsty, where earlier timbers have been used in the construction.

There is an oft-repeated legend that house beams were old ship's timbers, because they are often obviously notched for other purposes. Some beams may indeed have been salvaged from ships if the houses were near the coast, but in an age of muddy tracks and no wheeled transport, dragging oak timbers up the fell would have been a mammoth task.

The twentieth century brought the outside world much closer to the fell farmers. Motor transport was a novelty but delivery vans from Windermere brought goods and news to outlying farms. The railways had increased mobility in the previous century, and farming families could seek opportunities further afield. A branch of the Taylors of Thorphinsty Hall became cow-keepers in Liverpool - the calves were sent home by train to be reared in the country. Eggs were sent to Liverpool by the same means. The local roads were still largely unsurfaced until after the Second World War and electricity did not arrive until the 1960s, though one or two enterprising farmers had water turbines built on their becks as early as the 1930s.

There are not many roads traversing the contours of the fell, so in order to make it easier to identify the farmsteads, I have arranged them as though one were traveling from south to north, with diversions. The maps are taken from the 1888-1893 Ordnance Survey, 25 inches to the mile.

Parish Government

UNTIL the dissolution of the monasteries, the task of looking after the populace was largely an affair of the church. The priors at Cartmel would have provided for the poor of the parish, whilst extracting tithes which helped to pay for the service. Apart from relieving the local poor, mendicants and travellers would be helped on their way with a penny or two or a meal, and the system was too good to scrap altogether when Henry VIII reformed the church and its powers.

In Cartmel, the mother church of St Mary still held its position over the chapelries of the seven divisions. These were Upper and Lower Holker, Upper and Lower Allithwaite, Flookburgh, Staveley-in-Cartmel and Cartmel Fell. Dues were paid to the mother church, but each chapelry had its own group of men who could be termed a management team. The principal members were the chapelwarden, who ran the ecclesiastical affairs, the constable, who was responsible to the magistrates for law and order and collection of taxes, the overseer of the poor and the grave. This last post is ill defined. It used to mean the official who collected the lord's rent, but in this area he probably assisted the constable when necessary. The area being managed within the greater parish was known as a 'township'. Some such townships had many other officials including overseers of the highways, hedge-lookers and moss-lookers. Cartmel Fell had only by-ways, but someone must have seen that they were negotiable, at least with pack-horses. It was noted that no wheeled traffic was to be found on the fell in the seventeenth century. Papers from Cowmire Hall show that disputes on hedging responsibilities were settled 'by ancient custom', meaning that whichever farm had maintained the fence or hedge in the past, continued to do so. Changes in ownership might result in such disputes. The moss-lookers controlled the digging of peat, but in this township this must have been deemed an un-necessary post. As in other parishes, such as Hawkshead, this body of men were known as the twenty-four, but as each parish contributed four men, and four times seven equals twenty-eight, another parish must have been added at some time in history. Possibly the system existed in pre-reformation times, and the priors, as representatives of Cartmel, were not counted.

In most south Cumbrian parishes, all the men, and occasionally women, held their posts in rotation. It seems from existing parish records, that only yeomen held parish office. If a man had more than one estate, he did duty for each, and often in successive years. Some parishes had a rotation of two or even three years for those holding office, but this was not the case in Cartmel Fell. The account books of the seventeenth and eighteenth centuries are in Kendal Record Office and from these one can see that a steady progression around the fell was the way the various offices were apportioned. For instance, in the case of the constable, in 1726, John Philipson of Hodge Hill held the post and in the successive years the position rotated from Pool Garth, Blewthwaite, Burblethwaite, Collinfield, Goswick Hall, and so on, past Addyfield. It was a democratic system, and the time-consuming work was over in a twelve-month.

The constable had to make journeys to the petty sessions or quarter sessions, and if there was some sort of township disturbance, this had to be dealt with summarily. An instance in the account books is where an entry for 18 May 1759 brings an intake of breath: 'By cash pay'd to Mr. Thomas Atkinson for costs on account of William Harrison's Tryal for Murder of his wife Allis.' In the margin is a note 'Moorhow.'

The overseer of the poor had an unenviable task, and his accounts open a window into the life of an eighteenth-century pauper. If the bread-winner died and he had been only a farm worker, his widow had no means of moving to find work, as only her parish of origin was bound to help. Widows, widowers and children were dealt with in enterprising and ingenious ways. There is an instance where two paupers helped each other mutually. John Philipson was widowed in 1736, leaving him to cope with a new-born baby. He was a poor man, so the parish paid for his wife's burial, the child's clothes and then a series of wet-nurses for the baby starting at 1s.5d. a week and reducing to 4d. a week when the child was two-years-old. The first of these nurses was the wife of pauper Stephen Crackelt who had lost her own child, so the two families were mutually supportive.

Some years were more of a drain on the community coffers than others, and the funds were managed in several ways. Men of substance and standing had moneys in their own hands for investment, and they paid interest on the capital. House-to-house collections were made to collect what would now be called rates or community tax, and these were divided between the roads, the church and the poor. After a bad year, the rate would go up, but these were quite separate charges from the national taxes for windows, land, hearths, or whatever the government devised. In Jersey, an identical system exists today. The parish principals, headed by the constable, assess the needs of the district and set the rate accordingly. Where the community is closely knit and its needs are understood by all, there is a common will.

None of the upland areas were wealthy, so what little money there was had to be used on the residents, but it was also national policy to serve the needy only in their home parish. To this end, vagrants were either arrested or hustled on. An entry for 1742 in the constable's accounts is for two shillings to a Captain Simpson, for making a search for vagrants. In that same year, there were bills for the militia of £3.16s., and to cleaning their muskets, six shillings. Earlier, in 1739, Joshua Poole charged the parish two shillings for drawing up a warrant to 'take' Edmund Warriner.

Even though money was tight, there are several entries in the overseer of the poor's accounts which show that compassion sometimes overcame guidelines. A woman called Scotson had a bastard child within the parish in 1737. Maybe she was a farm servant, but her birthplace was in Colton not Cartmel Fell. This child seems to have been born with a double hernia, and the sum of 1s.6d. was spent on hernia belts before the mother and child were despatched back to Colton the following year. Another instance is where a collection was made to relieve the sufferings of French Protestants, but this was in response to a national appeal or 'brief'.

Orphaned children were boarded around the township at the expense of the parish, and this could be a big drain on resources. As soon as possible, apprenticeships were found for them and several such cases can be followed through the pages of the account books. The children of pauper Henry Garnett were scattered round the fell in the 1720s. Thomas Kilner of Pool Garth took in Mary and Esther, and then we see that Mary has been 'bound' later in 1729 at Newby Bridge. This meant bound as an apprentice, but in what trade it does not say. Girls were often just bound to learn housecraft or farm work, but as with the boys, they were unpaid until they were 21, receiving only their keep, but this was true of the farmers' sons and daughters also. We know from Jonathan Wilson's diary of this period, that his apprentice malt-maker ran away, but he did not get very far before his master caught him and brought him back.

In 1749, a decision must have been made to provide a 'Poor House'. This was built on land acquired by the parish to let, the income from which would swell the parish chest. The house was called Low House, and is off to the west of the road up to Foxfield and is now a total ruin. As was the custom of the day, a sort of party was held at 'the rearing.' This was when the timber frames for the roof were hoisted into position and fixed, a task requiring many strong men from the parish, but also an occasion for merrymaking. In this instance, the overseers paid out 2s.11d. for bread and cheese, and often a wealthy landowner would provide ale for the workers, but this would not appear in the parish accounts. In 1755 heavy expenses were incurred at Low House for fencing, walling, leading stone and for drawing a contract for letting the land. It might have seemed a good idea at the time to have a custom-built poor house, but on paper it appears to have been a constant drain on funds.

It would seem that this very personal grip on township affairs worked reasonably well in the north, but when poverty in the southern half of the country was seen to be acute in the early nineteenth century, central government intervened. In 1834, localities were divided into 'unions', the guardians of which fixed the rates for a much larger area than was formerly the case. Whereas this was welcomed as a vital step in the south and midlands, at first it was bitterly resented in the northern counties. One of the changes was that succour was refused to the able-bodied poor, except in the workhouse. These were places of dread, from which the only hope of escape was by being hired. In the case of children under sixteen who became apprentices or servants, the relieving officer was expected to inspect the conditions under which they were living. This meant twice-yearly visits, and an enquiry into the working conditions and food. Only the larger towns had custom-built workhouses, so paupers from rural parishes might be many miles from their friends and relations, though in this respect they were no worse off than ordinary farm servants.

The establishment of urban workhouses was not new. They had existed since Tudor times in the form of hospitals such as Christ's Hospital and St Thomas's, which were for the sick and infirm, and Bridewell for the vigorous idle. What was new in Victorian times was the huge increase in extreme poverty. The poor-rate became too much of a burden on the ordinary parish, and instability threatened everyday life in the south. Between 1837 and 1872, the total expense of poor relief doubled in England, but the overall national pattern seems to have hardly touched Cartmel Fell. Because the population of the parish remained fairly constant, and because there was no decline in agriculture or woodland management, workers were earning far more than the national average (see Thorphinsty Hall). There was no pool of casual labour to call on, but there were itinerant labourers who came from Ireland at harvest and potato-picking, though only in ones and twos.

In hindsight, central government seems to have resorted to a drastic measure to cope with a situation that threatened national stability, but the overseers of the poor in each parish had more humane solutions to a timeless problem, or so it would seem from the Cartmel Fell account books.

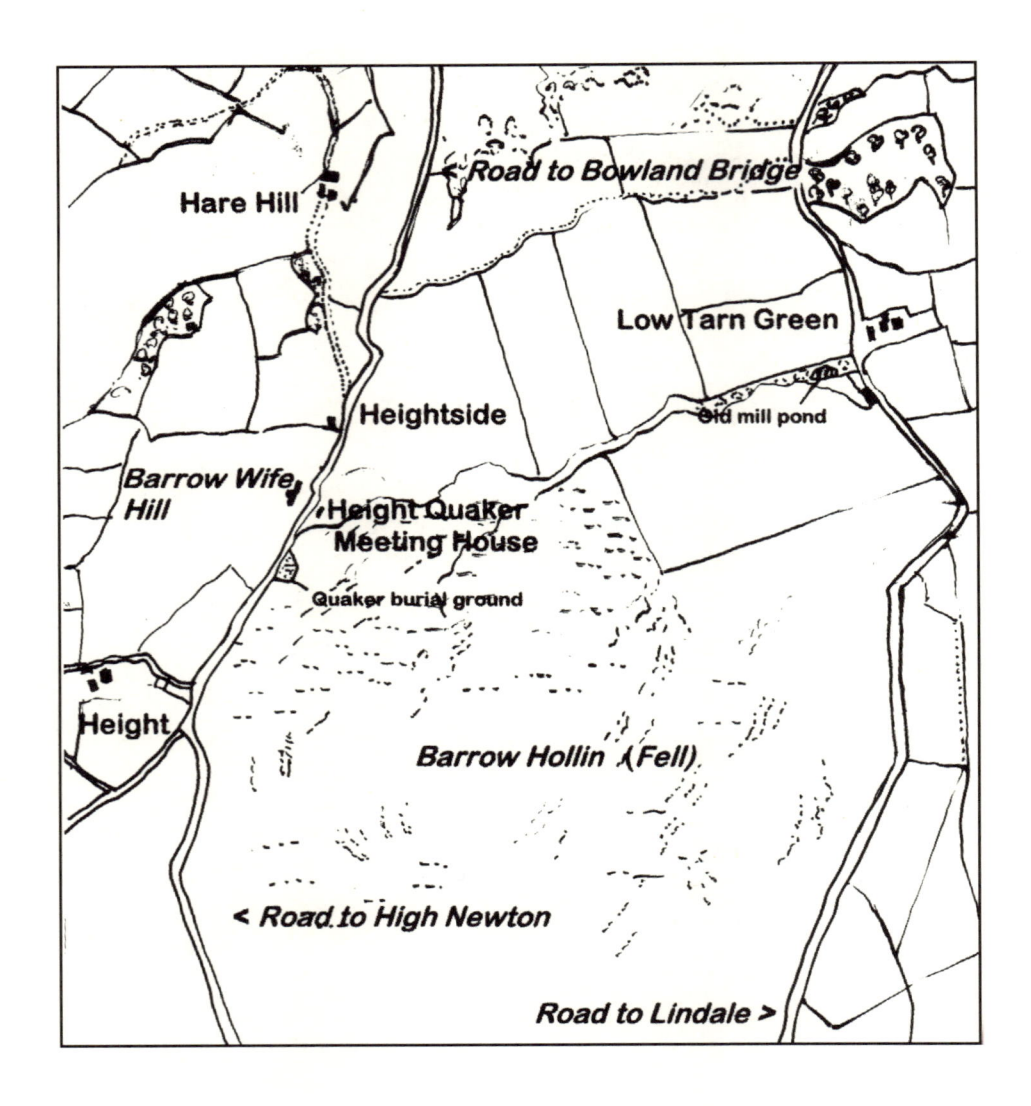

CARTMEL FELL

Height

THERE are two areas known as Height or Heights on Cartmel Fell, and these are now differentiated by parish boundaries, one being in Upper Allithwaite, the other in Cartmel Fell. In earlier times there was no such distinction, so it is not always possible to identify a farm which is referred to in the parish registers or wills. A further confusion is in the use of 'Height' in old documents to cover a very wide area, some farms being a mile apart; in fact, Height was a district.

Today, the most imposing building known as Height is a farm at the southern end of the fell, near the summit of the road to High Newton. It is in the symmetrical Georgian tradition, smooth-faced and displaying no traces of vernacular architecture externally. It was built to make a statement, and is a monument to the Gibson family who commissioned it from the locally well-known firm of Websters, architects and masons. There is an inner core of an older house, invisible from the outside. Just below this farm and to the north is the Height Quaker Meeting House.

Behind the present-day Height farmhouse is a yard and farm buildings, but on closer inspection, some of these appear to have been dwellings also. One, with no less than three fireplaces, has been restored by the present owner with guidance from the Lake District Planning Board. The other, with a small wooden mullioned window, is still in farm use as a barn.

One of these old houses was probably the home of Lawrence Newton. It was he who willed land and money to the Friends to build their Meeting House in 1677 at Height. We know from Quaker records that early meetings were held in Lawrence Newton's own house many years before the Meeting House was built, and a marriage was recorded there in 1660 on the tenth day of the fifth month, (July) which style of dating was the Quaker usage as they shunned the month names commemorating Roman gods, (the year at that time began on 25 March). The marriage was between Hugh Tickell of Portinscale and Dorothy Pearson of Pow (Pool) Bank in Witherslack. The Pearsons of Pool Bank were staunch Quakers until the twentieth century, and founder members of the Friends in this area after George Fox's visit to Pool Bank in 1652. Lawrence Newton was buried at Height in 1676, the year before the Meeting House was built.

An early record of the Newtons is in the Cartmel Priory burial register, when John of Height died in 1653. Without doubt, the entry refers to this Upper Allithwaite area, but earlier records are less clear. In 1594, at Crosthwaite, William Wallas's wife, of 'Heytsht' in Cartmel Fell was godmother to Janat Wilson's bastard son, John Lewis. Two years later, William Rowlandson died and left his property at Height to his son James. It is possible that these references are to the tiny ruin of a house behind a bothy on a fell track to Sow How. The track continues to the now almost levelled site of the farm once known as Prentices, and this too was 'At the Height'. Prentices was demolished in the nineteenth century, and the stone was used to build the dams for the artificial tarns nearby.

Thomas Bigland of the Height christened his

daughter Anne in 1663, and in the following years christened John, James, Jennet, and finally Elizabeth, at Cartmel Priory in 1673. This was roughly contemporary with Lawrence Newton and it seems that the Biglands and Newtons were close neighbours in the mid-seventeenth century. An extract from the Cartmel Priory accounts reads as follows: 'February 2nd, 1661. John Bigland of the Height hath given £5 for the use of the Poor in the upper end of Holker Townshippe, and the same to be put furth, and the use thereof to be distributed yearlie at Easter... the use thereof to be given so that it may not ease the rich. John Burns of Speel Bank hath the money, and he hath laid a gaige for it.' The donor of this money was probably the John Bigland who was buried at Cartmel Priory on Christmas Day 1667. The family were related to the Biglands of Bigland Hall.

Towards the close of the seventeenth century, the names which occur specifically at Height in the Cartmel parish registers are those of Barwick, Newton, Bigland and Gibson. George, James and Jennet, the children of Thomas Bigland were buried at Cartmel, as were husband and wife John and Margaret Gibson and their son Edmund, also Agnes Barwick who was entered in the register by her maiden name, but was actually Edmund's widow. In a Cartmel Priory rental of 1539, one of the tenants was Lawrence Newton of Cartmel Fell, so the somewhat unusual family christian name was a long-standing one.

The Gibsons were the most enduring family at Height, however, having been there at least since the mid-seventeenth century, but maybe well before that. In 1662, the Cartmel parish register noted the baptism of John, son of John Gibson of Height. The last of the Gibson line was George, who died in 1859, but more of him later.

Lawrence Newton must have been a man of substance (but maybe no heirs) to have left both land and money to the Friends. He also made many other charitable bequests within Cartmel parish, so his relationship to the Quakers is slightly ambiguous. For a while at least, he seems to have had sympathy for the Friends and their ideals whilst maintaining a foothold in the parish church. He was buried in the Friends' burial ground eventually, and had meetings at his house, so perhaps he had a gradual conversion. In the Cartmel churchwarden's accounts for 1675 there is an entry: 'Payd Lawrence Newton for killing Mould warpes (moles) these being the first yt was payd for in this parish.' It seems likely that this was the same man, as had there been several of the same name in the parish, some identification might have been made, such as 'the elder', or 'of the Height'.

Lawrence Newton's bequest to the Friends engendered quantities of documents, copies of which are now in Kendal Record Office. From these we can find names and addresses of the trustees who were Quakers in the area, but in 1996 an even richer source came to light, and a unique record of a house and its occupants. The farm in which these papers were found is now the only one to bear the name 'Height'. The present owner began a programme of restoration and reclamation when he inherited the farm, and during the course of clearing and sorting, he came across some photographs and books which he thought might be of interest to Cartmel Fell Local History Society. The ledger with a torn leather cover was a mixture of a day-book, diary and accounts. This in itself is perhaps not unusual, but this long, narrow volume had been used by whoever had lived at the Height for over 250 years. The first entries were the diary of a Quaker who later lived in the cottage adjoining the Meeting House. Later entries in the mid-eighteenth century include farm records, buying and selling of stock with current prices, dates and names of cows bulled, and recipes for medicines. Another user of the ledger was a Stockholm tar dealer, and he lists his customers and some addresses all over the district. A few pages have been used by one of the Gibson children to practice copperplate handwriting, together with embellishing scrolls.

After this interesting find had been taken to Kendal Record Office for copying, yet another discovery was made, but of a different nature. Dr John Marshall and other local historians have shown that the standard of education was unusually high in the counties which now comprise Cumbria. The levels of literacy and numeracy were well above the national average, and not just limited to the gentry and wealthier merchants, and the exercise-books from the Height endorse this. Between the years 1811 and 1816, young George Gibson was walking daily to Staveley-in-Cartmel village school He must have been a clever and diligent child, but his schoolmaster must have been a brilliant and far-sighted man also. Among the books, which are of varying thickness, are all kinds of imaginative ways of teaching mathematics. All of these have a strongly practical application to trade and industry, and in particular, to surveying. The diagrams which the children drew in their copy-books are as precise as steel engravings, the arithmetic involved changing currencies for foreign trading, changing yards to ells for exporting cloth to Paris, even explaining 'Forty Pieces of Silver' in shekels. In particular, land surveying was covered extensively, and methods of measuring uneven ground are shown in detailed diagrams. It may be that there was a family connection between the Gibsons of Height and two well-known eighteenth-century Gibsons in the mathematical field, but so far this is not clear. As mentioned in the section dealing with Hollins farm, William Gibson or 'Willy o' the Hollins' was known internationally for his mathematical genius, and he was known to have kept a school, but this was said to have been in Cartmel and these exercise books are clearly labelled 'Staveley School'. The other Gibson was John, a surveyor who died in Cartmel in 1824, but there is no evidence that either of these namesakes had any influence at Staveley School. We do know however, that the last schoolmaster to combine the office with that of minister, was the Rev. Martin Wilson Lamb, who died in 1828. He was mentioned in a Government Charities Report of 1820, so it was probably his flair for teaching which is illustrated in George Gibson's many school books.

It seems that the Gibsons were originally farmers, but by judicious use of any spare cash, they gradually accumulated property in the Newton area and in Grange. The first written evidence of this family comes from another leather-bound notebook. This had a metal clasp in its heyday, and could perhaps have been locked. It begins in August 1753, 'Edmund Gibson, Hic Liber est Meus' and opens with prosaic household accounts. Agey (Agnes) Redhead had an advance of 10s. 6d. from her annual wage of two guineas, and this entry is followed by a remedy for a beast that is thought to be 'in the Fellon,' that is with mastitis:

1 pennerth of Aneseeds
1 pennerth of Fennel seeds
1 pennerth of Turnbrick (Turmeric)
1 pennerth of Longpepper
Diepenty half ouns. (This was a mixture of five ingredients)
Genson (Gentian?) half an ouns
Galinkel, (Gallingale) half an ouns
Medersat (Meadowsweet) half an ouns
Comon treackel half a pound
Two good Drams of Brandy & a small Butter kek, all put in Qart of frish Drink hung ofer the fire but not give to the beast Boild, Lukewarm.

It is very doubtful whether this cow drink could have had the slightest effect on mastitis, but at least the farmer was doing something. All those herbs might have been used to better effect to keep flies off the beast's udder.

Page two of this notebook goes back four years to 1749, and contains a series of sales to different people. These include sheep, nine at a total of £2.11s.6d., a calf at 8s.6d., fifteen stones of wool at £4.0.0d. and 'Tow Keslop skins, 6d.' This last item is the dried stomach of a calf or sheep, which contains the rennet for cheese making. A slightly mystifying item in December of 1754 was seven 'Crismos skins' at 10d. each. Were these also keslop skins? It seems too cheap for hides. The following year in June, an entry shows that charcoal burning was part of the Gibson enterprise: 'Livered 3 Lod & a half of Cols to Martin Harriman (of Lightwood) for Backbarrow Compony, valey £5.12s.6d.' This charcoal would have been used for smelting at the iron foundry in Backbarrow.

Much money was lent over the years, and 'Ould' Betty, Edward Noble and Edward Barrow seem to have been frequent borrowers. The men borrowed in guineas, old Betty a few shillings only.

Edmund had a son John who was born in 1747, and a daughter Mary who was still under 21 at her father's death in 1766, so John was charged with overseeing her continued education. We can deduce from various entries in the notebook that Edmund had also been responsible for his younger sibling's education. This was George Gibson, who became the vicar of Biggleswade in Bedfordshire. Over £600 of George's money was invested at a rate of 9d. in the pound per annum. One of the largest investments was in a mortgage for William Jopson, a maltster from Lindale. This amounted to £420, not an impressive amount today, but the equivalent value in 2005 was around £31,000, according to the Bank of England figures.

Amongst the several rent books, spanning 100 years or more of the Gibsons' tenants, is a list of the varieties of apples used in replanting an orchard. The only one which is readily recognisable today is a Ribston Pippin. Some of the others include: Winter Scarlet, White Hawthorn, Irish Codling, Daker's Delight, Gray Oakhams, White Massock, Margels, Greenup Pippins, Brickarts, Crawfords, Green Soldiers, Ten Shillings, White Squares, Prussian Pippins and Wigan Virgins. All these apple trees were planted at Widow Postlethwaite's in Grange on 13 March 1814. At this period, John Gibson was married to a woman from a Quaker family, so perhaps it was she who entered this transaction as the third month of the year. An interesting footnote on the page reads: '4 Newtown Pippins from America planted in highest row in new orchard at Grange next Greenw'd House. All 50 trees cost £1.13s.4d.' A couple of years before that, we had been at war with America and this last variety is not listed in the 1812 catalogue of new plantings as it would not have been obtainable.

The Gibsons were slowly and very carefully consolidating their farming interests and accumulating property. The various ledgers found at Height show accounts for cottages all over the townships which make up Cartmel parish. The rents are recorded on the credit page, and the debits show repairs to these properties, but also many outgoing annuities, and it seems that one financed the other. An example is on 29 December 1823 for £3.9s.0d to James Rowlandson, and the same amount at mid-summer. Fifty years earlier, Mary Hartley signed receipts for her annuity of £2.10s., which was paid twice yearly. By slow accumulation of properties, the Gibsons had transformed their farming interests of the seventeenth and eighteenth centuries into what was in effect, a private building society. They had enough capital to advance loans, invest the savings of others, and purchase houses, the rents of which paid dividends to the investors. The account books in the mid 1700s are somewhat haphazard, maybe half a page of one transaction being ruled off to make out a receipt for an annuitant, and ending with prices paid for labour. There are a few pages of one account book devoted to mortgages, and the terms on which money was lent. On the same pages were sums lent on mortgage for £134, £25 and £60. Some of this was being invested for Edmund Gibson's younger brother George, the vicar mentioned above.

This small notebook in the Height collection recorded other accounts. Towards the end of the book, and six years before he died, Edmund wrote:

'5 of August. Mary Gibson went to Cartmel 1760. Be it remembered I have paed 8 shillings towards her bord to Betty Trimble all p'd for by me, E. Gibson.' Evidently Edmund's daughter Mary was going to have some education in Cartmel, but unfortunately there is no indication as to where this was to be obtained. When her father died, Edmund's will shows that Mary was still a minor, but she received the handsome dowry of £300, including a £10 bequest from her uncle, the Rev. George Gibson. John, her brother, was to see that she continued her education and he was to provide her clothes until she was 21.

John was only 20 when his father died, but his mother Ellin lived for another forty years and must have helped her son to run the various enterprises. There was their own farm to manage, the tenanted farms to keep an eye on and various financial affairs involving loans, mortgages and bonds to many people. Woodlands in Newton were coppiced for charcoal burning, and maybe there were other business schemes not included in this one notebook. Edmund Gibson and his son John have both used it but their hand-writing differs greatly, the son's being elegant and embellished on occasion with beautifully executed flourishes. In the 1760s, John Gibson began to enter his own accounts and occasionally he turned his back on the day-to-day records of salving hogs (2 days on Nov. 29th, 1775, 1s.3d), and he entered a little poem, 'Inclined to Marry.' Unfortunately, this poem has no date, so we can only guess that it was written between 1766 and 1773, as it occurs between those pages. John was born in 1747, so he might have been in his late 'teens when he copied out the following:

*Would not have you, Strephon, Choose a Mate
from too exalted or too mean a State;
for in both these we may expect to find
A creeping Spirit, or a haughty Mind.
Who move within the middle Reason, Shares
the least disquiets and the smalest Cares.
Let her Extraction with true Lustre shine;
if something brighter, not too bright for thine;
her Education, Liberal, not great;
Neither inferior, nor above her state.
Let her have wit, but let that wit be free
from Affectation, Pride and Pedantry:
for the Effect of Woman's wit is such,
too little is as dangerous as too much:
but chifly, let her humour close with thine,
Unless where yours does to a Fault incline;
the leas Disparity in this Destroys
like Sulphorous blasts, the very buds of joys.
her person, amiable, straight and free
from natural or chance, Deformity.
let not her years exced, if equal thine;
for Women past their vigour soon decline.
her fortune competent; & if thy sight
Can reach so far, take Care t'is gather'd right
if thine's enough, then hers may be the Less:
do not aspaire to Riches in Excess
for that which makes our lives delightful prove
is a genteel sufficiency and love.*

This charming ditty is sandwiched between orders executed for tar and a receipt from Mary Hartley, who had invested her lands at Ayside in an annuity with Edmund Gibson for £2.10s. half-yearly.

If the rhyme was written by a romantically inclined young man, it was a long time before he found the desirable and fitting companion. John Gibson did not marry until 1796 when he was close on 50, his bride being Susannah Hall of Newton, and they were married at Cartmel Fell by John Allenby. This was a mixed marriage of Protestant and Quaker, the Halls of Newton being Quakers until the twentieth century. History does not relate what the respective families thought of this marriage, but relationships must have been maintained, as the Halls were the main beneficiaries of the Gibsons' only child. Susannah gave John a son and heir in December 1799, and they christened him George. Susannah died ten years before her husband in 1824, aged 62, and may have died suddenly as she left no will, but her estate was worth £100. John lived to be 86, as the burial entry for 4 October 1834 records in Cartmel Fell parish register. Although the Gibsons seem to have been close to the Friends, both as neighbours and in business, they were members of the Church of England, but Susannah's burial was not recorded in Cartmel parish.

In William Pearson's memoirs, he recalls how anxious John Gibson was to have a rookery at Height. He was convinced that rooks did far more good than harm to the land, eating the chafer grubs which destroy grass roots, and devouring many other pests. He procured rooks' eggs from neighbours, and experimented with putting them in magpies' nests in his own trees, but to no avail. Finally, the rooks took pity on him, and came of their own accord. Despite there being plenty of tall trees around, there are no rooks at Height farm today.

When his father died, George inherited all the Height estate and many rented properties in Newton and surrounding districts, but his real-estate kingdom was still expanding. After inheriting the estate from his father, he may then have commissioned the firm of Websters, architects, to enlarge and gentrify this old farm, but the accounts for these transactions are not amongst the many documents.

On making enquiries as to whether anyone had done research into the Websters, the writer was introduced to Angus Taylor through Kathleen Hayhurst of Burton History Society. Angus came to look at Height and proclaimed it undeniably Webster, and identified it as the work of George of that family in *The Websters of Kendal*. The exterior is austere, but the two front rooms have exuberant plaster-work, somewhat in the Strawberry Hill style, with the marble fireplaces of different hues in either room.

In 1848 George Gibson bought Pool Bank in Witherslack, the old family holding of the Pearson family, and in the same year he had a public house built in Low Newton. This building can be identified by a carved datestone over a window at the roadside, G.G. 1848, and the architect was again George Webster. In 1851, this house was listed as an inn in the census, and it was farmed then by Robert Barber who had 100 acres of land and four labourers. Those familiar with Low Newton will recognise the farm by the recently converted barn (1997) on the opposite side of the busy road. The work for the inn was put out to tender and William Matthews was the successful bidder for the walling and slating; presumably a member of the well-known family of master-wallers from the Lound in Cartmel Fell. At this period, George Webster was living just down the road from Low Newton at Eller How, the house his father Francis had begun.

The paper-backed cash book in which the building costs of the inn are recorded has a mixture of entries. They vary from the mundane, such as frequent purchases of floor cloths and black lead, to very substantial bank statements. One entry was an account of a violent affray at Newton, possibly written in court, in which a man called Young from Witherslack was arrested and three other men were named by Joseph Stones, the police officer. Later in the book we find that on 5 May 1851, George Gibson held £555 in the Joint Stock Bank and £4829.18s.8d. in Wakefield's Bank; he paid in that day £140 and took a note for £722.

This methodical accounting for all his activities seems to stem from his schooldays. One of the school books from Staveley is entitled 'The True

A school book of George Gibson's.

Station Method of Keeping Double Entry. George Gibson 1814'. This had many imaginary household accounts and must have been the model for his real accounting in later life. One item from the school exercises was 'To a Writing Master, a quarter, 10s.6d.' This lesson was very well learned by the pupil. Apart from household needs, the notebooks record many farming orders. In 1847-8, Mr. Meldrum supplied 35lbs. white clover seeds, 12lbs. of Timothy (Common Cat's Tail, named for Timothy Hanson) and a little rye grass. From the same source came a gallon of port, two gallons of sherry and four gallons of wine, which cost £1.2s.

George Gibson died relatively young, shortly before his sixtieth birthday. He had never married and all his properties and fortune were willed to numerous cousins, the chief beneficiary being Benjamin Hall, his cousin on his mother's side, and Benjamin's second and third sons, Basil and Edmund. Other bequests were to friends including the Pearsons of Pool Bank in Witherslack and several thousand pounds to his female Hall cousins. One gets the impression of a kindly man who thought of many ways to help his friends and relations. All his servants had £50 apiece, and the rents of his properties were to be invested for the education of his heir's children. At his death, George Gibson's estate overall was worth £18,000, but the extraordinary feature of this fortune is that so much of its careful amassing can be followed in all the various notebooks for well over a hundred years. The last of the Gibsons of Height have an imposing marble memorial tablet in Cartmel Fell chapel. The plaque came from the same Webster workshops that fashioned the marble fireplaces at Height, and was erected by relatives 'as a token of their esteem.'

IN MEMORY OF JOHN GIBSON OF THE HEIGHT
WHO DIED SEPTEMBER 30th 1834
AGED 86 YEARS
ALSO OF SUSANNAH HIS WIFE
WHO DIED OCTOBER 13th 1824
AGED 62 YEARS
ALSO OF GEORGE GIBSON THEIR ONLY SON
WHO DIED APRIL 4th 1859
AGED 59

A gentleman farmer, Francis Wilmot, aged 56 and who was born in Derbyshire was at the Height in the 1861 census, with 118 acres of land. His wife Ann was born in Upper Clapton, Middlesex and they had two living-in servants, a cook and a housemaid from Bristol and Derbyshire. Eventually, Francis and his wife retired back to his home county, and in 1881 they were living in Allestree, Derbyshire. In that year, the Height was owned by a farmer, Edward Stanley, who was born in Eton. He was 51 and his wife was 53. Their unmarried daughter Annie Jane Elizabeth Cross Stanley aged 25 was described as 'Manager of Household,' and they had five other living-in servants. Seven years later, Mrs Stanley was dead and the entry in Cartmel Fell burial register, 14 March 1888, is for Mary Ann Elizabeth Stanley of The Height, aged 60. Amongst the many papers at Height were a few pages written by a farm servant girl, and although it is not dated, the writing could be contemporary with the Stanleys' occupation. The account is of a few weeks during haytime, the master getting up at 3am to mow. When the women-folk had completed their washing, they all went into the fields to turn the drying grass and the un-named author took great satisfaction in recording the number of loads safely housed.

In the twentieth century, Sir John Fisher of Barrow bought the estate. It was tenanted by Richard Dixon before the turn of the century, a noted local shorthorn breeder, then by his son George who later had the opportunity to buy the farm as a sitting tenant. Sir John kept the rough shooting, which was his original reason for buying the farm. The present farmer is a descendant of the Dixons.

Height, Quaker Meeting House

HEIGHT, the district, encompasses a considerable area of Cartmel Fell, many farmsteads bearing this definition in times past, but the Meeting House of the Religious Society of Friends bears the same name and cannot be confused with other holdings. A date stone above the porch proclaims it was built in 1677, and the house is fronted by a high stone wall with an unusual 'lych door', which is echoed in the graveyard across the road.

The land and money to build the Meeting House was bequeathed by Lawrence Newton, who died in 1676, and this bequest was used at a time when Dissenters were not allowed to own property, or use existing premises for the purposes of religious meetings. Therefore very few Quaker meeting houses existed before 1689, the year in which the Act of Toleration was passed. The conveyance for this piece of real estate still exists, and copies of the documents relating to Height Meeting can be seen in Kendal Record office.

Lawrence Newton of Height paid a Hearth Tax in 1664 for four hearths. This was well above the average of one or two, and it would seem that Lawrence had no direct descendants, as his will mentions neither wife nor children. He was buried in 1676, and it was probably his father, John, who was buried at Cartmel in February, 1653/4. The Newton family seem to have had their branches spread locally, and may have originated in Lindale.

A Lawrence Newton of Lindale married Agnes Burton at Cartmel in 1622 and when his daughter Mary was christened in 1627, Lawrence was recorded as the reader at Lindale chapel. There is reason to believe that early Quaker meetings were held in Lawrence Newton's house, which was probably behind the present-day Height farm. Three fireplaces can be seen in what is now a barn, and there was a roofed entrance into a small enclosure in the lane leading to Height, which may have been the first Quaker burial ground. This lych gate was in a ruinous state in 1995 and has now gone.

There is a minute book belonging to the Friends, which gives details of individual costs and the total overall building expenditure of the new Meeting House, which was £106.9s.7d.

Wood	£29. 2s.0d
Limestone, leading and breaking them	£ 2. 2s.0d
Coal, to burn them with	£ 1. 6s.6d
Stones, flags & Sand, laths & spars	£ 3. 19s.1d
Freestone	£ 5. 15s.2d
The Wright's diet	£ 4. 9s.7d
Malt & drink at the rearing	8s.8d
Getting moss and plaster, making, etc.	£ 1. 2s.2d
3 Trees & drawing them, & leading boards & joists	£ 2. 12s.6d
Meat & drink for slate & sand leaders, several times	16s.9d
Glass & casements	£ 3. 10s.6d
Hair & plaster & a barrel	£ 1. 7s.7d
Slates and dressing of them	£ 7. 0s.0d
Nails, smith's work and iron	£ 4. 6s.4½d
Men's wages	£25.14s.3d

The plan of the original building did not include as much partitioning as there is today, but the continuous screen on the right of the door as one enters dates from the first construction.

In 1677, Thomas Preston of Holker was the tithe farmer for the Bishop of Chester. His was the responsibility to see that all tithes were paid on time and went straight into the coffers of the Established Church. The recipe for his confrontation with the Quakers was set in concrete, since they had so many beliefs at odds with each other. The Friends were opposed to the payment of tithes, and also abominated a paid clergy. The Preston family loathed the dissenters with a burning intensity, and when Thomas Preston junior succeeded to his father's post he took up the cudgels with renewed energy. He devised traps for unwary Friends, imprisoned some in Lancaster gaol and seized goods far above the value of the unpaid tithes.

Gateway into the first Quaker burial ground?

This was a time of great national insecurity. In the previous century, Henry VIII had dissolved the monasteries, and this inadvertently removed the main source of Poor relief. The new religion had patchy support and many families, especially in Lancashire, still supported Catholic priests albeit covertly. When Cromwell threw the whole country into turmoil once again, many were searching for a new and better way to lead their lives, and the Quaker ideal began to gain support. George Fox criss-crossed the land preaching and evangelising, and came to the Winster valley on more than one occasion. His reception was varied; at Pool Bank on the Crosthwaite/Witherslack boundary he made converts of families who continued to be Quakers into the twentieth century, but in Lindale, they threw him in a horse trough. On Cartmel Fell there seems to have been a considerable impact from Fox's visitations. Pockets of families began to meet in each others' farmhouses, and although nothing is recorded of those early discussions, (and the Quakers later became meticulous in their paperwork) one can half-imagine the earnest discussion that ensued whilst the movement was coalescing.

Spooner Close, down by the lake was one centre of early Quakerism, and Pool Bank in Witherslack another. There were many families who were divided by religion, such as the Birkets of Birket Houses and The Wood, but on the whole, relationships seem to have been amicable. Many documents survive showing opposed cousins as witnesses to wills, or being recipients of bequests from relations of another persuasion. It was only the law-enforcers who were so totally opposed to these tiresome, obstinate, iron-willed Friends. It must have been utterly mystifying to the tithe-farmers to find that there was no resistance offered to arrest, and the prisoners meekly submitted to the sufferings they endured, many dying in prison for refusing to pay a few shillings.

The year in which the Meeting House was built, Thomas Preston junior brought some Dissenters to the Court Baron in Cartmel. Some Friends queried the Court's right in respect of tithes, 'Upon which demur, the said Thomas Preston, Farmer, brake forth into great wrath and rage.' Three months later, informers told Thomas Preston of a meeting at Height, maybe one of the very first. His tithe gatherer, one George Rigg, 'A man of no repute among his neighbours,' and a fellow informer, Edward Stone were despatched to Height to note the congregation. Thomas Preston waited outside and shouted, 'Where are the rogues? Where is your preacher? I'll take a course with him. And where is Thomas Atkinson, that rogue of rogues?' A note in the margin says that Thomas was, 'An antient man of about 72 years old, a man of good conversation and good repute in all his time.'

Thomas Preston issued an ultimatum to the assembly: either they submit to the Cartmel Court, and let him recover the tithes, or else, 'He wod persecute us so that he wod root us out, root and branch, Foundation and generation, and that he wod also pull the house down over our heads, and trail us in carts.'

Thomas Preston's brother-in-law was Miles Dodding, a Justice of the Peace, and using the informer's evidence, he issued a warrant for thirty five people, four of whom were not at the meeting, and two in another county.

On 19 August 1677, the high constable of the north side of the sands went into the field where the preacher Francis Fleming was working and demanded £20 for preaching, and five shillings for his wife, who was not at the meeting. Francis refused, so three constables and the informer George Rigg took his two cows, valued at £8.17s.0d. Thomas Preston, still in a fury, declared that if Francis had had twenty cows, he would have taken them all. Other members had fines imposed between £3 and 8s.

On 22 August, the seized goods were sold in Cartmel, and Thomas Preston said that if the cows were not sold, then he would make the officers buy them at 2d. a beast. Francis Fleming, standing by, said to the people in the market place, 'Ye are many living witnesses that hear these things.' Thomas Preston called Fleming a 'Rogue and a Knave', at which he calmly replied: 'Thou accuses me falsely, for I am neither of these things.'

The wrangling went on for some time, revolving around the legal right of trial for non-payment of tithes at Cartmel. Thomas Preston's only desire was to be rid of these tiresome non-payers and install willing payers from other parts, which he declared he had already done in Rigby, Lancashire, and in Cheshire. Then, a surprising turn of events took place on 25 August. Francis Fleming met George Rigg by accident on the road, at which the latter confessed he was sorely troubled at the part he had played in informing against the meeting. He desired forgiveness, and said he would go with the Friends, to the King if necessary, at his own cost. Apparently, his wife later got to work on him and he grew slightly less humble, but nonetheless agreed to hand over his dues as informer to try and make amends.

In 1683, further fines were imposed on the Friends by Thomas Preston and William Knipe. Edward Myles of Ludderburn in Cartmel Fell paid 4s.6d, and Francis Fleming lost his kettle and three pewter dishes, presumably because he had no money. The following year he was imprisoned and released in 1684. He was buried at Height in 1694.

Thomas Preston's position then, could be compared with officials trying to collect the Poll Tax in Margaret Thatcher's era. Many withheld their payment on moral grounds and in the end, common sense or pragmatism won the day. The Act of Toleration was passed in 1689, allowing free worship, mainly for the benefit of Catholics, but greatly benefiting the Friends. The numbers gathering at Height for worship must have swelled steadily, as in 1691 stables were erected at the rear of the building, the equivalent of a car park today.

In 1712, a cottage was built adjoining the Meeting House at a cost of £22.10s, less than a quarter of the cost of the original structure. The family who own both buildings today, say that the quality is reflected in the price, the Meeting House having walls three feet thick, but the cottage being far more flimsy. We now know that this cottage was designed for a caretaker, but with the possibility of self-sufficiency, as more acreage had been acquired together with barns across the road.

In 1775, an indenture was drawn up between Myles Birket late of the Wood in Cartmel Fell, merchant, and seven trustees. Only two of these were really local, Thomas Pearson of Pool Bank and Isaac Hall of Newton, both yeomen. The document lists the holdings which provided income for the Friends. The land amounted to about seventeen acres, and all the fields are named; 'Now in the occupation of Jonathan Wilson, farmer thereof.'

Jonathan Wilson had been born at Birket Houses, and his family had lived at Hare Hill, just below the Meeting House when he was a child. A great deal is known about him as his day-book and diary were discovered with other papers at Height in the 1990s, copies of which are in Kendal Record Office. The whole family removed to Witherslack when Jonathan was a young man, but he came back later to Height, and lived in the cottage. He was a small-time farmer, and made his living first by malt-making for inns to brew with, and later by chair-making. When he returned to Height, he was dismayed to find that the records were not being kept, so began at once by listing the visitors who came to the Meetings. 'Shall indever to keep account of all public friends that may come to visit this meeting for the future, and the first, Mary Dixon from Bishop Aukland in the County of Durham, 24.8.1738.'

The list grows to over 200 over the years, most visitors coming from the northern counties, but many from London, Ireland and 'Wails'. There were also regular visits from the eastern states of America: 'Joseph Jordan from Virginia, 9.6.1725.' This and many other early visits were recorded in Jonathan Wilson's hand, so he must have taken on the task in his twenties, but then went to work in Lancaster, and nobody else filled his shoes. Later, after his return, he records other Americans: 'Arthur Joans from Pencilvania, 21.11.1738' and 'Micall Lightfoot from Pencilvania was at Kendal, 10, 1740.' Quite often, women ministers travelled from America as in 1743 when 'Elisabeth Shipley and Easter Whittle, both of Pencilvania, attended Height in 1743, 1st of the 10th month.' One tends to think of Dissenters taking a one-way passage to America, but this was far from the case.

Jonathan Wilson was often the Height representative at the Kendal Monthly Meeting, and he also went to Quarterly Meetings further afield. He married Elizabeth Leech at Crook in 1735 when he was forty one, and the couple seem to have been childless. Elizabeth died in 1779, and there is a note of her funeral expenses in the ledger. By Quaker standards,

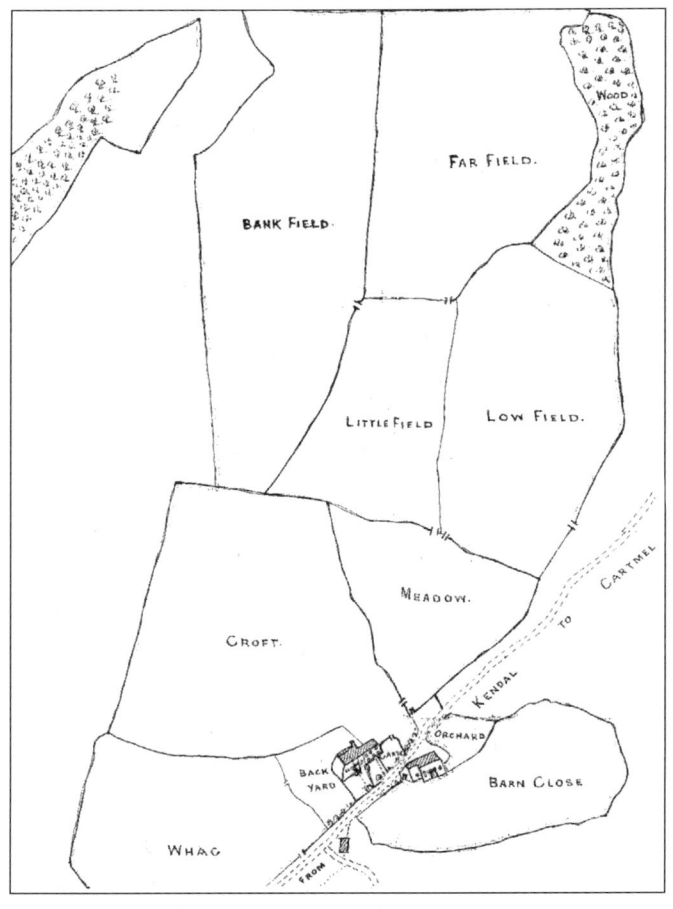

Nineteenth century map of the Meeting House estate.

this seems quite a lavish affair; in the Height Preparative Meeting book of 1699, an injunction read: 'Where Friends provide to accommodate such as are invited to Funeralls, Meat and Drink that then are the customary way of giving Bread and Cheese be laid outside being altogether superfluous and unnecessary to such. And where it may happen in Country places, Bread and Cheese and Bread and Drink being the most suitable, let it be in moderate plain manner, and not above one loaf at most to one person, and in some places, one half may be sufficient.' Times must have changed by the time Elizabeth Wilson died, because the fare was much as one might find today at a country funeral:

```
2nd. mo. 27th,
Pd. For a Shroud......................8s. 8d.
For 4 pieces of Beef..................18s.10d.
For 2 quarters of veal and
    2 Leggs of Mutton....................12s. 9d.
For a ham, 19lbs........................... 9s. 6d.
Groceries, 14s.9d...................... £1. 4s. 3d
Ale..................................................... 8s. 2d
Bread & Flour from Matson
    and Preston............................. 14s. 3d.
Coffin.................................................. 18s.
Tea....................................................... 2s
Apples 1s.......................................... 3s
Inviting to Burial etc....................... 2s.
```

Jonathan continued to live at Height after his wife died, and apart from keeping account of visiting Quakers, he also seems to have been librarian for the religious books kept there. He entered the book and the borrower in the same ledger as his personal business accounts, and these included his farming activities. As the years advanced, his handwriting betrays failing sight. He died in 1787, and the ledger he used was taken over by the Gibsons of Height mansion. They too used it for ordinary domestic accounts.

There is a stone structure in the garden of the cottage which was built to house bee skeps. It could be described as a roofed cupboard, having slots for shelves, facing south-east. More of these buildings are being identified as people become aware of their purpose, and there are several remaining on the fell.

The Meeting was well attended until the nineteenth century, when numbers began to dwindle. By the 1842, attendance was at a low ebb, and was discontinued about 1890. A brief revival occurred early in the twentieth century.

The author Mary Wakefield visited Height and wrote: 'In those days, the caretaker was a woman, a gaunt figure with a voice like a man. On being asked what one paid for a grave, she replied, 'Nay, there's nowt to pay, save me for diggin' on't.' The book was published in 1909, but she was obviously referring to an earlier time. She goes on to give a description of the interior: 'The seats were of unpainted wood in rows each side of the apartment, the males on one side, the females on the other. At the top of the room there was a long raised seat in which sat three Friends, two men and a woman. Behind us was an apartment raised over the adjoining cottage, where the Women's Meeting conducted their own discipline. On entering, there was no bowing or taking off the hat; each sat down and assumed the appearance of perfect stillness. The wood of the floor was green.'

Fortunately, the interior was photographed by the present owners before renovation was begun, so we

Bee shelter at Height Cottage or 'Barrow Hollin'

mostly dating from the last half of the nineteenth century, or the first half of the twentieth. There are a number of children's graves from the same family, due, a relative confided, to the incompetence of the local doctor.

The tombstone inscriptions at Height have been recorded by Claude Harrison for Cartmel Fell Local History Society and passed on to Kendal Record Office.

can see the meeting room just as it was. The interior has been little altered, but for some years in the first half of the twentieth century, the building was used as a hay-barn, so needed some restoration.

Today, the house is called Barrow Wife, from the name of the field which surrounds it on three sides. The Barrow family lived at Height in the sixteenth and seventeenth centuries and this parcel of land must have been inherited through the female line.

Although the Meeting House is no longer used as such, the little burial ground up the hill is occasionally put to use. It has the same slated porch entrance as the Meeting House, but whereas the former has a double door, the burial ground has one. There are neat rows of identical tombstones,

Heightside

THIS is one of the newer dwellings on the fell, and its name derives from its position. Height Meeting House and Height farm are further up the fell to the south. It is recorded in the first document of the deed that, on 14 July 1926, Mr George Hodgson of 8, Rose Bank, Lancaster, purchased the Height Farm, Cartmel Fell, High Newton, in the county of Lancashire, from Mr Norman Briscoe Barrow of Height Farm, but formerly of Stainton Hall, near Dalton-in-Furness. The Height Farm, (not to be confused with the mansion at the top of the hill which has its own farm), comprised the farmhouse now re-named Barrow Hollin, and the attached Quaker Meeting House now called Barrow Wife, together with the barns opposite, now Hollin Foot. Adjoining land, to the extent of 36 acres and 37 perches was also mentioned in the conveyance.

Recently married, Mr Hodgson was a disenchanted solicitor of independent means who came with his bride to Cartmel Fell to be a gentleman farmer. He had two sisters, Mrs Cross and another who was unmarried. Robert Matthews, the joiner from Bowland Bridge, built a wooden summer-house for the sisters in a corner of the field about 50 yards to the north, just down the hill from the farm, and this is the origin of Heightside.

Mrs Hodgson did not like the quiet country way of living, and hankered after the bright lights of Lancaster. After about ten years of marriage, she could stand it no longer and left George to return to the city. In due course they were divorced. George sold off some of the land and concentrated on poultry farming in the fields nearest to the farm, and these could still be seen until the millennium.

At the beginning of the war in 1939, Mr. Hodgson was too old for military service but joined the Home Guard and became the commanding officer of the local unit. During the war years of 1939-45 the summer-house fell into disrepair. The sister who had made most use of the hut was no longer interested and was quite happy that her brother should let it in 1947 to a young couple, Mr and Mrs John Nixon, for a nominal rent, having regard to its poor condition. As the law stood at that time, John Nixon, as a tenant, could expect his landlord to carry out repairs to the summer-house to make it habitable, but Hodgson was not prepared to spend money on it, so the Nixons left to find accommodation in High Newton.

Sometime in the spring of 1960, George Hodgson had a visitor. This was the former Private Fred Lightburn who was then living at Beechwood Cottage, Arnside. The two had not met since they were in India during the First World War when George was an officer in the army. Mr Lightburn thought he recognised in the derelict summer-house a means of making a profit, and managed to persuade Mr Hodgson to sell it to him for £200. The conveyance, dated 12 August 1960 refers to the property as 'Heights Bungalow', and includes a small parcel of land as a garden.

Fred Lightburn and his wife Ada had moved temporarily into an old caravan on the site, and started renovations and alterations to the hut. There was much work to be done, including re-arranging the internal walls to make a bathroom. Fred Lightburn did the plumbing and electrical wiring, fitted a picture window, and covered the outside with chicken wire and pebble-dash to make it look like a conventional house. He added an extra bedroom at the side and built a garage, outhouses and a greenhouse. The work was all accomplished by Fred, with the occasional help of his son when he was on leave from the RAF. They used salvaged materials such as odd lengths of copper pipe, electric wiring, floorboards, window frames etc. on the principal of 'waste not, want not'.

It is understood that Lightburn had worked as a gardener and subsequently became a lengthsman employed by the council to maintain the roadside verges. Ada did floristry and made wreaths, selling at local markets. With this expertise and experience, it is not surprising that they made a pretty garden with well-chosen trees, shrubs and plants, many of which are still thriving, to make the garden a mature setting for the present cottage.

George Hodgson was still living alone next door at Height Farm, with the help of a housekeeper, but he frequently had a couple of old friends from Warrington to stay. During the course of one of these visits, his friend was taken ill and subsequently died, and George married the widow. Eventually, when George himself had medical problems, his wife persuaded him to move to Grange, as she did not drive. There, George died aged 76, some time in the 1970s.

At this period, the Lightburns sold Heights bungalow to the Misses Doris Webber and Kathleen French, both of Rockwood, Elterwater. The conveyance was dated 3 November, 1970, and the price was recorded as £6,250. It would seem that the purchase was made to provide a home for Miss Webber's brother George and his wife Iris, returning from Rhodesia where they had lived for many years. George Webber was a civil engineer, engaged by a Liverpool firm to oversee a sewage project in Langdale. The couple had considered retiring to England, but it soon became apparent that Iris could not tolerate the Cumbrian climate, and longed to return to Africa.

Douglas Martin, a dentist from Eastbourne, was driving past Heights bungalow one December afternoon in 1972. Unable to find the address he was seeking, he called in to ask the way. Mrs. Webber could not help, but this chance meeting eventually led to the purchase of the premises by the Martins, some eighteen months later.

Mr. Webber finished his engineering contract in Langdale and sold Heights bungalow, on behalf of his sister and Miss French to Douglas and Ailna Martin for £8,000, the conveyance dated 3 May 1974. As the Webbers did not want to take all the contents of the house to Africa, a deal was struck for the items they did not require. In fact it was later learned that they had made similar arrangements with the Lightburns, so some of the furniture present today has been in the house for a long time.

The Martin family and their children, Clare (16), Alistair (14), and Julian (12), moved in over the weekend after contracts were exchanged, and had their first holiday at 'Heightside', as they re-named the bungalow. By this time, the other buildings which formerly had constituted Height Farm had been sold. Height Farm and the Meeting House had become three dwellings and all had undergone a change of name. 'Height,' once a district, then whittled down to a mansion and a farm, finally became the sole name of the Webster mansion.

Over the following seventeen years, holidays at Heightside were enjoyed by the Martins, their relatives and friends. However, attempts at maintaining the progressively rotting timbers of the 1928 summer-house were becoming ineffective. Thus it was, on the advice of the architect Arthur Frearson of High Newton, in June 1988, it was decided to rebuild the cottage to modern standards. Planning regulations would not allow much variation from the original, so the present house is the same basic design as before, but marginally bigger. The building work was carried out by Bryan Hill, then of High Newton, and supervised by Arthur Frearson.

'Heightside Mark 2' was recommissioned on 2 April 1989. Meanwhile, a piece of land to the north had been purchased from R. Howard & brothers, scrap metal dealers in Lancaster and owners of the adjacent pasture, where they graze their trotting horses in the summer. The additional land more or less doubles the size of the plot and accommodates a modern septic tank.

Unlike the other houses on the fell which all have private water supplies, the five dwellings comprising Height have water from the reservoir to the south. This causes the Water Board many problems with pumping and filtration, but this hamlet is exempt from the worries of drought.

Hare Hill

ALTHOUGH hares are becoming scarce on the fell, they can sometimes still be seen around this area, and the farm must surely be named for these elusive creatures. For lack of evidence, it might be supposed that this holding is not as ancient as many of the others on the fell. Today, it is not in Cartmel Fell parish, but within Upper Allithwaite because of the re-drawing of parish boundaries, but it is well and truly a fell farm, commanding splendid views over the Winster valley and it was once part of Cartmel Fell as an indenture of 1766 shows.

The present farmhouse and buildings were built by the Robinson family at the end of the nineteenth century, relations of the Robinsons of Low Moor How, but the holding is far older than that. It can be traced in various records, at least to the early 1700s. Frequently it is referred to as 'Height', which encompassed many dwellings in the region, so positive identification is sometimes difficult. A number of documents which came to light in 1996 have helped to clarify many things. One ledger was written by Jonathan Wilson from the 1720s onwards, but others have used the book for similar purposes. From the book we learn that Robert and Dinah Wilson's younger daughter Rachel was born at Hare Hill in 1701. Their book also tells us that they came to Hare Hill via Winster and Birket Houses, and that they brought four small children with them - David, Jonathan, Elizabeth, and John. For whatever reason, the Wilsons migrated to Witherslack for many years, and when Jonathan returned to the Height in later life, it was to the Quaker Meeting House farm, and not Hare Hill, but the farms shared a common boundary.

After the Wilsons left, it seems that the Fells were the next occupiers of the farm. The whole area had become a Quaker stronghold, and the Fells occur frequently in the records of the Friends, so that we know Hare Hill was the Fell family home for at least two generations. Thomas buried his daughter Margaret in 1722, and when he died in 1734 he was buried at Height Sepulchre, as the little graveyard was known. Christopher and Jane Fell had a daughter in 1731, but sadly, Jane died soon after, and Christopher was re-married in 1746 to Mary Braithwaite of Crook. She died in 1754, and the address was still Hare Hill. A cross reference to Christopher Fell occurs in an account book from the Height farm, kept first by Edmund Gibson. The Gibsons kept careful records of their transactions, great and small, and gradually they amassed a fortune over a period of about a hundred years. Part of the basis of this wealth was making their money work, and one way was to act as financiers to their less fortunate neighbours. Christopher Fell was short of ready cash on several occasions and borrowed two guineas in August 1773, and 15s. in June 1775. Both sums have a cross against them in the account book, meaning that the debt was repaid. The Hare Hill branch of the Fell family were probably related to those who were at Tarn Green at the

Hare Hill

turn of the seventeenth century. Thomas Fell and his wife Sarah had a son called Thomas in 1699, and a son James in 1705, and Christopher Fell of Tarn Green was buried in 1705 at Height. All these names are recorded in the Friends registers of births, marriages and burials. In the collected documents of Height, there is an indenture which partly explains the relationship of Thomas Fell and his inheritance of Hare Hill. It appears that Thomas's grandfather, Christopher Fell, deceased by 1766, had left Hare Hill to his grandson, Thomas the younger of Sunbrick, but he and his partner leased the whole to Thomas Fell the elder, i.e. his father, for a peppercorn rent.

By 1766 there is a new name at the farm, and it seems they were not Quakers, in this hamlet of the Friends. John and Elizabeth Wilkinson christened their daughter for her mother on January 1st at Cartmel. There is no way of knowing if the Wilkinsons were yeomen, tenants or servants, and the same is true for John Storey of Hare Hill. He was drowned crossing the sands in January 1792, but his body was not found until the spring and was buried at Warton on 26 May, 'after the coroner's inquest had sat upon the body.'

After this, there is a gap of some years before other evidence of ownership comes to light. At some period around the turn of the eighteenth century, Hare Hill became the property of the Robinsons. Another branch of the family was living at Moorhow at this time, but there were many brothers and sisters, most of whom were unmarried. Thomas Robinson sent a bill to his tenant at Hare Hill in 1807 for three years' rent up to May Day 1810, a total of £108. The tenant was John Whaley, a name which is unfamiliar in the various parish registers, though there were variants of Wallas, Walles and Wales. In the 1829 Parson & White directory, Thomas Robinson is farming Hare Hill himself, but he was nearing the end of his life. His wife Lucy died the following year, aged 64, and Thomas followed her in 1834. Another generation was growing up meanwhile, and young Thomas Robinson and his wife Lucy christened their daughter Agnes the year her grandfather died. They had living-in farm servants, as little James Holmes was christened at Cartmel Fell in the new year of 1838, and his father, James, was described as 'labourer of Hare Hill.' Like many farm servants on the fell, the Holmeses were related to their masters, but this is not always apparent. The comparison of the local census often brings enlightenment as in this case.

Another member of the clan, William Robinson, continued to work and trade from the family holding during the middle of the nineteenth century. He had brothers and cousins who were merchants, importing timber and guano to local ports and to Liverpool. According to Mr and Mrs. Coward, descendants of the Robinsons, William used to travel to Liverpool on foot with a horse and cart before the days of the railway, with only a pocketful of apples for sustenance. Once the iron horse arrived, he went so far as to enquire the price of first, second and third class tickets. The shock was too much, 'Nay, I'll tak t' fourth class,' he said, and set off once more on foot. The 1851 census shows William living unmarried at Hare Hill, aged 56. He calls himself a landed proprietor, farmer and woodcutter (with 70-80 acres), employing four servants. Two of these share his name, so are probably his brother and wife, James who was 54, and Mary, the same age. The oddest member of the household was Hannah Kellett Elam, a lodger aged one year, but a glance at the Moor How census shows a Mary Ann Elam aged 24 employed as a servant to old Ann Robinson. Mary Ann was in fact born a Robinson, the daughter of Thomas of Moor How (1765-1834) and Ann's niece. She had married a man from East Anglia and had gone there to live but her husband died shortly after the marriage, so one of the Robinsons took a horse and cart across England to bring Mary Ann, her little daughter and her belongings home. Living with Ann, who was then 79, was her nephew James Holme, born at Hare Hill and aged only thirteen. The two households seemed intertwined. This was the James who was christened in 1838, but the vicar added an 's' to his surname.

Ten years on, all had changed. Wilson Wildman was farming 80 acres with his widowed mother to keep house, together with his sister Jane. We know that the Robinsons still owned the farm, but they had a succession of tenants, the Bibbys following the Wildmans (who moved over the crest of the hill to Pattinson How) and then, before the farm was completely rebuilt, Bryan Batty and his wife Sarah moved in. By the time the 1891 census was taken, they had seven children, and Sarah was only 32. They went on to have another six boys, and their grand-daughter Ella remembered visiting Hare Hill to find Sarah cutting out 22 cotton shirts for her vast tribe of menfolk. She had no sewing machine, so all had to be very well hand-stitched to withstand heavy work. Sarah used to bake huge quantities of bread, setting it to rise in a massive earthenware bowl or pancheon before the fire. At least the Robinsons had built them the most up-to-date farmhouse and buildings in the district. The quality of stonework was high, the house spacious and well planned, and the joinery was done by the craftsmen Robert Matthews & Sons, then of Strawberry Bank. Even the calf pens have a standard of workmanship that many modern houses do not receive. The corners of the posts are all nicely chamfered, and the section of timber is far more generous than in modern house construction. The barns were built first, flanking the entrance, and have a datestone of 1895 and the initials R.L.A.R. The house has a datestone of 1907 with the same bold initials. This was Robert Robinson and his wife, descendants of the same family of owners, who by that time were living in Darlington. The rooms were spacious and there were two ranges to cater for large families, and a utility room where boots could be left and the washing done. There was no interest in the splendid view across the Winster, and the main windows faced the barns and shippons, all far more important to a farmer. The only glimpse of the panoramic view was from the landing window. We know from the Inland Revenue return of 1911 that the rebuilding cost £2,070. 13s. 8d. The same document has a nice plan of the buildings and states that the rent was then £80 yearly and the sporting rights were worth £100. There were still small sums to be paid as of ancient custom, such as the knowing rent of 2s.6d.every two and a half years, and a fee farm rent of 4s.2d. There was also a tithe of 7s.4d. one year and 7s.8d. the next.

There was a great age range between the large family and the older members began to marry whilst the younger were still scholars. A wedding photograph of about 1905 shows Mary Batty and her new husband, Joseph Wilson with family members outside Hare Hill. The brothers who were eligible enlisted in the First World War as gunners, but some were badly injured. Robert was gassed and died aged only 35 after taking a farm at Seatle. Another generation followed Bryan and Sarah at the farm, the oldest son William and his wife Betsy, who had previously been farming at Hodge Hill. Old Sarah Batty had circulatory problems, but she struggled with her workload for years before finally succumbing to gangrene.

When Bryan retired, he fenced off a corner of his own land and built a modern villa. His second wife was from just over the hill at Lightwood and it was she who laid out and planted the garden with many shrubs and trees. They called their new house 'Silver Birch' and it has a fine view over the estuary towards Arnside. Until the post-war period, it was probably the newest house on the fell.

The house at Hare Hill faces south and there is a level space in front on which grow two massive yews. A visiting parson with an interest in yew trees proclaimed them to be about a thousand years old. Here again is the association of an ancient holding and these trees of well-known toxicity. The belief or superstition which caused so many to be planted near farmhouses must have been stronger than the fear of the effects of the poison on livestock.

Low Tarn Green

LOW Tarn Green stands out in the open, surrounded by flat land, now well drained, but with a peaty sub-soil. This was the flood plain of the melting glacial ice, later to become bog-land and in places the peat is said to be over 100 feet deep. When there was an earthquake around 1993, most of the houses on the fell merely shuddered, and perhaps a plate fell off the dresser, but they are built on rock. Low Tarn Green wobbled on the peat, cracks appeared, and the plaster came off the cellar walls.

The house is large and unusually high for the area, and obviously built later than most. A feature at the roadside is an old water wheel made of iron, once operated from a mill dam higher up on the other side of the road, but this has been removed. The old mill at Thorphinsty is only just up the road but in another parish, and it would have been decaying at about the time the one at Low Tarn Green was constructed. The flat valley land would have been good for growing corn, but it was and is very liable to flooding, and no amount of draining can save it, because the river Winster bursts its banks several times a year. Sometimes, looking down from the top road, a stranger might think he was looking down on Lake Windermere or paddy fields. Maybe because of the nature of the sub-soil, the unusually spacious farm-yard has been painstakingly cobbled with beck-stones, and these are bisected with drainage channels. Further up the fell, the rocky nature of the ground prevents the farm-yards being churned up in bad weather.

For almost the entire nineteenth century, several generations of the Clark family farmed Low Tarn Green. In the copy of the 1814 land tax valuation book, it states that the owner of Tarn Green was Lord Cavendish as lessee under the Bishop of Chester, and Francis Clark was the tenant, and this is cross-referenced at the time of the Witherslack enclosures in 1815, when Francis Clark was a landholder in the same area of Low Tarn Green. This was presumably the father or even grandfather of a later Francis who was recorded as farming there in the 1851 census. He was then 46 and born in Lower Holker. Elizabeth his wife was 42, and they had four children. Francis and William were seventeen and fifteen and worked for their father, as did thirteen-year-old Ann. John Beck Clark was still at school, being eleven. Apart from his family, Francis Clark senior had four agricultural labourers living in, three local but one Irish, and a female servant aged fourteen, Jane Oliver from Kendal. This is a bigger farmhouse than most, but when servants outnumber family, one wonders where they all slept. Three or four in a bed may have kept hypothermia at bay in the winter, but must have been unbearable in summer.

An article in the *Kendal Mercury* of February 1857 shows that this Francis Clark was a farmer with cash to spare and was of a generous nature. He had sometimes lent small sums of money to a labourer, William Jackson. Evidently Jackson was not reliable in the repayment of these transactions, and on one occasion Francis had asked for a guarantor to sign for the loan. Jackson had forged the signature or mark of Ann Paisley, and admitted it in court. He was sent to prison with one year's hard labour.

The Clark family continued at Low Tarn Green into the next generation. Francis junior was there in 1891, by then aged 57. His wife Jane was 54 and they had six unmarried daughters living at home. The four oldest were employed as 'Farmer's Daughters', the next to youngest was an elementary school teacher, aged 21, and the youngest, Annie, had no occupation filled in, so presumably she was no longer a scholar. Apart from the six girls, there were five male farm servants, ranging from 23 to 13. There is a note in the margin of the census form to say that this farm was formerly part of Upper Holker.

At the turn of the twentieth century, the Clarks had left Low Tarn Green and Thomas Mansergh was the tenant. He was a bachelor whose sister Elizabeth kept house for him and they had five servants living in. Two servants were described as cowmen, two were horsemen and one was a general servant.

An interesting probable link with the Wilkinson foundries can be seen in the splendid barn at Low Tarn Green. This is on the western side of the road and has tall iron columns supporting the lintels for the open front. The barn design is itself unusual for this area, and the construction unique. On the opposite side of the road is an equally impressive barn, built in 1991 by Tom and Richard Cornthwaite. Today, the farm is still leased from Holker Estates.

CARTMEL FELL

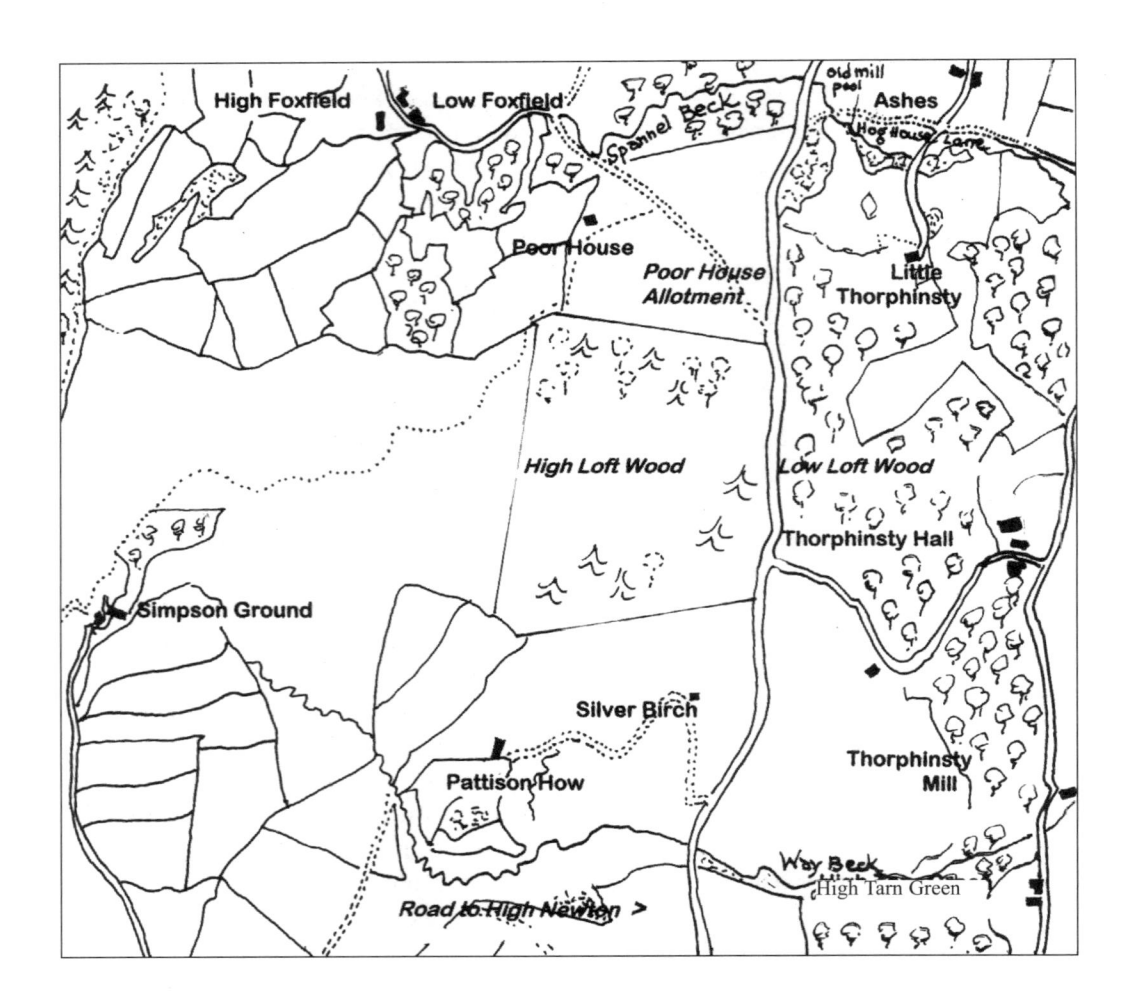

Thorphinsty Hall

THE name, according to Brearly's *Lake District Place Names,* comes from the Old Norse, Thorfin being a proper name, and sty, derived from *stig,* being a pass, therefore Thorfin's pass. The farm is on the lower slope of the fell, and close to the flat valley land of the Winster. The present low road is within yards of the hall, so it is quite easy to imagine that today's road follows an ancient track, keeping above the boggy land lower down. On the other hand 'sty', in Norse, means exactly what it does in English, the place where pigs are kept. The woods around have a large proportion of oaks, so pigs could fatten in the autumn on the acorns. To a farmer, this would have the added bonus of preventing acorn poisoning of sheep and cattle. The third possibility is that the 'ty' element was absorbed from the earlier Welsh culture, tigh or ty being a house. Maybe Thorfin's wife was an old Cambrian?

A History of Lancashire notes the earliest mention of Thorphinsty Hall in 1275-6, when it was held by Henry, son of Henry de Thorphinsty. He claimed the messuage and plough land against the prior of Cartmel, and a law-suit went on for some years, but the record of the result has been lost. This was in the days before surnames were general, but the plaintiff's grandfather was Thomas, son of Ketel, a Norseman by descent it would seem. The new owners of Thorphinsty South Cottage discovered sherds of thirteenth century pottery and Cistercian ware when they were excavating in the garden in 2004.

It is not until 1508, in a Cartmel Priory rental, that another reference to Thorphinsty reveals the surname of the owners. It would seem that the Priors of Cartmel had won their claim, at least to extract fines and tithes from the Huttons of Thorphinsty. There was extraordinary continuity with this family, because they held the estate until the nineteenth century, when it passed through the female line to William Uthwatt, of Maids Moreton in Buckinghamshire.

In 1508, Henry Hutton of Thorphinsty paid taxes in two directions. One was to the priors of Cartmel, from whom he held the estate, and this amounted to 62s.8d. a year. The other was a 'Decima Furne' payment of two shillings to the Duchy of Lancaster. It seems likely that this was a kind of hearth tax, but in this case not a household one, but a tax on a forge. If there was a furnace of some kind, the fuel needed would be charcoal, and in 1565 a complaint was brought against the Duchy's tenants at Thorphinsty who were accused of spoiling the woodlands by using them for fuel, instead of burning peat. Remnants of slag have been found beside Way Beck to the south of Thorphinsty Hall, which show where the forge operated, and, though this may be quite unconnected, the remains of a huge pair of bellows could be seen above the beck until the late 1990s.

These small insights into the ways and means of exacting tolls, taxes or tithes in the early sixteenth century, give us an idea of the general administration of holdings on the fell. If people were too poor to pay in money, they paid in kind or in labour. There must have been many who could

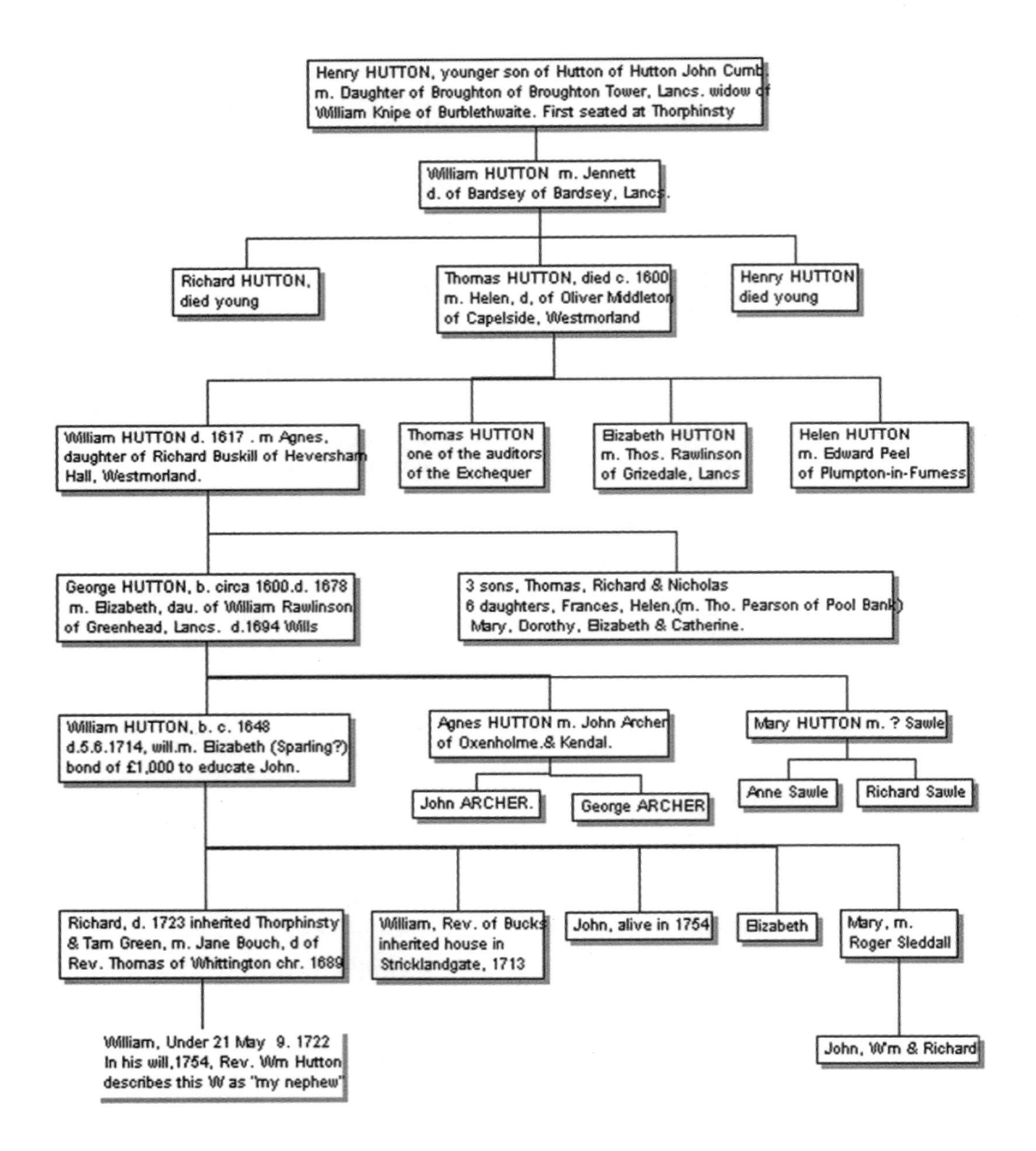

Cartmel Fell

```
Henry HUTTON, younger son of Hutton of Hutton John Cumb.
m. Daughter of Broughton of Broughton Tower, Lancs. widow of
William Knipe of Burblethwaite. First seated at Thorphinsty
         │
William HUTTON  m. Jennett
d. of Bardsey of Bardsey, Lancs.
         │
 ┌───────┼─────────────────────────────┬──────────────┐
Richard HUTTON,   Thomas HUTTON, died c. 1600    Henry HUTTON
died young        m. Helen, d. of Oliver Middleton   died young
                  of Capelside, Westmorland
                         │
 ┌───────────────┬──────────────┬──────────────┐
William HUTTON d. 1617. m Agnes,   Thomas HUTTON    Elizabeth HUTTON    Helen HUTTON
daughter of Richard Buskill of Heversham  one of the auditors   m. Thos. Rawlinson   m. Edward Peel
Hall, Westmorland.                of the Exchequer     of Grizedale, Lancs   of Plumpton-in-Furness
         │
 ┌───────┴──────────────────────┐
George HUTTON, b. circa 1600. d. 1678    3 sons, Thomas, Richard & Nicholas
m. Elizabeth, dau. of William Rawlinson  6 daughters, Frances, Helen, (m. Tho. Pearson of Pool Bank)
of Greenhead, Lancs. d.1694 Wills         Mary, Dorothy, Elizabeth & Catherine.
         │
 ┌───────┴───────────────┬──────────────────────┐
William HUTTON, b. c. 1648   Agnes HUTTON m. John Archer    Mary HUTTON m. ? Sawle
d.5.6.1714, will.m. Elizabeth (Sparling?)   of Oxenholme.& Kendal.
bond of £1,000 to educate John.           │                   │
                                   ┌──────┴──────┐        ┌──────┴──────┐
                                   John ARCHER.  George ARCHER   Anne Sawle   Richard Sawle
         │
 ┌───────┼──────────────┬──────────┬──────────┐
Richard, d. 1723 inherited Thorphinsty   William, Rev. of Bucks   John, alive in 1754   Elizabeth   Mary, m.
& Tam Green, m. Jane Bouch, d of    inherited house in                                   Roger Sleddall
Rev. Thomas of Whittington chr. 1689  Stricklandgate, 1713                                     │
         │                                                                           John, Wm & Richard
William, Under 21 May 9. 1722
In his will,1754, Rev. Wm Hutton
describes this W as "my nephew"
```

barely survive, and Richard Hutton of Thorphinsty was one of the founder members of the Bryan Beck charity which helped to alleviate the sufferings of the poverty-stricken. Another Richard Hutton left £20 in 1723 for the use of the poor, and this ultimately bought Low House field, (now known as Jinny Lot) and the interest was distributed by the curate at the chapel table to fifteen needy parishioners. Apart from these charitable acts, the Huttons seem to have kept a very low profile within the parish, though occasionally they are mentioned as executors of wills, as in 1668, William Harrison of Sow How, when making his will, names 'My good friend George Hutton of Thorphinsty.'

A document in very obscure Latin relates to this period. It mentions the Thorphinsty water mill and 'Ternegreene' messuage, together with 24 acres of which George Hutton was now in possession, because of the failure to pay the fee-farm rent by Peter and Dorothy Palmer in 1629. The king had been the beneficiary of these premises as a result, until the matter was resolved by paying the debt.

At the dissolution of the monasteries most of the farmholdings in Cartmel parish were annexed and united with the Duchy of Lancaster, which set the annual rent. Excepted from the parish of Cartmel Fell were Tarn Green and Thorphinsty, or as it was termed in the document, 'Thornepanstye or Thorfinstye'. These were granted to Richard Cartwright in fee-farm, a man who may have been a dealer in monastic lands. Tarn Green's rent was 4s.4d. and Thorphinsty's was 62s.8d. Although most of the influential families of the district are named in the document, the Huttons are conspicuous by their absence. They must have been tenants of Richard Cartwright at that time and purchased Tarn Green and Thorphinsty later.

A number of Hutton wills survive, and these show the inter-marriage with other minor gentry in the area such as the Briggses, the Sleddalls and the Archers of Oxenholme. The wills also show a kindly disposition towards servants with many small bequests.

When Elizabeth Hutton made her will in 1690, she was said to be 'of Tharfinsty', indicating the pronunciation of the day. She was then a widow and the estate had passed to her son William, so her bequests were of personal belongings. She left a clock to her son and heir, but also a steel trap and a gun, which seem surprising treasures for a woman to have. The grandchildren received silver spoons and a piece of gold, but William's heir, Richard, was left his grandfather's wainscot bed and grandmother's great Bible. Elizabeth's servant, Isabell Barwick was left 'the Bed of Cloethes in which she now lies', and all William's servants received 2s.6d.

William died in 1713, leaving the messuages of Thorphinsty and Tarn Green to his son Richard. He had other properties in Kendal and Underbarrow and these were to be administered for William's children, John and Mary Hutton who were minors, by Myles Sandys of Graythwaite and others. The will reveals that these other estates came to him through his wife, Elizabeth.

Richard died before his mother, and made his will in 1722. His son William was under age, but Thorphinsty and Tarn Green were left to him, including water corn mills and all estates in Cartmel. Many small monetary bequests were left to tenants and servants, including five shillings to each member of the Fell family, Quakers, who were

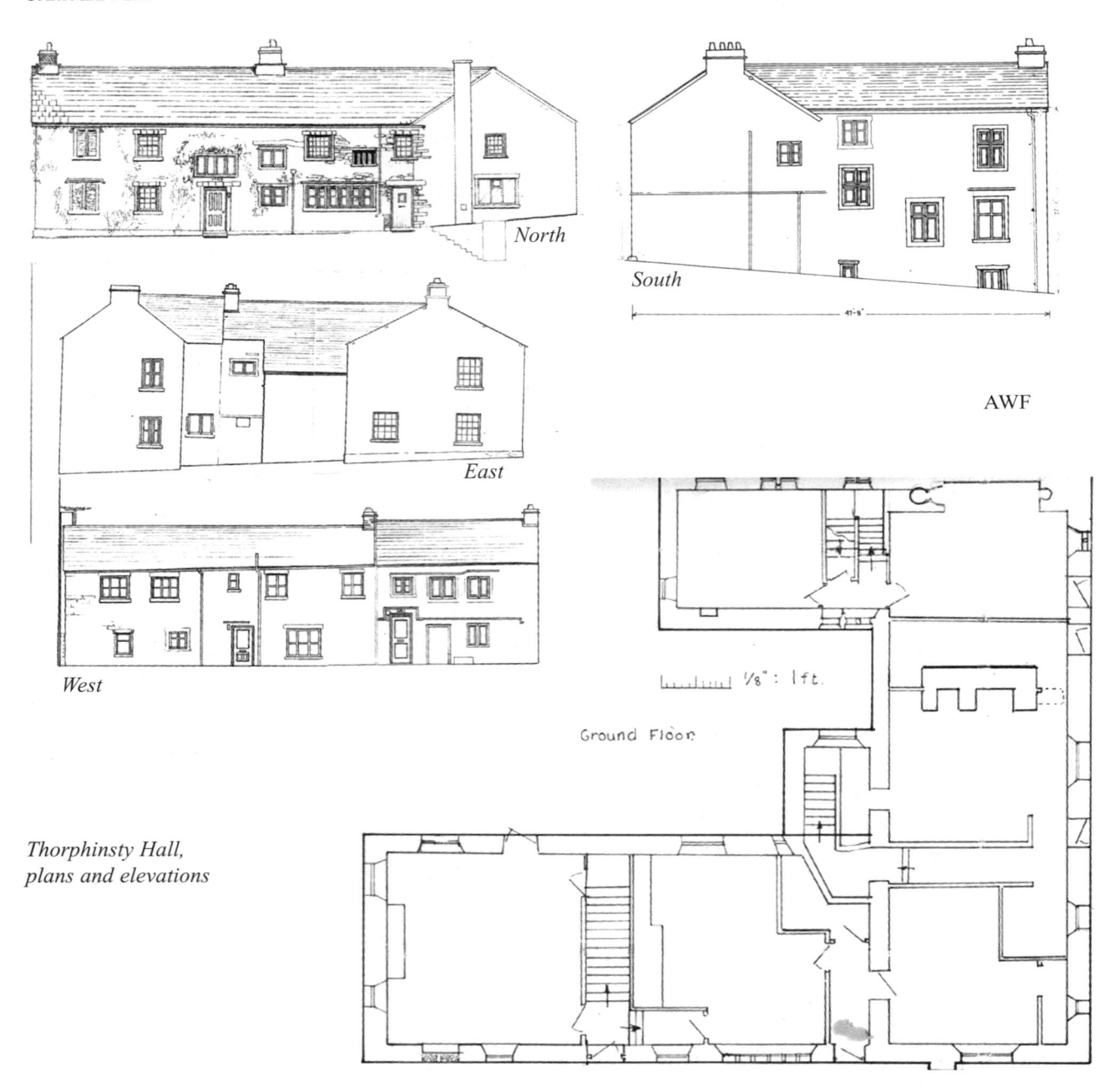

Cartmel Fell

North

South

East

West

AWF

Ground Floor

Thorphinsty Hall, plans and elevations

living at Tarn Green. In a codicil, Jane Hutton, Richard's widow was to have his bay gelding called Ball and a dun colt. Owing to him at his death was a sixteenth share in the ship *Thomas and Mary* of Grange.

Somewhat confusingly, another Richard Hutton, but a bachelor of Thorphinsty, made his will in that same year of 1722. He left his sisters Elizabeth and Katherine all his share of the lease of Tarn Green, out of which they had to pay Jane Poole £7 in two instalments, £3 the first year after Richard's decease and £4 in the second year. He left many bequests of £10 to individuals and £20 to purchase land, the profit of which was to be distributed yearly among the 'Pore old People of Cartmel Fell.' A list of the first beneficiaries is in Kendal Record Office. Items at Grange and Flookburgh were for his sisters and he gave to William Britton's wife, 'my table in her husband's house.'

At the time of the enclosures around the end of the eighteenth century, the only Hutton to receive an allotment award was the Rev. Hutton Long, the 'Thorping Stye' road passing over his allotment. It seemed as though the male line was dying out, for the Long surname was derived from a marriage to a Hutton female.

The hall itself is rambling, on a roughly E-shaped plan, which lends itself well to today's division into three. On the north wall where the stonework is not rendered, one can see where mullioned windows have been blocked up (perhaps for Pitt's window tax) and later Georgian ones put in. A datestone of 1704 is above a window, though this is a replica of the original, which is on another side of the house.

Mary Burkett, who was then director of Abbot Hall, thought that there had been a pele tower where there is now only a square space, and indeed, a stair can be seen spiralling into the wall and ceiling of the house adjoining this space, but it ends abruptly. There have been so many alterations and divisions over the centuries that the original design is lost in the jig-saw. The grandest staircase today is in the southern end of the complex, ascending three stories. The nicely turned banister rails go up to the loft and the stairs are twice the width of those in the north-east section of the house. In this southern end, now called South Cottage (though certainly not of cottage proportions) a large cellar had been accessed by an internal stone stair, but at some stage, this had been bricked up, leaving only the stair-well. The earth of centuries had washed down the fell and piled up to window level outside, whilst the inside of the stair-well had similarly been filled up with household waste until only four stairs remained out of eight.

At the time of the renovations in 2002, a large open hearth was revealed in South Cottage, and on either side of the inglenook are slate lined bread ovens, one with a seat below it. This would have been one of the warmest places to sit on a bitter winter evening, but the fire would have been only of peat and would not have produced a roaring blaze. The massive beam above this hearth spans a ten foot opening and the beams which supported the rannel-baulk can be seen high in the chimney. This portion of the house was used partly as a granary and partly as a temporary shooting lodge in 1868, when the shooting and accommodation were let for £10 a year each to two un-named men.

In the nineteenth century, there is much more light shed on the activities at the Hall. There are census returns which show large numbers of people in residence, parish records, estate records, memorabilia and photographs of various events and families. The parish register shows that in 1820, James Coward, a cooper, and his wife Jane, christened a son John. The next year, Robert and Ann Atkinson christened young William. The question is whether they were operating a cooperage from Thorphinsty, or were they employed elsewhere? The Parson & White directory of 1829 names Richard Barrow of 'Thorpingstyle' Hall, but by the 1851 census, the Wright family were farming 160 acres with only one labourer employed. Despite this, the household consisted of Joseph Wright, 41, his wife Hannah, two sons, James aged fifteen, and Joseph aged two, a daughter, Hannah Maria, aged thirteen, and no less than six living in servants, one female, and all the others described as agricultural labourers. A separate household, but at the same address in 1851, was Catherine Long, aged 61, retired shopkeeper and born in Crosthwaite, so she probably lived in South Cottage. In 1830, already at Thorphinsty, she had christened a son Robert, and in the 1841 census she is described as charwoman.

The Taylor family arrived at Thorphinsty in 1863. They had begun married life farming Wattsfield, which was then on the outskirts of Kendal but the fields are now engulfed by housing estates. The Taylors had three daughters before moving to Cartmel Fell, and then Margaret Taylor bore her husband five sons and another daughter. By all accounts, the family was hardworking and canny, but to earn a little extra money for his growing family, John Taylor used to go to the Mason's Arms for two weeks between haytime and harvest, there challenging all comers to bare-knuckle boxing contests. A photograph in the local collection shows him with a distinctly black eye.

The estate papers of this period in Barrow Record Office show all aspects of management. Some relate to the buildings and farmland, others to insurance and hiring, but a large proportion relate to woodland management, and it is evident that timber accounted for a high percentage of the estate income. There are posters from 1847 advertising forthcoming sales of woodland, with records of purchasers, estimates and related correspondence.

The woodlands at Thorphinsty were separately managed by the Holme family in the nineteenth century, but by this time the landlords were absentees. The Hutton-Long's inheritance passed to the Uthwatts of Maids Moreton in Buckinghamshire, and they employed the same woodland agents as did the Wakefield family of Kendal. James Holme of Blakeholme was related by marriage to the Robinsons of Moor How, and he kept meticulous accounts and letter-books of the transactions he undertook for the Uthwatts, his son John succeeding to the post later in the nineteenth century. The correspondence generated by the absence of the landlord makes fascinating reading today.

In 1874 the Rev. W. A. Uthwatt could not believe

Mrs Mary Uthwatt

the high wages that James Holme was paying his foresters at a time when unemployment was rife in Buckinghamshire. He wrote to his agent in February: 'It surprises me to hear of such scarcity of men in the North, as I should think that they had been too well off for some years that emigration should be quite out of the question. Plenty of labourers are to be had here for 12s. to 14s. per week, finding for themselves in everything.'

The difference was in the semi-independence of most of James Holme's seasonal workers, many of whom had small farms and were similar in origin and education to their employer. Mr. Uthwatt wanted the Wakefields and other men of substance to build a hundred cottages on the fell and then he would send poor unemployed agricultural labourers from Maids Moreton to swamp the labour market. He mentioned that the railway company had built houses at Wolverton and Bradwell near him, and now 2,000 workers were occupying them. In May William Uthwatt wrote again: 'I was quite astonished at the offer to pay the woodcutters 6s. per day. I think it ought not to have been done. It only causes dissatisfaction in others working for less money. Employers in my opinion ought to determine beforehand what was a fair price and hold to it, but it appears you want more men in your neighbourhood, and to supply this want, houses, I said before, must be built, which would soon be filled and cause the price of labour to come down to what is fair and right.' After more in the same vein, the landlord intimated that he could supply woodcutters who would work for 2s.6d. a day, and that agitators stayed away from his parish as his tenants had allotments, though low wages.

Apart from timber, the by-product of bark for tanning and dying was an important part of the woodland management, and huge amounts of correspondence were devoted to this. An instance in December 1864 is in the form of an urgent request for 200 sacks as the bark was ready; 24 sacks of larch bark had already been despatched from Moor How.

The insurance of the farm and buildings was part of the land agent's remit, so the values placed in 1886 are a useful comparison with today's. The main house was valued at £600, and the cottage adjoining at £150. Amongst the buildings was a horse-walk, which must have meant a circular shed in which the horse was the motive power for a mill in the centre. The total value of all the buildings was £1,600, and the premium a mere £1.17s.6d.

Among the Thorphinsty memorabilia still in private hands, are tenancy agreements. The Taylors were to keep the fences and ditches in good order, pull docks and burn them, cut thistles and apply twenty shillings-worth of crushed bone each year. There was to be no cropping or lopping of trees, except for fence repairs, no sub-letting and the tenants were to live in the house and keep a dog for the landlord. The rent was £245 a year, though by 1888 this was reduced to £225, payable in two halves. In 1891, the census shows the Taylor family still in residence. John, the head, was 60, a farmer, born in Whinfell. His wife, two daughters, and five unmarried sons were all living at home.

Apart from farming, the Taylors supplied game to various customers, and there is a notebook with a record of game taken showing the current prices received in 1891, 1892 and 1893. Rabbits were surprisingly dear it seemed, at two shillings each, whereas in the 1930s, they were only six pence in the market. Woodcock were two shillings also, and a hare three shillings. Snipe were four pence and plovers six pence Game pie in those days might contain anything from waterhens at four pence to a seagull for six pence. Much of the bag seemed to have gone to Grange, presumably to local butchers and poulterers or hotels, but some went to farms in the neighbourhood.

The household account books, now in the hands of a descendant, shed an interesting light into the economy of the day. The regular grocery orders were for dry goods such as flour, semolina, dried fruit and sugar, but coffee was in far greater demand than tea, and the whole bill was offset by the sale of butter to the grocer. In peak production times this would be up to 70lbs, but towards the time of the farm sale, it had dwindled to around 18lbs. The family's indulgencies were cough sweets and tobacco. The Taylors sold their farm in 1921, and the auction poster is retained in the photographic archive of the fell, together with a notebook of all the prices realised. The auctioneers were Messrs. M. B. Hodgson & Son, and the sale took place on 6 April. The low prices for hand tools, harness and implements is almost shocking by today's standards; a hammer nine pence, sod cutter 1s.6d., hay spade one shilling, but when it came to modern technology, the 'Side Delivery Rake' was £27, no less.

The Taylors must have been potato producers as there were many bags of seed potatoes to sell, varying from four to twelve shillings a sack. A dog-cart was £2, but motor transport was creeping onto the fell by then. The ewes and lambs fetched consistent prices, and most must have had twins at foot in April, as a typical entry is: '5 Ewes , 9 lambs (blue horn) at £7.10s... £37. 10s., and one tup was £2. The sheep totalled about 60, with nearly 100 lambs. Some of the cattle must have been exceptional quality and as so many are described as roan, they must have been mostly Shorthorns. The top price for a roan cow was £71.10s. and a similar bull, £57.10s. Heifers averaged about £27. There were six horses altogether - two mares, two fillies, a colt and a foal. The mares brought £65 and £59, and the filly foal fifteen guineas. Horse power still had a future. Towards the end of the sale came poultry, furniture and dairy implements; a cradle made £5 and a churn the same.

The new farmer was a descendant of the Wrights who were at Thorphinsty in the previous century when Joseph Wright had lost a fortune on the farm, but his grandson said he would retrieve it. James Wright of Goswick was a baby when his father took over the farm, and grew up there. When the young James was fourteen, his father gave him a start in farming. He bought six Herdwick hogs from Beatrix Potter for 30s. and from that beginning, his son progressed from sheep to pigs, then from cows to horses.

William Lydell became the new owner of Thorphinsty before the Second World War. He was a Yorkshire man, and brought fellow countrymen with him as workers. He was dissatisfied with the auctioneer's valuation of the stock, which sold for maybe less than half the estimate, and he asked for compensation. William Lydell was progressive, and had the first electric-powered milking parlour on the fell in the 1930s. The water of Way Beck was used to drive a turbine built by Gilbert Gilkes & Gordon of Kendal, and its crumbling housing still spans the beck, but it became obsolete when electricity came to the fell in 1960. His daughter and her husband built themselves a bungalow on land above the hall, calling it Thorphinsty Crag. The council tried to have it pulled down, because they said it was built on a public footpath, but Jim Wright was called as a witness with lifelong knowledge of the land, and told the council that it was not a footpath, merely a bracken track, well worn with leading loads of brackens for winter bedding to the farm.

Today, planning permission has been allowed for the conversion of most of the outbuildings into dwellings, and Thorphinsty Hall is a farm no longer. It will be a hamlet of seven dwellings and to date, the greatest concentration of housing on the fell. The mediaeval barn to the north of the house was converted in 2002, and retains the four cruck beams which bear the weight of the roof. After cleaning, these look as though they were made yesterday. An old man who was once a farm hand at Thorphinsty said his initials are carved on one of the cross beams, as that is where the hands used to retire on a Sunday afternoon, to lie in the hay. At the eastern gable-end, the six pigeon-holes have been retained, with their landing ledges. Another great barn, higher up the road, was demolished in the twentieth century.

A few hundred yards along the bottom road is Thorphinsty Mill, or what remains of it. There is an old bread oven in one corner, but the roof has gone and the walls are disintegrating. From evidence in baptismal records, it seems to have been used to house labourers, though was often uninhabited in census returns. The last known occupants were the Airey family in 1891. The first recorded burial, in January 1780, was that of Robert Routledge. There are no further entries in parish registers until 1802 when Mark and Agnes Crow christened their daughter Ellin, but at this stage, no occupation is entered, though when another daughter is christened in May 1804, Mark is described as miller. In 1772 Joseph and Agnes Crow of Thorphinsty Hall christened their son Mark, so it seems more than likely that it was he who rented the mill on his doorstep 30 years later. There were many Crows on the fell in the eighteenth and nineteenth centuries and the men were all called Jacob, Joseph or Mark, so it makes for difficulties in sorting them out. They were also particularly mobile, and there is scarcely a farm which has not had Crow tenants or owners at some time, and today there are still Crows and their descendants farming on the fell.

In 1851, a pauper called Ann Atkinson was living at the mill house with her son Richard who was a bobbin-turner. There is no evidence that the mill was used to power bobbin machinery, except that in 1839 James and Hannah Watson of Old Mill House christened their son Robert, and James was also a bobbin-maker. In other parishes this was a common trade, but the few in Cartmel Fell were in the Gill Head area.

Descendants of the Taylors of Thorphinsty refer to Mill House as the gamekeeper's cottage, but the only gamekeeper recorded there was in 1861, when 28-year-old Robert Dickinson and his wife were living there. They were followed by Robert Atkinson, his wife Agnes and toddler Isaac. Rather surprisingly, they had a fourteen-year-old servant girl from Dalbeattie living with them, but she may have been employed at the Hall. The girl was called Elizabeth Taylor, so one is tempted to imagine a relationship with the family at the Hall, but actually she was one of a large family which came down to Cumbria with her parents, and she eventually married into the Pearson family of Borderside.

The last time the mill occurs in a written record, apart from the census, is for insurance in 1886. It was then in the private occupation of John Airey and was valued at £100, with an adjoining peat-house worth £50, all stone built and slated. The 1891 census states that John was a wood-cutter, born in Troutbeck Westmorland aged 34. His wife Mary had six children, the oldest, a boy of twelve being an agricultural labourer already. Ten years later, the Aireys had moved to Burrow Cottage near Tower Wood, and the mill house was uninhabited again.

From this period onward, there are no entries in the parish registers of baptisms or burials from the mill house, and one supposes it was in terminal decline, together with the mill itself. Scraps of pottery and glass lie around the ruins to show that they once held life, and a kettle appeared on the broken hearth of the mill in the 1990s, looking strangely forlorn.

M. Davies Sheil has had a look at this mill, and has found a reference to 'the great beam at Thorphinsty' in 1660. This was because the valuable hammer beam was by then disused, and could be re-located. By this, we can infer that the mill was originally a forge, hence the tax of 'Decima Furne' referred to earlier, and the Huttons' reprimand for spoiling the woodland.

High Tarn Green

SITUATED on the south side of Way Beck, High Tarn Green lies on the edge of Cartmel Fell township; in fact it is now in the township of Upper Allithwaite. Low Tarn Green was a detached division of Upper Holker until the Divided Parishes Act of 1882. Originally, there was only one holding of this name, the farm that is now called High Tarn Green, and that seems to have been part of the Thorphinsty Hall estate, at least since the seventeenth century. Low Tarn Green was built about the turn of the eighteenth century, at the time of the enclosures.

The name describes the unexpected bulge of the river Winster, where it forms the peaty, reedy Helton Tarn. Legend has it that the iron master, John Wilkinson of Lindale, built the first iron ship (actually more of a barge,) and when it was carrying peat to an experimental furnace, it sank in this tarn. There have been several unsuccessful attempts to find the boat, the last in 2003 using up-to-date techniques, but nothing has been discovered.

James Stockdale asserts that in the reign of Elizabeth I, or James I, both Thorphinsty Hall and Tarn Green were granted in fee farm to Richard Cartwright. Who this man was, or where he came from is hard to tell, as his name does not occur locally in parish records. The evidence for the Huttons being the ancient holders of these properties is much stronger, and their name appears on a rental of 1508, when they held the whole Thorphinsty estate from Cartmel Priory for an annual rent of 62s.8d. There must have been a manorial change of ownership after the dissolution of the monasteries, whereby the Huttons held their customary tenement from a new lord, Richard Cartwright.

Dugdale's *Visitation of Lancashire*, 1664-5, states that Henry Hutton, a younger son of the Huttons of Hutton John in Cumberland, was the first of his family to occupy Thorphinsty. A pedigree does not give early dates, but Thomas Hutton was dead by about 1600 and he was the grandson of Henry, so one can surmise that Henry might have been born in the early 1500s and died about 1550.

Inside Tarn Green, high on the staircase wall, is a datestone with the initials W. H. E. 1694. Without doubt, this is William and Elizabeth Hutton, but whether this was commemorating an alteration or anniversary is hard to determine. The house is thought to pre-date the inscription, but changes have certainly been made, as there are windows in internal walls and it seems that the house was once two dwellings. Underneath the wooden stairs is a much older stone stair, and although the date-stone is now above it, the suggestion is that it was moved there when the facade was rendered. The kitchen wing, which is to the south-east, is an eighteenth-century addition in which there is a large, high fireplace with a corbelled lintel, and the sub-floor, which is concrete, was laid by Italian prisoners of war from Bela River camp, near Beetham, during the Second World War. When the two buildings were joined, the whole roof would have been turned through 90 degrees and it also appears to have been raised at some stage.

The earliest tenants that we know of at Tarn Green were Quakers. Thomas, son of Christopher Fell of Newton, married Sarah Birkett in 1684 at Height. Their first two children were born at Nether Newton, but by 1696 when their daughter Margaret was born, their address was Tarn Green. Thomas followed in 1699, and James in 1702. It would seem that Christopher of Newton had moved with the younger generation, for when he was buried at Height in 1705, he too was of Tarn Green.

We know that the Huttons were prominently Anglican at this period, as their pew in St Anthony's carries the date 1696 and there is a marble wall plaque for them in Cartmel Priory. One could assume that they had a fairly liberal attitude to Quakers, at a time when the gentry were largely hostile, or they would not have admitted the Fells as tenants. An especially close relationship is shown when William Hutton of Thorphinsty died in 1714 and his inventory was compiled by Thomas Fell of 'Turn Green', a phonetic rendering. Helping Thomas with the appraisal of goods was John Pearson of Witherslack, another Quaker. He was later of assistance in taking the inventory of Richard Hutton of Thorphinsty, who died only eight years after his father in 1722. This will shows the relationship between John Pearson of Low Wood and Richard Hutton, (they were cousins), and it also makes clear that Tarn Green was part of the Hutton estate in Cartmel parish, though they held lands elsewhere as well. The Pearsons of Low Wood and Pool Bank were early converts to Quakerism. The Huttons were traditional adherents of the Church of England, but this did not come between family and friends with a small 'f'. There are many instances on the fell of trust and co-operation between the families of the Established Church and their Quaker neighbours, especially as evidenced in legal matters, but this is almost a subject in itself.

By 1733, the parish register shows that Anthony Strickland was living at Tarn Green, almost certainly one of the Hartbarrow Stricklands. Knowing that John Pearson of Low Wood was a Hutton cousin, it is yet another example of the local dynasties being interwoven, and showing their mobility. An instance of these flitting families comes in a letter from John Brockbank of Witherslack (who was a witness to Elizabeth Hutton's will of 1690) to his son Thomas: 'Anthony Strickland is removed from Low Wood to his own house at Hartbarrow in Cartmel Fell.'

Later in the eighteenth century, the then famous William Gibson lived at Tarn Green. He is the same man as 'Willy o' the Hollins', farmer and mathematician, and then of world renown. We do not know exactly when he moved from the Hollins, but he and his wife Isabel (née Jerman or German) christened their son Thomas in January, 1756, and their home was then at Tarn Green. In that same year, Edmund Gibson of the Height made a note in his day book: 'Desember the 2 day, 1756. I sould two parshels of spring wood at Lower nuton with a parshel of ashes above the hiway with it going back beneath the way at Hier nuton to William Gibson of tarngreen for 13 pounds and a day plowing and 3 par of Rallstoops he paying at Candlemas, 1758.' Rallstoops may have been the alternatives to gate stoups, that is the pierced upright stones which held rails instead of gate hangings. It would be interesting to know if there was any relationship between Edmund Gibson and William, but the latter's obituary gives away little of his origins. There is more about Willy in the section of this book relating to Hollins. Willy Gibson kept a gentlemen's school at Tarn Green for some years as evidenced in his obituary. Between twelve and fourteen boys were lodged at Tarn Green during this time, but it seems that the Gibsons eventually moved to Cartmel.

Evidence of Tarn Green's occupants is scanty at the close of the eighteenth century, but at the time of the enclosures (circa 1797,) Francis Hutton Long was awarded an allotment for Tarn Green. He had inherited Thorphinsty Hall also, evidently through the female line since Hutton was his middle name, so the two properties were still hand in hand. At this period the last of the Huttons must have moved down to Buckinghamshire, as in William Hutton's will of 1754, he mentions 'My nephew William of Thorphensty', and from then on the Huttons were absentee landlords. A generation of Hutton Longs must have succeded the Rev. William, and then we hear of the Rev. James L. Long who was vicar of Maids Moreton in Buckinghamshire. The Longs and then their daughter's husband, the Rev. William Uthwatt retained their Cumbrian estates until the early twentieth century. There is a rather touching tombstone in Maids Moreton, erected by the Rev. James Long in memory of a servant (who was a Methodist), Ann Lane. She died suddenly aged 47 and 'Her Affectionate Friend' paid for her headstone. It seems the ecumenical tolerance of earlier generations of Huttons had persisted.

There is a gap of thirty years or so before further evidence of occupants appears. A William Hall lived at High Tarn Green in 1832, and he remained there for the next thirty years or so. His retiring sale was advertised for Thursday, 2 April 1863 on the premises, and the auctioneer was Mr John

Hodgson. There were no cattle in the sale, but three work horses and a filly of two years, and two flocks of sheep, 33 of which were half-bred ewes and 41 Herdwicks, all put to Leicester tups, one of which was also to be auctioned. Refreshments were at twelve o'clock before the sale commenced, as many prospective bidders would have travelled on foot or by horse and cart for some distance. Detailed aspects of the new tenancy agreement dating from 1863 set out the terms for a nine-year lease. Robert Atkinson was the new tenant and he agreed to pay £150 a year for 103 acres, 1 rood, 9 perches. He might not sub-let, he was not to lop or crop any trees except thorn and hazel for fence repair, and he had to lay 40 roods of hedge each year. He should cut all thistles, briars and weeds, and pull docks and burn them. The crop rotations were specified, and so was the cow grass, which had to be timothy, rye and red and white clover. Each year he had to apply 40 bushels of crushed bones to the turnip crop and a change in attitude to the game laws made the tenant responsible for killing all rabbits on the farm.

In 1865, Robert and Isabella Atkinson had a daughter Mary baptised and in April 1868, their son Robert was christened. Both these entries at Carmel Fell list Robert as 'farmer'.

An article in the *Kendal Mercury* describes in detail a disastrous fire at Tarn Green in September, 1869. Robert Atkinson had been the tenant for six years when the adjoining barn caught fire during the night. By the time the servants were awoken by the crash of the floors collapsing, it was too late to control the flames. Volunteers climbed onto the roof of the house and sawed through connecting rafters and so stopped the fire from spreading, but all the hay and corn were destroyed and also the seed of Italian rye grass which he had hoped to sell. It seems that there was no insurance, and a subscription fund was set up at various banks to help with the estimated damage of £200. Robert Atkinson was quite newly married, but his wife was at the time an invalid and was carried from house to house of their neighbours during the fire. *The Westmorland Gazette* described Robert as 'a young and industrious beginner in farming,' so maybe he housed his hay too quickly and it continued to heat up. The previous year, he had won several prizes in the Crosthwaite and Underbarrow Agricultural Society Awards, including best heifer calf and best breeding cow. In the year of the fire, he won best yearling heifer and the best crop of turnips. From the baptismal registers of St Anthony's, we learn that Isabella Atkinson was pregnant at the time of the fire, and their baby Isaac was christened on Christmas Day of that fateful year, but by that time the couple were 'of Height', and Robert was described as a labourer, not a farmer. Either the subscription fund proved helpful, or Robert and Isabella started again from scratch, because eventually they went back to Tarn Green, and when their next children were born in 1871, 1873 and 1877, Robert was again described as farmer.

In 1880, the incoming tenant was Robert Webster and his wife Elizabeth Ann, and their infant Robert was born at Tarn Green that year. The rent was reduced to £145 yearly and he had struck out the clause relating to the landlord's right to hunt, shoot or fish on the land. It must have been a time when the big landowners faced opposition from their tenants, for the same thing happened with the Bryan Beck agreement. Perhaps the rising standards in education had something to do with changing attitudes, or possibly the local press encouraged individuals to make a stand, publishing articles on the game laws by rebels such as William Pearson of Borderside. The letter books of the Holme family, who were land agents to the Thorphinsty and Tarn Green estates, indicate a shortage of manpower in the region, so that if there were only two or three tenders for the lease of a farm, and maybe only one was known to be an efficient farmer, then he would have a certain amount of leverage to negotiate a good deal. This same Robert Webster had also struck out the clause which obliged him to apply manure to the value of £15 a year.

We can learn quite a lot about the Webster family from the 1891 census. Robert was then 39, so he must have been only 28 when he took the tenancy. He was born just down the Winster valley at Foulshaw, and Mary Elizabeth, his wife was 35 and a Beetham lass. They must have married young, for their oldest son, Alexander, was 18. There were seven other children, the youngest being two years old, but the places where they were born point to a tenant farmer looking for better opportunities. The first two children were born in Beetham, perhaps at their grandparents' house? The second two were born at Hare Hill which is almost vertically above Tarn Green. That farm was then owned by the Robinson family who were cousins to the land agents, so there must have been reliable information as to the kind of farmer Robert Webster would make. The four youngest children were all born at High Tarn Green. The three oldest Webster children were employed on the farm in 1891, so there was need of only one living-in servant, Henry Stewerson (?) who was sixteen and from Witherslack. Earlier in the century, the 1851 census shows that the then tenant, William Hall, needed to employ four agricultural labourers and a girl, all living in. He was 44 and his wife 43, so they were not past their prime, but they seem to have been childless.

The Taylor family of Thorphinsty Hall had several sons, and when John junior married at the beginning of the twentieth century, he and his wife Sarah took the tenancy of Tarn Green, then still part of the Thorphinsty estate. John was a keen sportsman, and a family photograph shows him in his Cumberland and Westmorland wrestling kit, all beautifully embroidered by his sisters. John and Sarah had seven children spread over twenty years whilst they were at Tarn Green, and then they moved back to Thorphinsty Hall for a couple of years, but farming was beginning to be a struggle, and they sold up in 1924 and took a boarding house in Arnside. Sadly, Sarah Taylor died suddenly of a brain haemmorhage, and so her sixteen-year-old daughter took up the reins of the household.

Until locating the archive of estate papers, it was often difficult to tell whether High or Low Tarn Green was being referred to in local records, since they were seldom differentiated. Once the acreages were made clear, it was an easier task. We can be fairly sure that William Hall was at High Tarn Green since he was said to farm 100 acres in 1851, and there is a record of his sale. This was actually computed to be 103 acres in the estate books, but very different to the other Tarn Green which was 400 acres at that time, half of it in Lower Holker. Today, the whole complex of houses and barns and sheds at High Tarn Green has been divided by Holker Estates. The barn to the south has been converted to a house with a joinery workshop at the front. The old orchard on the opposite side of the road, now covered in buildings, still belongs to a descendant of George Airey Parkin, the owner earlier in the twentieth century.

George Parkin was a practical joker and a story is still told in the neighbourhood of an impending cock-fight which he had heard about during the Second World War. This was to take place in an old potash kiln in Ashes Wood, long after cock-fighting was made illegal. George borrowed a policeman's uniform and came upon the main from the road above: 'Hello, 'ello, 'ello!' Great was the consternation among the gathered throng!

High Tarn Green has been owned by John and Beryl Offley since the 1990s, and they have done much restoration to the house and barn. They have also contributed a great deal of research into the property.

Foxfield

THE sites of these farmsteads are surrounded by rocky outcrops, ideal for fox borrans, and the hunt will usually find foxes on this land today. This is by far the most likely reason for the name of the farms.

The complex of buildings is roughly half way between the Gummers How road over the fell and the one from Kendal to High Newton. Although gated, the track is now tarmac up to Foxfield, but beyond that it is a rough track over open fell. The area is very exposed, with sweeping views to the east and across Morecambe Bay. Despite its height, the house has an excellent and unfailing supply of spring water, which may be why it was built there in the first place. There are two farms, and now a third dwelling made from a converted barn in this complex, but first we will deal with the original house.

The earliest documentary evidence so far to be found, is when Michael Rowlandson, yeoman, purchased the estate in 1662. It seems likely that he was the tenant at the time of the purchase, as he was said to be already of Fox Field.

The main farmhouse consists of a very old northern section, with a much larger addition, probably of eighteenth-century date. The older part is basically one room up and one down, connected by an oak staircase with quite elaborately turned banister rails. There was a fireplace in both rooms, the upstairs one of an unusually large size for a small room. This was not the house of a labourer for all its simplicity, and the Rowlandsons or Rawlinsons (the spelling varies and is occasionally Rollinson) were men of substance for more than two hundred years when they lived on the fell.

The farmhouse of the lower Foxfield was probably the home of the Muckelt family. They intermarried with the Rowlandsons and occupied the site for at least fifty years in the second half of the seventeenth century. Widow Muckelt of Foxfield held moneys which were invested for poor relief in the parish. In 1696, 'The Intrest belong the Poore of Cartmel Fell' from her holding of £17.13s.3d. amounted to 17s.8d. It does not seem of much value today, and the bi-annual disbursements to the poor amounted to only £1 between eighteen people in 1703. In 1707, a Margaret Muckelt received 1s.6d. for poor relief, but whether she was related is hard to say.

John Muckelt of Foxfield had his daughter baptised at Cartmel in 1676, and from wills, one can see the continuing entwining dynasties. James Rowlandson of Foxfield made his will in 1723 and names a grandson, Richard Muckelt. This James was a moderately wealthy man, and his total assets were valued at £92.12s.0d., but his bequests outstripped his assets. Mary, the oldest daughter was to have £100 and her married sister, Agnes Becke, £70. His heir and namesake had to pay 20s. a year to Richard Muckelt until the young man was 21, and then give him a further £20. There was a fierce penalty if this were not paid; the whole estate was to be sold by the testator's friends, Richard Rawlinson of Simpson Ground and Robert Halhead of Chapel House. In the way of stock the Rowlandsons had a plough team of a pair of oxen and fourteen other mixed cattle and 'sheep of all sorts' worth £33.15s.

James Rowlandson (born circa 1725) and his wife Grace had four male children, but their son James died in infancy as did his brother William. Michael, the next brother was born in 1772 and married in 1804, but died a month after his son James was christened in 1805. This infant must have been the one to carry the family name into the nineteenth century, when he and his wife Elizabeth had James and John baptised in 1833 and 1835 at St Anthony's. (The name here spelt Rawlandson.)

There is no differentiation between the upper and lower Foxfields in any documentation at this stage in history, but the higher one was probably the first to be built, maybe in the last years of the sixteenth century, and the lower one to accommodate the growing clan, though the upper house was enlarged greatly somewhere around the middle of the eighteenth century. The 1814 land tax return shows that Rawlinsons still owned both Foxfields, though occupied neither. James owned the higher and had a tenant James Leak, (whose descendants continued the tenancy until the 1840s) and Eleanor owned the lower, with John Bowness as the occupier. This land tax information is confusing, because the Cartmel Priory bishop's transcripts have other names at this date. James and Mary Long baptised three children between 1810 and 1816, and James was entitled farmer, not labourer, implying that he was the tenant.

After such a long reign at Foxfield, the Rawlinsons appear to have had troubles or needed money to finance some venture. A James Rawlandson mortgaged the property in 1833, and then again in 1838. In 1846, the estate, or part of it, was bought by Mr John Pool, and by then James

Rowlandson was living at Newby Bridge. The Cartmel Fell burial register shows that Elizabeth Rawlinson, James's wife died aged only 29 in 1836, so that event may have caused the family to move. In the 1841 census James Leak and his family were still farming at Foxfield, and they christened a son William from there in 1838. This must have been James junior, as he was only 35. His wife Mary was 26 and they already had three children and employed three farm servants.

In the 1851 Mannex directory, Foxfield was being farmed by Richard Pearson and William Carr, cattle dealer. This is confirmed by the census, which adds the information that Mr Pearson was a widower aged 40, farming 115 acres. He seemed to have been in sole charge of his son of eleven and daughter of five. Ten years later, High Foxfield was being farmed by young James Hayton and his wife Bella. He had 50 acres of heath land and 45 acres of 'old' land, i.e. pre-enclosure.

At Low Foxfield, John Goodman farmed 20 acres of old land, plus 40 acres of enclosed heath. We see in the burial register that John Goodman died in 1869 aged 58. Both farms employed a farm lad, one of fifteen, and the other of thirteen. Both these little farms seemed to change hands regularly, because tenant farmers struggled on poor land. Three years later in 1871, both had new tenants. Anthony Prickett was at Foxfield, he being 40 and his wife Ann 45. Anthony's 85-year-old mother-in-law Margaret Kirkbride was living with them, and was returning to her old home. She and her family had previously lived over the hill at Simpson Ground, but Margaret and her husband Thomas had begun their farming life at one of the Foxfields in the early part of the century when Thomas was a labourer.

Isaac Kirkbride, Margaret's son was living with them as a labourer, but they had a farm lad of fourteen living in too, John Howson from Hutton Roof. Only three years later, Anthony's wife and mother-in-law were both dead, and we later find him lodging and working at the little holding that belonged to the Quaker Meeting House. There is a photograph of Anthony at the gate to Height Meeting House, looking very much in need of wifely care.

The Inland Revenue review of 1909/10 has a surprise. After two and a half centuries and evidence of financial need, the Rawlinson family were still the owners of High Foxfield, but by now, Rowland Rawlinson (a christian name much favoured by his forebears) was of Waterfoot, near Manchester. The old house was stated to be in good condition and together with the buildings, had recently been repaired. At this period, many of the farms on the fell were in a poor state, especially if they were tenanted.

The estate was bought by the Bentleys, a family from Yorkshire, before the Second World War, and for a while was farmed by Jack Myers and his wife Mary. They got married just as war was declared and went to New Brighton for their honeymoon, somewhat to the alarm of their families, but they returned unscathed as the bombing of Merseyside did not begin for some time. Their first son was born at Foxfield, and the doctor's fee for attending (but after the event) was eleven guineas, an enormous amount for a tenant farmer to find at that time. The minimum wage for a farm worker was raised to £3 during the war, and prior to that, some payment might be in kind, e.g. milk, firewood or housing.

Unfortunately, the two farms were rarely

differentiated in parish documents, and it is only because the Rawlinsons have been traced at High Foxfield until the censuses began, that assumptions can be made as to the lower farm. There must have been practical reasons for setting the house where it lies, but they are not immediately obvious. The road is quite steep, but the building does not follow the contour, it faces the track. The ground below it is fairly level and seems a better site, but may be prone to flooding. Very often, as the National Trust have proved in Langdale, the single farms of today were once hamlets of families, and around 1600, the number of families working the land was at an all-time high. This could have been the period when Low Foxfield came into being, perhaps to equip cadet branches of Rawlinsons with a means of livelihood.

Above Low Foxfield but below the converted barn are a series of bee-boles built into a south-facing wall. As mentioned elsewhere, these recesses gave shelter to the straw skeps in wet weather, and these are perhaps unusually high on the fell, but in earlier times the land above would have had more heather where today there is forestry.

The earliest residents of Low Foxfield are not easy to identify, but once the census began and the local directories were published, more can be gleaned, though even the census returns do not differentiate between the two farms. By 1910, the estate belonged to John Taylor of Laithbutts, Kirkby Lonsdale, a son of the Taylors of Thorphinsty Hall. The pasture-land, described as 'fair' by the Inland Revenue, was farmed by William Harrison, but the cottage was described as being in poor condition and uninhabited.

Apart from the Rowlandsons, so many different names appear in the baptismal registers, one assumes that there were ever-changing tenants at the lower farm. Undoubtedly there were farm servants living with the Rowlandsons, but they were usually unmarried. Among the surnames of couples who had children baptised from 1779 to 1835 were: Holme, Sewart, Barker, Tyson, Long, Fleming, Kirkbride, Mitchell, Robinson and Jackson. These were most likely young couples who wanted to get a foot on the farming ladder and maybe move on to something bigger or better.

The newest dwelling at Foxfield is called Rankthorn from a nearby intake. It was converted from a barn in 1994 by the farmers of Foxfield who were nearing retirement, and was perhaps built in the eighteenth or early nineteenth century. This was once a bank barn on two levels, so it lends itself well to conversion. The living quarters are on the higher level, so have commanding views over the Winster valley. Rankthorn plantation, lower down the hill is now commercial conifer woodland, but was once the origin of a local red apple named for its location. If anyone knows of a surviving Rankthorn apple, Cartmel Fell and District Local History Society would be interested to record it.

Pattison How

AT some distant period, this elevated portion of the fell must have belonged to a family by the name of Pattinson, often abbreviated to Pattison. The surname is said to originate in Patterdale, and it was recorded in a lay subsidy roll of 1332 in Cumberland.

At the time of writing, in 2005, this farmhouse is a bleak windswept shell, and though there was once hope of restoration in 1996, the Lake District Planning Board would not allow it. The case went to appeal, with letters of approval and support from locals, but again it failed. Now, the entire structure is unsafe, and part of the roof blew off in winter gales.

The interior has two snug little rooms each side of the door with fireplaces, and extensive larders and pantries behind, half set into the hill. There are two floors above, the first with four bedrooms and then a loft covering all the roof space. The loft was intended for frequent use, as the once fine staircase shows, maybe as servants' quarters. Today, the only footsteps on the stairs are those of sheltering sheep. The land around the farmhouse is poor, either boggy and acid or rocky and thin-soiled. The house and barns adjoining are unique in this area, being constructed with massive slate slabs set on edge. The appearance is of facing stone, but the blocks are an integral part of the building. The interior walls seem to be made in the usual way, the core being filled with lime and rubble, but the style is so unusual that it is hard to date. The Cartmel Fell Local History Society thought that possibly a great renovation took place in the early nineteenth century, and the facing blocks were to improve the weather-proofing. Certainly it is one of the most exposed settings of any farm on the fell, commanding a sweeping view over the estuary to the distant Yorkshire peak of Ingleborough. The mystery has since been solved, as a grand-daughter of Bryan Batty tells us that her grandfather made this change in the facade early in the twentieth century, and also installed the cast-iron range.

Amongst the collection of deeds found at the Height Farm are many relating to Pattison How, and they tell the story of ownership, leasing, and mortgages which could not be repaid. All the details from these documents come from the same source and I am indebted to Geoffrey Wightman for letting me borrow them.

The first of these is dated 1688, when Thomas Ashburner of Marsh Grange in Furness sold the property to William Simpson of Flookburgh for £207. There was the understanding that the 'Knowing Rent' of 2s.6d. had to be paid by the new owner every two and a half years. As mentioned elsewhere, this must have been a relic of monastic dues, but the rent had become privatised by this date. Most likely, the holding was let on a tenancy agreement, as surnames changed often. From documentary evidence, it seems that there were religious divisions at Pattison How at this period. Quaker records and the Cartmel Fell parish records show that there were families of both persuasions living in close proximity. The Cartmel Priory register notes that Margaret Stones of Pattison How, a Quaker, was buried at the Sepulchre on 9 December

1702. In the Friends records, Jane Garnett was buried in 1695 at Height, and James a year later, both of Pattinson How. In 1707, according to the Cartmel Fell chapelwarden's accounts, Lawrence Swainson, son of Christopher of Pattinson How, 'A Younge man', gave £6 to the good of the chapel, whilst at the same address in the same year, Agnes Garnett made a Quaker wedding with Daniel Rawlinson of Arles Beck (Old House Beck). There had been much hostility between the Friends and the officials of the established church within living memory at that time, so one wonders if living in such close proximity fanned their loyalties or submerged them. Certainly, £6 was a huge gift for a young man to make to chapel funds, and far more than most people gave. The wealthy and generous Rowland Briggs of Swallowmire was recorded as giving £5 in the same account.

The property seems to have been tenanted throughout the first half of the eighteenth century, for the names on the deeds do not tie up with those in the births, christenings, marriages or burials. The landowners had money problems, and this property was the subject of a number of mortgages for over a century, during which it changed hands several times.

Thomas Bowes was a tailor and when he made his will in 1714 he described the dwelling as Pattyson How. He owned a property in Witherslack (possibly Low Wood) which he bequeathed to his son Thomas. He had two other sons, George and Peter, who were left 5s. and 2s.6d. respectively, and his daughters' children received a total of 30s. From the way in which the will was couched, it seems that Thomas Bowes was already a widower, so maybe he was lodging at Pattinson How whilst his heir ran the farm in Witherslack.

In 1718, William Simpson of Marsh Grange in Furness leased the whole property, with fields and closes totalling about sixteen acres for 99 years. The fields were described as 'Several small closes and parcels of arable land, meadow and pasture' and the closes were named: Moor Close or Foils, eight acres, Cross Dales, three acres, Gate meadow, two and a half acres, New Close and Gillbrow about two acres. The new lessee was Thomas Dicconson of Crosthwaite, and he agreed to pay three instalments of £100.10s. every year on 2 February, plus an initial payment of £50. There was also an annual rent of one peppercorn to be paid at Pentecost if so demanded. This seems to be a large amount of money at this date for so few acres on such poor land. In 1737, a mortgage for securing the repayment of £200 was drawn up. It was from Tobias Knipe, eldest son and heir of Mr John Knipe of Flodder, to John Ponsonby of Hale Hall in Cumberland for one year, in which 'Pattison House' and its lands were included with others at Flookborough. This move seems to have been a temporary expedient to recover some of the money owed by Thomas Dicconson. By 1741, both William Simpson and Thomas Dicconson were dead, as a further deed shows, but the debt was still outstanding, so the property was re-conveyed for another 99 years to Mr John Dodgson of Wilson House, which was a couple of miles away in Lindale. We also learn from these transactions, that Tobias Knipe, John's son, was also William Simpson's grandson, so the property had merely been shuffled round the family descending through the female line to the Knipes. John Knipe must have married William Simpson's daughter.

The relationship between the Dodgsons and the ironmaster John Wilkinson does not seem to have been recorded, but it is thought that Wilkinson moved to Wilson House around 1748/9, leaving in 1755 to go to Bersham in North Wales, though he retained ownership of Wilson House. Maybe he offered to buy the property in order to have ready access to the peat mosses, as at that time he was experimenting with smelting using peat. If he had made a tempting offer for the property, this might have persuaded the Dodgsons to buy Pattinson How, but without access to the Wilson House deeds, this is pure speculation. On the rough track up to the house on Cartmel Fell, in places the hardcore can be seen to contain lumps of slag. In all probability, this came from the furnaces at Wilson House, but it might have come from Backbarrow, as the Gibsons at Height were selling charcoal to the Backbarrow company in 1754, and would not like to return with an empty cart.

It seems that the Dodgsons lived at Pattinson How for most of the rest of that century, but when the father, John, died in 1781, he could not have known that his son and heir, Matthew, would follow him to the grave only four years later. Matthew's will shows that they now owned the freehold of the property, and as he was unmarried, he left it to his mother, Isabel. She also inherited two more freehold estates at Hubbersty Head, one of these being Yews. Isabel had no other children to inherit her properties, so she divided them between various nephews and great nephews. Pattinson How was to be shared between George and Richard Howgarth or Hoggarth, the sons of her nephew George and niece Dorothy Hoggarth, of Pattinson How. (When she made this will, Isabel was living in Kendal, so she must have leased Pattinson How meanwhile to her niece and nephew.) From the wording of the will, it seems that the Hoggarths arrived when Isabel lost her own menfolk. She stipulated that the two brothers were to pay their mother Dorothy a £10 annuity out of the estate, in half-yearly instalments, so it would seem that Dorothy was also widowed and needed support.

Apart from the sons, George and Richard, there were eight daughters, seven of them unmarried. They were to have their great-aunt's clothes, both linen and woollen, and all her household stuff and furniture, hangings, table and other linen. They were also to have £30 apiece. There were numerous other bequests to nieces and nephews including three sums of £200, so if her only son had lived to succeed his father and had his own family, they would have been rich indeed.

The Hoggarth brothers decided not to farm jointly, and George's son George must have tried to buy his uncle's half by borrowing money from John Gibson of the Height. This amounted to £300 and the interest thereon. Unfortunately, his efforts to repay the mortgage failed, and the wealthy Mr. Gibson became even wealthier.

Piecing together the evidence, it seems that Jacob Crow, maltster of Winster, and his wife Agnes bought out George Hoggarth, who was then able to pay his debt to John Gibson, but Jacob also had to borrow money to buy Pattinson How. He went to the man who seems to have been the private banker of southern Cartmel Fell, none other than the same John Gibson. The amount was now inflated to £400, due no doubt to the Napoleonic wars, but if it could not be repaid within a year, i.e. in 1814, the property became Mr Gibson's for a 1,000 year lease. Yet again, there were problems with repayment, and the day came when the money was due, but it could not be found. The solution this time was to sell the estate, which now amounted to about 90 acres. The purchaser was Jacob Wakefield of Kendal, and Jacob Crow was able to pay his debt and the interest on it to John Gibson, and an amount was set aside to pay Dorothy Hoggarth her annuity of £10 until her death.

From parish records, it seems that the Crows stayed on as tenants or leaseholders, at least for a while. They had a son, Jacob junior in 1813, and a daughter Ellen two years later. John, another son, was christened in 1821 from Pattinson How, but when Mark was born in 1825, the family had moved to Swallowmire.

During the 1830s and 1840s, John and Isabella Robinson were farming up at Pattinson How and between 1841 and 1849 they had five children, but this was a decade when their family name occurred frequently in the parish burial register. Some were infants, two were in the prime of life, and John must have been a great-grandfather, aged 93 when he died in 1842.

Shortly after this period, the Crows re-appear on the scene. In the 1851 census William Crow, then 28 and married to Hannah, was farming 50 acres at Pattinson How with no hired help. The 90 acres which were mentioned in 1814 had shrunk. The couple then had two children, Ann and Jacob, and William followed in 1852, then Agnes who was born in 1855. A separate household, but at the same address were John and Mary Lowd, 22 and 21 years of age. There is no obvious way of dividing this house, but a now derelict addition to the northern end of the main house could have been a two-roomed dwelling in the past, but appears to have been a wash-house latterly, as old wash-coppers rust among the ruins. John Lowd was an agricultural labourer, possibly at Pattinson How or Height farm.

The Crows were there long enough for their daughter Ann to be married on Boxing Day, 1861. She was 21 and her husband was Henry Dodson Thornborough of Little Thorphinsty. Henry must have moved into Pattinson How, as that was his abode when his first son, Thomas, was christened the following year. His middle name, Dodson, seems to indicate a relationship with the owners in the previous century, although the spelling is variable. Further investigation shows that the Rev. Thomas Thornborrow married Esther Dodson in 1806, and Henry was a descendant of this line. The families of Crow, Dodson and Thornburrow were continually on the move during the late eighteenth and nineteenth century, shuffling between the farms of Swallowmire, Ashes, Little Thorphinsty and Pattinson How. Reading and comparing the census records of the decades is bewildering, as grandchildren move in and out, as do nieces and nephews, then entire families exchange farms. Sadly, Ann Thornborrow died in early January 1868, aged only 25, and the farm changed hands yet again. After the Crows flew, John Bennett, a widower from Broughton, moved in. He was 53 in 1871 and his daughter Mary looked after the house. She was 25, and must have had a lonely life, but they had a young farm lad living in, sixteen-year-old John Warrener from Windermere. John Bennett claimed to be farming 80 acres then, so the land had changed shape yet again.

As an aside at this point, it is often believed that

farms stayed much the same size, but in most cases that are detailed on Cartmel Fell, this certainly was not so. The houses and land were split just as often as they are today, and for the same sorts of reasons.

After the Bennetts left, some time between 1881 and 1891, Wilson Wildman and his sister Jane arrived at Pattinson How from Hare Hill, the adjoining farm. In 1891 Wilson was described as a widower of 47, and his sister was unmarried and 51. Their mother must have come to join the household prior to the census, for in 1890 she was buried, aged 85, and she had been with them at Hare Hill. The parish registers have neither baptisms nor burials from Pattinson How after this date. Wilson Wildman stayed on for at least another ten years, but in 1901, his sister's place had been taken by Margaret Hoggarth. Her relationship, if any, to the Hoggarths who inherited the farm 100 years earlier has not been investigated. This middle-aged pair had a young lad living in to help on the farm, and this was 15-year-old Bryan Batty, who in later life was to farm it himself.

A descendant of the Battys who farmed Hare Hill in the late nineteenth century sheds a little light on this era. Bryan Batty senior farmed Hare Hill and Pattinson How as well, first as a tenant, but later buying Pattinson How and 148 acres from the Robinson estate. This was probably around 1913, and when Robert Robinson died. Bryan had a large family of fourteen children, mostly involved in agriculture. His son Bryan was farming at Sow How around 1918, establishing himself as a shorthorn breeder, but his father decided that he would like Pattinson How to be managed by one of the family. Young Bryan was loath to move, as the acreage was considerably less at Pattinson How, so it meant selling some of his stock, and the family felt even more isolated than they did at Sow How. The water had to be fetched from the well outside, and little Ella Batty used to watch her mother carrying two buckets at a time to fill the wash copper, making nine journeys in all. When she was still in the infants' section of the school, Ella had to walk three and a half miles there, and three and a half miles back every day on her own. If it was raining hard, her heavy coat was sodden by the time she got to school, and still wet when she came to go home. By the next morning, it might still be damp on the shoulders, and eventually this took its toll on the little girl and she contracted pneumonia. Their doctor was at Penny Bridge, but he had no transport, so in order to fetch him, Bryan had to harness up the pony and trap and make the double journey to bring and return the doctor. On her return from school, Ella often walked with the postman who was returning to Newton. She was always afraid of meeting a deranged man from Grange who would walk up Cartmel Fell, muttering and stuffing his pockets with grass, and this strange behaviour terrified the little girl. She would scuttle away, but the man walked faster, so she always hoped for the postman's protection.

Farming at Pattinson How was not successful for the young Battys, and eventually they retreated down the fell to take up the tenancy of Burblethwaite Hall, where everything was more congenial and the children could get to school in twenty minutes.

After the farmhouse became uninhabited, it was used for a while by visiting troops of Boy Scouts as a base for summer camp. It must have been on one of these visits that the floorboards of an upper room were burnt through. A footpath to Simpson Ground goes past this lonely outpost, and one can see on the left the remains of a little enclosed orchard with stumps of damson trees. Red deer can sometimes be seen in this vicinity.

Simpson Ground

AT the dissolution of the monasteries, many farmsteads which were held by the church became the property of the tenants or new landlords. They might owe service to the new lord, such as boon shearing, and they might have to pay a fine on the death of the lord or on the death of the owner. It is thought that most of the 'Grounds' date from this period, the name of the farm being that of the family which held it. Around Coniston and Hawkshead such Grounds abound. Atkinson Ground, Roger Ground, Keen Ground, Walker Ground etc., and from a Duchy of Lancaster Rental of 1508, we can be fairly certain that Simpson Ground was named for the occupant. This was John Symson, and that is about all we know of him. It may have been one of his descendants however, who lived at Height and left a will in 1645. Height, the district, encompassed Simpson Ground, so Jennett, widow of Michael Simpson could have been of Simpson Ground.

The farmhouse is situated near the 600 foot contour and faces south. There are buildings on either side, and a road runs between the house and barn onto an ancient track across the fell. Part of this has been built up into a causeway across the bog, but how long ago this was done is hard to say. On the Enclosure map of 1797, this track was marked and was called Rapier Meadow road, but the rapier meadow is not named. There is a very long narrow field running alongside the track, but its shape is more like a broad sword than a rapier. The fields to the south of the farmhouse have an interesting shape. It looks as though a wall has been built, and then the area within the enclosure has been divided into narrow strips. This is the nearest thing to the mediaeval form of strip lynchets that can be seen on the fell, and may be a pointer to the antiquity of Simpson Ground. This is an area of flat land, and might conceivably have been shared with the hamlet which centred around Height farm. The other alternative is that the occupants of Simpson Ground used the strips to practice their own rotational system.

There is a big gap in the continuity of records from John Symson until the Rowlandsons appear in the mid-1600s, but the wills of Michael and Jennett Simpson of Height indicate continuity of Simpsons, in the Height area at least, until 1645. This couple appear to have been childless, as all bequests were to brothers, sisters or nieces and nephews. Michael, who died in 1642, left two shillings to his namesake to buy a lamb. When Jennett, his widow died, a full inventory was taken, and this had the usual household and farm gear, and like many other of their neighbours, the Simpsons had spinning and weaving equipment. The raw materials included hemp and hemp yarn, and four stones of wool. Money which was due to them included six guineas lent to Lawrence Newton. This was very probably the same Lawrence Newton who eventually left money to build the Friends Meeting House at Height in 1677.

A Rowland Rowlandson of Simpson Ground baptised three daughters at Cartmel, and when he died in 1704, he left a will and inventory. From the will we can see that he had yet more daughters, and he is termed yeoman, that is owner occupier. The house was very small, but the Rowlandsons had some items which added to the style and comfort of life. There were curtains in the chamber, and these were probably to keep draughts off the bed. A new "tukin" covercloth may have been a Turkey carpet cloth, which can be seen in some paintings of sixteenth and seventeenth century life as a table covering. There were sheets and table linen, and 'quishons' to make the wooden chairs and stools more comfortable. Outside, there were four cows and two stirks, horses and sheep, so the farming was not on a large scale, and wool and hemp were worth £1.8s.6d. The total value was £43.16s., but like so many of his neighbours, his debts exceeded his assets, and came to £60. One always wants to know what happened next? Did the daughters forego their inheritance? Did they sell up and take rented accommodation or go into service? We can see from the chapel accounts that Rowland had borrowed money from the chapel funds, because an item in 1696 notes his repayment of interest for two years, £3.13s. 'To the chapel and poor of Cartmel Fell.' Whatever the outcome was, by 1726 a new name appears at this farm. John Elerah (Elleray) who was the Overseer of the Poor for his holding at Simpson Ground. In the same box of documents at Kendal Record Office, there is a memorandum of the goods and fences belonging to the Simpson Ground estate, and from this we can make a guess at the sequence of events following Rowland Rowlandson's death. The document shows that the estate was purchased from Richard Rawlinson (Rowlandson?) in 1722 by the late Queen Anne's bounty. The estate was to be used for funding the chapel, and a quarter of the rent was still used to augment the curate's salary in the first part of the twentieth century. The memorandum of 1722 deals in great detail with the fences and boundaries of the estate, but there is an interesting little domestic aside headed 'The Goods'. This is a brief inventory of the household furniture and includes 'The great table in the house' and 'all the boards, fast and loose in the Dwelling House and outhouses.' There are recollections of great tables in many farms on the fell, and they were deemed to be fixtures, having been made of large oaken planks and joined inside the house. There used to be one at Thorphinsty Hall which the purchasers expected to find there when they moved in about 1970, but when they arrived, the table had been removed. Another such table was at the Wood in the early part of the century, and was used for weddings and funerals in the parlour. In the autumn, it was used for storing apples in what was a seldom-heated room.

The parish became responsible for repairs and maintenance to Simpson Ground, and there are accounts for walling, glazing and a new lock. The tenant seems to have been one of the officers of the parish, and they did their turn as chapelwarden and so on. John Elleray who was the tenant when the estate was bought for the parish was overseer of the poor four years later. It is possible that the Rawlinsons or Rowlandsons continued to live at Simpson Ground even after John Elleray became the official tenant, as their name occurs a year after the official purchase, when Richard apprised the worldly goods of James, who died at Foxfield. Spelling was still phonetic to a certain extent, so the official rendering of the Rawlinson surname had not gelled.

Towards the end of the eighteenth century, many names occur for Simpson Ground in the parish registers; Mattinson, Backhouse, Lesh, and then Holme in 1821, when John gave 1s.6d. towards the curate's salary. Somewhere between 1821 and 1823, Thomas Kirkbride took over the estate. The chapelwarden was unfamiliar with his name and spelt it Churchbride, when he too gave 1s.6d. towards the curate's stipend. We know a good deal about this man and his family, thanks to an account written by his descendant, Mrs Lucy Holmes of Staveley. The Kirkbrides hailed from Inverness originally, probably victims of the Highland clearances. A legend in the family was that they had no name, being serfs of the clan McLeod. When the minister asked the surname of the man about to be married, he said he was nameless and so the minister gave him a name in memory of the church and his bride.

Three generations of the Kirkbrides farmed at Simpson Ground, but the first had worked on several farms before taking on his own tenancy. Thomas senior had children baptised at Tarn Green in 1812 and 1814, and then three more when he was at Foxfield, and finally the last three from Simpson Ground. Thomas worked very hard to improve his new farm. He improved the drainage, built retaining walls and enclosed fields to enable him to keep more stock. He employed two men for a while, to cart the stone and do some walling. The couple were of such disproportionate sizes that they were known as Cuckoo and Li'le Bird. The second generation of Kirkbrides had ten children with seventeen years between youngest and oldest. Seven were boys, and according to their niece, all near six feet tall, due to their Highland genes no doubt. The boys wore kilts when they were young, and one wonders if they were heirlooms. Kilts don't wear out on the knees like trousers, so they can be handed down for generations. On one occasion, John Kirkbride was saved from drowning by his kilt, probably around 1866 when he was four. He fell in a pool near Witherslack, but was buoyed up by the kilt floating out around him. One of the Cockertons happened to be nearby, fishing, and helped to land a bigger catch than usual. He asked: "Whose lad are you?" Answer: "Me Dad's." "Where are you from?" "Home."

Lucy Holmes relates many of the methods of household management and farming practice in her memoir; smelly candles were made from mutton fat with cotton twine for a wick, and soap was made from fat and washing soda. When the soap had been cut into blocks it was put to harden on the shelf which hung just below the ceiling of the kitchen. In the same mouse-free zone were placed the small sheep's cheeses. All manner of products were preserved, including fish. Mrs. Kirkbride would buy fresh flukes from Flookburgh, and when they had been gutted and split, salt was rubbed over them and the children stitched them together in pairs through the tails. These were then hung up like washing, to dry above the fire. Before cooking, they were soaked in a little milk. Pea pods were hung up in the same manner.

In the nineteenth century, all the cooking was still done as it had been for hundreds of years, over the open peat fire. Pots were hung from the crane in the chimney, and white bread was a Sunday treat. Without an oven, this too had to be cooked in an iron pot which was covered over with peat. When the peat had burnt away to a white ash, then the bread was ready. For everyday, the family ate haver bread, and this was made once or twice a week and stored in an oak kist to keep the mice out. The oatcakes were cooked on a bakestone which was heated with wood shavings. Oatmeal porridge was the daily breakfast, and almost all food was home produced. When fresh meat was not available, there was home-cured fatty bacon or ham, and salt beef. Mutton was sometimes pickled with vinegar and spices, and of course there was always poultry for meat and eggs.

There was no running water, but the boiler in an outhouse was used for all kinds of purposes. It boiled the washing, heated the weekly bath water. was used for the dolly tub and for scalding pigs after killing, and for boiling up animal feed such as corn or potatoes. The Kirkbrides rarely drank tea, milk being the usual drink, but in the summer they made a kind of herb beer with nettles, burnets and dandelions. Sugar and yeast were added to ferment the brew, and no doubt this was done in the wash boiler too. Of course, all the children had to pull their weight, and they all had their own jobs to do. When they got home from Staveley School, they had to thrash a few sheaves of corn with a flail on the barn floor. Some would have to put the turnips through the crusher and others chop straw for the horses to eat. The cow tubs would have been prepared before they set off for school, so the morning must have begun very early, as it was quite a long walk to Staveley. Mrs. Holmes comments on the excellent education the children had, her father having a beautiful clear hand, and also being able to reckon up as fast as a calculator. Along with reminiscences of a bygone age, Lucy Holmes includes remedies which her forebears used at Simpson

Simpson Ground in 1933.

Ground. Some, like goose-grease rubbed into the chest for a cough, were probably universal at the time, but fresh cow dung as a drawing poultice might not have been so widely used. Another poultice for a septic wound was boiled potatoes and epsom salts, applied hot, and buttermilk was a soothing remedy for sunburn.

The first Thomas Kikbride died when he was only 57, leaving his wife Margaret to farm with the help of her children. She was five years her husband's senior, and was widowed at 61. Her oldest son Thomas was then thirty, and it was he who took on the tenancy. Although Thomas Kirkbride improved his farm, it did not benefit him as the rent was increased to match the improvements. We know from parish accounts that in 1868 the rent was £60 a year for 148 acres. The family decided to move in the face of the unequal struggle, but Thomas had became so depressed that he took his own life by hanging himself. His widow had to make the move on her own with eight children, the youngest being only nine months old. Ironically, by the end of the nineteenth century, the rent of Simpson Ground was only £25, but times had changed and land values had fallen.

In the following decades a number of families moved in and out of Simpson Ground. The censuses record Ellwoods and Prestons, and the parish registers show Cassons, Atkinsons and Nicholsons in the early years of the 20th century. In 1901, George and Emily Birkett were the tenants with four children, all born on the fell, but Emily came from East Bergholt in Suffolk. By 1906, the Carruthers family had taken over the farm, and their son William was christened in that year, named after his father. This family had relations at Cowmire Hall, and an old photo exists which shows some huge family gathering at Simpson Ground, and an old post card shows the farm as it was before it was enlarged. Two little girls sit on the window sill, and these are probably Carruthers too. When Peggy Carruthers got married in 1943, the wedding breakfast was held in the barn at Simpson Ground, and until quite recently, all such occasions would have been celebrated on the farmstead. A winter wedding would be more difficult, as the buildings would be full of fodder and stock.

The roof level must have been very low in the original house, but the upstairs rooms were merely lofts at first, so there would have been more headroom but more draughts. At some period around the middle of the twentieth century, a dormer window was installed, to be followed by another at the opposite end of the house some years later.

Between the wars, the land around was owned by Sir John Fisher of Blakeholme Wray, and he used to hold shooting parties using Simpson Ground as a base. The farm has dwindled to a smallholding now, but some of the land was sold to create a new small farm called Summer Close. This was the field name of the site that the new bungalow occupies.

Little Thorphinsty

DESPITE the name, historically this farm seems to have been unconnected with Thorphinsty Hall. It could possibly have been part of the hall estate before the Dissolution, but there is no evidence, since the priory archives have disappeared.

The earliest documentary evidence of the holding is oblique. James Swainson of the Kit Crag (now Swallowmire) died in 1625 and left the estate to his heir, Nicholas, and also 'Theorphinstie'. We know that Thorphinsty Hall was not his to bequeath, so this must be Little Thorphinsty. Nicholas died the same year as his father, leaving five daughters and a son, James. As the heir, James would have inherited Kit Crag, but the family seem to have been ailing, and Elizabeth, the eldest daughter was to have 'Thorpensty' if her brother died without issue. Money was left to pay off a £5 mortgage with Nicholas Robinson, borrowed by Ann Raisbecke and William Atkinson's wife, on the proviso that they came to the aid of James's sick children, and in later years, the Robinson name crops up again in connection with Little Thorphinsty.

There was a large contingent of the Robinson family at Staveley-in-Cartmel in the seventeenth and eighteenth centuries, associated with Tower Wood and Fell Foot. Over several generations, they acquired property on Cartmel Fell, and they became constables and overseers of the poor for their estates.

It would seem that for a while at least, Little

Thorphinsty had tenant farmers because a family called Scales lived there in the first part of the eighteenth century. The name of the farm is not always given in the Cartmel register, but 'Cartmel Fell' is added. The surname was quite a common one in Cartmel and in the Lyth valley at that period, and indeed there is a farm in the Lyth called Johnscales, which must simply have meant John Scales's house, and the Crosthwaite registers show members of the family living there in the seventeenth and eighteenth centuries. The name was uncommon in Cartmel Fell however, and there are only a few mentioned in the Cartmel Priory registers. A positive identification is when John Scales of Little Thorphinsty christened his son John, at Cartmel, on 10 June 1722. The christian name John seems to have been a family tradition. Six years earlier, another John of Cartmel Fell was buried, and although the farm is not named, it seems likely that he too was of Little Thorphinsty, since the surname is not linked with any other holding at that time. Earlier still, a poor widow, Ellin Scales, had relief of 1s. from the parish in 1703, and 2s. in 1707. In 1734, Dorothy Scales, widow of yet another John, applied for letters of administration for her husband's estate, and the attached inventory gives us an idea of the size of the farm in those days. Unfortunately, the goods in the house are not itemised as in some inventories, but the rooms are named:

His purse and Apparrell...	2...0...0
In House and Buttery...	15...6
Goods in the Chamber...	1...1...0
Goods in the Back Chamber...	5...0
Goods above stairs...	14...0
2 Heifers and 2 Cows...	7...10...0
5 Young Heifers...	4...10...0
Goods in the stable,	
* Cowhouse & Peathouse...*	7...0
In the barn, Hay, Oats and Barley...	6...0...0
Two geldings...	2...10...0
Nine Hogs...	13...6

From this inventory, it seems that John Scales was obtaining his income mostly from cattle. He had no breeding flock of sheep so was probably wintering his nine hogs to sell the following season. They must have been poor little things at just over 1s. 4d. each, because at a similar period in 1734, Humphrey Senhouse computed that his lambs were worth 4s. each. There is no mention of poultry in the inventory, though it is hard to believe that there was none, nor any trade tools, such as a spinning wheel or loom, but that might come under the heading of the unspecified 'Goods'. Without being able to read between the lines, one could assume that the only source of cash for this family was the sale of livestock at market. The two cows were in calf with any luck, as this was November, and he had two heifers which might calve the following year, and five young ones. The newly-calved heifers might be expected to bring £2 apiece, and the fattened hogs perhaps 3s. each, so that would bring in over £5. A small farmer might make a little extra by selling his services when needed to wealthier neighbours, such as Thorphinsty Hall, at haytime or harvest, but that expedient had to be weighed against the importance of getting his own crops. A better way to earn a little money was to make saleable items when the weather was too bad to work outside. These might include woodland products such as hurdles and besoms, or baskets, which were used for all types of transportation, and the actual measure for such items as apples or pears. We do know that there had been a certain amount of hemp grown and processed on this farm, as indeed it was on many others. Hemp was widely grown in Tudor times for sails and cordage for the Navy, but of course for use in sacking and even heavy-duty clothing on the farm. Apparently, the quality of northern-grown hemp was much finer than the imported fibre. Until the almost universal use of paper or plastic sacks, many farmers in the twentieth century preferred to turn the rain with a sack across the shoulders, and maybe another for a hood, and Beatrix Potter, in farming mode, often would do likewise.

There is a scrappy map of the fields of Little Thorphinsty in the Kendal Record Office. It has no date, but the handwriting looks as if it could be about 1800. The fields have their amended acreages but no names, so it may have been made for land tax purposes. A separate list of fields and farms exists (without a map) for the 1814 Land Tax, so it has been possible to work out field names from the acreages. One field above a beck has the name of Hemplands, but to clinch the deduction, the watercourse has a series of retting dams still visible. The banks are lined with small walls making shallow oblong stepped pools, each with a small dam, not fully blocked. If a stone is dropped into the gap, the pool instantly fills. Normally, these pools are overgrown with ferns and other plant life, but after torrential rain, the sides are scoured out and the shapes are visible again. The newly-cut hemp, or flax possibly, was laid in the dammed pool, and for a few weeks was trampled at intervals until the outer casing degraded and washed away. The process was quicker in stagnant water, but more obnoxious and polluting, or it could even be carried out by the dew and rain if the hemp was spread out on the field. This latter took a good deal longer, maybe six to eight weeks, dependent on the weather conditions. I am told by flax growers in Ulster that the smell of stagnant flax-retting dams is like stale flower-vase water magnified a thousand-fold. No-one will approach a flax treader until he has had a bath and left his clothes in a distant building. There is no suggestion of hemp in John Scales's inventory however, but of course it could be part of the 'Goods'. When William Pearson wrote his diaries and letters in the mid-nineteenth century, he guessed that few young people would recognise hemp if they saw it growing, though he remembered it was widely cultivated in his youth, so we might guess that it ceased to be grown here around 1800.

Another field on this estate with a descriptive name was 'Grindstone Haw'. Having identified this by acreage also, on investigation it seemed that superficially the outcrops of rock looked the same as all the others in the neighbourhood, but on breaking off a chunk, the inside surface had a glittering appearance and felt abrasive. It sharpened an axe quickly, and when a piece was rubbed on a slate, it was the slate that wore. Another mystery was solved by this little map. In the lists of field names with acreage which are in the 1814 land tax book, many farms have a field called 'Whagg'. None of the local farmers knew the meaning of this word and dialect dictionaries were no more fruitful. It seemed likely that it might be connected to hag, as in peat-hag, or quag, as in quagmire, and this was confirmed on the ground. There is a permanent bog between two rocky outcrops in Whagg field.

It appears that Spannell Beck has been diverted at some distant time. The shape of the land indicates the natural course, and it used to be very boggy until re-drained in 1994. The most usual reason for diversion was to create a mill leat, and the Ordnance Survey map calls the wood alongside the beck 'Mill Wood'. The map confirms the speculation, for the fields bounding the diversion are called Great and Little Mill fields. Here and there are the remains of stone slabs which lined the sides of the beck to keep it in its new course. There is a sudden fall in the land which creates a waterfall and an artificial pile of stones in parallel with the beck may have supported the launder. Today, the scene looks totally rural, but further up this little beck are two other mill sites. They would probably have been used for fulling in medieval times, and there are remains of potash kilns nearby which would have produced the basis of the soap used to clean the cloth. So far, there is no evidence to show who the local industrialist was who built these mills, but it is interesting to speculate. The Knipes at Burblethwaite Hall were the lords of the manor, but it was a very little manor which seemed to extend to the oft-disputed boundaries with Cowmire Hall, and probably ended at the road above the hall. The Huttons at Thorphinsty had a forge on Way Beck, but there is little evidence to point to their ownership of any land at Little Thorphinsty; indeed, existing estate maps for the hall cease at the boundary. The most likely family to develop the woollen trade were the Briggses of Cowmire, Bridge House, Kit Crag and Swallowmire. Their wealth came from the wool trade, and what more natural than that they should have the processing on the doorstep, where an eye could be kept on the business.

After the Scales family left, the next record is of a Mr Robinson, who was overseer of the poor for Little Thorphinsty in 1752. This does not necessarily mean that he lived in the house, though he may have done, but that he owned it. The title of 'Mr' seems to denote one of slightly superior standing in the community since nearly all other entries give the christian name instead. Richard Robinson was one of the appraisers of John Scales's inventory in 1734, so was maybe his landlord. At the same period, i.e. in 1754 and 1755, Mr Richard Robinson was overseer for his holdings of Kit Crag and Swallowmire, so he may well be the same person, as the lands run together along what used to be called Kit Crag road, and is now Hoghouse Lane. A deed in Barrow Record Office, dated 1700, details the sale of Little Thorphinsty from Richard Robinson to John Walker of Fair Ridge in Cartmel. The estate changed hands for £260, plus the yearly rent of 6s.7½d. and 8d. for milling. The woods and trees had already been sold to Anthony Addison.

At the end of the eighteenth century the farm was leased by Matthew Dodgson to Joseph Crow and his wife Agnes. The parish register shows that they settled down to produce a line of daughters; Agnes in 1774, Betty in 1776, Mally in 1778 and Nanny in 1781. As mentioned elsewhere, the Crow or Crowe family were numerous and mobile. They seem to have farmed most of the holdings on the eastern side of the fell and are still in evidence today.

In 1798-9 Roger Russell was the occupier. He seems to have taken on many parish duties for a few years, and his name appears in the parish documents as chapel warden for Little Thorphinsty in

1789, and then he went on to do the same for other estates in the succeeding years. A bill in the parish accounts is to Roger Russell for roofing.

In the 1814 land tax list, Esther Thornborrow is the owner-occupier. She was the daughter of Matthew Dodgson, the previous owner, and wife of the curate of Kendal, formerly of Greenthorn, but she did not stay long at Little Thorphinsty. Her husband died just four years later, aged 36, and his widow moved up the hill to the Ashes. It is probable that she owned both properties, because after a short break, there were Thornburrows in both farms. The name is spelt in different ways on each and every document, 'barrow', 'burrow', ' borrow' and occasionally 'burough'.

The next family were the Capsticks, an unusual name for this immediate area, but they seem to have been birds of passage. John and Jane christened three daughters between 1820 and 1825, but then disappear.

In the 1841 census, Catherine Thornbarrow was the head of the family, aged 52 and a farmer. She had three children, Thomas, Mary and Selina, all in their 20s, and an unexplained child of four years, Esther Coward. They also had a farm lad of thirteen, John Martindale. Ten years later in the next census, Thomas is married, head of the household and with three boys, Thomas, Richard and John. They had two living-in servants, fourteen-year-old Jane Hodgson from Witherslack, and William Mason from Dent. Tombstones in the churchyard tell us that Thomas died in 1883 aged 68, and Margaret his wife died in 1875, also aged 68. Their grandson Thomas went to Cartmel Fell school and was taught by John White who gave him an excellent reference in April 1886:

School House, Cartmel Fell
I have known Thomas Thornborrow since 1880. Whilst under me as a pupil I always found him steady, careful, obedient and honest.
Since leaving school he has been with his uncle on the farm and his conduct during that time has been all that can be desired
I can confidently recommend him to any office of trust, firmly believing that he will strive to do his duty cheerfully and honestly.
I shall be glad to answer any further questions if necessary.
J. White, certificated teacher.

By 1891, there is a large family of Taylors in residence at Little Thorphinsty. They may have been related to the family then at Thorphinsty Hall as many of the Christian names tally. The oldest member was grandfather William, a basket-maker of 73, but his son John was head of the family, aged 40, a farmer and basket-maker. His wife Elizabeth was a Kendal woman of 36, and they had seven children, from fifteen downwards.

This was not a farm with long-term family occupation and the 1910 Inland Revenue assessment shows that the Crowes had winged their way back, and Birkett was the occupier on a yearly tenancy of £40 per annum. He had to give 2s. to the chapel salary, the fee farm rent was 7s.7d, and, very surprisingly, he was still paying the ancient 'Knowing' rent of 2s.8d every two and a half years. This is the latest record of this payment that I have come across, but there is still no clue as to who received this odd rent. The gross value of the whole farm was estimated to be £900, and the comment of the assessor was 'Fairly old property in fairly poor condition.'

In the 1920s and 1930s, the Mallinson family were the tenants. The boys slept in the back bedroom which had a window almost at ground level as the hill rises steeply behind the house. One dark night, they were alarmed when there was a tapping at the window and a dim face loomed at the pane. It was a tramp who wanted to sleep in the barn for the night. In those days, tramps were quite common, but they often used hay and bracken barns as bedrooms without asking permission.

The Mallinsons used to take large numbers of summer visitors from the mill towns of Lancashire during the Wakes weeks, maybe 30 or 40 at a time. These families were accommodated in wooden huts in the fields, bunk-house style. Mrs Mallinson was accustomed to catering on a grand scale as she used to provide wedding breakfasts and on-site catering at auctions, and all this was done on the old cast iron range, as electricity did not arrive on the fell until fifteen years after the Second World War. She had no running water in the house either, only a little spring by the back door, which ran into a stone trough. The mill workers would arrive at Grange station and walk the steep six miles or so, but their luggage was transported for them by pony-trap. Though it seems impossible today, the track down Little Thorphinsty Wood was negotiable for a pony cart in those days. For the mill workers, this was paradise. They used to walk down to Bowland Bridge, to the shop or to the pub, and residents could hear them coming from half a mile away, their clogs clattering and strains of popular songs wafting on the breeze, blending with cheerful chatter. An oral history account of how hard Mrs Mallinson worked came from a Mr Worrall. He used to stay at Little Thorphinsty in the 1940s and was charged 4s.6d. a day, for dinner bed and breakfast. Mrs Mallinson used to stay up all night to bake bread, cakes and pasties for the following week. Eventually, the family moved to High Cark, but satisfied customers returned there for ham-and-egg teas.

Another document which throws some light on farming activities is the 1941 farm survey, made country-wide by the War Agricultural Committee. Whereas the house and buildings were in poor condition in 1910, by 1940 they were good. The landlord was a Mr Cockerton of Dublin, a descendant of the Cockertons of Ravensbarrow Lodge, and the tenant was Mr J. Mallinson. There was no water in the farm buildings, no motive power on the farm and no hired help. The annual rent was £56. Because of Ministry of Agriculture directives, every farm had to increase its ploughed land, not an easy matter in this region. In the 1940 harvest, the Mallinsons had one acre of corn, and in 1941 this had trebled. Sadly, this extra ploughland destroyed the wild daffodils which thronged the old hay meadow in earlier times. Jim Mallinson remembered a golden field when he was a boy in the 1930s, but all that remains today is a swathe on a steep breast, too awkward to plough.

A comparison can be made between the stock levels in 1941 and those in 1734. The Mallinsons had eight cows and heifers in milk, and the Scaleses had four. In assorted young cattle, the Mallinsons had twelve, and the Scaleses had five, but whereas the Scaleses had nine hogs, by 1941 there were no sheep on the farm. Two horses were kept in 1731, and only one 200 years later. The war effort was helped by poultry farming, for the Mallinsons kept 60 hens and 20 pullets, and the ploughland not laid down to oats carried half an acre of maincrop potatoes and an acre of turnips for fodder. Apart from these last two items, the pattern of crops can hardly have changed in 200 years, except for the production of hemp.

The farm briefly became part of Thorphinsty Hall property when it was bought by William Lydell in 1943, and he willed it to his daughter Marie Chambers in 1951. She and her husband made most of the alterations to the house, virtually gutting downstairs, making one large room where there had been three, and building a new fireplace, for which the huge larder slab became the hearthstone. Two windows were put in the east wall where there had been none and the three little bedrooms were made into two larger ones, the fourth becoming a bathroom. The holding was sold by Robert James Cockerton of Dublin in 1967 to Marie Chambers' son, who put it on the market again in 1982, when it was bought by Alan and Jennifer Forsyth. They bought back some of the land which had been sold off and added a studio behind the barn adjoining the house. Part of this barn was made into an extra bedroom in 1991. Because of its location, the barn was always very difficult to approach with laden trailers or carts. Jim Mallinson remembered having to get the old horse almost cantering to get up the slope, with all the family pushing behind, but because there was a sharp corner, the cart would sometimes overturn.

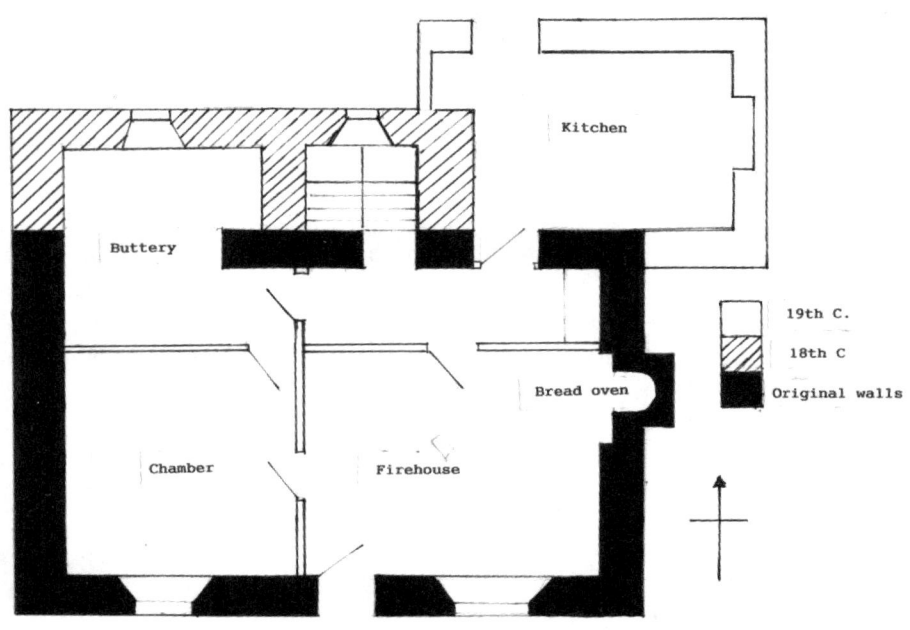

No modern wagons could even get down the lane with hay or straw, so in 1984, a new barn was erected near Spannell Beck. Even that is difficult to approach with large trucks because of the narrow bridge, and turning is impossible.

A small pasture near the house was set aside in 1992 to create a little copse of forty American Red Oaks *(Quercus Rubra)* to commemorate the Forsyth's ruby wedding, the oaks being a present from their son and daughter in law, Andrew and Elaine. Another alteration has been to turn a very boggy area into a pond. This land was probably part of the old river course, and frequently flooded when the artificial course of the beck burst its banks. Two days' work with a digger created a large pond, and as the subsoil turned out to be grey clay, no artificial liner was needed. The woods around had not been coppiced since the war, which meant that the sun did not reach the house from November to March, but a start has been made at the lower end of Low Loft Wood, and it is hoped to restore this section to coppice status.

The Buildings Conservation Officer, Andrew Lowe, made a visit of inspection to determine the ages of various parts of the fabric of the house and barns. He thought that the smallest barn, with its cruck beams could be as early as the fourteenth or fifteenth century, the big barn eighteenth century, and the house had continued to grow outwards and upwards for centuries, evolving from a single storey oblong.

Ashes

ASHES is such a simple name, but there are several theories as to the meaning of this farm's title. Since there is no obvious answer, the reader may make his or her own choice from a selection. There is an abundance of ash trees in the vicinity, but these cannot be the same trees that were there hundreds of years ago when the house was built, for the name Ashes was used at least from 1635. G. P. Jones, in his *Short Account of Cartmel Fell till 1840* suggests that the farm names like Oaks and Ashes might suggest that these trees were not common in the area. It could be argued that the opposite might be true, with a preponderance of one particular variety in a given location, since these were the species at the core of the woodland industries, together with hazel. Another suggestion comes from Michael Davis-Sheil, who says that if there was a potash kiln on the land, the house acquired the name, and frequently it was a superior kind of building, because potash meant wealth. In this case, it seems a likely conclusion, because there is a kiln in the wood above, which is called Ashes Wood. The quality of the building does not match the theory of wealth however. When the tenants recently put in a new window and lintel, they were amazed at the poor quality of the wall that they exposed. It is likely though that the owners of the kiln did not live in the associated farm-house, since it was frequently tenanted.

The archaeology of the area takes us further back

than the written records. Spannel Beck, which runs through some of the Ashes land, has the remains of three mills on a stretch of less than one mile. These would have been fulling mills associated with the several potash kilns in the neighbouring woodland. Potash was made by burning bracken, and the resulting ash was used to make soap. Newly-woven lengths of cloth were put into the fulling mill, together with the soap, and heavy paddles pounded the fabric, cleansing and felting it in one action. The owners of these mills have not been identified, but suggestions have been put forward in the section on Little Thorphinsty.

The road or track which leads over the fell above Ashes and which links the ancient mills, has evidence of a cobbled surface along its length to Foxfield. In its heyday, it must have been one of the best roads in the district, and the fact that it still has a dense surface after centuries of rain, frost and snow, shows how well it was constructed. This was not a mere bracken-track, and someone must have thought it worthwhile to invest unknown man-hours to make an enduring road. At one section of this bridleway, the little bridge has a double arch, and when the beck is low, one can see the positions of slots where sluice gates were inserted to create a mill pond upstream. The mill race ran down to a natural ravine where the remains of the wheel pit can still be discerned. In the field to the east of the road below, another mill pond can be made out, and the foundations of the ancient mill below it. There must have been a bridge of some kind from the track to this mill, as the ground is very boggy between the two, and the mill is on the far bank.

The inhabitants of Ashes farmstead appear in the parish registers of Cartmel Priory in the late seventeenth century. Nicholas Robinson christened two daughters, Jane in 1694 and Margaret in 1697, and he was still at Ashes in 1721-2, when he was chapel warden for his holding. Possibly his younger daughter inherited the farm, because in 1727 Francis Turner, yeoman of Ashes Beck made his will and left the farm to his son Henry, and his widow Margaret was to have £3 a year for the rest of her life. This family had the status symbol of a clock in the buttery, though one wonders why it was kept in there and not on show. They also had a pair of looms and some hemp and hemp yarn, though there is no mention of woollen yarn to make a connection with the potash kilns.

The farm appears again in the records of Cartmel Fell from 1735, when a Richard Rawlinson was chapel warden for St Anthony's. In 1753, another or the same Richard was overseer of the poor for Ashes, but rather confusingly there is a reference to Mr Philipson in the same period and of the same address. The house has two doorways side by side, so possibly it was once two dwellings. Isaac Rawlinson of Ashes was a trustee of the Bryan Beck charity in 1773.

In the Crosthwaite parish records, an account book of 1739-50 has a note of receipts for interest of moneys lent. Mr Philipson of Ashes lent £50 to the parish fund, and as most folk are referred to by their Christian and surnames, 'Mr' implies a certain respect. Probably he was related to the Philipsons of Hodge Hill who were minor gentry. A nice little oak cupboard in the parlour wall next to the chimney breast may have been installed at this period, but is un-dated.

In the 1790s, John and Rebecca Rowlandson of Ashes were buried at Crosthwaite. Cartmel Fell chapel had its burial licence by then, so maybe the couple originated in Crosthwaite. In the same year as John's death, another family from Ashes baptised their baby, again implying two households. They were William and Ann Nicholson, and their son William later lived at Brigg House, then later still at Gummers How.

By 1821, John Storey was in residence, and he gave 8d. to the fund for the curate's salary. This was about the middle range of payment, James Birket of Birket Houses paying 3s. for his twelve estates, and Betty Stewardson of Beech Hill giving 3d.

The 1829 Parson and White directory placed an asterisk by the names of yeomen farmers who subscribed to the publication, but John Wilson of Ashes had no such designation so was presumably a tenant. There was a succession of young couples throughout the 1830s, as evidenced by the baptismal records. Between 1834 and 1839, the families presenting their children for christening included Atkinson, Swainson, Leak, Taylor and Barrow. In the parish registers of Cartmel Fell, these fathers were designated labourers, indicating that they were not the owners of the farm, all that is except the Leakes, who had moved down the fell from Foxfield. It is likely that the owner at this time was Esther Thornburrow, a daughter of John Dodson who owned many properties on the fell and left them to his children in 1801. Esther was the widow of the curate of Natland. He had died in 1819 aged only 36 and was buried in Kendal, though he has a tombstone in Cartmel Fell graveyard. Esther owned Greenthorn when she was married in 1806, but lived at the Ashes in later life with her unmarried daughter Selina. Her son, Thomas Dodson Thornburrow lived down the lane and farmed Little Thorphinsty, but Esther always had one or two grandchildren or great-grandchildren living with her, and her grandson John eventually ran the farm at Ashes.

Esther died in 1883 aged 94 and John became the head of the household. He married around the time of his grandmother's death and his son Thomas

Bee recess in a barn at Ashes.

William was born in 1891. Selina and another of his aunts, Mary Woof, continued to live at Ashes with their nephew. Selina died in 1893 aged 75 and Mary Woof was buried the previous year aged 81, so it would seem that the Thornburrow-Dodsons had strong constitutions.

The Thornburrows moved from both Ashes and Little Thorphinsty at this period and at the turn of the twentieth century Edward and Annie Fox were the tenants with a boy named after his father. They were not there very long and at around this time the farm was owned by Alice Carr wife of the vicar of Newlands, near Keswick, later inherited by her daughter, Lucie. The vicarage was near Littletown and this was Beatrix Potter's Lucie, Mrs Tiggy Winkle's friend.

The occupier in 1909 was David F. Cockerton, a descendant of the Cockertons who built Ravensbarrow Lodge. He became friendly with the new curate, Thomas Price, and the two used to go fishing together. Soon after his arrival on the fell, Thomas Price noted in his diary that David Cockerton had supplied him with seed potatoes, and he consulted him on the restoration of the church. They agreed that a glass case should be made for the vestry, in which to protect the various curios and artefacts, such as the pitch pipe and the key.

In the early twentieth century, there was a pattern of quick successions of tenant farmers, just as it had been a hundred years earlier. If a farm had been improved by a tenant, the landlord would often increase the rent, so couples would have to search for another which they could afford. It must be said that erstwhile tenants often speak well of their landlords, but it was not always so.

The Ashes and many other properties in the district were inherited by Miss Lucie Carr, who died in 2001 aged 103, and her tenants were able to purchase their holdings. Two generations of the Clarkes had been at Ashes for upwards of thirty years and they have again become yeomen.

Cartmel Fell

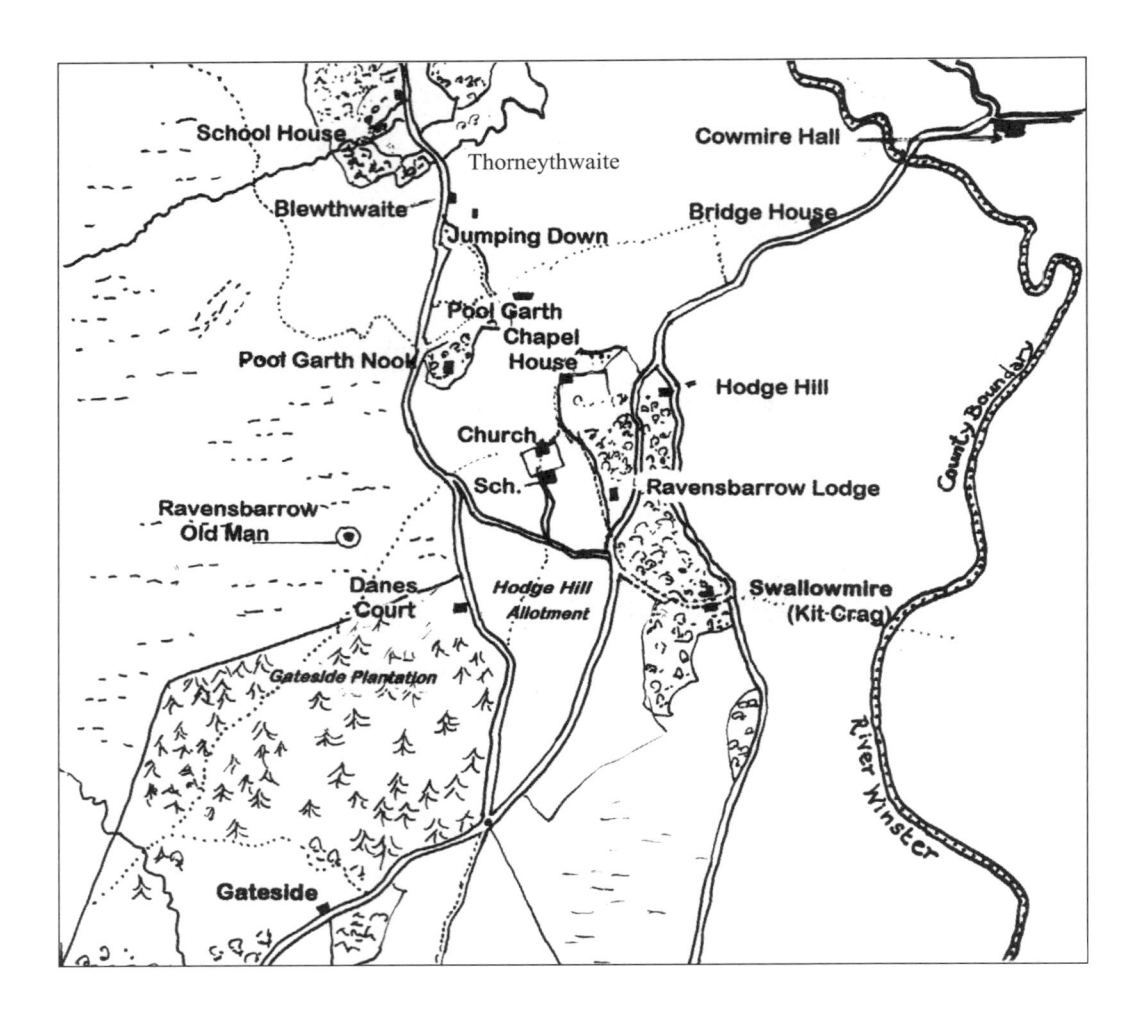

Gateside

AS in many place names in Cumbria, 'gate' in this instance is taken from the Norse *gata*, and means a street or road. The first Ordnance Survey map of the district shows this area of the fell to be called Gateside allotment, but that was in 1846, over sixty years before the house was built.

Gateside Plantation, as it was called by 1911, was sold to Anthony Taylor, then aged 43 and one of the large family from Thorphinsty Hall. The vendors were Edwin and Benjamin Hall, formerly of St. John's Wood and then of Willesden Green, London. The Halls had once been of Grange and High Newton and were Quakers in the eighteenth and nineteenth centuries. The land they were selling was probably their inheritance from their uncle, George Gibson of Height in Cartmel Fell who died a bachelor.

Anthony Taylor was one of five brothers who helped to run their parents' farm, but when the Boer War began, he felt patriotic enough to enlist, and sailed away from all that was familiar. By the time the ship berthed in South Africa, the war was over, so Anthony returned to Thorphinsty Hall and continued to work the farm with his brothers and sisters. It seemed as though nothing had changed since his brief months in uniform, until one day, perhaps when sorting the washing, one of his sisters found a note in Anthony's pocket which began 'My Dear Husband.' The cat was out of the bag and the questions began.

It seems that Anthony and his wife Annie had been secretly married. She was a seamstress with the Stanley family at Witherslack Hall and already had a son. The couple were living as tenants at Yew Tree farm in High Newton when they decided to buy their own property.

John Taylor of Thorphinsty Hall must have been a successful farmer as he left each of his children £200 when he died in 1897. Anthony drew his money out in 1911 and bought Gateside Plantation and a pre-fabricated bungalow. Whether this was the whole purchase price is not recorded, but a memorandum in Anthony's hand reveals the source of his new home: 'Today, a man arrived from Sheffield to put up the bungalow.' It was made of corrugated steel on a timber frame, and the interior was lined with tongue and groove pine.

As soon as he was in possession, Anthony Taylor began to cultivate his land. He established a market garden, planting fruit trees and bushes, and began a business of supplying the market with rabbits and game. A friend who went out with him one day to check his rabbit traps recalled that they came home for lunch with a hundred couples in the pony cart! Possibly the story became distorted in the telling, and the total was a hundred, but either way, Anthony Taylor must have helped to keep the fell rabbit-free. He used to cycle to Kendal on a bicycle with a huge basket on the front. In season he would load up with strawberries, raspberries and gooseberries called Golden Droppers, which were a dessert variety and still remembered by older people. Apparently, his wife used the bicycle as well, and went to Grange once a week with produce. One day Anthony found her preparing to depart on a different day to her usual trip, and was scandalised.

'Folk will think you're never off the road!' he remonstrated. The saying passed into Taylor family folklore.

The Taylors of Gateside had a daughter called Annie, named for her mother, and known as Annie Bracken by her numerous relatives, to distinguish her from the many other Annies in the family. Before the bungalow was built, the site was regularly visited by gypsies. The Taylor children scurried past on their way to school, as everyone was somewhat wary of these nomads. They were said to roast hedgehogs when other delicacies could not be caught, and one family were such regular campers that their name, McFarlane, is still remembered.

Anthony Taylor died on 2 April 1953 aged 85, but his widow continued to live at Gateside until she died in September 1958, and then the property passed to their daughter who lived in Grange. She rented it out for a couple of years and then decided to sell. It was bought by the present owners in March 1960, and they erected the barn behind the house, of similar construction.

Spannel Beck runs through Gateside allotment, and there is archaeological evidence of a mediaeval fulling mill higher up the fell. Down by the roadside is a huge rhododendron ponticum, which must have been planted by the Taylors, together with two Scots pines either side of the entrance. The latter were planted to commemorate the 21st birthday of Anthony's step-son, and many friends and neighbours attended a large party to celebrate the event. Afterwards, the young man emigrated to Australia, and was never seen again. The Scots pines are now reaching old age, and in recent years storms have wrenched limbs from the main trunks.

Ravensbarrow Lodge

THIS house is amongst the most recent to have been built on the fell, probably at some time in the 1830s. It takes its name from the hill behind, which has a cairn at the summit, into which is built a recessed seat. This cairn is known as Ravensbarrow Old Man, and is shown on the Ordnance Survey map of 1846, so it was already a landmark at that date. A possibility is that it might have been erected by the Cockerton family who built Ravensbarrow Lodge, perhaps to celebrate the event, but nothing is known of the cairn's history.

Robert Cockerton was the curate of Cartmel Fell from 1829 to 1861. He was the son of the vicar of Dalton and married Eleanor Birket, daughter of William Higgin Birket of Hodge Hill. The land surrounding Hodge Hill belonged to the Birkets at that time, so Robert's father-in-law must have provided a site on which to build a convenient house for the young couple, but they must have lived in Winster whilst the house was being built, as that is where their son George was born in 1834. Two years later Mrs Cockerton gave birth to Eleanor, and she was born at Ravensbarrow Lodge. The children followed on almost every other year after that; James Birket in 1837, David in 1839, Amelia in 1841, William Higgin Birket in 1843, Robert Blackburn in 1845 and then a gap before Martha Jane was born in 1850. The Cockertons must have been very pleased with their modern house in which to raise their large family.

A track behind the house leads to the church in just a few minutes' walk, and the principal rooms face out across the Winster valley, catching all the morning sun. In the garden wall behind the house, also angled to warm up with the first sun's rays, are a pair of bee-boles. These recesses might be amongst the last to be made for this purpose as the modern bee-hive was about to be introduced, thus doing away with the need for straw skeps.

According to the 1851 census, apart from the Rev. and Mrs Cockerton, there were four sons and three daughters living at home, as well as Myles Birket who was Eleanor's brother, and a servant, Isabella Robinson. The oldest son, George, was seventeen, but he had a tragic death in 1877 when he drowned in Windermere lake. Ten years later, in 1861, both the Cockerton parents died, but Amelia, one of their daughters, had died two years earlier, aged only eighteen. Another daughter, Martha, died in May 1861, aged eleven. One wonders if perhaps tuberculosis was the cause of four comparatively young deaths in two years, for the parents themselves were only in their fifties.

The Cockerton heir who was to inherit Ravensbarrow was James Birket. He was born in 1837 and married Jane Graham of Cowmire Hall in 1860, the year before his parents died. Presumably, the young couple moved into Ravensbarrow Lodge after probate was granted, and by 1871 they had two girls and three boys. James was described in the census as having no occupation. His unmarried sister Mary was still living in the house where she was born, and so was Myles Birket, their uncle. He was by this time 62 and described as 'landowner'.

By 1881 only the two younger boys were at home, fourteen-year-old David, and twelve-year-old Robert. Their cousin George was living with them, and he was almost certainly the son of George Cockerton who drowned in the lake. He was thirteen, so came neatly between his cousins' ages. Myles is recorded as being 70 in this census, but we know he was born in April 1808, so someone had got their sums wrong. James was 53 by the time of the 1891 census, and though termed a farmer in parish registers, in the census he is still of no occupation. His wife Jane was 52, so it is something of a surprise therefore to find that they have a son of four, called Myles Birket Wennington. Their other children had flown the nest by this time, and

James Birket Cockerton.

the oldest, Elizabeth, was nearly 30, so little Myles probably was already an uncle at his birth.

David Frederick Cockerton, the second son, was born in 1867, and by the time the Rev. Thomas Price wrote his diary in 1910, he was living at Ashes, just up the road. His little brother, Myles Birket, was the one who inherited Ravensbarrow Lodge, probably because the older brothers and sisters were well established in life when Myles was still a child. Some time in the 1920s, Myles Birket Cockerton decided to marry. His bride-to-be was Flora Frances May Holyday of Cartmel, and the banns were duly read, but on the day of the wedding and already in the church, Myles had an argument with the officiating clergyman and stormed out of the building. Miss Holyday's furniture had already been transported to Ravensbarrow Lodge, and she was loath to part with it, so she moved in with it and kept house for Myles. The arrangement must have suited them both very well, and they both had their own interests. Miss Holyday played the organ at St Anthony's every Sunday and she died whilst feeding the cats outside her back door in 1977, aged 93.

Maybe it was something to do with being the baby of the family, but apparently Myles Birket Cockerton had a very short fuse. He quarreled violently with his brother Fred and renounced the name of Cockerton on his seventieth birthday, reverting to his grandmother's name of Birket. It makes genealogy very difficult when trying to sort out the Cockertons, as so many had Birket in their forenames and then changed their surname to Birket for inheritance or other purposes.

Myles was a land agent for Wilfred Bentley and his employer used to take him for an annual check-up with his doctor and optician. They used to have

Myles Birket Cockerton.

a good lunch and a drink or two, and then Mr Bentley would drive Myles back to Ravensbarrow Lodge. On the last occasion of this event, Myles went down to Chapel House to tell them about his marvellous day out and died in the chair there, so Mr Bentley had to return from Windermere to take charge of matters.

The present owner inherited the house from Myles Birket (Cockerton) with a proviso 'That he turns out all right'. It should be mentioned that the Birkets and Cockertons were all keen on field sports, and could not abide the thought of anyone living in their property who thought otherwise, so

'Turning out all right' meant having similar interests. As an example of the family's intense interest, in May 1893, *The Westmorland Gazette* reported on the Preston Dog Show: 'Mr. J. B. Cockerton took the gold medal in the English Setter class with Lune Belle, and the gold medal in the brace class with Lune Belle and Guy, and in the open bitch class, a first with Ellen Terry.' The family were also poultry fanciers and bred game birds as well as judging at shows.

There was no immediate heir of course, and the other Cockertons had dispersed or died. The Cockertons who changed their surname to Birket had moved to Birket Houses, but they too died out, the last of the line, Myles Higgin Birket dying in 1947.

In 1978, the house was almost unchanged from the day when it was built. There was no electricity and no piped water, only a well. Windows have since been inserted in the south wall and the dining and sitting rooms have been combined, but otherwise the appearance is unaltered. A range of kennels at the back of the house must have housed the prize-winning setters.

In the 1990s, Dixie Cockerton, a distant relation from New Zealand arrived on Cartmel Fell to seek her ancestor's home. She was the grand-daughter of the orphaned George Cockerton whose father drowned in the lake. Michael Bentley invited her in and she was thrilled to sit in the house of her forebears, but she died shortly after returning to New Zealand. Dixie was the headmistress of a junior school and a national netball coach, with her own website promoting the game. The Cartmel Fell Women's Institute has an unexplained relationship with one in New Zealand, and it is thought that the Cockertons must have established the link.

Swallowmire

THIS farm, like so many others, has been added to and altered over the centuries. The name may relate to mud washing down the fell, causing a mire which engulfs or swallows. The track through the farm from the higher road is still unsurfaced, and can get very mirey; another possibility is that mire has evolved from mere. The two words were frequently interchanged in the seventeenth century, Grasmere often being spelt Gresmire, so maybe there was once a small tarn, long since drained and forgotten. Swallows collect mud for their nests from suitable water margins, so maybe they had been observed nearby, and even today, when swallow populations are declining, there are still plenty at Swallowmire.

There seems to be no evidence of the name Swallowmire before about 1680, but the core of the house is surely much older than that. The massive fireplace with its inglenook is built on a scale which implies wealth and status, and the high panelled double doors at the end of the house look fit for a regal entrance. The question is, who were the owners, and why have they left no trace? In parallel with this question is another; where was the large farmholding of Kit Crag, and where has it gone? Perhaps the two are synonymous. For the purposes of this chapter, the two names will be taken as being twinned, with justifying evidence interspersed.

On the map drawn up for the enclosures in 1796, Kit Crag is a geographical feature, a large rocky outcrop on the river Winster side of the road. What is now called Hog House Lane was then called Kit Crag Road. At some period during the next hundred years, the name of the crag transferred to the other side of the road, and Kit Crag is marked on today's O.S. maps as being the rocky area to the south of Swallowmire. No signs of any habitation can be seen, and yet there are wills and inventories of the seventeenth century, all relating to a farm of this name.

The owners' names are of the important families of the day; Swainson, Birket, Briggs and Addison, to name a few, but the size and value of their inventories far exceed the worldly goods of most others in the neighbourhood. An example can be found in 1625, when James Swainson of Kit Crag died. The inventory is written on a long thin strip of parchment, no more than three inches wide, but it goes on and on. The cattle included four oxen worth £3.10s. each, twelve kine, three heifers and three steers, six calves, cows and steers sold, and 'one heffer claymed by the wyffe to bee hers'. There were three work horses and an old mare, three little stags (young horses), a little old mare, and perhaps about 70 sheep, the value of which was £11. The list of farming gear and household goods extends down the parchment and includes 'silver spoones and other little jewells,' but by far the largest item was the list of debtors. These necessitated more strips of parchment being stitched onto the roll, and in bills, bonds and mortgages, the total of debtors was over 50, and the amount they owed to James Swainson's estate was £666.13s.4d. In 1625, that was serious money and not the preserve of a subsistence farmer. In that same year of 1625, the inheritor of Kit Crag died too - Nicholas Swainson of 'Theorpinstie and Kittcragge'. He had five daughters and a son James, but if James were to die without issue, then daughter Agnes was to have Kit Crag, and daughter Elizabeth to have Thorphinsty. It is not clear from the wording whether this refers to Thorphinsty Hall or Little Thorphinsty. We know that the Huttons had been at Thorphinsty Hall for centuries, but that did not mean that they owned it outright. The hall has been divided into two (now three) separate dwellings, and the southern end has all the marks of a quality building. Without further evidence, it cannot be said which house was intended, but in all probability, the property bequeathed to Elizabeth was Little Thorphinsty. If all the children died without heirs, then Robert, the testator's brother, was to have Thorphinsty. Another brother, Thomas was to have £120 out of the Kit Crag estate, and 40s. each was allotted to Cartmel Fell chapel and to twelve of the poor people of the parish on Easter Day. Maybe the testator's children were sickly and ailing, because there is an odd proviso at the end of the list of bequests. Nicholas Robinson was to be forgiven a mortgage of £3 if he came to the aid of the sick children. Nicholas Robinson's wife was to have the price of three pecks of malt as her portion. Two of the oxen mentioned in the earlier inventory must have been sold between March and October, as these are worth only £7 in Nicholas Swainson's belongings, and half the cows had been sold too, the sheep had almost doubled, being worth £19. The biggest item was a mortgage at Height, for £20. Was this the farm of that name one wonders, or another farm in the Height district, as the upper fell was known?

In August 1666, Miles Birket of Kit Crag was buried at Crosthwaite. His will must have been stored in damp conditions as portions were missing when it was copied in 1883, but the inventory survives. We learn from the will that Miles had a wife Margaret, a son Edward who was to inherit Woodside farm on the Crosthwaite side of the Winster, and a daughter Barbarie who was to receive £80 in two instalments, three years apart. The supervisors of the will were to be his friends Robert Briggs (of Swallowmire?) and William Garnett of Cowmire Hall. If only Robert Briggs' address had been added it might have further clarified the division between Kit Crag and Swallowmire. Each of the supervisors were to have 3s.4d. for their pains. Robert Briggs signed his name as a witness, but Miles Birket left his mark and seal. Unlike previous inventories from Kit Crag, this one names very few stock. One might infer that this was either a smaller farmer or else one who was semi-retired. There is still a team of three oxen and there are five 'kye', but only twelve sheep, young and old, worth £2. For transport there were 'Tow meares and Tow load sadles', with a hackney saddle also. Because it was September when the inventory was made, the barns were full with unthreshed corn, bigg, oats and peas. Although some of this would be for human consumption, a lot would be for animal fodder and the value was £13. A single hive of bees was worth 6s.8d., apples, crabs, butter and cheese were reckoned to be worth 14s.6d. Unlike the average farmer's purse which contained about £3, Miles Birket's had £68.16s.8d., and he had £120 owing to him in bills, bonds and other specialties. Unfortunately, his own debts exceeded the total value of his goods, as he owed £198.5s., whereas his assets were only a total of £189.6s.8d. What happened to his widow? Did she live with Edward at Woodside, and did Barbarie get her inheritance? This is a conundrum posed with so many inventories.

It is probable that the Briggs family of Cowmire Hall were the builders and settlers of Swallowmire and they may have intermarried with the wealthy Swainsons. We know that the Briggses owned the estate in 1688, because Robert Briggs leaves all his messuages and lands at Kit Crag, Swallowmire and Addyfield to Rowland, his son, and he may well be the same Robert Briggs who witnessed Miles Birket's will. Perhaps he bought the next-door house from the heirs. It is tempting to speculate.

Rowland Briggs is more widely known by visitors to Cartmel Priory as it was he who left money in his will to provide bread for the poor in 1703. This investment of £52.10s. has provided bread to this day, and as long ago as 1870 James Stockdale estimated that 10,000 loaves had been distributed by the priory. Rowland also provided 5s. to the sexton of the priory, to be given on Christmas Day, 'provided my grave is unbroken up.' This money came from the rent of Addyfield, and Stockdale comments that the owners had paid it for 166 years, and that he was the sole executor in 1870. The owner then was Mrs Susannah Newby of Carke Villa, who has a marble plaque in Cartmel Priory.

There is another will of Rowland Briggs, but two generations earlier in December 1644. This is much damaged by damp, and the farm's name is missing, but is almost certainly Swallowmire/Kit Crag. The inventory was appraised by George Hutton of Thorphinsty Hall, Tobias Knipe of Flodder Hall and two others. This must have been a rather more well-to-do family than average, because amongst their possessions were table cloths and table napkins worth £1.15s. and 'curtain cloathes' worth 13s. Other items not found in usual listings were a bow, arrows and a quiver, worth 3s.4d. This might mean that Rowland Briggs had hunting rights, but although his weapons were by that time antique heirlooms, it might also mean he was ready for militia service. Another item in the inventory is 'Ox yoakes, hames and traces.' Although a horse and mare are listed, these must be quality animals, for their value is ten guineas; obviously not for ploughing or carting purposes.

The answer to the puzzle of the seemingly intertwined farms of Swallowmire and Kit Crag may lie in their close proximity. If the western end of what is now called Swallowmire was first called Kit Crag, and then the owner built on a newer wing, calling that Swallowmire, the two names could have marched side by side for a hundred years or so. A new and separate wing was added at right angles to the older structure, and appears to be eighteenth century in style, and this could have been a modernisation when the farm was owned by the wealthy Dodgsons, but more of them later. If the owner had no financial need to farm himself, he might have retired to his own wing, calling it by another name. His tenant would manage the farm from next door, but when the properties came under one owner/occupier at a later date, the old name of Kit Crag could have lapsed. If any reader has further evidence to solve the riddle, please contact Cartmel Fell Local History Society.

The parish church documents for Cartmel Fell list the constables and graves who did parish duty, and there are two consecutive entries for 1723 and 1724 for the post of grave, that is an assistant to the constable. Both entries are for Mrs Briggs, but one for her estate at Kit Crag, and the other for Swallowmire. The list tends to work its way along the fell year by year, taking the yeomen farmers in turn, until by 1746 it is at the far end of the parish, where Joshua Pull is grave for Moorhow, and then by 1752 the list dives into the valley below, and James Birket is constable for his property at The Wood. This sequence in itself indicates very close proximity for Swallowmire and Kit Crag. Mrs Susannah Briggs was the widow of Rowland, giver of bread to the poor. She too had a charitable disposition and left £10 to be let out at interest by the overseers of the poor for the benefit of Cartmel Fell poor folk. This money was to be distributed on Shrove Saturday. Another £10 was to be invested to pay for a sermon on Shrove Sunday, or the Sunday before Easter. Mrs Briggs obviously had strong feelings about the subject matter of such a sermon, and she decreed that the text was to be from Hebrews 13: 'Ye Marriage is honourable in all, and ye bed undefiled, but whoremongers and adulters God will judge.' This sermon was to be preached first at Cartmel Fell in the morning, and again at Cartmel in the afternoon. A further £20 was given to the overseers of the poor to pay for the education of four poor children. This money would be paid to the curate who was also the schoolmaster, and at that period it was George Walker, who then also lived at Swallowmire.

There was a family of Addisons at Kit Crag in the mid-seventeenth century, possibly related to the Addisons of Tower Wood and Lightwood. Anthony Addison had his son and daughter baptised at Cartmel priory in 1677 and 1683, but records for Swallowmire in parallel are hard to find, as if it had not yet been built.

By the eighteenth century, the name of Kit Crag is fading away, and the last entries in parish registers are for the Brittain family in the early part of the century. Christopher was the father, and he had a daughter Ann christened at Cartmel in 1717, and a son John in 1723. In between, his infant son Thomas was buried at Cartmel in 1720. Ann Brittain of Kit Crag was married in 1741, almost the last mention of this dwelling. She married into the milling family of Garnetts, her husband George then being of Mansriggs Mill. Later, they moved to Reston Mill at Staveley and had nine children. George died in 1784. The last mention of Kit Crag in the parish papers was when Richard Robinson was overseer of the poor for this holding in 1754, but he may have been doing duty for someone else.

In 1728, Judith Heysham of Swallowmire married into the Bigland family of Hartbarrow. Judith may have been a farm servant, as the surname Heysham was not a local one. James, her husband was described as yeoman, and a bondsman at the wedding was Timothy Strickland, also of Hartbarrow. Timothy was the clockmaker who made the Witherslack church clock three years later at a cost of £19.

If we assume that Swallowmire was next door to Kit Crag, then at this period, the curate of Cartmel Fell was neighbour to the Brittains. This was George Walker, curate of St Anthony's from 1715 to 1758. As the clergy had had a better education than most farmers, they were often called upon to witness signatures or to supervise wills, and when George Lindow died in 1731 at Pool Garth Nook, he made George Walker of Swallowmire a supervisor of his will. There was no vicarage as such in those days, and the incumbent either lodged with one of his flock, or found his own property if he had private means. The stipend was being slowly improved by bequests and investment, and in 1731 it was about £14 a year, having been a mere £10 in 1700. From the mid-eighteenth century onwards, so many names crop up at Swallowmire, it seems reasonable to suppose that there are now two or three households at the same address. The Crow family were in residence for well over a hundred years, Jacob and Betty baptising a daughter in 1792, and at first we know of them through parish documents, but later through the censuses. Probably, they were tenant farmers, as we know that the land baron Matthew Dodson owned Swallowmire in 1800, when he made his will. This document extends to many pages because of the large property holdings and the large family, but since it illustrates the wealth of the Dodgsons, a condensed version is given:

The will of Matthew Dodson, yeoman of Poolgarth, dated 1800: Very far advanced in years, but of sound mind, memory and understanding. His wife Betty to be paid a £40 annuity in lieu of widow's 'thirds'. His messuages included Oaks, Great and Little Ludderburn, Sow How, Little Thorphinsty, Swallowmire, Poolgarth and Greenthorn, all in Cartmel Fell. Elsewhere he owned Gateside in Cartmel, and Hawthrigg and Low House in Kentmere. In Underbarrow he had Low Gregg Hall, which was to be his widow's until her decease, and then was to be their son John's. There was only one son and heir, but five daughters, all of whom inherited property from their father. Esther later became the wife of the Rev. Thomas Thornburrow, marrying him in 1806, and the Swallowmire Crows were witnesses. At the end of the will there is a surprising codicil. Since the preamble indicated Matthew's failing physical condition, the revelation that Betty is pregnant again is unexpected. The unborn child was to have £1,000 at 21, to be paid out of Low Gregg Hall's estate. It appears that all the children were under age at the time of their father's death, and whatever schooling they had had up to that time was continued. William Pearson, later of Borderside, but then of Yews in Crosthwaite became their private tutor for a while. His own education had been at Underbarrow school where by his own account, he had received a thorough grounding. After leaving school, he continued to read avidly and was particularly interested in natural sciences, so the Dodsons probably acquired knowledge on a broad canvas from their tutor. John, Matthew Dodson's heir, seems to have stayed on at Swallowmire, and he had an entry in the 1829 Parson & White directory, but when he died in 1835, he had come into his Gregg Hall inheritance and was buried from there aged only 42. The following year, Elizabeth Dodson, by then of Broughton, was buried at Cartmel Fell, aged 78.

In the copy of the 1814 land tax assessments, Thomas Pattinson is the occupier of 'Swallowmire Kit Crag', which included most of the fields bordering the Winster in today's farmholding, a total of 119 acres. The owner was John Dodgson, but the 'g' has been struck out when the writer realised his spelling mistake.

In 1841 Matthew and Hannah Pattinson of Swallowmire had their son christened on Christmas Day. He was named Matthew Dodgson, but whereas the church register gives the father's occupation as labourer, the census of that year declares him to be of independent means. Were the parents hoping to attract some Dodgson (a 'g' has crept in by now) wealth in their son's direction, or were they actually related? By this time, no Dodgsons were left at Swallowmire, all having dispersed, or changed their name by marriage. The same land tax document shows that Jacob Crow of Swallowmire was farming 233 acres in 1814, so it seems that at that period, the house and land were divided between the Pattinsons and Crows, the latter family having the high land which included Ravensbarrow allotment of 96 acres. In the main house, the Crow family continued to expand. Joseph and Agnes were running the farm in the mid-nineteenth century, and the census shows that it was then 211 acres, 150 of which was heath or enclosure land. One generation took over from the last, Jacob dying in 1853 and being succeeded by Richard. In the census for 1851, Jacob's son Birkett was 21 and still at home. He was described as an engineering draughtsman, and that must have been an imaginative leap for a farmer's son to take at that time. Where did he work, and how did he get there one wonders? His elder brother Edmund occupied the adjoining part of the house with his wife Ellen, but he was termed 'agricultural labourer,' and may have worked for his father, but by 1861 he had moved.

The census returns for Swallowmire show that the Dodgsons actually did not disappear, and in 1881, through marriage with Thornburrows and Crows, there were descendants of Matthew Dodson still in residence there, though not as owners this time. The Mannex directory for 1851 has an asterisk beside yeomen farmers, and Jacob Crow was not among them. We know from papers in private hands that the owner of Swallowmire in 1863 was a Mr. Thomas Pearson, probably of Pool Bank. He raised a mortgage on the farm of £280, borrowing the money from Roger Moser, solicitor of Kendal.

The Finance Act return of 1909/10 provides a lot of information, not otherwise available. The acreage of Swallowmire seems to have changed very little, being 217 acres, 1 rood at that time. The owner was Myles Higgin Birket who owned no less than twenty pieces of property on the fell in the same schedule. From abstracts of title to some of these properties, it is possible to see that they were mostly bought through failed mortgages when times were hard in the nineteenth century.

The twentieth century has seen two families at Swallowmire, the Hodgsons who have farmed it, and the Flemings who were also carters. The Flemings began at Thorneythwaite where father William was a waller. His son John farmed first at Chapel House where his son and namesake was born in 1906, and then at Swallowmire. Sadly, young John died long before his parents in 1936, but there are photographs of his father with the team that constructed the new barn at Hodge Hill in 1904. The curate, Thomas Price, notes in his diary that Hodgsons' sale was at Swallowmire in March 1916, but does not say if it was a dispersal sale.

In 1971, Celia Hodgson had just been married and whilst she was away on honeymoon, she left all their wedding presents at her old home. A fire broke out in the lower half of the house, causing a lot of damage, and all the presents were destroyed, but fortunately there was no loss of life. It happened to be clipping time, but because the household was so disrupted at Swallowmire, Mrs Clarke from the Ashes brought down tea for the clipping team in a milk-bucket.

Hodge Hill

THE *Oxford Dictionary of Surnames* places 'Hodge' as a diminutive of Roger, so maybe an early settler of that name cleared a bit of woodland here, and it became known as his hill. Until the eighteenth century it was quite common to omit the possessive 's', so one would not expect the place to be called Hodge's Hill. Alternatively, Hodgsons had been on the fell at least since the seventeenth century, so maybe owned some acres here. A more direct association comes from the work of Dr Terence Fahy, who researched the Philipson family in depth. It seems that the tenant-right of Hodge Hill was owned by the Hodgson family until 1651, and this seems the most plausible explanation for the name of the estate.

This impressive farmhouse is one of the few remaining in the district to retain its lattice windows, most others having been modernised to sashes in Georgian or Victorian times. The approach from the road is by the back door with an attractive so-called spinning gallery above. The current opinion is that these galleries were never intended for spinning as most face away from the sun, and much spinning was done by firelight after the day's work was done. The term was introduced in Victorian times and caught the public imagination, but by then, few remembered the practicalities of spinning. Both the front and back doors are massively constructed in oak, with heavy studding and large locks.

In 1998, the Cartmel Fell Local History Society made a rough survey of the house, measuring wall thickness and window sizes, and noting detail, such as carved cupboards. From this evidence and that of wills, the society concluded that there was a solid but smaller house built first, and then the eastern wing had been added, more than doubling the size. The earlier house now comprises the kitchen regions, and has capacious larders with slate slabs or 'sconces' for safe storage of food and dairy products, and flagged floors of blue-black slate.

The actual builders of Hodge Hill are something of a puzzle, but the property was sold in 1651 for £650 to William Harrison yeoman of Cartmel Fell. The next purchaser was Brian Philipson of Cawsey, (Causeway) in Applethwaite, son of John and Mary of Orrest, Windermere. This branch of the Philipsons were descended from an earlier Brian of Undermillbeck, about 1487. The first house might have been built as an investment, and evidence taken from an inventory of 1719, following the death of Brian Philipson, shows that part of the dwelling was used as an inn. 'Item. Goods in the Kitching Inn…£3. Item, In Licquor and other things in the cellar….£10.' This building is at a meeting of two roads, or tracks as they were in earlier times. The church and school were a few hundred yards away and there was no village centre where an inn might otherwise have been useful, so this seems a logical place for rest and refreshment. The inn was most likely the cottage which is at right angles to the house, and it has its own very large pantry or dairy.

South aspect, Hodge Hill, AWF

The earliest date in the house is on a carved cupboard in the largest room downstairs. This has the initials E S H 1678, and is thought to be for Edward and Susan Harrison, part of the widespread clan on the fell. Another cupboard upstairs has a ferny pattern and the date of 1692, with the initials B A P. This was made for Bryan and Agnes Philipson, whose descendants lived at Hodge Hill for the following hundred years or so.

The Philipson wills that survive do not shed much light on their Cartmel Fell holdings. They leave property in Little Langdale and Tilberthwaite to their heirs, although Bryan's will of 1719 mentions messuages and tenements, (plural) in Cartmel Fell, but these are unspecified. John Philipson died in 1712, naming his son Bryan, and grandsons John and Bryan. He had a nephew Bryan in London who had four children and they all received £1 apiece.

A PATCHWORK HISTORY

His grandson John had £20 and the promise of the properties after his father's death. One wonders if John's son Bryan was even then showing signs of ill-health as he died only seven years later.

Both father and son showed kindly tendencies in their respective wills, John leaving small bequests of money to all his servants at Hodge Hill and Bryan doing the same. He also left money to his tenants in 'Longdale' and Tilberthwaite and to their children, and he desired his son John to be kind to these tenants.

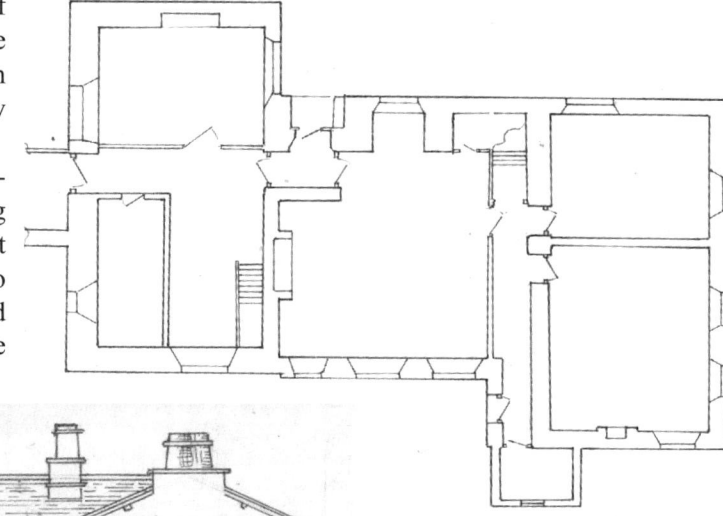

Although there were farm buildings attached to Hodge Hill, these must have been run in a separate enterprise. Father John Philipson did have forty sheep worth only £9.4s, but

Plan and elevations of Hodge Hill.

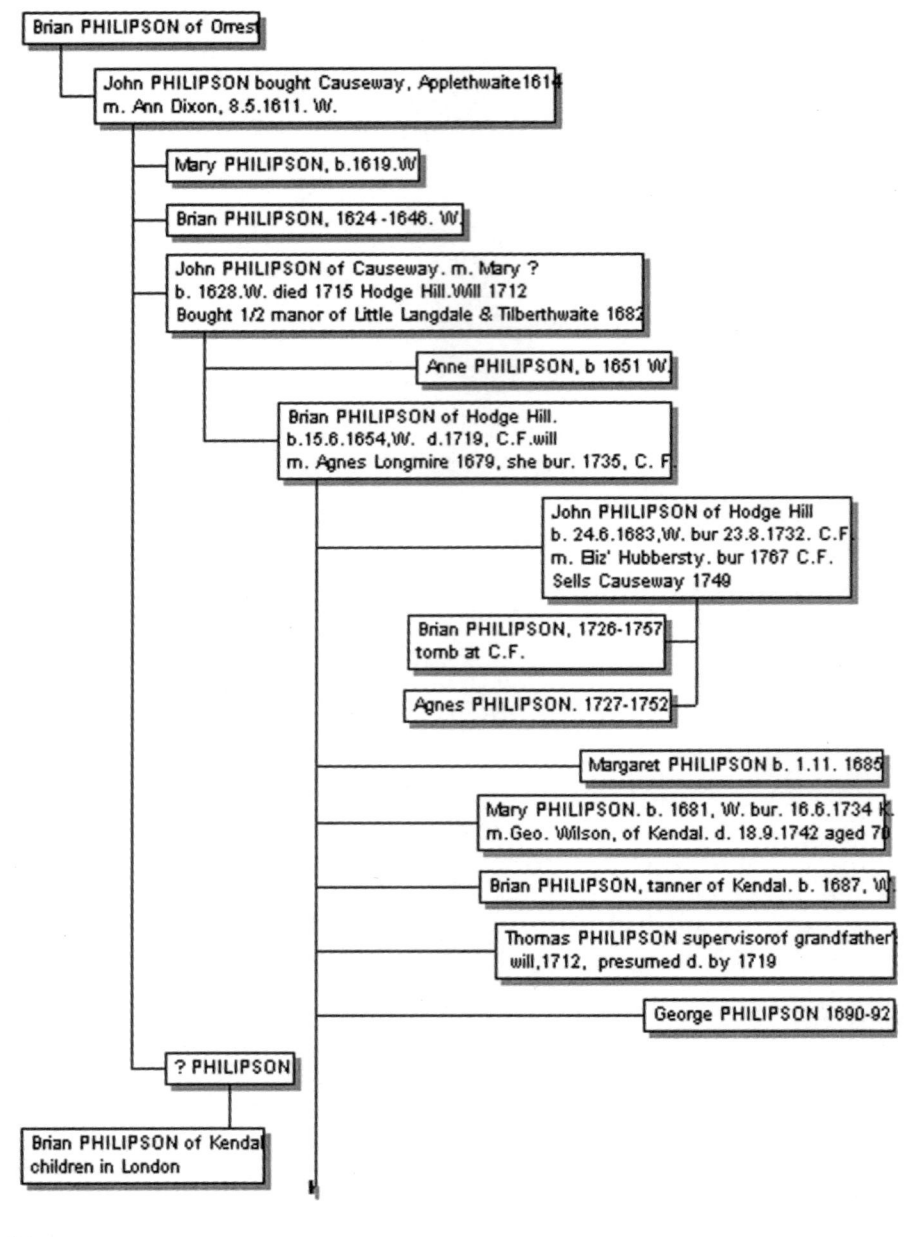

CARTMEL FELL

Philipson Family Tree

- **Brian PHILIPSON of Orrest**
  - **John PHILIPSON** bought Causeway, Applethwaite 1614. m. Ann Dixon, 8.5.1611. W.
    - Mary PHILIPSON, b.1619. W.
    - Brian PHILIPSON, 1624-1646. W.
    - **John PHILIPSON of Causeway.** m. Mary ? b. 1628. W. died 1715 Hodge Hill. Will 1712. Bought 1/2 manor of Little Langdale & Tilberthwaite 1682
      - Anne PHILIPSON, b 1651 W.
      - **Brian PHILIPSON of Hodge Hill.** b.15.6.1654, W. d.1719, C.F. will m. Agnes Longmire 1679, she bur. 1735, C.F.
        - **John PHILIPSON of Hodge Hill** b. 24.6.1683, W. bur 23.8.1732. C.F. m. Biz' Hubbersty. bur 1767 C.F. Sells Causeway 1749
          - Brian PHILIPSON, 1726-1757 tomb at C.F.
          - Agnes PHILIPSON. 1727-1752
        - Margaret PHILIPSON b. 1.11. 1685
        - Mary PHILIPSON. b. 1681, W. bur. 16.6.1734 K. m. Geo. Wilson, of Kendal. d. 18.9.1742 aged 70
        - Brian PHILIPSON, tanner of Kendal. b. 1687, W.
        - Thomas PHILIPSON supervisor of grandfather's will, 1712, presumed d. by 1719
        - George PHILIPSON 1690-92
    - ? PHILIPSON
      - Brian PHILIPSON of Kendal children in London

otherwise there is no mention of farming stock or implements in the inventories. Both father and son had bonds and specialities worth £140 and £347 respectively, and they were probably both lawyers. A tombstone in St Anthony's churchyard (1757) of a fourth generation of Hodge Hill Philipsons describes this Bryan as being 'bred to the Law', as though this was the family calling.

From a combination of wills and tomb inscriptions one can construct an incomplete family tree for this branch of the Philipson family. The earlier generations of Philipsons were buried at Cartmel Priory, but once Cartmel Fell was licensed for burials, they constructed two of the most imposing memorials in the churchyard to their dead. One large sandstone tablet is on the east wall of the church, and is much weathered, but fortunately it was transcribed from the Latin around 1910 by the Rev. Thomas Price. Translated it read:

*John Philipson of Hodge Hill in Cartmel Fell,
Gentleman.
A comrade of ready and witty speech,
Of all the graces and conversation
He excelled without an effort.
A neighbour at once hospitable and kindly
Withal, a Trusty and loyal friend
He earned the esteem of those who knew him.
A lover of Plain Truth, a stranger to Guile,
Of that probity he loved in others
He was himself an example.
A devoted adherent of the Anglican Church
To which, scorning all deceipts of false doctrine
He firmly clung.
He shall rest here in the Lord, awaiting
When Death itself, the Vanquisher of all
Shall be swallowed up in Victory.*

*He died on the 20th August 1732,
in the 50th year of his age.
On the left hand lies the body of
Agnes Philipson, mother
Of John, aforesaid,
who died on the 31st March 1735
In the 50th year of her age.
On the right hand lies the body of
Agnes Philipson, daughter
Of the aforesaid John, who died on the
22nd April 1752
In the 25th year of her age. Models of Prudence.*

The other slab is equally fulsome in its praise of the deceased, who was Bryan, son of John and Elizabeth Philipson of Hodge Hill. This tombstone is also very weathered, but with some difficulty was finally deciphered by Cartmel Fell Local History Society. As with the Latin inscription, only the dates had to be left as queries:

'A man of amiable disposition, of manners candid and humane, the inheritor of his father's generosity, who (had?)... been comfort and solace to his mother's ageing widowhood, benefit to all the neighbourhood, being bred to the Law, in ascertaining claims and prevailing on various disputes, If his life had been prolonged, but Death, alas, has snatched him. He died 11th Day of December 1757 in the 34th (?) year of his age.'

As with other parish duties, the Philipsons took their turn at the office of chapel warden. A new book was produced in 1721, with John Philipson's name and the date on the cover. He may well have paid for the ledger, which is bound in leather and tooled with gold leaf, and he remained as chapel warden for three years running.

After the Philipson dynasty ended their tenure of Hodge Hill with the death of Elizabeth in 1768, a number of new names appear at the farm in the parish registers. George and Elizabeth Tomlinson christened their daughter Barbary in 1772, four years after Elizabeth Philipson was buried. In the year following, they had another daughter baptised Susannah, but also in that year, Jane Pearson of Hodge Hill was buried. In 1784, Thomas and Mary Clarke had a son christened for his father, so possibly these were servants or caretakers, but the register's next entry for Hodge Hill begins a new dynasty which is remembered locally to the present day.

The Birket family had owned land in Cartmel Fell since the sixteenth century, and maybe even before that. It is highly probable that the new occupant of Hodge Hill, William Higgin Birket, was merely moving into family property, he being the grandson of James of Birket Houses. William was born about 1765 and married Ellen Cartmel from Broad Oak, Crosthwaite. They had six sons and three daughters, but for whatever reason, none of the sons married and one died in infancy, so there were no direct Birket heirs. Eleanor was born in 1806 and married the Rev. Robert Blackburn Cockerton who became the curate of Cartmel Fell in 1829. An older sister, Betty, lived on at Hodge Hill after her parents died and is registered as a separate household in the 1841 census, and of independent means. Alongside is a farming family, Joseph and Deborah Airey with their three children and three servants. (Hodge Hill has three doors and two staircases, so dividing the house was no problem.) The Aireys worked the farm for twenty years or so, and in later life, Betty Birket left her family home and moved into Bridge House, just down the hill, which had been built for her widowed mother.

The farm-land that went with Hodge Hill was something in excess of 200 acres according to two of the censuses. This was much larger than most farms on the fell, and it must have attracted ambitious tenants. A family of Taylors followed the Aireys and continued their tenancy for two generations. By 1891, John Thomas Taylor had taken over the farm from his father, and had married another Taylor, though of a different family, from across the fields at Thorphinsty Hall. Margaret was several years older than her husband but did not have the upper hand in her marriage. Her descendants tell of her isolation when the day's work was done. She would sit unhappily alone in the kitchen whilst her husband joined his parents in the parlour.

John Greenhow Fawcett was the tenant in 1901, with his wife Mary Ann and four young children. Elsie, the oldest child was eight and had been born in Underbarrow, her brother William Greenhow was born in Holme, and the younger two were born in Cartmel Fell, with two more following in 1901 and 1903. The family had two living-in servants at this period, Esther Middleborough and George Gaterix, both seventeen years old.

It was at about this time that there was a disastrous fire in one of the barns at Hodge Hill. Fortunately, this was across the field on the opposite side of the road, so the house was not threatened, but was said to have been started maliciously by a farm servant who had been dismissed for some offence, though nothing was proved. A splendid new barn was built on the opposite side of the road, and a date-stone proclaims the year, 1904, with the initials MHB, for Myles Higgin Birket. Several photographs record the building progress of what was probably one of the last traditional barns to be commissioned on the fell. The builders were John Kellett's family and the stone was carted by John Fleming of Swallowmire. The joiners were Robert Matthews, Midford Dewhurst and John Long.

For whatever reason, the Fawcetts gave way to the Preston family in 1905. John and Ruth Jane had their daughter baptised Maggie on 5 December 1905, and then, rather surprisingly, their son James was christened the following month on 7 January. The following year, they had another daughter who was named after her mother.

Farming was in the doldrums in the depression years of the early twentieth century and several young families passed through Hodge Hill. Many tenants found rents unrealistic, so this may be the reason for so many changes. One of the tenants identified in Bulmer's Directory of 1910 was William Batty, a member of the large family born at Hare Hill. William and Betsey were at Hodge Hill for several years, their daughter Betsey being baptised from there in 1918, but later they took over the family farm. The Batty menfolk were known locally for their cattle-breeding and fine horses, and they enjoyed showing their stock at local agricultural shows. Many generations later their surname can still be seen among the prize-winners at today's shows. Eventually, William took over the family farm of Hare Hill when his father, Bryan, retired to Silver Birch in the 1920s.

The survey made for the Inland Revenue in 1909/10 found that part of Hodge Hill was then ruinous, but the habitable part consisted of a sitting room, kitchen, back kitchen and a dairy, plus four bedrooms. This must have been the older, working end of the house.

A couple who found a successful formula for diversifying, as it is now called, were Henry and Mary Johnson. They came to Hodge Hill before the Second World War when times were hard. He was the farmer, but his wife capitalised on fresh farm produce and ran a very well-known restaurant for many years, employing local girls and teaching them her skills. Many of these lasses became splendid cooks in their own right. From plain ham-and-egg teas, Mary Johnson developed her culinary skills and began to serve what she called 'simple English food.' The ingredients may have been simple, but the results were unsurpassed, and in later life, after being widowed in 1963, Mary and her son and daughter-in-law moved to Tullythwaite House in Underbarrow, where one had to book weeks in advance to get a table.

The Birket line had almost come to an end on several occasions, through lack of heirs, but had struggled on with several name changes when the female line took up the cause. The last link with the family was broken when Mrs. Mason Burgess of Birket Houses died. She had first been the wife of Myles Higgin Birket and had inherited his holdings when he died.

Hodge Hill went on the market in 1967 and it was bought by Beryl Blades and her husband. Beryl continued the fine English cooking tradition of Mrs. Johnson's restaurant, but the farm-land was sold separately. One of the several large barns was converted into a dwelling in 1980 by the architect Jonathan Prichard, husband of Beryl Blades' daughter Bridie, and is now called Wicklow Barn, after a racehorse.

In a house of such antiquity, one must surely expect a ghost or two. Visitors staying for bed and breakfast have had varying experiences, some alarming and others enjoyable. The most recent was in 2002 when a clergyman's wife wondered who the young woman was in the pink dress (since she had not been introduced) who met her on arrival and later passed on the stairs. Another visitor from Austria said a young woman warned her to close the bedroom window, but she did not. Later in the night, a flurry of hailstones landed on the bed and she remembered the warning. When premature baby Robert Prichard cried, his mother would find the cradle being gently rocked, but a visiting man said he would never return to Hodge Hill. He had been pressed back into his bed by a woman in the night, and he was quite unable to sit up.

Chapel House

THIS farm lies just a few hundred yards to the north east of St Anthony's chapel, but there is now little chance of finding which is the more ancient. If the farm was already in existence when the church was built in 1504, it must have had another name. Without doubt, the back of the house is much older than the front. The windows are irregular and small, and the staircase is of a stone spiral construction. From across the fields, it has a look of great antiquity. The south-facing main entrance has all the features of a late-seventeenth century yeoman's dwelling, and must have been added on at that time of increased farming prosperity. There is a central porch, a large window to illuminate what was the firehouse or living kitchen, and the three upstairs windows are equally spaced. There must be hundreds of farmhouses in the Lake District which conform to this pleasantly familiar pattern. There are no dated stones on the front of the house, but inside is a little cupboard with the initials IAC, and the date of 1698. In all probability, this was the date of extension, and the owners were John and Catherine Addison. At that period, the letter J was always rendered as I, as in Latin. The initial of the surname almost always came in the middle, and the wife's initial at the end. From the Cartmel Priory registers we can discover that John Addison of Chapel House baptised his daughter Agnes on New Year's Day, 1683. His wife's name is not given, but there were so few girls' names beginning with C at that time, that Catherine seems the most likely, and was a popular name locally. There were several branches of Addisons on the fell in the seventeenth century, and they were probably kin to one another. One family was at Tower Wood and another at Kit Cragg, (later called Swallowmire) but for whatever reason, the families melted away, maybe for lack of male heirs.

One of the first names to come to light for Chapel House is John Strickland in 1638, the year he had his daughter christened Anne at Crosthwaite. Strays from Cartmel Fell often turn up at Crosthwaite at this period, as Cartmel Fell had no licence for marriages or burials until the following century, and Crosthwaite was only half the distance of the journey to Cartmel. John may have been a twig off the Strickland family tree at Hartbarrow. Oddly, almost all the baptisms for Chapel House, whatever the family were girls. Some farms retained the family name for generations, but without a great deal more research, it is not possible to say if this farm descended through the female line.

An un-dated entry in the parish records lists moneys given for investment for the benefit of the poor of Cartmel Fell, and James Harrison of Chapel House gave £13.6s. to Thomas Knipe. This was probably a relation of John Harrison of the same address who made his will in 1638.

Edward Becke had his three girls christened at Cartmel between 1668 and 1672, Jennett, Margaret and Isabel. We can imagine that Edward and his family still inhabited the oldest part of the house, that which is now at the back. One can compare this very small, but substantially-built dwelling with the original house at Foxfield. This too is virtually one room upstairs and one room downstairs.

The Addisons were probably the family who enlarged and improved the farmhouse at the end of the seventeenth century and after them came the Halhead dynasty. This family were at Chapel House for most of the eighteenth century, and their names crop up as witnesses to wills or indentures. In 1723, Robert Halhead was a trustee for James Rowlandson's estate, and 21 years later, when described as 'Yeoman of Chapelhouse', he was a trustee for Richard Rawlinson of Simson Ground. He was also a trustee for the Bryan Beck Charity in 1727. Yeomen did parish service, but for some reason, the Halheads do not appear in the lists of parish officials, which rotated around the yeomen farmers. In 1757, Rowland Rawlinson took on the task of overseer of the poor for Chapel House, but several times he took on this office for other yeomen, maybe for payment, having proved himself effective. It could be that the Halheads were only semi-literate and unable or unwilling to do the necessary book-keeping. Much later in the century in 1766, Isaac Halhead was paid from the chapel funds for six days carpentry work at 1s.6d. a day, the wage of a skilled man. He too had daughters, but one of them, Mally, was buried in 1777 aged only three. It seems that at this period there were two brothers and their families all living in Chapel House as they both christened children in the 1700s. Isaac was married to Betty and Thomas was married to Anne. They seem to have had a succession of daughters, Betty, Mally and Anne, and that is maybe why the farm became the property of the Greenwoods by 1812.

In 1782, Mary Barrow of Cartmel Fell had married Robert Greenwood, of Turner Hill in Witherslack, and he also owned Chapel House and here we have a glimpse of the status of the farm, as it appears in the Burblethwaite Manor accounts. It was liable for a literal peppercorn rent of five ounces to the manor, but little else. Other estates in the so-called manor had to do boon service and supply peat or a day's shearing, but Chapel House was free of those obligations. Robert's brother William Greenwood then lived at Pool Garth Nook, and from William's will we know that Robert had two daughters, Susannah and Elizabeth, and they eventually were left their mother's family messuage at Turner Hill. The will was made in 1820, and it reveals that Robert was already dead. It also mentions 'My nephew John Greenwood', and indeed, John Greenwood was the owner of Chapel House in the 1814 land tax return, though not in residence. The following year however, he was living at Chapel House and from there baptised his daughter Anne after her mother and was styled yeoman in the baptismal register.

The next piece of documentary evidence for this farm comes from the 1841 census. It appears there as two dwellings, one of them uninhabited. A bachelor aged 35, William Birket was the head of household and perhaps living in the newer front of the house. He was probably the son of William Higgin Birket of Hodge Hill. If so, he never married and retired to Cark Villa, Cark, according to a pedigree of the Birket's, published in 1873 by J. Footes. Living with William were Ann and John Gibson, probably mother and son. She was a 60-year-old farm servant and he an agricultural labourer of 30. There were many Gibsons on the fell from the sixteenth to the nineteenth century, so it is hard to pinpoint this pair.

Ten years later, a master-shoemaker had taken

over the farm which was then of 22 acres. John Stables had moved from Blewthwaite, just across the fields, with his wife, daughter and two sons, but he was not long for this world. In 1852 he made his will, though his burial is not recorded at Cartmel Fell. The census told us that he was from Langdale, and his will names the family farm as Walthwaite, which he left to his ten-year-old son James, with his brother Henry and two brothers-in-law as trustees. A writing desk was left to James also, but not until his mother died or re-married, and the other son, John, was to have his clock. His daughter Mary was to have a corner cupboard under the same terms. It would be interesting to know if these items are now family heirlooms. If their mother re-married, she was to sell the furniture and invest the money for their children until they were 23. In an illustration for *Annals of a Quiet Valley,* published in 1894, Bertha Newcombe portrayed the shoemaker, sitting on the Philipson tomb in the churchyard, chatting to the parson. Maybe someone had told her that this is where John Stables carried out his work on fine days, but this is mere conjecture.

It seems that both Stables parents must have died before the next census, because in 1861, two aunts are in charge of the farm, Eleanor and Hannah Mason from Wharton. Their teenage niece Mary and nephew James Stables were farm servants in what was their parent's farm, but their brother John had left the family unit. Eventually, the sister and brothers were re-united, at least for a while. John had become a warehouseman with a woollen manufacturer, but was living at Chapel House again by 1871. Probably, John married and moved away again, but his brother and sister continued to farm their small acreage until the end of the nineteenth century. In all the census returns from 1861, a relative who is a visitor is present at Chapelhouse. In 1861, this is an infant of two, Joseph Swindlehurst, mistakenly entered as a niece on the census, but then small boys wore dresses. In 1881, Emma Swindlehurst of Claife is in residence and also in 1891, by which time she is 28.

The 1901 census shows that the farm was tenanted by Airey Mansergh, his wife Hannah and their baby son Walter Herbert. Airey was born in Dunnerdale, but his wife came from Undermillbeck on the eastern side of Windermere lake. This property was owned by Alice Carr of Newlands Vicarage by this time, and the status of her tenant was described as 'hind'. The 1909/10 Finance Act describes the property as it was then: 'Parlour, kitchen, back kitchen, dairy, pantry, 4 bedrooms, stone, slate, fair. Land, fair. About 8 acres of rough pasture. Extent, 26 acres. 2 roods.' This acreage was unchanged from the mid-nineteenth century. Alice Carr's tenant in 1910 was John Fleming who was born at Thorneythwaite in 1869, one of a large family. Because the acreage of the farm was so small, John needed another source of income and was the local carter. This was mentioned in a skit of 1910 called 'The Tory Social', explaining why there were so few radicals in Cartmel Fell. The poem implied that John would vote for whichever party employed him, and since he carted the fuel for the stoves at the school and the church, it was inevitable that he would vote for the Establishment. John Fleming must have become the tenant some time before 1906 when his son John William was born at Chapel House. The family moved to Swallowmire, but their son died before his parents in 1936 aged only 31.

In the 1940s, the Pearson family were tenants at Chapel House. Leslie Pearson remembered that the farm rent and the 'knowing' rent were due at about the same time, and it was difficult to find the money when farming was depressed. The ownership of the farm passed to a Miss Carr who died in the year 2000, aged 103, and was the daughter of Alice. When their landlady died, her tenants had the opportunity to buy their holdings and to become yeomen again. Today, Chapel House has one of the few remaining dairy herds in the parish and the Kitching family have a milk round.

Bridge House

THERE has been a house on this site for several hundred years, but the one you see today was built much later than its nearby barn. The name would seem to be self-explanatory, but the bridge is about one fifth of a mile from the furthest boundary, so not exactly adjacent. In earlier times the dwelling was called Brigg House, but although this is just dialect for bridge, it could also mean the house of the Brigg or Briggs family. This wealthy and influential family owned the adjoining lands of Cowmire Hall during the fifteenth and sixteenth centuries, so a cadet member of the family could have been accommodated nearby.

The Cartmel Parish registers have a number of entries for people living at Brig House or Bridge House in the eighteenth century, but 'Cartmel Fell' is not appended, so there may be another dwelling in one of the other parishes of the same name.

There was an existing dwelling of this name in 1561, when Miles Briggs claimed a right to the messuage of Brigg House and eight acres in Cartmel Fell. The dispute was with Anthony Knipe of Burblethwaite, who claimed that this was part of his demesne, and by a deed of 1532, he had put in tenants, Thomas and Miles Barwick. The dispute was eventually settled, and the Briggses gained or re-gained the property, but the enmity rumbled on in other disputes for several generations.

'Lobby' bridge spans the river Winster, once the county boundary between Westmorland and

Lancashire. In the Cartmel bishop's transcripts for 1810, 1816 and 1818 there are three entries, one for Lobby Hame, and two for Lobby House. It seems likely that this was briefly the name of Bridge House, but the origin of Lobby is obscure. Maybe it was once just a little bridge, maybe a couple of poles lobbed over the river?

The present dwelling dates from the nineteenth century, and the specification for its building still survives on fourteen pages of closely written foolscap paper. The house was to be built for Miss (Elizabeth) Birket at Bridge House, implying an existing homestead. We know from censuses that Elizabeth's mother Ellen lived there in 1841, with her unmarried son Miles. Ten years later, Elizabeth was the sole owner/occupier, as the Mannex directory states, and she continued to live there until she died in 1862. Old Mrs Birket must have moved elsewhere, as she died only one year before her daughter. She was the widow of Higgin Birket of Hodge Hill who died in 1836, and from parish documents, it can be seen that Bridge House was part of the Hodge Hill estate by the nineteenth century.

This new dwelling must have been the envy of everyone in the township. No detail was left to chance, from the Whitbarrow limestone for the windowsills to the downspouts and guttering; these to be of differing quality, front and back. The latest and most exciting innovation was an indoor water closet, but as yet, no bathroom. There was a description of the brass bell to be installed, but disappointingly, no date is attached to the specification. All one can say, is that it had to be before Elizabeth died in 1862.

The Kidd family followed Miss Birket. Henry Kidd was a shoemaker, and had worked his way along the fell from Low House Beck to Poolgarth, and from there to Poolgarth Nook. His last child, Jane, was born at Bridge House in 1870, but Henry died the following year, aged only 41. He left a widow and six children, the oldest of whom was ten. Life must have been very hard for Mary Kidd, and when the next census was taken she was a charwoman with two children still at home and three lodgers. The lodgers must have been brothers - Thomas, Edward and Samuel Gass - all unmarried and all general labourers.

Three years after her husband died, Mary's second son, William, followed him to the grave. Only six months previously, another lodger had died, John Dickinson aged 44. When death sweeps through a household, one thinks of tuberculosis, but without death certificates this is mere supposition. By 1891, Mary was still a charwoman, but had only her last-born, Jane, living with her. She disappears from local records at this point, but one hopes she had a more comfortable life with a married son or daughter in another parish.

Early in the twentieth century, Bridge House was home to Thomas Lishman and his family. Like so many of their clan, these Lishmans were timber merchants and woodcutters. In 1912, Thomas and Clara Fanny christened their son John, and Daisy followed in 1916, but died a few weeks later. Mrs Gladys Dunn, née Lishman, remembers visiting the family, and the welcoming homely atmosphere of the household before the First World War. Mrs Clara Lishman was deaf, and famous for her delicious plate pies. Tom Lishman was a concertina player, and the family delighted in showing off their step-dancing skills. The table would be pushed back, the mats removed, and great fun was had by all. Step-dancing is undergoing a revival, but for those not familiar with this activity, it could be likened to Irish dancing, where the upper body moves little, but the feet twinkle as the intricate steps are performed. A hundred years earlier, a family of Lishmans had a dancing academy in Cartmel, so perhaps these were descendants. 'Lish' in dialect means lively or active, so a very suitable surname for the family. Two decades later, another generation of Lishmans began, when John and Gladys christened their son John in 1940, but this family later moved to Bryan Beck, still following their trade as woodsmen and wood merchants.

The outbuildings at Bridge House are those which would be expected on a small farm. They pre-date the house by about two centuries, but an addition on the south east side might interest bee-keepers. This is a stone built bee shelter, constructed in a lean-to fashion. The sides are two huge pieces of limestone and one giant flag-stone forms the roof. The straw skeps would have been placed on the shelf, or shelves, and the west wall would protect them from the prevailing wet winds. The garden wall has bee-boles in it as well and these may pre-date the shelter.

Cowmire Hall

COWMIRE Hall is on the northern side of the River Winster and therefore not in old Lancashire or the township of Cartmel Fell, but nonetheless, the families who lived there had much influence on the parish. The name has been spelt many ways down the ages; Caluemyer in 1332, Calmire in 1535, Cawmire in 1589, and Cowmire today, and the pronunciation may have been as variable too, but locally it is known as Comer. The 'mire' element can be easily explained, for this ancient farm is situated on the relatively flat valley land, where the Arndale beck joins the river Winster. It must have taken hundreds of man-hours to drain adequately, and there might have been a tarn or mere here in early medieval times. As a comparison, Grasmere was often spelt Grasmire in the seventeenth century and might reflect the local dialect. The Cow or Cal prefix has been explained as either cow or calf, so one might assume that there was a dairy farm of some size from early times.

The house itself began as a pele tower, and it is said to be the last one to be built in Westmorland, probably in the fifteenth or early sixteenth century. Certainly, it seems to be less concerned with defence than many others, as it has quite large windows which are very similar to those in the church. The worst of the Scottish raids in the Furness area was in 1321, so the memory may have been all too fresh locally when the name was first recorded, and there were still many border raids further north.

Tudor windows in the pele tower.

Possibly the pele tower was built on the site of an existing house of less robust structure. At the base of the tower is a double vault, one of which was obviously used as a dairy, but when the seventeenth century section was added, the second vault was divided to accommodate the stairs.

The Brigg or Briggs family are the first known owners of Cowmire, and it is this line who were the great benefactors of the chapel of St Anthony. The glass in the windows of the church has been restored to a degree, and the kneeling lady in the east window is the wife of the donor, Anthony or Robert Brigg. In the well-understood symbolism of the day, donors had lecterns and there would have been a representation of her husband in another section of the windows. An inscription in the north window makes the family known: *orate pro animabus Antonius Brig et (uxor) benefactores isti locis* (Pray for the souls of Anthony Brig and his wife, benefactors of this place). One could speculate that the chapel was dedicated to St. Anthony because of the donor's christian name, and Anthony was also a family name of the Knipes, fellow-donors. In another panel in the east window other family members have mention, Robti, i.e. Robert Brig and his wife.

Four years after the chapel was built, in 1508, the Duchy of Lancaster survey shows that Robert Briggs paid 16d. rent to Cartmel Priory, together with various tithes and service. Cowmire seems to have been the only holding in Westmorland which held their lands from the Priory, but possibly this could mean that the Briggses originally had an estate in Cartmel Fell (Brigg House) which extended over the river into Crosthwaite, and there they built the Cowmire pele. Robert died in 1520 and his will shows that Brigg House was held from William Knipe, son of Anthony, of Burblethwaite Hall, and this was the cause of family feuding for several generations. Apparently, the grant to the Briggses had been made by William Knipe's guardian before he came of age, and so in 1532, William re-entered the property, claiming that without his consent, Thomas Briggs had put in an under-tenant. The following year, this case went to arbitration, confirming the tenant-right of the Briggs family, but adding to the Knipe's resentment. This particular dispute flared up again in 1561 and is recorded in the Burblethwaite papers.

Unfortunately, although there are several wills extant which show rather broken pedigrees of the family, it is not possible so far to construct a complete family tree. Robert Briggs the elder made a will in 1588, naming his heir Roland and three other sons, Miles and Henry and Thomas. His daughter Isabel was to have £20 for her marriage portion together with apparel and bedding, and 'if she would be ordered and do her friends' counsel,' she was to have an extra twenty marks. Robert's widow Jennet was executor and left her will in 1614. Robert's will was supervised by (among others) Thomas Briggs of Cowmyer. The attached inventory showed that the Briggs family's wealth was then in cattle, although they possessed studdles, wheels and cards, all of which imply textile production. The cattle of mixed ages totalled 32, but in addition there were four draught oxen and a flock of 50 old sheep with seventeen lambs. The whole assessment of Robert Briggs' worldly goods was £95 19s 10d. Amongst the little luxuries in the household were silver spoons and bordcloths which were probably Turkey carpets for covering tables.

There was an inscription relating to William Briggs in the east window of St Anthony's. It was thought to have been added after the glass was fired, maybe with ink, and has now all but disappeared. When the windows were restored in 1912, it was recorded thus: 'William Briggs goeth to London upon Tuesday xith day of Aprill. God fend him.' There is no way now of calculating which year William Briggs went to London, but it obviously caused great anxiety for the rest of the family. It was usual for travellers to go in convoy for their mutual protection, and they might accompany the strings of pack-horses which regularly plied the road which has become the A6. In Jenet's will, she leaves her grandson Thomas 'at London' £3 6s 8d, and this may have been the link with William's worrying journey, and possibly was the family of Miles Briggs mentioned in the Burblethwaite papers.

Miles Briggs was evidently a man of high profile in the sixteenth century, and comes into focus largely through disputes of one kind or another. Earlier in the century, he or another Miles Briggs was granted a pardon in 1509, but the offence is not recorded. He was then said to be of Calmire. Much later, in 1554 a man of the same name was again pardoned for an unspecified offence, and then described as 'late of Crostewhate, and marchaunt, alias late of Colymire Hall, in the parish of Heversham, chapman, alias the son and heir of Thomas Briggs late of Cartmelfell, marchaunt, deceased.'

Nowadays, we tend to think of a chapman as being in business in a small way, perhaps with a pack on his back and going about the dales on foot. The Briggs must have been engaged in much larger commercial ventures which financed the building of such a pele tower, and then with money to spare, to subscribe to the building of a chapel. The wool merchants of the fifteenth century grew rich through the home and continental markets, and many became benefactors of the beautiful churches which sprang up, most notably in the Cotswolds and East Anglia. St Anthony's chapel is not quite in the league of, say, Burford, but it reflects a local style. The wool of fell flocks was anyway not as valuable as that of Lincolnshire or Cotswold sheep. The Briggses were probably among the many wool-merchants who sent their product to London or

Southampton with the strings of pack horses travelling the north/south route continuously.

The disputes between the Briggs and the Knipes of Burblethwaite rumbled on over several generations and seem to have rivalled those between the Montagues and Capulets, some incidents resulting in physical violence. A document in the Public Record Office shows the extent to which the parties gave vent to their feelings. In 1561, Julian, the wife of William Briggs, was attacked in the chapel of St Anthony, dragged outside thereby tearing her clothing, then her adversaries 'hurte her in such sorte that she then and the same tyme did lye in an deade swone by a long space and not without great danger of her lyfe. By reason of wch great assalte and affraye, the said Julian a long tyme thereafter did lye sore sycke and not like to have recovered her health againe.'

The perpetrators of this act were Anthony Knipe, William Knipe, Miles Poole, Anthony Harrison and Michael Matson. Apparently the ill-feeling was inspired by the belief that because Julian had been born in Crosthwaite she should worship there, not in the nice new chapel of Cartmel Fell. Actually, Cowmire Hall is on the far side of the Winster as mentioned, and therefore technically in Crosthwaite parish, but the Briggs chose to endow a church accessible to the community of Cartmel Fell and more convenient for themselves. The Briggs and Knipe families had been the principal donors, so the logic of the argument against Julian is hard to understand, but probably logic had little to do with the case.

The original pele tower seems to have had some land attached and is described in a fragment of a Crosthwaite rental of 1582: 'Thomas Brigges holds of the Lord their by tenande righte accordinge to the custome of the manor there... a tenement with an orchard ground.' Elsewhere in the document it states that James Briggs held of the lord only a parcel of land, being a leek garth, containing one fall of ground. James Briggs may have lived in Brigg house, now called Bridge House, just up the road, and this has only a small enclosure of land, enough for a leek garth.

The Briggses were conservative in their choices of Christian names, as were their contemporaries. They favoured Thomas, Miles and William for their menfolk, and this makes it difficult to sort the generations. It is possible to pinpoint the family in 1615 however, when St George's Visitation was published. Thomas Briggs had married into another wealthy family of clothiers, the Braithwaites of Ambleside. His wife was Isabell, and they had four daughters, the third of whom was Frances. She had been widowed and was married for the second time to Arthur Benson of Skelwith. The Bensons were an ancient family of fullers from the Ambleside and Rydal area, so the links with the cloth trade were again fortified. Unfortunately, the only two boys died in childhood, so Thomas had no male heir. The Crosthwaite parish register records the death of four members of the family in the 1590s. Myles Briggs and his (nameless) wife, and John of 'Cawmire' who was buried in 1597 and in the following year, Isabell of Cawmire, wife of John.

In 1662 there was a conveyance by Anthony Byerley, a magistrate of Midrigge Grange in County Durham, to Henry Newby of Hazelrigg, Cartmel, yeoman. The Newby's family must have lived at Cowmire for perhaps twenty years, as Anne, wife of William was buried at Crosthwaite in

1693. Thomas Machell, 'the Antiquary on Horseback', rode to Calmire as he called it, probably in 1692, through the woods from Witherslack. He likened the old-fashioned house to a monastery, all overgrown with ivy, but he was very interested in the painted glass, some of which had coats of arms and others depicted the symbols of the woollen trade, packhorses and carriers, spinning wheels, a basket of wool, carding hands and wantaracks[1]. In a window in what Machell calls 'the clay room' was depicted a man in yellow with a pikestaff on his right shoulder and a whip in his left hand, driving four pack-horses. Here and there were letters TB, IB, MB, which he assumed were the initials of members of the Briggs family. He relates the purchase of Cowmire by Henry Newby, father of William, and must have had a conducted tour and been given the history by the Newbys themselves.

According to a reference in an article in the *Transactions of the Cumberland and Westmorland Antiquarian & Archaeolgical Society*, in the papers belonging to the Burrow family of Hilltop, Crosthwaite, in the same box of papers containing the conveyance, were plans and an elevation of the proposed additional wing of Cowmire Hall, but I have been unable to track this down. At the end of the seventeenth century, Isabel Newby married Richard, the eleventh child of Sir Daniel Fleming of Rydal Hall, and they came to live at Cowmire Hall. Richard was 30 at the time of his marriage, and until then had acted as his father's steward at Rydal. Isabel was a considerable heiress, whereas Daniel Fleming had lost a great deal of money during and after the Civil War and had fifteen children, so it was probably her money which produced the up-to-date façade and hall, which more than doubled the size of the old pele tower. The medieval tower was completely obscured by the symmetrical frontage with many windows, and the servants were banished to their own quarters instead of sharing the master's table.

Richard died in 1717, a relatively young man, and his only son, Daniel, died unmarried, as did three of his four sisters. The inheritance descended through the only married daughter, Catherine Compstone of Ambleside, and she had two daughters only.

Thomas Machell's sketch of Cowmire.

CARTMEL FELL

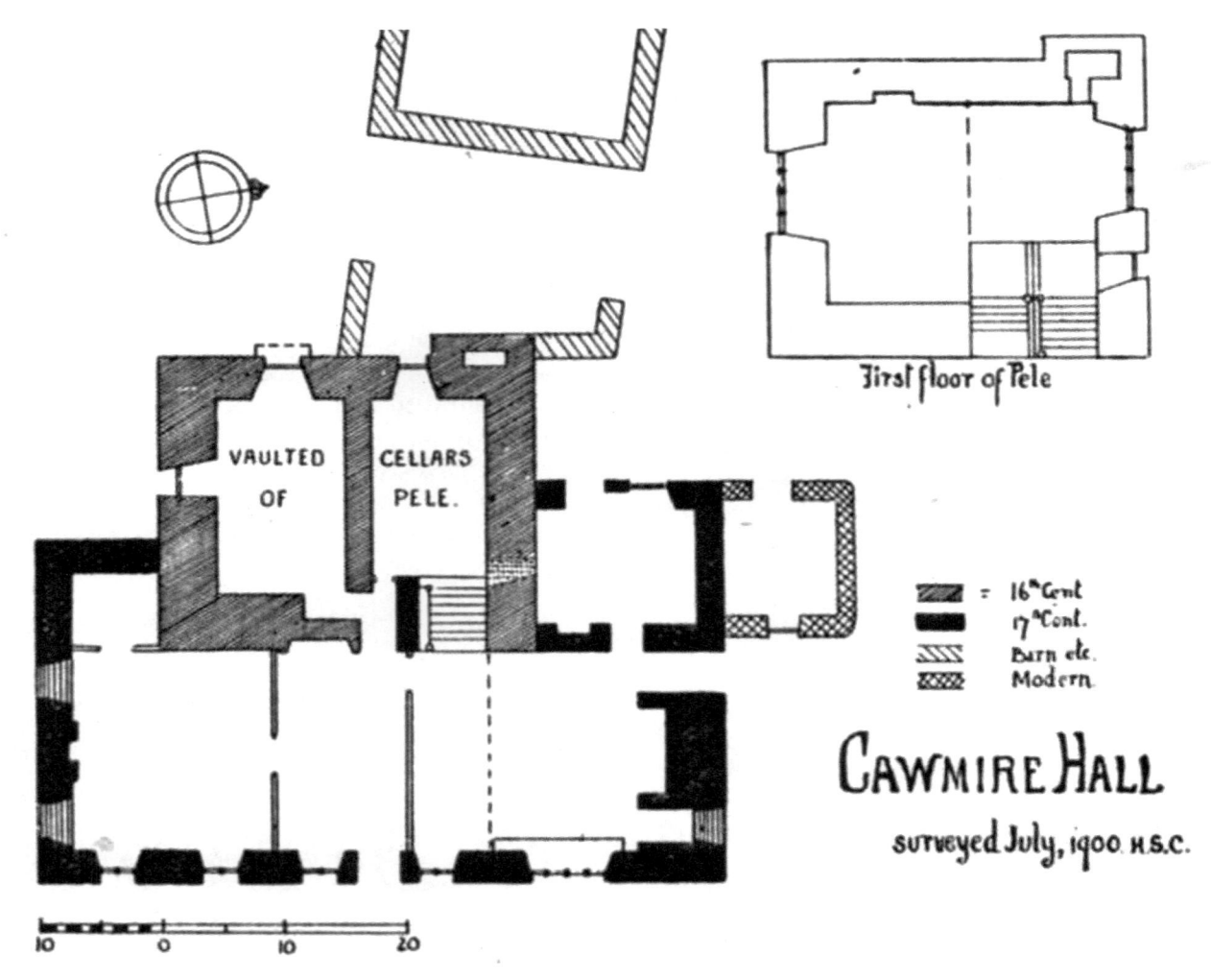

First floor of Pele

VAULTED CELLARS OF PELE.

= 16ᵗʰ Cent
= 17ᵗʰ Cent.
= Barn etc.
= Modern.

CAWMIRE HALL

surveyed July, 1900. H.S.C.

About ten years after Richard Fleming's death, another dispute arose between Burblethwaite Hall and Cowmire, though by this time different families were involved. There is a small sheet of paper, written in a fine neat script in the collection of papers relating to Cowmire. It declares that Edward, Thomas and James Garnett, farmers, but formerly servants at Cowmire, swear that the fence in Scale Meadow belonged to Burblethwaite, then the property of William Robinson. They described the fence as beginning at a certain eller tree (alder), and going to where the watercourse runs out of Burblethwaite field. What was more, they declared that farmers of Burblethwaite had repaired that fence for 40 years without using a single stick out of Scale Ground, that is to say, the boundary was the responsibility of Burblethwaite. Scale Ground is still retained as the field name today.

The owners of Cowmire Hall did not necessarily live there, and from the eighteenth century, several tenants are recorded. Among the Cowmire papers is a list of the freehold and customary lands attached to the estate. The document was generated because of a query from a tenant as to the way in which the rent was apportioned. There were the lands which had been held from the manor by ancient custom for which annual fines were due, and there were also freehold lands. The former were Daniel's portion as the son and heir, and presumably the rest were the daughters' portion. Customary holdings were hereditary, but on the death of the owner, a fine was paid to the manor.

James Wilson was the tenant in 1793, and he did not think that £60 15s (which was one third of the rent) was equal to the acreage of the customary land. Roger Fleming replied that there had been arbitration in 1765 as to the divisions, and he attached a complete list of the fields, orchards and gardens.

In 1772, Barbara Fleming, spinster of Ambleside and the oldest of the three sisters, sold her share of Cowmire to George Knott of Monk Coniston for £500, but apparently the money was never paid. In 1782, it was re-sold or possibly re-possessed by Roger Fleming of Whitehaven, and the document noted the yearly customary rent of 13s 4d. This was paid to the Lowthers as lords of the manor. Catherine Compstone's share of Cowmire descended through her granddaughters, one of whom, named for her grandmother, married Christopher Wilson. The Wilson family were then of Abbot Hall in Kendal, and later of Rigmaden in Kirkby Lonsdale. Because of having been divided down the generations, the estate was becoming eighths, but Christopher Wilson began to pull it together again by buying out his sister-in-law's share for £1,100 in 1805. When Christopher Wilson's heir died, his share of the annual rent was £36 13s 4d, and the tenant of Cowmire was James Maudsley.

The enclosure acts were awarding allotments to the various farms in the area at the turn of the nineteenth century. The Cartmel Fell awards came in 1797, but the Heversham enclosures were not until 1821, and Cowmire was then allotted 62 acres, three roods and two perches of unimproved land. A great deal of timber was sold from the estate at this period, as the advertisements of the time show. For instance, in 1838, 100 oak trees were auctioned and realised £122, and seventeen acres of fourteen years' coppice growth made £88. Compared with the rent from the farm, the timber was a good investment.

Christopher Graham from Heversham was the farmer in 1851. He had a large family living in with him including two nephews who were farm labourers, two other farm servants and a housemaid. His own children ranged from five to seventeen, but were not designated as either scholars or farm workers.

As late as 1906, a general fine was still being paid to the Lowther Estates, though by this time it had dwindled to 7s 4d with a fee for four shillings which was not explained. It can hardly have been worth collecting at Kendal, where it was paid by John Barrow.

We know from the diaries of Thomas Price that

in 1913, the Carruthers family were in residence at Cowmire. Cicely Price, the curate's daughter, persuaded Mrs Carruthers to be the first district nurse for the area. This included Low Birks, Woodside, the Fellside area and Pool Bank. Mrs Carruthers had been at Cowmire since the end of the nineteenth century, and she recalled in later life that the garden had then been sunken, with the approach to the front door up a flight of steps.

In *Some Westmorland Farmhouses* published by the 'Westmorland Gazette', the author notes that the fireplace in the hall, which has an opening five feet square, is identical to the one at Thorphinsty Hall, though the Fleming coat of arms is an additional embellishment at Cowmire. He comments that they were probably made by the same craftsman,

The owner of Cowmire at the end of the nineteenth and early twentieth century was J D Burrow of Hill Top in Crosthwaite, and in 1919 he leased it to Colonel Wellwood, late of the Indian Army.

Among the Cowmire papers are a few relating to the defence regulations of 1944. They are not in this instance concerned with defence, but give an indication as to what was required of farmers by way of their war effort. The owner was still J D Burrow, and he was served with a 'Cultivation of Land' order. This laid down specific requirements for cultivation, for instance: 'Plough part of 404, seven and a half acres of oats and one and a half of spring wheat. Part of 375 to be ploughed for one and a half acres of potatoes, oats and seeds in another six acres. Four acres of turnips and two and a half acres of greencrop elsewhere.' The War Agricultural Board must have scratched its head when trying to find ploughland in Cartmel Fell, but Cowmire Hall had a better choice than many farms.

In 1954, Major Gordon was visiting his sisters at Haverthwaite and saw that the Cowmire estate was for sale. He had previously farmed in Scotland and must have been about 70 years old when he decided to take up the reins in the Winster valley. He continued to farm it until he was 83, and then sold it to the Barratts in 1967. The farm is run as a separate enterprise today, and a house was built to the south of the hall to accommodate a farmer.

The second generation of the Barratt family to live at Cowmire is re-planting the woodland, and in 1988, six tulip trees were planted to commemorate the golden wedding of Roger and Diana Barratt. In 2005, the exterior of the hall is undergoing a facelift. The sombre pebble-dash rendering must have been applied at some distant date to keep out the worst of the weather, but this has been removed and replaced by a warm ochre lime plaster.

[1] Wantarack, a merchant's mark, maybe derived from *wantoe,* the band which held the pack-saddle frame.

The School

THERE is evidence of a school on the fell for 300 years at least, but even before this time, it is possible that the incumbent of St. Anthony's would have given some basic education in reading, writing and arithmetic to his parishioners' children. There were endless difficulties in providing education for the children on the fell, as will be seen, but public-spirited members of the community fought long and hard to gain it, often dipping deep into their own pockets.

In June 1695, Benjamin Fletcher left £200 in his will to the twenty-four of Cartmel, the interest thereof to pay four readers and schoolmasters in the chapelries of Lindale, Staveley, Flookburgh and Cartmel Fell. The first schoolmaster to receive his share of this bequest is not known by name, but we hear of him in a letter of Thomas Brockbank's. Writing in December 1697, he thought that the master lacked diligence and care, and he suggested that William Myles should be the replacement, as he had a good reputation at Blawith. It would seem like an early example of head-hunting. The appointment was made, but by March 1700 Myles was already out of favour, according to a letter to Thomas Brockbank from his father, John. Thomas Brockbank was by then the vicar of Garstang, and he thought the trouble might be partly caused by the vicar of Cartmel, who wished to dismiss Myles, but we do not know if the reason was personal or professional, or even political. From other sources, there is evidence that the Rev. Thomas Proddy of Cartmel had become a victim of senile decay, so maybe that was a contributing factor. Here it is a little difficult to read between the lines, but there must have been a just grievance on Myles's part too, as he seems to have been unpaid. This could have been a deliberate policy to hasten his departure, or merely inefficient administration of the funds. Thomas Brockbank's diary comments: 'Admittedly the Cartmel Fell people were Factious and Headdy, yet they had too just cause for Complaint.' Myles went to see the bishop of Chester in his own defence, armed with petitions from persons of 'Note and Quality', to show that the people of the fell had not kept their promise to augment his salary, and as a result, the bishop withdrew his inhibition. We presume that an uneasy truce next ensued between the schoolmaster and his pupils' parents, but it did not last long.

In September 1706, Thomas Brockbank became the vicar of Cartmel, and kept a close eye on the seven divisions. In that year, he noted that Jonah Walker, reader and schoolmaster at Cartmel Fell, had not taught school for about two years, and at Easter had vacated the place, 'leaving the Chappelry in a Manner Desolate ever since.' His whereabouts was not known, or even if he intended to return, but it seemed that there had been a casual arrangement for a neighbouring schoolmaster to read prayers on some Sundays. Thomas Brockbank wrote a flurry of letters in an effort to find the missing teacher. After an exchange with Brian Philipson of Hodge Hill, who was probably involved in the management of both school and church, Thomas wrote to the Rev. William Scott. This gentleman was a senior Fellow at the Queen's College,

Oxford, and the letter enquired whether he had knowledge of a pupil by the name of Walker, and if so, what he intended to do about his deserted post of reader and schoolmaster. Since the letter was delivered by Mr. Walker's own brother, one supposes that he was also the informant on his sibling's whereabouts.

The reply pleased no-one: 'Queen's College, Sep. 16, 1706. Rev'd Sir, Mr Walker, Sometime a neighbour of yours at Present my Pupil here, is under some concern about a Letter which You lately sent to Mr. Scott. If the Gentleman that he left to supply, either by his negligence or want of due Qualifications throwes a burden on you, he has more reason to Begg your Pardon than to make an excuse. His good Temper makes me believe that he will be glad to work out part of the Obligation upon his return, and his Industry promises fair for his being better qualified for it than when he left you. If his absence can be born til he has kept the Michaelmas Term, he will come both to do his Duty and to thank You, and in the meantime You can render it easier by a little of Your Assistance in Baptising, etc. I shall be glad to take the Obligation of that a favour upon myself, & ready to answer it by any humble service that you can command from your Affectionate friend & humble servant, John Gibson.'

A second letter was enclosed. This was from the errant Jonah Walker and repeated almost word for word his accusation of 'leaving the Chapel in a manner Desolate,' but saying that he had made an arrangement to supply another reader and he had heard the inhabitants were well satisfied with this man. Both these letters were sent to Thomas Brockbank by Brian Philipson, together with a copy of the enquiry, and a request for instruction. The reply was one of restrained exasperation. Philipson did not believe that the parish would have heard one word of Walker's intentions had they not pursued him, and his excuses were mere pretence. Walker's tutor declared that there was more reason for his pupil to beg their pardon than to make an excuse. With winter drawing on, the school matter must be settled quickly and a meeting was necessary.

The temporary curate summoned a meeting, and among those present were Captain Fleming of Cowmire Hall, Mr. Hutton of Thorphinsty Hall and Brian Philipson of Hodge Hill. Thomas Brockbank was asked to attend and give guidance, but his wife was due to give birth, so he sent a very diplomatic letter instead. The entire parish was angry and exasperated by Jonah Walker's treatment of them, and yet they baulked at dismissing a figure in authority. It seems that Thomas Brockbank had learned that the Cartmel Fell post, with its salary of £10 a year, was not Mr. Walker's goal. He offered to write the letter of imminent dismissal himself, thus clearing the way for withdrawing the licence and electing a new man. In fact, a full six weeks earlier, Jonah Walker had taken a curacy in Somerset at £25 a year, and had not even had the courtesy to inform his northern parishioners. The teacher and reader to succeed the absent Jonah Walker was the temporary incumbent, Mr. Hotblack.

There was no school-house at that time, and lessons took place in the chapel, as they had at Cartmel, Blawith and other places. William Wordsworth was attracted by the Seathwaite curate 'Wonderful' Walker, and has left us a description of a rural schoolmaster and pastor. 'His seat was within the rails of the altar; the communion table was his desk, and like Shenstone's schoolmistress, the master employed himself at the spinning wheel, while the children were repeating their lessons by his side.'

Within the Cowmire box pew in Cartmel Fell church is a table with benches surrounding it, and this must have been the teaching area. There are carved grid patterns on the seats, which are probably methods of teaching fractions and multiplication. The oak is far too hard for casual schoolboy carving, and the incisions would have taken a considerable time to complete, so these grids must have been made for a serious purpose. The sixteenth-century Scottish mathematician John Napier devised (among other tools) logarithms, but also a simple method of multiplication using rods. These are now known as 'Napier's bones' and can be translated into a grid.

The church would have been numbingly cold in winter, so Bryan Philipson's worry of approaching winter shows that schooling in Cartmel Fell was a seasonal affair in the early eighteenth century.

There is no longer any record of the first school building, but there must have been one prior to 1780. An H.M.S.O. pamphlet of 1900 quotes from an indenture of 15 February 1780, showing that Thomas Walker conveyed to John Pool and Henry Herd (respectively the chapel warden and overseer of the poor of Cartmel Fell) a dwelling house, peat house, and garth or garden thereunto belonging, adjoining Cartmel Fell school, for the sole use of the township. The sum exchanged was £3 and a peppercorn if demanded, paid annually to the chief lord. Even allowing for far higher monetary value of the pound in those days, (£1 = £63 in 2005) it seems hard to believe that the house was anything more than a flimsy bothy, and sixty years later, there was nowhere for a schoolmaster to live. The 1780 document mentions the school, however, so some kind of a building had been erected or utilised.

A report on the *Public Charities of Lonsdale* of 1820 sets out the educational possibilities available to the boys of the seven divisions of Cartmel, and Cartmel Fell is one of these divisions. It states that the Bryan Beck estate was purchased in 1714 for £220, and its trustees used the annual rents for the relief of the poor of Cartmel Fell, and also for the curate and the maintenance of the chapel and roads. Individual bequests were specific. Lawrence Harrison left £10 to the curate to teach a school, and there was an endorsement to that effect in 1727, and another in 1743. Small bequests and gifts were beginning to accumulate throughout the eighteenth century, and serious efforts were made to get continuity of teaching. The H.M.S.O. pamphlet of 1900 refers to a memorandum of 1726:

One of the grids on a bench in the Cowmire pew.

'Whereas such small encouriagement hath been for severall years by past for keeping a constant school in Cartmell-fell to the detriment of the children thereof, whose parents would constantly send them to school, Wee, whose names are hereunto subscribed [and there were no less than forty signatures, unfortunately not quoted] and inhabitants in the chapelry of Cartmel-fell, being verry sensible of the loss occasioned thereby, Do hereby give our severall consents to take up and appropriate the graseing and eatage of a piece of Common, already and time out of mind almost enclosed and called Stock Moss, for the sole use of a teaching schoolmaster.'

There is more, which provides for peat cutting access for those with rights, and watering for stock in time of drought at the Stock Moss ford. The land is about 34 acres, and in 1900 was let by the school managers for £9.10s. a year to Mr R. Crowe, and the shooting to Mr. Birket Cockerton at £2.8s. This same pamphlet goes on to describe the dilapidated state of the schoolhouse in 1871, when it had not been used for six years. The schoolhouse had been occupied for upwards of 40 years by James and Ellen Robinson, having been placed there by the overseers of the poor, and the garden had been cultivated by the schoolmaster, rent free. The document continued:

'The buildings, which are so delapidated as to be entirely unfit for habitation, are in their present state unproductive of profit and useless to the inhabitants of Cartmel-fell. The buildings are adjoining Cartmel-fell school, which is intended to be rebuilt and enlarged during the course of the present year; and by laying the site of the dwelling house and peat house forming the subject of this Charity to the site of the old school, and appropriating the garden for the erection of offices [i.e. toilets] for the said school, sufficient ground would be obtained for the erection of a new building. There is no ground belonging to the school except the site on which it stands.'

It is interesting to note at this point, that the comments that the original school was an encroachment on un-inclosed common, and as such had no title. At the enclosure of 1809, the site was indicated and recognised.

At a public meeting of the ratepayers of Cartmel Fell held on 15 November 1870, a resolution was unanimously passed, recommending the appropriation of the premises. The previous year, Mr William Robinson, the owner of Moor How, had left £300 in his will, to be invested in consols, and two thirds of this income was to benefit the school. It seems ironic that the institution was by then defunct. A new and brighter future was at hand however. For the outlay of £271, a new schoolroom was built in 1871. It was very modern, with a high, airy ceiling and large windows above eye level, to avoid distraction of the pupils' attention. The new building was on the east side of the road, the allotment land having been acquired from Mr James Birket of Birket Houses. There was still a difficulty in finding lodgings within a reasonable distance for a teacher, so a plot was donated by F. A. Argles out of the Greenthorn plantation, and a new house was built in 1877. It cost £370, and was largely paid for by voluntary subscriptions.

Having a new school seemed to encourage the benefactors of the parish, for small and large sums began to accumulate. In 1881, James Robinson of Brindle, the brother of William of Moor How, invested £100 in L.N.E.R. debentures, the money from this to provide books as prizes for proficiency in reading, writing, arithmetic, religious knowledge, and good conduct. Miles Birket of Ravensbarrow Lodge left a further £250 in 1884, but £25 was swallowed up in death duties. The school needed enlarging by 1914, and a second room was added to the south. Photographs from this era show open common with scarcely a tree to be seen.

An Act of Parliament, decreeing primary education for all children, coincided with the rebuilding, and we have a more personal record of the scholastic life of the day. Teachers were obliged to keep log books of daily events, and the guidelines stated that, 'No reflections or opinions of a general character to be entered.' The log books are beautifully bound, and have strong brass corners and brass locks. No prying eyes of pupils or parents could discover the teacher's comments, until today that is, because they are now available from the Lancashire County Archives, and have been transferred to Barrow. Sadly, the early teachers do make very generalised comments, despite the injunction, and they make dull reading ('The infants are making good progress with addition') but occasionally local people are named. On 3 September 1873, Isaac Robinson records: 'Summer ended wetly. Poor attendance averaged 7.6 the week of Aug. 8th. Sep 3rd, School visited by Mrs. Cockerton (the curate's wife) and Mrs. Pearson, who were pleased with the conduct and attention of the children, and the songs sung by them. 31 Oct. 1873, The school only open half a day on account of having to attend the funeral of Mr Jos. Pearson.'

A new teacher, Thomas Chadwick, came in 1875, but he is no better at bringing the log to life, though his inspector comments that the standard of arithmetic is much improved. Joseph Waring was installed in 1879, and his strong, vigourous hand makes one hope for lively notes, but it is not so. The most tantalising titbit was, 'I had to punish a boy on Tuesday for using bad language,' but it does not say whom, what he said, or even what the punishment was.

There seems to have been a fairly rapid succession of teachers in this new school, and one wonders why. Perhaps it was a stepping-stone to greater things, or maybe the managers were dissatisfied with progress. Joseph Waring followed Thomas Chadwick in 1877, but he only stayed three years. His successor was Joseph White, and he settled down to a stint of thirteen years. The census of 1881 records him living in the new school-house, then called Shanty Cottage. John was aged 23 and his sister was keeping house, but also teaching sewing at the school. Ten years later, sister Mary had departed, but John had a wife and three children. In February 1888, the school log records: 'Several of the children are sick and two sent word to say they have no shoes... One is a free scholar.' This last entry is a reminder that free education was not yet for all, and the school pence had to be brought each week. An entry for June 1888 records children being sent home for their pence, as yet again they had come without them.

12 March 1888, 'We have several serious sick cases, and I am sorry to say Scarlet Fever has broken out amongst us. Three scholars belong to that (un-named) family. Some others are afraid to come already.' This entry reminds us of the dread with which a disease such as scarlet fever was viewed. Before antibiotics, it was a frequent cause of infant

and child mortality and as late as the 1960s it was still a notifiable disease. On 29 March of the same year: 'Our average is again 23.3 [out of 33]. Many of the children want sharpening up, or at least their parents do. They keep them away to work, and make frivolous excuses to screen themselves.'

John White left Cartmel Fell in 1893 and was followed by Henry Broadbridge, but he only stayed for two years. He complains a good deal to the log book about illness and poor attendance, and on 1893, 15 December he gives a list of the children who are ill: 'Beatrice Wilson, Crayston Webster, Richard Taylor, William Pearson, Robert Crosthwaite, Harry Lishman, William White Kellett, Emma Kellett, Edith and Frank Atkinson.' Then he adds, 'The master is very unwell indeed and is hardly able to keep on teaching 'Sweet and Low'.'

In 1896, a new teacher came to the fell. This was Richard James Craghill, and his entries show much care and affection for his charges. Mrs Edith Taylor of Crosthwaite, who was a pupil of his, confirmed that he was a lovely man. The school was about to begin a settled existence under the same head teacher for the next 35 years, and fortunately for posterity, Mr Craghill was a keen amateur photographer.

In April, 1899, the school began a collection of wild flowers, shells and bird's eggs. Mr Craghill was troubled at the idea of robbing birds' nests, and had a word with the inspector who gave him guidelines:

1. Not more than one egg from a nest.
2. A nest must have at least three eggs, and
3. The eggs advertised in the Westmorland Gazette must not be touched, i.e. all owls, buzzard, merlin, kestrel, falcon (peregrine?), goldfinch, kingfisher, dotterel, raven, heron, dipper, woodcock and golden plover.

He adds, 'I have two Barn Owl eggs got from the top of a hay mow that was being carted away and could not be saved at Collinfield.'

The following week, the teacher was trying to recruit pupils for a butter-making class to be held at Thorphinsty Hall, presumably by the Taylor womenfolk, but under the auspices of the county council. There must have been a county-wide effort to improve the quality of local butter at this time. The *Westmorland Gazette* of 6 August 1898 was highly critical of butter standards, declaring it little better than cart-grease, and wondering why, with the best pastures and the best cattle in the kingdom, we produce the worst butter. The methods employed were out-dated and slovenly they declared, but Mr Craghill was doing his best to improve matters on Cartmel Fell. The week after that, a new intake of three boys and a girl brought his class up to 40, and so far, no infant teacher had been deemed necessary. The school log reflects the strain: 'New infants interfere with steady work. I find my hands very full, and a bit bewildered what to do next.' By June, the total of pupils was 46, the highest ever, and two of the older girls were attending the dairy classes.

A party was held at Strawberry Bank for schoolchildren, but it seems to have been a rowdy affair. Poor Thomas Batty sustained internal injuries when some boys from an un-named neighbouring parish ran over him. He was stooping to lace up his boots at the time, but there must have been parish rivalry. On 12 June the teacher noted primly: 'The party has been held for three years, in opposition to our own children's party, simply because we cannot see our way to providing dancing.'

A feature of the school log books is the intermittent comments of visiting inspectors. In August of 1899 the comments seem unfair. 'The master has to give all instruction except needlework. Discipline should be better, and quieter methods of teaching prevail.' With 46 pupils and no help, it seems a tall order.

The pupil numbers were getting too large for one teacher to manage, and the single room was cramped, so in 1914 a second room was added and an infant teacher engaged. In those days, female teachers had to be single and lost their jobs on marriage, so these ladies boarded with local families. In an oral history interview, a former infant teacher, Mrs Pearson, remembered her days of walking or cycling to school and wrestling with the smoking fires, trying to keep the classroom warm enough to dry out her sodden charges. Fires were not lit until November, so until then, there was no means of helping the children to dry out. She said that the inspectors simply had no idea of the conditions on the fell in winter, and the reasons for children's non-attendance or being late. Winters were very severe, and children from the high farms were frequently totally cut off by snow. The log books report closure of the school on occasions when weather conditions made the journey too difficult.

It seems that the future lives of the children were always uppermost in Mr Craghill's mind, and as well as teaching the three Rs, he devised ways of making the breaks instructive as well. The boys would build small walls on the allotment, and they grew potatoes during the First World War. The girls learned cookery as well as needlework from Mrs Craghill. She would teach cookery in her own home, but determinedly showed no favouritism. Mrs Edie Taylor remembered that if she liked you, then your task might be gutting rabbits or plucking a hen, but if she thought less of you, then perhaps you could learn how to make fairy cakes. Another former pupil, Ella Wilkinson, dreaded needlework, recalling the pain of having a thimble rapped on her head when her stitches were not neat enough.

In February 1923, the School Inspector's report must have been very gratifying to Richard Craghill: 'For nearly thirty years, Mr Craghill has maintained a high standard of instruction and an excellent tone in this isolated school. Owing to closure for epidemic, (mumps) there was no inspection last year, and this year's results are fully up to previous standards. Despite the difficulties of access and situation, few of the children exhibit shyness, and it is noteworthy that in class one, answers are obtained to questions that are constantly missed in more advantageous areas.'

That autumn, an experiment in adult education began at the school. There were evening classes of veterinary lectures for the men, and home nursing for the women. These were to be six in number, and fortnightly. At the first men's lecture there were 40 in attendance, but at the next only 30, whilst 17 women enrolled for home nursing. There is no comment on the weather conditions, but when most people would have gone on foot in the dark, the programme might have been more attractive in the summer.

During the 1923 Christmas holidays, the school was thoroughly swept and cleaned. The walls were distempered and the ceilings whitewashed, but this had not been done since 1916.

It is a matter of regular irritated comment throughout all the available log books, that children were forever being kept away from school to help with seasonal work on the farm, though Richard Craghill was more understanding than some of the other masters. In the early days of the logs, schooling was not compulsory and had to be paid for, so it is easy to see why parents felt that they could choose when and when not to withdraw their children. It was vital for the families' livelihood that crops should be harvested when the season and weather dictated. Throughout the logs, there is no mention of a half-term break, though in the mid-twentieth century this used to be a two-week holiday in October, especially for the potato harvest. Maybe the authorities bowed to the inevitable and made it official. In the days of living-in farm servants, the six-monthly hiring contracts usually ended in November, and this was the time for servant's holidays and another reason for needing the children to work at home. Practical reasons for absenteeism were many and various, but still anathema to teachers. Apart from work, severe weather and distance were factors; there was only Shanks's pony for transport, and Mr Craghill had remarked in 1899 that six children came over three miles, and only eleven under two miles.

In September 1927, both the Craghills were seriously ill. She had pneumonia, and he phlebitis. Hilda Turner of Dalton took over temporarily, and she too must have had soggy memories of Cartmel Fell. On November the second she recorded: '2¾ inches of rain fell, and 3.4 on the third. Great floods, and all roads impassable.'

The school log closes on 30 September 1931. 'Today, I, James Cragghill conclude my office as headmaster of this school of which I have been in charge since 1st. January, 1896. Mrs Cragghill also resigns as cookery teacher. It is with great regret that we leave such a nice school, scholars and district, as well as the inspectors, and L.E.A. Success to the school, and my successor, Miss Cooper.'

The subsequent log will not be available for public scrutiny until 2031.

The school continued to flourish throughout the next three decades with the older scholars progressing to Cartmel or the Lakes School at Troutbeck Bridge. The school photographs reveal family likenesses of today's children, but the numbers were dropping. This was partly due to the 1944 Education Act, which gave secondary education to all, thereby cutting off primary school pupils at eleven years old, and partly to rising salaries for teachers, which made small schools uneconomic. There was a brief wartime influx of evacuees which swelled the numbers of pupils, one of the most famous being the actor Derek Nimmo, but by 1968, the school photograph shows only nineteen children and these were taught by a single teacher again.

In 1971, Cartmel Fell school ceased to be, and is now used as the parish hall, home of the W.I., venue for dances, parties, flower shows and the like. The building had always been used for the various societies and social activities, but in those days there was a caretaker who cleaned after the children had left, lit the stoves and maintained orderliness. For many years of the twentieth century, this office was performed by Lucy Woof, and she was dinner-lady too. There were plans for a caretaker's bungalow adjoining the school, but costs escalated from around £6,000 when first mooted, to unreachable targets, so maintenance is in the hands of the hall users. The societies which meet there are continually fund-raising to make gradual improvements. The cast-iron stoves were replaced with electric heating in 2001, and in 2002 the kitchen was re-furbished and a large oven installed, and the water supply had to undergo ultra-violet treatment to comply with health regulations. (The children and adults all seem to have been immune to the pollution which frogs in the water tank incurred). A disabled access and toilet were added in 2004. In that same year, a ceramic mural was designed by Hans Ulrich, with the help of local children, and it depicts life and customs on the fell. The idea of the mural was to commemorate the 500th anniversary of the founding of St Anthony's, but the church authorities would not allow it to be put in the church porch, so it was decided to decorate the school wall instead.

Visitors to the area will have noticed the polished rock slide on the hill opposite, worn smooth by countless small bottoms, and lasting evidence of generations who were taught and played there.

St. Anthony's Church

THE chapel of Saint Anthony, set in its woodland clearing, was built as a chapel of ease at the beginning of the sixteenth century. Literally, this meant that the folk on the fell had their worship made easier, in that they no longer had to go to the mother church of Cartmel Priory for Sunday services.

It is quite possible that a much earlier place of worship existed on the fell, but to date, no archaeological evidence has been found of any building, though a tantalising clue exists which suggests a very distant Christianity. This is an almost life-sized stone arm, crudely carved and with an indentation like a nail hole in the palm. It is on show intermittently in the Kendal Museum and has been ascribed to the ninth century A.D. The whereabouts of the rest of the figure has yet to be discovered, and since this piece was being used as a coping stone in an old bothy known as Jumping Down, the remainder could have been used in walling anywhere in the vicinity. It could be of relevance that the site of discovery is only a few minutes walk from the present church.

Cartmel Priory was the mother church for the seven divisions of Cartmel, of which, Cartmel Fell is one. For all major Christian festivals and for weddings, funerals and baptism, the fell community had to walk or ride between six and nine miles to the priory, and of course, back again. In the winter, it must have seemed like double the distance.

A few generous benefactors caused the chapel to be erected around the year 1504, according to a deposition of Anthony Knipe in 1561. He said that his father William Knipe, and others, built the chapel 55 years before. This ties in with the date of 1504, when Robert Briggs of Cartmel Fell gave to the priory a chalice and a pese, to housel with, but it had to be returned to St. Anthony's for the Easter service. This word comes from the Norse, husl, a sacrifice, and had come to mean the administration or reception of Holy Communion. This Robert Brigg or Briggs (the spelling varied) was probably of Cowmire Hall, and in his will of 1520, he left 33s.4d yearly, for life, to John Holme, priest, and he was to be given his board by Robert's son, Thomas Briggs. For these considerations, the priest was to pray for the souls of his benefactors, and take no wages of the parish. It appears that John Holme Briggs was the priest's full name, and almost certainly related to Robert.

There is a board inside the church, with the names of subsequent priests or curates, but with continuity gaps. One who does not appear is John Brooke, who was followed by George Inman in 1658. This may be a bit of clerical whitewash, as John Brooke was described as 'An old malignant, not reconciled' meaning that he still had Catholic leanings and did not embrace the Cromwellian Presbyterianism.

Until the Reformation, a rood screen separated the congregation from the altar, and this, it was said, subsequently formed the Cowmire pew. As Robert Briggs probably helped to pay for it in its original form, the Cowmire household no doubt felt that they had first claim. However, recent research suggests that the pew was actually made for the Briggs family and has always been in situ, just in front of the rood screen. The evidence for this is in the jointing of the base of the pew. The aisle slopes down hill quite markedly, so the corner post nearest the altar is longer than the one at the western corner of the pew. Professor Marks, visiting in 2004, thought that the jointing was original for the post and the panels, and therefore constructed to accommodate the slope. The carving of the woodwork is still crisp, though some has been restored, and around the cornice are letters or symbols, once thought to represent Mary and Jesus, but now are

Tudor windows at St Anthony's

considered to be guild emblems. 'M' is for the mercers, and 'J' is actually a wool-hook. This makes sense when one remembers that the Briggs family made their money as chapmen and wool merchants. A little of the green paint still adheres to the outside of the box pew, and in strong light the ghosts of saints can be made out on the back wall. In the Kendal Museum is the crucifix which would originally have been displayed on the rood screen. It languished for years in the vestry, and has lost its feet, gilding and paint, but small vestiges of colour can still be discerned. This early carving is one of the oldest of its type still surviving. In 2003, it was displayed in the Victoria and Albert Museum's Gothic exhibition, placed well above eye level as it would have been in pre-Reformation times. Two other rood figures of similar date are Welsh. The canopy which surmounted the crucifix, now forms part of the Cowmire pew, no doubt salvaged by the Briggs family. A story has grown up that the rood figure was once used as a poker, because the feet are blackened and burned, but in pre-Reformation times it would have had candles burning below it. In continental churches, similar scorching can be seen on wooden crucifixes.

Even though the people of Cartmel Fell now had a chapel, it was not licensed for baptisms, weddings or funerals, and these were conducted at Cartmel Priory. Winter funerals must have been a particular trial, and some went to Crosthwaite or Winster if they lived at the north-eastern end of the fell, and a few to St. Martin's in Bowness. In *The Annals of Cartmel,* James Stockdale says that for country funerals it was customary to invite a hundred or more mourners, so that the bearers did not become exhausted. He had seen the two parish biers belonging to Cartmel Fell, 'One rather new, and one very large (of oak) very old, very strong and very heavy - a load in itself!'

Wheeled traffic had not arrived on the fell when Thomas Machell, author of *The Antiquary On Horseback,* wrote of his travels in the seventeenth century. He said that it should be known as CartLESS fell, on account of its lack of roads. This then, was another way in which the parish of Cartmel Fell was isolated in the post mediaeval period.

It would be interesting to know whose idea it was, but there is no record of the person who suggested that the Bishop of Chester should be petitioned to allow a burial license for St. Anthony's. At an extraordinary visitation in 1712, this was granted, and the chapel warden's account of that year can be seen in the County Record Office in Kendal: 'To my journey to Kendal when I fetched the Licence, 1s.0d.' That was a twenty mile round trip. It was later in that century that christenings and marriages were allowed, in 1764 and 1765 respectively, or so the records say. However, in the transcription of the Cartmel Priory registers, there is an interesting amendment. In the index was a heading 'Weddings forgotten.' This alluded to a piece of paper stitched into the margin of the parish register which is headed 'Weddings forgotten in the yeare 1593 to enter in the book.' One of these was the marriage of Myles Harrison and Elizabeth Gurnell on 15 June, but it states 'Maryed at Cartmelfell'. It may be that some baptisms and weddings and even funerals had been performed at St. Anthony's from the first, but had not been regularised.

These books of old parish records are a fascinating

source of the day-to-day business of the church in the previous centuries. There were many small charities to be administered, apprentices helped by funding and outgoings for repairs. There are also regular receipts for monies which are not explained. For instance, John Pull (or Pool) of Waterside paid £1.10s. for two years interest in 1711. The church acted as a bank or building society for reliable members of its congregation. The funds were kept in a 'chist' or kist in the church, as a footnote shows in 1750, and other funds were in private hands, to invest as they thought fit.

It is difficult to select just a few items from the chapel wardens' accounts, as all are interesting, but below is a sample of the year's activities. Note the dialect spelling:

For Rushbearing...   *6s*
For a load of sleat for the chapel...   *1s*
For a diel poost. (i.e., for the sundial)...   *3s.6d.*
To Mister Jakson for Preachin...   *5s*
For gadering of the Salery for Mister Magdenel (Macdowell) to Johen Roobeson.   *1s*
1697. Charge concerning the rem (hole in paper) of the pulpit and making the pew and putting in a window and other works. Imprimis to Tho. Seatle, 13 dayes...   *13s.*

(This last refers to the three-decker pulpit, which has the date 1698 carved on its door, maybe at its dedication. The window was to provide light for the now elevated preacher.)

To Edward Robinson, for ringing in the year 1711...   *5s.*
For one bell Rope (The very next entry!)...1s.10d

There are regular disbursements for mossing or draught exclusion, and for linning (sic) washing, also for Strewing or Strawing in the days before the floor was flagged. In 1720, there is a bill for the large sum of £9.3s.4d. for bringing flags down the lake to Bowness, and thence by road, to pave the nave. This was a big proportion of the annual expenditure, but the committee of the day must have thought it worthwhile, and it ended the need for strawing. It took four days to transport the flags from Brathay to Bowness, and a boat had to be hired at a cost of 4s.6d. Sixty yards of flags were brought overland from Bowness, and the workmen were boarded at nearby Chapel House while they were laying the floor. Their wages were a further £2.2s.3d. In the days when important people were buried inside the church, a flagged floor was desirable. James Stockdale remarked upon the odour at Cartmel priory before it was all flagged.

The windows seemed to need constant repairs. Almost every year there are bills from glaziers for amounts which varied from 2s. up to 10s. After seeing the accounts, it comes as less of a surprise that the windows are such a patchwork. In 1706, an attempt was made to secure the Great Window. It had been mended five years earlier, but five new stanchions were bought, these being the iron bars which support the great weight of glass and lead. Richard Crewdson was then paid 4s.6d. for new glass.

In the days when it was widely supposed that the greater part of the populace was illiterate, it is gratifying to see that so many yeomen on the fell could set out accounts and write a good clear hand. The offices of the parish were held in annual rotation, so it was not one learned person doing all the paperwork. The chapel warden, overseer of the poor, constable and his assistant the grave were held by the various men of property, even if that property amounted to only a few acres. Nearly all the parish paperwork was performed very competently.

Although the chapel never had great wealth, it nevertheless attracted small sums and bequests over a long period. The interest on these was used for specific and general purposes, according to the donor's wishes. In 1724, Bishop Gastrell's *Notitia Cestrensi* mentions £10 left to the church by Lawrence Harrison, probably of Greenthorn, the interest on which was to pay the curate for administering the sacrament once a year, and a Mr. Shaw (of Burblethwaite) gave the same amount for a sermon once a year. The paper details the augmentation of the living: 'Income certified, £8.10s.2d., viz. £6.0s.2d. collected by a salary bill from the Possessours of land within the Chappellry; and £2.10s, the interest of £50 given by Mr. Fletcher.'

Most local people know of the loaves at Cartmel Priory, which were the bequest of Rowland Briggs of Swallowmire to the poor. He made his will in 1703 and the money came from his Addyfield estate. Less well known is his widow's bequest. Susannah Briggs left £10 to be let out at interest to provide money for the poor of Cartmel Fell to be distributed on Shrove Saturday. Another ten pounds was invested for a sermon on Shrove Sunday, or Palm Sunday as we now know it. Another twenty pounds was to go to the overseers of the poor to pay for four children's education. The schoolmaster and curate at the time was George Walker, who also lived at Swallowmire.

In 1707, there is a long list of 'All those Neighbours wch hath given any monie to the good of this Chappell.' These include four families of Swainsons who gave between 10s. and £2 with a special note of Lawrence Swainson of Pattinson Howe, son of Christopher, 'A Yonge Man,' who gave £6.

In 1771, an attempt was made to drain the churchyard which cost £3.11s.6d. Drainage, or the lack of it, had always been a problem, and there is apparently a spring which runs parallel with the north wall, so in particularly wet seasons, coffins had been known to float before the service was over. Small stones in the ground indicate where the drains run, but no plan exists of either graves or drains. It is open to speculation whether the chapel might have been built near the site of an early 'holy well', inadvertently causing the drainage problems.

In 1912, an article was written for the Cumberland and Westmorland Antiquarian & Archaelogical Society by John Curwen, FSA, RIBA. He said that in 1707, the Burblethwaite pew was 'all ruinous,' and over a century later, an application was made to the Bishop of Chester to rebuild it. This application was probably made by James Adam, who bought Burblethwaite Hall in 1811 and was an associate of John Wilkinson, the ironmaster. In the previous century the Hall had been owned by the Robinson family of Fell Foot, who must have neglected the fabric of the pew.

There is a drawing by Bertha Newcombe which shows the clerk's pew, beneath the three-decker pulpit. The chapel warden has his pitch-pipe ready to sound the key, having announced the hymn from his central position from the pew below the pulpit. Until very recently, the same blackthorn pipe could be seen in the vestry, but it was stolen in the Millennium year. A reproduction of this drawing and several others which Miss Newcombe made of the area can be seen inside the church, and the originals are at the Wordsworth Trust in Grasmere.

Another pew of interest is the small enclosed one nearest the altar. It belonged to the Hutton family of Thorphinsty Hall and has the initials W H (for William Hutton) carved on the door, with the date 1696. This cannot have been the Huttons' main place of worship, as they have a very prominent marble memorial tablet in Cartmel Priory and probably rode there, but their servants could easily have walked to Cartmel Fell chapel. The Huttons must have been thrifty, because one of the small benches inside the pew is obviously cut from an old door or cupboard, complete with keyhole.

The east window is an incomplete jig-saw of very old stained glass. There seems to be no record of Cromwellian defacement of this remote chapel, and the glass just became damaged over the centuries, as chapel accounts show. As early as 1754 the windows were in a poor state. Dr. Richard Pocock wrote of Cartmel Fell: 'We soon came to a chapel, where are some *remains* of good painted glass.' James Stockdale, writing in 1868, said that a quantity of old glass was kept in a box in the vestry for repairs to breakages, but a great deal more was discovered when the church was re-furbished in 1911. This was walled up in the space which now reveals two small windows to the north of the east window. A letter from this era has been retained by William Matthews, and is from one of his forebears. It sheds a little more light on the reasons for the mis-matching of stained glass. The letter is headed Strawberry Bank, Cartmel Fell, 1911.

'Dear Sir, In answer to your inquiry about the glass in the Church window, I asked my father about it. He said he remembered helping one Thomas Atkinson to put it in. He said it was when he was a boy, and it is nearly eighty years since it came from Cartmel, but how they got it, he cannot tell. He says the man Atkinson went by the name of 'Putty Tom.' I remain, Yours, J. Matthews.'

The general consensus used to be that the glass dates from the reign of Henry IV or early Henry V, that is the first quarter of the fifteenth century. The fur tippets, the long straight hair and the shape of the chalice are the indicators used for dating, but there is an anomaly here. Henry V came to the throne in 1413, so these windows were unlikely to have been made for Cartmel Fell chapel, which was begun in 1504, unless fashions lagged very much behind in the north. The east window has flat headed arches, typical of the Tudor style, and the painted architecture of the windows clearly has had pointed arches, which have had to be truncated to fit the flatter arches of the windows. However, Professor Richard Marks visited St. Anthony's in the autumn of 2003, together with a colleague, Eleanor Townsend of the Victoria & Albert Museum, and they deciphered some of the fragmentary inscriptions on the glass. The 'Brig' family are mentioned three times, including Antonius, his wife and Robti (Robert). Their opinion was that it seems highly probable that the glass was commissioned especially for St. Anthony's, and paid for by the wealthy Brigg or Briggs family. Part of the inscription reads: *Orate pro animabus Antonius Brig et (uxor)... benefactores isti locis.* 'Pray for the souls of Anthony Brig and his wife, benefactors of this place.' Did Anthony choose the patron saint of the church and why is there a discrepancy in the dating?

Several visitors to St. Anthony's have left their

impressions over the centuries. In the late nineteenth century, Mary Wakefield wrote a chapter about the fell in her book *Cartmel Priory and Sketches of North Lonsdale*. She described the ascent: 'If you come up, it is a terrible tug; if you go down, it is all the pony can do to keep the vehicle behind him in its place; yet such is the approach to the chapel, and many a coffin has to be carried to its last resting place up that steep fell side which is known as the Corpse Road.' She goes on to remark on the battered firs to the south, which were shorn of their beauty in the great gales of 1893, and also quotes from Nicholson and Burn's *Guide to the Lakes* of 1771.

'There was no road over Cartmel Fell, but just when guidance and help was most wanted, we find a quaint little chapel, dedicated to the patron Saint of hermits.' Mary Wakefield also commented on the way the earth had washed down the fell and piled up against the west wall, 'Looking as though the chapel had sunk.'

When Thomas Price arrived in Cartmel Fell as curate in 1910 he was shocked at the state of the church fabric and he was responsible for overseeing the necessary repairs and restoration. His granddaughter, Joan Duke, has deposited his diaries and some letters in the Kendal Record Office, so we have an account of those days. Thomas wrote to his brother, the Rev. Clement Price with an enclosed photograph:

'This gives you a good idea of the "History" which Mr. Benson would have preserved. You see the boxes and pews which the "Restorers" of 1800 or so placed upon the cut down foundations of the old oak benches – the break in the nave is caused by their having fastened some short pews onto the front of the old oak four poster on the N. side of the church, which threw the East end out of centre. They then made a platform and placed it under the South lights of the East window. The space around the altar, you will notice, was crowded up with pews and boxes. The pews were mostly of pitch pine. The boxes, I should say, were rather later and made of deal. The little window that you see near the East window in the first photo is interesting. There is another down below it, about the level of the present floor - when the workmen were taking off the roughcast from the outside, they found this lower window built up, but the plaster on the side had not been removed. On it was scribbled in pencil, James Field, 1819, between the windows and the East window were the foundations of the chancel wall. Evidently, about 1819, they took down the old chancel wall and threw up two small chambers which were behind it, into the Church.'

The architect who first alerted the Archdeacon of Furness as to the state of the church was John Curwen, and he deduced that this little space was a tiny room for the use of the visiting priest. Further on in the letter, Thomas Price refers to the windows: 'On Saturday, we had Canon Fowler over from Durham to see the East window. He is a great authority – I believe put together a window from the Bastille which had been in some shop in Paris for Selby Abbey or Southwell Minster. His advice was that if we wanted to have the windows rearranged, to send it to Knowles of York. We are to have a meeting on Monday, to settle what to do.'

The church was out of use for a while, but had a grand re-opening in January 1911 or 1912. A poster survives of this event, but has no date. How fortunate that the architect concerned was also a member

125

of the Cumberland and Westmorland Archaeological and Antiquarian Society. The work was done with scholarly care.

A curious visitor will notice deep grooves in the stone door jambs of the porch. These are not carved in the true sense, but are said to be the wear from innumerable arrows being sharpened. In 1252, a statute of Edward III decreed that archery should be practised after church on Sunday, and NOT football. Yeomen were liable to be pressed into military service in times of national crisis and especially to repel border rievers, so it was necessary to have them all trained as good marksmen. Just beyond the school is a flat rock with similar grooves, where the archers could shoot up or down the hill, apparently a more difficult task than shooting horizontally. Henry VIII had decreed that yews should be planted in churchyards, to provide a supply of longbows, but whether the yews at the lych gate date from Tudor times is hard to say without the help of dendro-chronology. Of course, St. Anthony's had not been built at the time of the statute, but Scottish raids must still have been remembered locally, even in 1504.

After the church was re-furbished, the lych gates were made as a memorial to the men who fell in the Great War. These were made by local craftsmen, the Matthews family of Bowland Bridge, and John Henry Downham of Sow How and Goswick Hall. The panelling behind the altar was made in the 1930s by Simpsons of Kendal, and Hubert Simpson suffered a hernia, lifting the large section over the wall.

In 1993, a group of parishioners undertook to transcribe all the tombstones in the churchyard. Some are getting very weathered, but since none is much older than 200 years, the task was completed with only one gap where the slate had de-laminated. The first stone to be erected was only two years after the burial licence was granted, and is that of the curate, William Sandys, who was only 27 when he died in 1714. This is inside the church, by the vestry door. The Sandys family of Hawkshead had many links with Cartmel Fell having inter-married with the Birkets, and a William Sandys of Dale Park was part-owner of Burblethwaite Hall in 1696, though it could not have been this young man who would then have been only nine.

A stone at the eastern end of the north wall commemorates some of the Poole family of Gill Head. A touching little poem for Betty ends the list of deceased Pooles. She was three years, one month and five days old when she died.

Beneath this tone a mouldring virgin lies
Who was the pleasure once of human eyes
Her blaze of charms virtue will approv'd
The gay admired her, much the parents lov'd
Transitory life, death untimely came
Farewell, adieu, I only leave my name.

A board with the names of the incumbents at St Anthony's is just inside the door. The names of some appear on contemporary wills as witnesses, but little is known of them otherwise. A few, however, were documented at the time, and one who was notorious in his day was Jonah Walker who is referred to in the section relating to the school. Another curate whose relatives have been researched in detail was the long-serving George Walker. He was the brother of Thomas of Hartbarrow and Bowland Bridge, and was in his post for 43 years, from 1715 to 1758. From his signatures on various documents, it can be seen that he and his wife moved a number of times, and seem to have been lodgers around the parish. He must have had other resources apart from his meagre salary, as in his own will he left £393.4s.8d.

A curate who built his own house close to the church was the Rev. Robert Cockerton, the minister from 1829 to 1861. He married into the Birket family who then owned Hodge Hill, so it was on Birket land that Ravensbarrow Lodge was built and but a three minute walk from the church. Ravensbarrow was the unofficial vicarage at that period, but later in the century the diocese built a typically Victorian house for its incumbent, no doubt a great attraction to the living.

The Rev. William Summers was to lead his flock from 1867 until 1909, and is captured on film with the children from his newly-built school in 1872. After his retirement, his successor, Thomas Price began fund-raising for the church's restoration. He was worried when he heard that Mr. Summers was vexed as his own name had not appeared on the list of those who had collected money, so wrote to re-assure his predecessor on 4 April 1911. Postal deliveries were swift in those days, so Mr. Summers must have received the letter, but four days later he was dead, and Thomas Price conducted the funeral service at Cartmel Fell.

It is sad to report that Saint Anthony's few antique furnishings were stolen after a wedding party had left the church in the 1990s. The artefacts were not of enormous value, but they were unique. One was a carved chair of 1645, known as the bishop's chair, and another was the old oak chest which used to contain the chapel's funds. When it was stolen, it contained only the chapel's vacuum cleaner, but fortunately, the documents relating to the parish, which used to be kept in the chest, were all safely deposited in Kendal Record Office.

Thieves thought the churchyard was isolated enough to cache the frames of stolen paintings from Holker Hall in 1999. A certain tomb provided the flat surface which was used habitually by Eileen Lupton to arrange her family's flowers. One day, she noticed that the top of her table was not quite square and she could see a glint of gilt inside. A recent robbery at the Cavendish home of Holker Hall must have been done by people with local knowledge, as the canvases had been removed from the frames and the latter disposed of in what seemed like an unvisited spot. A municipal cemetery might have been a better location for consigning the frames to oblivion, because country people know everything about their own environment. The paintings were later recovered.

Directly and indirectly, the chapel of ease on Cartmel Fell has provided many varied sources of information about the inhabitants who worshiped there. Apart from the churchwarden's accounts, and the other documents connected with the work of the church and its early school, the requirement to keep parish registers can provide much information. The first attempt to keep national records of the baptisms, marriages and burials began in 1536, but it is largely a matter of luck as to whether all these rolls or books survive. The causes of loss range from civil war to damp storage conditions, mice and rats. Unfortunately, there is not a complete set of registers for St Anthony's, and as stated earlier, Cartmel priory was where most marriages, baptisms and burials were performed until the eighteenth century, and some families continued their loyalty to the mother church at Cartmel, even when their own chapel was licensed.

Probably, the occupations of the fell-dwellers changed very little over the centuries until the nineteenth, and this is where the registers are so helpful. The incumbent or his deputy was required by law to complete a standard number of particulars in the register. For a burial, the date and name were recorded, together with the dwelling and the age at the time of death. From this information it is possible to show the rate of infant mortality, the incidence of epidemics and the average life expectancy at a given time. In some parishes, such as Beetham, one eighteenth century vicar used the parish register as a semi-official diary. He recorded national events, unusual weather conditions, local building projects, and indeed anything which caught his imagination. Unfortunately, the curates of Cartmel Fell were less enterprising.

Taking every tenth year of our surviving registers, which was also the year that the census was taken, a pattern of death rates and ages can be seen. In the year of 1831, out of seven burials, five were infants under two years, one a woman of 39, and one a woman of 75. After 1962, there were no infant burials and the percentage of elderly deaths had increased greatly. Strangely, and as the parish is so small there may be no significance in this, the number of girls who died in the nineteenth century was higher than might be expected. One would expect boys to have more accidents, though cause of death is not recorded, and girls are supposed to be rather better at fighting infection. In the ten-yearly samples until 1931, there were no deaths of boys over two years and under seventeen, but six girls in the same age group. This trend was reflected throughout the register, so the sample is representative.

Infant deaths, however, show the opposite trend. In the hundred-year span of samples, that is from 1831 to 1931, there were six little boys buried (but four of them in 1831,) and only three girls under two years, and one of those was also in 1831. Not shown in the sample years were un-named infections. Sometimes over half a family would perish, as in the tragic few weeks of January and February 1855, when the Stott family of Thorneythwaite lost six of their children, from one month to twelve years with scarlet fever. As will be seen from the chart, the age at death tends to increase over the decades, and in some years the twentieth century, there were no burials at all. In 1971, there were two, both females, one aged 92, the other 91. For baptisms, the date of the event is of course recorded, but some of the clergy also added the child's date of birth. Usually, this was only a short time before baptism, but occasionally a whole clutch of children from the same family would be christened together.

Most valuable of all, from the social history viewpoint is the baptismal register, where one column gives the father's occupation. From 1830 to 1855, almost everyone on Cartmel Fell was in some way connected with agriculture or woodland industry. Most were farmers or farm labourers, a few were basket or swill makers; some combined farming with milling and malting, as at Burblethwaite mill. In certain families walling crops up regularly as an occupation, and there is an occasional joiner. Around the small industrial hamlet at Gill Head, before it was gentrified, there were bobbin turners and sawyers. There were one or two professional men such as the Poole family at Gill Head, most of whom seemed to take to the law, and of course the curate himself. Apart from a shoemaker and a blacksmith, those were the only occupations listed until the middle of the nineteenth century.

With the coming of the railway, new possibilities were opened up. Not only could the townspeople seek rural retreats, but the impecunious farm labourer could escape into a wider labour market. The patterns of life began to change slowly, roads were improved, and eventually, motor transport arrived. The fell-folk of a hundred years ago would have been amazed at the wide variety of trades and professions of fathers baptising their children in the 1990s which include: farmers and joiners as before, with farm managers, but then came all the new occupations, estate agent, company director, motor mechanic, publican, policeman, cafe proprietor, insurance agent, a stocktaker of wines and spirits, hotelier, architect, forestry contractor, frozen food dealer, dental surgeon, article-writer, timber feller, Milk Marketing Board consultant, teacher, lorry driver, scientist and civil servant, Public Health Inspector, student, roadman, boat-builder and furrier. Whereas the fathers of past centuries were almost all born nearby and living within the parish, the fathers of today come from as far afield as Derbyshire, Germany, Alberta, Argyll, Newcastle and Coventry.

Inside the church are four reproductions of drawings by Bertha Newcombe. These depict scenes from the mid-nineteenth century, around the time that Bertha was born in 1857. Bertha Newcombe was born in Hackney, the daughter of a schoolmaster. Unusually for girls at the time, she trained at the Slade, later illustrating many books. She was associated with what is now called the Women's Movement, women's suffrage and the Married Woman's Property Act, illustrating in 1870 the presenting of a petition for the latter to the M.P. John Stuart Mill. Among her associates were the Bloomsbury group, the Pankhursts and George Bernard Shaw, whose portrait she painted.

It is not known why this artist came to Cartmel Fell, but it seems likely that she was commissioned to draw these scenes of St. Anthony's for a book purporting to be written by a descendant of 'Wonderful' Walker. The author claimed that his father was a parson at Cartmel Fell, but the evidence is muddled in the book, an amalgam of several places, and it has been edited at a much later date after the author's death. *Annals of a Quiet Valley* was published in 1894, but Robert Walker, the purported author, was 70 in the 1851 census, and then curate of Longsleddale, so it would seem that his manuscript somehow came into the hands of John Watson the editor, a journalist living in Kendal in 1881. Bertha Newcombe's drawings of St. Anthony's and Hodge Hill are dated 1894, the year of publication.

Danes Court or The Parsonage

THIS house, now divided into three, was built as the parsonage in 1864. A cast concrete tablet on the wall facing the road testifies to this, but the four is in mirror image. Apparently there was a vogue for this kind of 'rusticity' at the time, but it could be merely the incompetence of the workmen with casting techniques. Unless the budget was very tight, one feels that they would have been obliged to do it again if it had been a mistake.

The land for the building was given in 1863 by William Wakefield of Birklands, Kendal. The Wakefields had been founders of the Kendal Bank, and several members of the family had been trustees of the Bryan Beck charity at various times. The architect was Miles Thompson of Kendal.

The money to build the house had come from several sources, and the total cost was about £1,100. Queen Anne's Bounty provided £400, a newly formed diocesan building society gave £150, and the remaining moneys came from public subscriptions. Tenders were invited, and the firm of Webster & Thompson was the successful bidder. The Websters were a local family of masons and architects, and although the business had removed to Kendal, George Webster had built himself an elegant house, Eller How, at Lindale. Miles Thompson was his clerk and assistant for many years, and by this date had pretty much taken over the business. The building took about a year, but as is so often the case, there were extra sums to find on completion. These amounted to £100, and were generously donated by William Wakefield.

Hundreds of houses were built especially as vicarages during the nineteenth century. Until that time the arrangements had been largely on an ad hoc basis. If a vicar had a private income, he could buy or build his own house. If a poor curate arrived in the parish, he took lodgings, and if they did not suit, he moved on. At one end of this scale was the very first incumbent of Cartmel Fell, John Holme Briggs. He had his bed and board provided by the Briggs family, and 33s.4d. a year in salary. At the other end of the scale, Ravensbarrow Lodge was built by the Cockerton family, earlier in the nineteenth century.

The first incumbent to live in the desirable new parsonage was the Rev. Thomas Carter, but he died in 1867 aged only 42. His fifteen-year-old son had died earlier in that year, so possibly they were tubercular. William Summers was then installed in the parsonage, as it was then called, and he was curate of Cartmel Fell for the next 42 years, until 1909.

A story which has been handed down orally illustrates the strict attitudes to Sunday deportment earlier in the twentieth century. Some boys were playing the old game of spell and knurr one Sunday on Cartmel Fell, and Mr Summers, (a formidable figure with a black beard) reprimanded them for not keeping the Sabbath properly. After he had departed, the boys decided to keep Cartmel Fell pure, and crossed the river Winster to desecrate Crosthwaite instead.

After Summers retired, the new incumbent was the widower Thomas Price, and one of the most illuminating sources of the day-to-day life of a country curate is the diary which he kept, now in transcription at the Kendal Record Office. Thomas Price came to Cartmel Fell just before Christmas 1909, and stayed until 1916. During that time the church was completely renovated, Thomas Price's family of three daughters and a son grew up, and the Great War began. All this and much more is related, on an almost daily basis. Thomas Price was a keen photographer, as was the schoolmaster, Richard Craghill. Between them, they recorded many aspects of life on the fell in the early twentieth century, including the renovation of St Anthony's chapel.

After reading the diaries, one is struck by the difficulties of transport and communication at the beginning of the century. The Prices arrived in the district by the early train from St Bees in snowy weather. Thomas walked the cats with his bike up Staveley Brow to Cartmel Fell and suffered a strained knee for some time afterwards as a result. There were problems with the vicarage drains at once, and their benefactor, Mr Wakefield, gave his permission to carry the cesspit overflow into the woods. Drains and the water supply figured largely in the diaries.

Though the family had a pony, Gypsy, who pulled a trap, the usual transport was the bicycle. The roads were not made up then, and punctures punctuate the paragraphs, together with brake problems: '17th February, 1910. Mended Dodie's tyre in the evening with little success... Aug. 16th, 1910. Fell off my bike at Kent's Bank and broke my bell... 13th Jan, 1913. Snow and frost. Took oil container from the greenhouse lamp to Mr. Craghill who kindly soldered it. Then went with magazines to Moorhow and Ludderburn. The snow much thicker up there and there was a frost. My bicycle lamp froze while outside at Moorhow. Punctured on the way back.'

This year of 1913 was when the Suffragette movement was beginning to inflame women throughout the nation, but it is a surprise to read that Thomas Price thought they might threaten the fabric of his church. On 12 May of that year, he recorded: 'I remained on guard, and showed a number of people over it.' (the church) The danger over, he planted potatoes in the evening. 'June 23rd, Punctured for the third day running. Sept. 26th, Called at Borderside and heard that Jim Pearson had gone to the Canary Islands.'

Frequently, the people he called to see were not at home, though not as far afield as the Canaries, but not even the curate had a telephone. When the war began, rumours abounded, and the only way to get some kind of verification was to cycle to Grange and get an evening paper. Even the press was full of speculation and a sample from the diaries for August 1914 may give some idea of the uncertainty:

'August 1st, I called at Bowness for a paper, but could only get an evening one. The only morning papers left were the *Manchester Guardian* and the *Liverpool Post*. (Did he not trust the veracity of the provincial papers one wants to ask?) Political news very threatening.

Aug. 3rd, Fred Cockerton called early in the morning to tell me that Mrs. Foster had died suddenly in the night. Went into Grange in the evening with letters. Got evening paper. There was a great rush for them at the station.

Aug. 5th, D. F. Cockerton went up to London for Mrs. Foster's funeral. Train full of reservists going up to join the colours.

Aug. 7th, In the evening, I went to Grange for the evening papers. The chief news was that the Liege forts were intact and that the Germans had asked for a 24 hour Armistice owing to the loss of 25,000 men.

Aug. 10th, I called and had tea at Mrs. Pearson's at Pool Bank. Ben Pearson told me that when he had gone to enquire about his train, they told him that they were taking thousands of soldiers through to the docks.

Aug. 11th, William Harrison had just come back from Grange and told me that Brearley at the Hotel had official news that 50,000 British troops had landed in Belgium.

Aug. 27th, Heard reports of trains full of Russians from Archangel coming down the LNWR (London North Western Railway.)

Aug. 28th, Met Miles Birket who told us he was going to join at Hull, where his brother is, next week. They are guarding entrances to the Humber. He confirmed reports of Russians coming through from Archangel. He understood that half a million were coming. 90,000 already said to have passed through.

Sept. 3rd, Called on Craghills to see if Mrs. C's niece (who lived in Natland) had heard anything about the transport of Russians. Apparently nothing, but Admiralty code (coach?) had passed through Oxenholme, but someone stated that he had seen thousands of Russians passing through York. Is it all a gigantic hoax?'

The parson's daughters were engaged in organising the production of knitwear for the troops. A depot for wool was formed at Hampsfield, and then it was distributed to home knitters who turned out socks, scarves and gloves. All the time, young men were calling at the parsonage to say their farewells before enlisting.

The medical examinations for physical fitness seem less than rigorous in the light of present knowledge: 'Dec. 3rd, Stormy. Went to see Mrs. Winder and Lishman. Ruth L. told me Harry had been rejected from the army on account of his eyesight, but had been told to stop smoking and come again in a fortnight.' Sadly, for whatever reason, Harry was considered fit enough when he re-applied, and his name is on the War Memorial in St Anthony's churchyard.

As the war progressed, Cartmel Fell still tried to sort hard fact from wild rumour, but with experience, Thomas Price was becoming sceptical. When he met his daughter at the Height in February 1916, she told him that she had heard of a great battle in the North Sea, with four British and eleven German ships sunk, but there was nothing in the evening papers. Thomas commented: 'Probably on a par with those (rumours) which came out at the beginning of the war.'

In May 1916, a letter from the bishop arrived, offering Thomas Price the living at Staveley-in-Cartmel. That very afternoon, T. P. as he called himself, set off for Staveley to take tea at the vicarage. The first impression must have been favourable, but remembering their initial problems with drains at Cartmel Fell vicarage, he set off again the following afternoon to check on the state of those at Staveley. All was well, and that evening, Thomas Price wrote to the bishop accepting the offer.

George Clayton was the next incumbent, and he had a family of teenage boys, one of whom was training for the church. These lads were full of fun, Ella Wilkinson recalled in later life. They used to all come home for the Christmas holidays and plunge into preparations for the annual concert. The girls' dressing room was a make-shift affair of a large clothes maiden and a sheet, but the Clayton boys had the knack of sending the whole apparatus flying, just as the girls had undressed.

In 1934, Charles Last took up residence in the parsonage. He was unmarried and lived with his widowed sister, but they felt they needed a cook-housekeeper as well, so they applied to a training school at Workington for such a girl. This school provided a crash-course in housewifery for school leavers, and Sarah Kellett was the chosen applicant. She had never been away from home before and found everything about the house and its inmates intimidating. Sarah's kingdom was the kitchen quarters and the larders and pantry. The flagged floors had to be washed daily and she wore a working overall and dress in the mornings, but changed into a more genteel outfit in the afternoons with a lacey apron. The large attic bedroom was shared with other maids, but they had curtained cubicles of their own.

It seems hard to imagine today, but once there was a tennis court for the vicarage, somewhere on the parish lot. The trees have sprung up everywhere since those times and the site is obliterated. During the Second World War, the vicarage vegetable garden was used by the school children of Cartmel Fell to 'Dig for Victory'. This plot was just across the road from the parsonage, but it is now completely overgrown. James Wright remembered that when he was a boy, the potatoes grown by the curate had a blue-black tinge to their skins, so were indistinguishable from the surrounding stones and very hard to pick. Today, a square patch of dogs mercury marks the spot.

Eventually, many separate parishes were amalgamated, and in the case of Cartmel Fell, the curate was shared with Crosthwaite which also had a vicarage, so one was to be redundant. Crosthwaite was more central and a nucleated village, so maybe that was one reason for the sale of the Cartmel Fell vicarage. After being a private house owned by the Kelsalls for many years, in 1991 they died within months of each other and it was sold again and divided into three holiday houses, all of a much higher standard than formerly. The men who worked on the development were alarmed by the sound of dragging footsteps on the corridor to the kitchens, but as soon as it was sealed off, the noises ceased.

Water, or the lack of it, had always been a problem at Danes Court as it is now called, so when it became three houses, a bore-hole had to be drilled for a more reliable supply. There seems no obvious reason for the house being called Danes Court, but the Kelsalls bred great danes for show purposes. They also bred dachshunds, but Dachshund's Court does not have quite the same ring to it.

Pool Garth

THIS farm was also called Pull Garth in earlier times, and it may be that it was built in the garth of one of the influential Pull or Poole family, though so far no evidence has been found for this. A small beck runs through the property, and forms a now ornamental pool just below the house. The beck must have been the original water supply and one of the reasons for the house being built here.

The first family recorded at the house were the Kilners, when Thomas was a witness to a deed relating to Blewet Tenement (Blewthwaite), when he was also a feoffee for the Bryan Beck charity in 1714. For well over 200 years, and maybe longer, Kilner was a local name, leaping into the limelight in 1576, when one Richard, of Witherslack, was murdered by Richard Taylor. The murderer was hanged and buried at Blackcrag Bridge End, in unconsecrated ground. Since Witherslack is on the limestone side of the Winster valley, the probability is that the surname arose there, the man who owns or tends a lime kiln. There are Kilners in the Crosthwaite registers a little later that century when Thomas married Agnes Brygges on 22 January, 1581, and when Edward was buried in June 1594. The first mention of Cartmel Fell as a Kilner residence is in 1663, when Thomas Kilner and Elizabeth Fell christened their illegitimate child at Cartmel. Thomas was the name of all the Kilners at Pool Garth, so it is tempting to assume that this is a forebear of the dynasty, but it cannot be said to be more than a likelihood.

In 1678, Thomas Kilner of Cartmel Fell (but no farm name) christened another Thomas at Cartmel, and then, in 1714, we have the first definite link to the steading, when Thomas Kilner was a trustee of the Bryan Beck estate. Here, Thomas is described as yeoman, so he owned the holding. It is probably the same Thomas who was buried in 1723. He may have died intestate, as there is an inventory of all his wordly goods in the Preston Record Office, but no will. As usual, the first item is the money in his purse and clothing, which amounted to £3.14s.0d. The other items were as follows:

Goods in the chamber, together with the widow's bed in the said room - £3.0.0
Bedstocks and bedding, and other goods in the brewhouse - 10s
Bedstocks & bedding & chists & chairs & other goods in the little loft - £4.15.0
In the great loft - 12.0
Iron gear in the house - £1.5.0
Clock and case and warming pan - £2.0.0
Meall and malt in the back chamber - £1.0.0
Ladders, Harrows & crooks in Bracken loft - £13.0.4
Cows - £10; one calf - 10s.; 3 yearlings - £4.5s.0d; 3 stears - £9.; 2 heifers - £4; 1 mare and 1 gelding - £6; Sheep - £26.5s.0d.
Wood in fields - £2.5s.0
Total: £117.7s.6d

As can be seen from this inventory, Thomas Kilner was living a reasonably comfortable life as an independant yeoman farmer. The furniture is not listed separately, but he had a long-case clock, which was most likely one of Jonas Barber's who began clock-making at Bowland Bridge. The brewhouse was a separate room at the back of the house with its own outside door, large fireplace and it later became a general utility room, with griddle oven and wash boiler.

The Kilner family was respectable, educated and fairly well off by the standards of the day, and this is shown in the parish records and their wills. They were trustees of the Bryan Beck Charity, and served their yeoman duties as chapel warden, constable and overseer of the poor. They also were witnesses to their neighbours' wills or appraisers of their property inventories.

There is a will, dated 1743, of another Thomas of Pool Garth, leaving the messuage to his son, who was yet another Thomas. His widow Isabell was left with six children, five of them under 21, and living with the family was her mother, Jennett Turner. As was commonplace at the time, the best bed features in the will, and Isabell was to have the feather bed, together with other bedding, 'fitting and suitable to make into a handsome bed.' Isabell was also to have a spinning-wheel and the oak chest in the bedchamber beneath the floor. This last reference is to the custom of the master and mistress of the house having the downstairs chamber as a bedroom. In traditional south Lakeland farmhouses of the seventeenth and eighteenth centuries, the main door opened into the principal room of the house, with its hearth, and larger window. To the other side of the door was a partition which divided off the chamber; this did not have a hearth, but had the other front window, usually smaller than that of the main room. Behind the chamber and firehouse would be the dairy on the cooler back side of the house. Thomas's son James was to be kept in

Pool Garth

'accustomed fashion' at school for one year after his father's death, 'with suchlike Meat, Drink, Washing, Lodging and other such necessary Apparrell to keep him at School for one whole year after my decease, such like he is now mentained at school.' The school was obviously some distance away as lodging was required, and young James may have been a pupil at Cartmel grammar school. All the children were to have £10 on reaching 21. Obviously, the Kilners were not only relatively wealthy, but they were educated and expected to be so.

The parish chest records list a Thomas Kilner as overseer of the poor in 1760 'for one of his estates', and then for the subsequent three years he held the same post in respect of other holdings. One of these was identified by the occupier, 'Lindow's,' so this must have been Blewthwaite or Pool Garth Nook, the properties which adjoin Pool Garth. On a tombstone in Cartmel Fell churchyard, is a memorial to Ann Robinson, born Ann Kilner of Pool Garth, who died in 1840 aged 83, and she seems to be the last of her line.

Matthew Dodson may have bought Pool Garth from the Kilner's estate, and this was where he was living when his daughter Susannah was baptised in 1791. Matthew made his will in 1800 and was still at Pool Garth, but after his death his widow went to live at Swallowmire, another of her husband's many farms.

The owner of the holding, according to the 1814 land tax, was Joseph Pearson, but the occupier of the land was John Bowness, and from the 1829 Parson & White directory, we see that he was then living at Pool Garth. He must have been there for some time, because he had two sons and six daughters baptised between 1820 and 1835. It seems likely that the house was divided at that period, because in 1831 another name appears in the baptismal register; Robert, son of Robert and Esther Matthews, waller. A burial of Robert Matthews of Poolgarth, infant, is entered in the register for same year, and also another infant of Poolgarth, James Robinson Atkinson. There may have been some kind of epidemic on the fell in that year, because out of a total of seven burials, five were infants, a number never again equalled. In the 1841 census, John Barrow, farmer, aged 55, was in one household with his wife Eleanor, whilst Mary Crosthwaite, labourer, aged 35, was in the other. She had three boys of thirteen, eight and three, and is the only case that I have come across on the fell where a woman is described as a labourer.

By the 1851 census, all had changed, and the Long family were in residence as one household, but Mary Crosthwaite was still in the other, now described as washerwoman, and living with two sons, one an 18-year-old agricultural labourer, the other a 12-year-old. In the ten-year period, Mary Crosthwaite had mysteriously gained fifteen years, but the 1841 census rounded down ages to the nearest five years, so she was now 50. Rowland Long was aged 36 and farming 81 acres, employing one labourer. His wife, Isabella, was a year younger and had two boys, William aged nine, and Rowland aged four. Jane Wilson, an annuitant of Underbarrow, was visiting on the night the census was taken, and James Wilson, aged 30, was the unmarried farm servant.

The Longs lived up to their name and were long-lived. Rowland and Isabella were still farming when they were 75, but Rowland died before the 1901 census and Isabella stayed on, entrusting the farm jointly to her two sons and her daughter Mary. The children were all middle-aged by this time, and none of them ever married. It is said that Rowland the younger and his brother Billy used to retreat to a building down the track to smoke and drink and laze away the day, where their mother's watchful eye could not see them. If a salesman called, Mary would cover up and say, 'Oh, they are in the office, I'll fetch them.' In 2001, the faint letters of OFFICE can still be made out over the door, and an old photo of them nicely sets the picture.

It seems that the Longs were only tenants at Pool Garth, because the 1909 finance act shows that Miles Higgin Birket of Birket Houses had by this time acquired yet another farmholding. It must have been he who erected the splendid new barn lower down the track, and it is built very much in the same style as the one he built at Hodge Hill in 1904. The stalls in the stable have beautifully chamfered timbers and all is on a grand scale. The upper floor of this barn was converted into living accomodation by the owner and architect Roy Manby in the 1960s. It is now called Long Garth, and the field below it rejoices in the name of Long Friday.

During the Second World War, the young Phizackleas farmed Pool Garth. Bessie was the daughter of the Walkers who owned Bowland Bridge, and John was the son of the family who farmed The Wood. In June, 1940, Bessie was delivered of twin boys, but she died in childbirth aged only 23, and was buried the day Edward and John were christened. The babies survived and were reared by their grandmother Mary Walker, who kept the shop at Bowland Bridge.

The Manbys came to Cartmel Fell from Mill Brow near Skelwith Bridge, where they were amongst the first in the area to breed Jacob's sheep. Judy Manby, Roy's wife, was a painter, better known professionally as Da Fano. Apart from painting pictures, she also designed and painted on porcelaine. After Roy's death, his widow sold Pool Garth to Michael Berry, and she moved to Milnthorpe.

In 1995, an extension of the house was allowed by the planning board, and a library was added at the upper end of the slope. When the builders began excavating for the footings, they uncovered a large and beautifully built covered passage, below the bank which abutted the end wall of the house. Although the level lawn appeared to be three to four feet up the outside wall, inside, the house was perfectly dry. This cavity was also a drain, and a similar construction was found up at Lightwood Cottage. Maybe others exist, but as long as they are functioning properly, no-one suspects their presence.

Pool Garth Nook

THIS farmhouse is now a total ruin, and it is hard to believe that it was lived in towards the end of the last century. 'Nook' describes the snug and sheltered position it holds, with its back to the fell and prevailing westerlies, and its face to the sunrise, which would quickly melt the snow or frost. Partly because the house fell into decay before twentieth century modernisation, one can see how other houses must have been in bygone days. The thick oaken mullions have not rotted yet, and the many small rooms can be discerned, as can the spring of water at the back of the house. Across the field is a barn of similar vintage, also roofless, in which are the huge crucks which supported the roof timbers. The positioning of these crucks looks precarious, because they are resting on the stones which flank the door opening. The design obviously works, since this wall is still sound, but it looks as though there could be too much pressure on a half-secured stone.

The first surviving record traced which relates to this estate is one of 26 March, 1731, when George Lindow of Pool Garth Nook made his will. In that same year he was also constable, indicating that the estate belonged to him. The next record, dated 1743, was when Thomas Kendall of Pool Garth Nook signed the Bryan Beck indenture. This again tells us that Mr Kendall must have been a respected man in the parish, and in 1741 he had been the chapel warden. It would seem that this farmstead was one which was going into slow decline, having been once of some importance and its farmers pillars of the community.

All the properties along this road were once subject to tithes, payable to Burblethwaite Hall, and Pool Garth Nook was no exception. In 1812, the occupier was Mary Greenwood, wife or widow of Robert, and she had to pay 3s.8d. and 1s. mill rent a year. She also had to do boon service, leading six carts of peat and assisting at one day's shearing a year.

In 1821, William Greenwood of Pool Garth Nook made his will in April, and died on 5 May. He was the brother of Robert, and left various properties to his nieces and the son of a nephew, but there is no mention of Pool Garth Nook, so probably he was a tenant there, although his will describes him as 'yeoman', but this title must have applied to his other properties.

By 1851, the census return lists the Rockcliffe family; William who was 50 and an agricultural labourer, and his young family of ten, six and one year, with their 31-year-old mother. Ten-year-old William was a scholar, so this must have been at the time that the old school was a near ruin. The parish registers show that the Rockcliffs had been at Low Green, otherwise known as Jumping Down, from 1838 until 1843. They had their children baptised, and a daughter of nine weeks buried during this period. Later, in 1849, they christened their daughter Eleanor whilst William was a labourer at Pool Garth, so they were slowly migrating south along the fell, before ending at Pool Garth Nook.

At some period during the last half of the nineteenth century, Pool Garth Nook itself was used as the school house, but as this information was verbal and second-hand, I cannot say just when. Apparently, Fred Cockerton (from Ravensbarrow Lodge) remembered running down the green lane from the top road to Pool Garth Nook when he was a boy, and related the fact to James Wright of Goswick Hall. This could have been at the time the school was enlarged, for the young Fred was about six or seven at that time. The new school must have seemed very grand after such homely surroundings. Very soon after this temporary arrangement, Pool Garth Nook must have slid into decline, and now it is a picturesque ruin.

Pool Garth Nook in the 1970s, photo. Tobias Harrison.

Jumping Down or Low Green

THE name defies analysis, sometimes being written in the parish register as 'Jumper Down,' but in the nineteenth century censuses as 'Jumping Down', though more often as Low Green. In earlier centuries it was referred to as Low Green in available documents, or even Low Side.

Low Green is a descriptive name and the bothy is set in fairly level grazing land, so there are few questions to be asked about that origin. Jumping, or Jumper can only be guessed at. The children would pass through the field as the most level route to school from the north, but there is nothing to jump in the vicinity. There is a difference of perhaps two feet between the upper and lower floor levels inside the bothy, and although there are steps, it was possible to jump from the side of these as the space is open. Another possibility, but more unlikely; a 'jumper' was the iron rod used by quarry-men to bore holes for the gunpowder, so was this a little forge in the past? The answer has long been forgotten. A nearby spring must be one reason for for the siting of this dwelling.

It has been difficult to find much evidence of the occupiers of this little house. In the nineteenth century it had become a rather humble abode, home to agricultural labourers and charwomen, but often unoccupied.

In the twentieth century, the upper storey became unsafe, so in the 1960s the roof was lowered by the Manbys, who were then the owners.

Whilst removing the coping stones under the eaves, a remarkable discovery was made. One of the stones was part of a crudely carved crucifix, an arm and hand with a hole in the palm. This is now in the Kendal Museum and has been assigned tentatively to the ninth century. This leads to other questions of course. Was there a very early church on this site, and are there other stones, part of the crucifix, buried in the bothy? The present church is within view across the fields, and the field below has the curious name of 'Long Friday.' Could this have been a processional route, or was there a preaching cross set up in an open piece of ground?

On safer territory, there is evidence for Low Green from 1662, when Edward Pearson, yeoman of Lowside was the owner of Blewet's, or Blewthwaite. This is the adjoining property and the two would have been a useful unit, even if Edward had only been a tenant at Lowside. In 1682, Bluett (as it was then worded) was sold to Rowland Hodgson of Green in Cartmel Fell. There are no properties in parish documents called Green, so this was almost certainly Low Green, alias Jumping Down. Rowland died at Oaks in 1702, leaving his properties to his daughter Agnes, but Low Green is not mentioned specifically.

Throughout the eighteenth century, little is heard of this house. It is not listed in the parish documents, where yeomen are listed to do their duties as constable, chapel warden, overseer of the poor or grave, so it was most likely tenanted by unlanded labourers. Rarely does it appear in the parish registers of baptisms and burials, but the nineteenth century censuses throw a little light on some of the inhabitants.

In the census of 1841, William Rockcliff, a forty-

CARTMEL FELL

Jumping Down

From that time onwards as far as the 1901 census, the house was empty, and maybe unfit for habitation.

By the mid-twentieth century, trees were growing from the roof and there was evidence that the building had become a cattle-shed, but now, with its roof made good, though one storey lower, the building is in good order.

year-old agricultural labourer lived at 'Law' Green with his 20-year-old wife and baby daughter Mary. She had been christened the year before and the baptismal register shows that they had a son in 1844, where the curate calls the house Jumping Down in both cases. By 1851 the house was not even listed. Ten years on, Mary Crosthwaite from Heversham was living at Low Green with her two unmarried sons. She was a charwoman and one son was a sawyer, the other an agricultural labourer.

A labourer called George Graves and his wife Agnes had their daughter christened Sarah Elizabeth in 1865, but by the following year they had moved to Lound Cottage when their next child was baptised. Little Sarah Graves died aged nine months and was buried from Jumping Down in December 1865. Once again the house was uninhabited by 1871, and by then it was called Jumping Down in the census, so the name had become official. To avoid any confusion, the census enumerator in 1881 wrote: 'Low Green or Jumper Down.'

Blewthwaite

TODAY, Blewthwaite farmhouse and Blewthwaite barn are separate households. The barn has a small dwelling attached to it, and this probably housed farm labourers. The present spelling of the farmstead is quite recent; in 1812 it was Blewit, in 1821, the parish clerk wrote Blue Tenement and in 1830 it was recorded as Bluett Tenement. In the 1841 census the enumerator wrote Blawthwaite Tennament, but the Taylor family who lived there from 1826 to 1882 erected a tombstone in St. Anthony's churchyard and there recorded their home as Blewit Tenimant.

The word tenement may conjure mental pictures of tall crowded buildings in Glasgow or Edinburgh, housing scores of families, but the origin of the word is the same as in tenant, that is 'holding.' Even though the occupier might own his property, he *held* it from the lord of the manor and paid what was in essence, a ground rent. His heirs could inherit the farm, but they had to pay fines to the manor on either the death of the lord, or the death of the owner. They probably had to pay annual tributes to the manor too, these being in labour or in produce.

The prefix Bluett could be interpreted in many imaginative ways, but it is merely the surname of an early owner, one John Blewet. His son and heir, another John, carpenter of Beathwaite Green (Levens), Westmorland, signed a deed which sold the property to Anthony Pearson of Ramshawe, County Durham in 1659. The farmhouse could have been built by the Blewetts thus acquiring their name, and they might have been tenants of Burblethwaite manor for generations, but the change in ownership engendered the first known surviving deed.

The deed sets out the terms under which Blewet's was held from Burblethwaite manor. The lord was Thomas Knipe, gentleman, and he had the right to charge rents, fines, heriots and 'Other Benefits.' These benefits are not named in this instance, but we learn from later documents that they entailed boon duties or services. As in the case of other properties held from the manor, one day's shearing was obligatory, and the leading of six carts of peat. There was an annual mill-rent of one shilling, and this must have entitled and required the owner to have his meal ground at Burblethwaite mill, and finally, there was a fixed annual rent of 6s.8d. This last item became almost worthless with continuing inflation over the centuries, but was of real value in the early years of the sixteenth century when we first learn of the Knipes of Burblethwaite. By local custom, the fine payable at the death of either the lord or the owner was nine times the annual fine which in this case was £3. This piece of multiplication varied from manor to manor and even from holding to holding. Failure to pay was the only way in which a yeoman could be evicted from his inherited property, and the threat sometimes led to ever-increasing mortgages and eventual sale. The heriot referred to in this deed was something akin to a death duty. It was the lord's right to choose the best item from his tenant's holding on the death of the owner. In the case of John Fleming of Rydal, at about this period (1670), the heriot was a sow valued at £6, but the heir bought it back. Since swine (plural) in his father's inventory were valued at 6s.8d, one feels that there was a certain element of extortion on the part of Rydal manor. To put these values into context, a labourer's daily wage was then 3d, according to the Rydal Hall account books, so the annual rent of Blewet's was about a month's wages, and the entry fine was equivalent to nine month's wages, though as a skilled carpenter, John Blewet would earn considerably more.

Anthony Pearson, the new owner of Blewet's was a native of Cartmel Fell. He was baptised at Cartmel in 1626, the son of Edward. He must have had a good education, because at the age of twenty he became secretary to Sir Arthur Haselrig who was governor of the north at Newcastle for the Parliamentarians. Anthony and Grace his wife must have developed Quaker leanings, as they entertained many prominent Friends of the time, including George Fox. The Fells of Swarthmoor Hall were amongst their circle, and Anthony was one of the trustees of Judge Fell's will.

After the Restoration, Anthony was appointed under-sheriff by the bishop of Durham, having diplomatically loosened his Quaker ties, but he died in 1666, aged only 40. His will proclaims him 'Gentleman' of the City of Durham. Thomas Pearson was Anthony's sole heir and executor and Grace, his mother, later re-married, but Thomas's sister, who was named for her mother, became famous in her own right. Grace the younger married Robert Chambers of Sedgwick in 1703 and became a Quaker minister. She travelled extensively in her ministry, overseas as well as in Britain, but she was also well known for her powers as a herbalist and apothecary. Her visit to Height Meeting is recorded in Jonathan Wilson's ledger along with a recipe for 'Grace Chambers' Salve'. The ingredients for this ointment are not very re-assuring as it contained large quantities of red and white lead, but the Countess of Suffolk endorsed her powers of healing, believing her to be far more efficacious than the doctors of her day. Grace was very friendly with the Darby family of ironmasters at Coalbrookdale, and was said to have been 'like a mother' to Abiah Darby. A contemporary description of Grace was that she was of dignified and simple manner, and plain in apparel.

The next deed relating to Blewet's is dated 1662, and acknowledges the new owner to be Edward Pearson, yeoman of Lowside, Cartmel Fell. (This property might be the same as Low Green, alias Jumping Down, which adjoins Blewet's.) Anthony must have realised that his life was now entirely in the north-east, and decided to sell his native holding, but whether the incomer was his father or a cousin is not clear. The form of official entry was well-known locally and entailed a little ceremony. The deed relates: 'The attorneys did enter into a close of land called (blank) and therein did deliver quiet and peaceable possession and seizin to Edward Pearson, by delivery of a clod of earth and a twigg, together with this deed.' If a dwelling was involved, a key was usually handed over at the ceremony, so maybe Blewet's was sub-let and Edward continued to live at Lowside.

In 1700, Thomas Knipe of Burblethwaite sold for £6 all the woods on the land of Blewet Tenement to Thomas Pearson of Co. Durham, son of Anthony. There is a memorandum attached to this document, as a sort of after thought to the agreement: 'If it soe fall out, as many times it hath been known, if there come any Beese which takes any hollow tree, commonly called Beestockes, that the said Thomas Knipe shall have the benefit, according to their former custom.' One could speculate that there was a known hollow tree with the smell of ancient honey to attract a new swarm. Bees can detect the aroma of honeycomb from great distances and will re-colonise old sites.

In the second half of the seventeenth century, little parcels of land, intacks and closes were added to the Blewet holding, and in 1682 it was sold again for £40 to Rowland Hodgson of Green in Cartmel Fell. 'Green' is not a name which appears in the parish records, but it may be the transitional name between the aforementioned Lowside and Low Green or Jumping Down.

There may have been business or family connections between the families of Rowland Hodgson and the previous owners, because Rowland's daughter Dorothy married a joiner, John Archbold from County Durham. In a document of 1698, John Archbold acknowledges that he had received 'A considerable competent summe of money as his marriage portion.' He goes on to renounce any future claims on the estate.

Rowland died in 1703, but his daughter Agnes inherited the farmstead and held it from William Sandys who was now lord of the manor of Burblethwaite. By the time Rowland made his will, he was of Oaks in Cartmel Fell, but whether as owner, tenant or lodger is not clear. Despite his son-in-law's disclaimer, Rowland left his family further sums of money in his will. Dorothy was to have 20s. on the fourth Candlemas after his decease, and his grand-daughters Margaret and Abigail were to have £2 each when they were 21.

Agnes Hodgson was now a woman of property, and in 1705 she married George Lindow at Crosthwaite and he was admitted to the holding of Blewet for the customary payment of the £3 fine.

Thomas Hodgson, Rowland's son and heir, was living at Bryan Beck when his father died, and in 1710 he finally received his share of the estate. This amounted to £15, and was paid to him by his brother-in-law, George Lindow; Thomas was by then described as 'Mariner'. At this period in Cartmel Fell's history, there were many families who were linked with the West Indies trade through Lancaster, and there were other Lindows who were merchants or otherwise connected to shipping in that area. The Lancaster Maritime museum has lists of mariners sailing from that port in the mid-eighteenth century. In the 'Contributions for the relief of seamen, 6d. list', William and James Lindow were masters of *Molly* and *Hawk* in 1752, and James Lindow sailed in *Ellen* to Jamaica in 1754. Other masters in that year were Francis Bowes and John Ormandy, and a John Bowes was many times captain of *Love*. The coincidence of all these names coming together at Blewet's seems to point to strong links with these sea-faring families.

George Lindow must have been a successful grocer, as when he died in 1731, he left numerous bequests of money to many relations. When his will was drawn up, he was living at the home of Thomas Bowes in Poolgarth Nook, the next farm along the lane, and his bequest to Margaret Bowes was 'My iron oven, Provided that I depart this life while I remain at the house of Thomas Bowes her father.' This useful article must have been the equivalent of a modern Aga, at a time when farmhouse cooking was done in a pot over the fire.

Another Lindow, Thomas of Arrad Foot near Penny Bridge inherited Blewet Tenement, but he declined the bequest in favour of his brother George. In a letter dated 31 January, 1734 he wrote: 'I do desire you tow pot my name ought of this admitens and pot my brother gorge lindow name in stead of mine, for I do cleme no title in my oncle gorge lindow stet (estate) at carkmell fell for it hase beene left by will severall times befoar now and so I shall be satisfied my brother gorge lindow shall have it. As witness my hand, Thomas Lindow.'

It is worth mentioning here, that the lord of the manor received a double benefit from the waiver. First he had £3 from the heir, and then another £3 from George Lindow junior. During his lifetime, George had to pay twice more. First, when William Sandys died in 1749, and then when William Robinson, his successor to Burblethwaite Hall died in 1760. At a time when the Lord of the Manor would have had a funeral of some grandeur, these dues from his customary tenants must have helped to offset the expenses.

George Lindow lived at Blewet Tenement for almost half a century, but then in 1781 he released the farmstead to his cousin, William Ormandy, yeoman of Rusland, 'In consideration of natural love', and five shillings paid by his cousin. By this time, George Lindow was described as maltster of Carlisle.

The Ormandy family kept Blewet's for the next thirty years, passing it from father to son, but John Ormandy of Newby Bridge seemed to have had a claim on the property, and it was he who finally sold it in 1811 to the Taylor family. Although the sale was in 1811, in the land tax document of 1812, John Ormandy was still the occupier of Blewet's which was described as a messuage and tenement. The annual rent to Burblethwaite was 3s.4d., half of the original 6s.8d., implying a division of the property. There was also a one shilling mill rent, so the corn mill was still operating at that time. Apart from monetary dues to the manor, Blewet's owed six carts of peat and one day's shearing.

In 1821, the Taylors were living at Blue Tenement, as it was then called, and they gave 6d. towards the curate's half-yearly salary. Three of their men folk died young, as their tombstone in St Anthony's churchyard attests. Isaac the father died in 1826, aged only 42, and his son Isaac died at eighteen, whilst little Joseph did not survive infancy. Another son, John, became a shoemaker and had come back to his family to live with his mother Agnes by 1851. She was living alone at 'Blawthwaite' as is recorded in the 1841 census, but a separate household was there also, the Stables family. John Stables was a shoemaker and had been born at Wallthwaite, Great Langdale and he later moved to Chapel House. In this household were two other shoemakers, one of them an apprentice, so at this period, Blewthwaite had become a colony of cordwainers, as they were then called. By 1851, they also had a master tailor living with them, Edward Wilson from Hawkshead. Agnes Taylor was described as 'landholder' or 'independent' in three censuses, so she probably leased the farmland and lived on the income. By 1881, both houses at Blewthwaite were occupied by Taylors, but their relationship is hard to fathom. John was a farmer of thirteen acres, aged 30, and next door was Benson, maybe a brother, aged 32, who was a basket-maker.

Ten years later, the Taylors had all moved on, and Henry Kidd was the farmer. If thirteen acres was the entire farm, it must have been hard to support his young family, but Henry was also a carter and general labourer. His wife, Sarah Ann had been born at Chatsworth, so it is tempting to speculate that she might have obtained a place at Holker Hall through the Cavendish connections, and thereby met her future husband. They had two children in 1891, but by the time their third child was born, they were farming up the fell at Foxfield. Next door at Bluethwaite, young Ralph Dixon, a woodcutter from Cumberland, lived with his wife and baby daughter.

By the 1920s, one of the Cartmel Fell flock of Crowes was living at Blewthwaite. Thomas and Jenny Crowe christened their son John Henry in 1925, and another son, George Alfred three years later. From Thomas's grandson, we now know that the next-door property of Thorneythwaite had been willed to Thomas's father. Birds of a feather flocked together in this corner of the fell.

Most of the foregoing information has been taken directly from the deeds relating to Blewthwaite or from the censuses, but there are other parish records which add to the picture. For instance, in the parish register for 1778, John and Ann Kilner of Blewit christened their daughter Mary. A branch of Kilners had lived at the nearby farm of Poolgarth for much of the eighteenth century, so probably these were junior members and possibly lived in the small house adjoining Bluethwaite barn.

The barn itself is of architectural interest. The turn in from the road is quite abrupt, so the corner of the building is not angled, but has a smooth curve so that overhanging hay or corn sheaves would not catch on the corner of the wall and be dislodged.

Thorneythwaite

IN the early nineteenth century this cottage was called Thorneythwaite, for instance in 1812, but in the various censuses until 1891 it was called Thorneythwaite Side. On the first O.S. map of 1846, the wood below the house is called Thorneythwaite Wood, so one might suppose that the wood was so named before the house was built, and therefore the house is at the side of the clearing in the thorns.

The name of this house does not appear in parish records before the end of the eighteenth century and it probably dates from this time. It does not have the traditional farmhouse appearance and there are no barns or shippons attached or any evidence of demolished buildings. It must have been built purely for residential purposes, and in that is almost unique amongst the older dwellings on the fell.

It is probable that the house was built by John Allonby (or Allenby), who was the curate of Cartmel Fell from 1790 to 1827. At the time of the Enclosure awards in 1796, the Rev. John Allonby was allotted a parcel of land next to that of Greenthorn's, and therefore he must have been already the owner of a small estate. There is no mention in the parish accounts of anyone from Thorneythwaite having to do their turn at parish duties, but maybe the parson was exempt. There is an anomaly in the accounts however, in that the Rev. Allonby of 'Thornthwaite Side', pays four pence towards his own salary in 1821/22.

In a conveyance dated 11 November 1799, a parcel of land near Poolgarth, being one acre three roods, was sold to John Allonby, clerk. The vendor was John Rawlinson who had inherited it from Isaac Rawlinson. There is a substantial amount of garden and orchard around the cottage, so an industrious family could have been self-sufficient in poultry, fruit and vegetables.

From the deeds of Burblethwaite Hall, it can be seen that both the house and land belonged to the so-called manor. The Allonbys paid to Burblethwaite two shillings annual rent and boon-service of three carts of peat, plus one day's shearing. John Allonby died in 1827 but his widow was still in residence when the 1829 Parson & White directory was published, and she too owed boon-service to Burblethwaite Hall. She died at home in October 1831 and was buried at Cartmel Fell.

The property was sold in October 1838 and was advertised as being auctioned at the house of Mr William Tyson, innkeeper at Strawberry Bank, at six o'clock in the evening. The vendor was Mr G. W. Reveley of Orton who had married Charlotte, the daughter of Rev. John and Mary Allonby, and the tenant was Joseph Graves. The property at that time had an orchard, garden and croft and pasture adjoining. The separate parcel of land of just over one acre was sold separately to William Tyson, the landlord of the Mason's Arms, for £47.

By the time the 1841 census was taken, the extended family of Stotts was living at Thorneythwaite. John was an agricultural labourer of 25, but his tribe is difficult to unravel. Jane was also 25, but the children were eleven, twelve, two and one, and living with them was Nancy Caroline Stott who was 30, so the older children could have been hers. Joseph, the twelve-year-old, was an agricultural labourer. The unreliability of the census is shown in the next one in 1851. Now we can see that John and Jane are husband and wife, but their daughter Ann, who was said to be eleven in 1841 was only fourteen-years-old ten years later. They have three girls and a boy, and the older woman has left, as have two of the children.

The parish registers reveal more about the Stotts. At the beginning of their married life they lived at Pool Garth Nook, and then at Pool Garth. The first of their many children was Agnes, born in 1838, and the next was Elizabeth, who lived only three months. When John was born in 1842, the family were in residence at Thorneythwaite, and they had another seven or eight children in the next eleven years. Tragedy struck the family in the new year of 1855, when the dreaded scarlet fever swept through the county and within one month the Stotts had buried six of their children, their ages ranging from one year to twelve.

The Stotts' much diminished family stayed on at Thorneythwaite for another fifty years or so, and by 1891 John had been widowed. He was still working as an agricultural labourer aged 78, but he was being looked after by his daughter Mary and her husband William Fleming. Four Fleming children were still at home, the oldest being named John after his grandfather and following the trade of his father, that of a waller and mason.

It seems that the landlords of Thorneythwaite had done very little to maintain the house, because in the Inland Revenue survey of 1909/10 the surveyor commented: 'Stone, slate, roughcast. Poor condition, very damp.' By this time John Crowe was the tenant, in the capacity of farm manager for Mary Long at nearby Poolgarth. Both the Long brothers had died, leaving their elderly sister, Mary Isabella, as the last surviving member of the family. When Mary died in

1936, she left the house at Thorneythwaite to John, together with a barometer and a framed photograph of her brothers. The last two items are still in the possession of John's descendants, together with a photograph of grandfather Crowe with a prize shorthorn heifer.

Mrs Sarah Crowe, John's wife, was originally a Pearson of Borderside, and it was she who brought a cutting of the wisteria that grew on her old home and planted it at Thorneythwaite. The climber had been planted at Borderside by William Pearson, who in turn had received it from William Wordsworth, though history does not relate whether it was from Dove Cottage or Rydal Mount. In 2005, this venerable plant decorates the whole of the front of the house and has a massive trunk. Sarah died in December 1952 at Thornythwaite, after having been widowed for nearly a year.

When Bill and Sybil Adam retired to Thorneythwaite they created a beautiful garden. In February, people passing along the road take delight in the thick fringe of snowdrops which lap against the foot of the wall, all planted by Sybil. Although considerably younger than her husband, Sybil died in 1994. Bill is an independent Scot who survived the Burma campaign, so he remained at Thorneythwaite until he was 94, maintaining the house and garden admirably and spending some of the winters with his son and daughter in Australia.

When Thorneythwaite was sold in 2006, the damp, which was remarked upon in 1910 by the Inland Revenue, was found to be partially caused by the ancient wisteria. Its roots had penetrated the foundations and tendrils had invaded the walls, so drastic action was called for. Neighbours have been invited to take cuttings, so Wordsworth's climber may yet survive.

School House

THERE were always problems in finding accommodation for a schoolmaster in the days before a special house was built. When the curate was also the schoolmaster, arrangements were made on an ad hoc basis until the parsonage was built, and the same problem prevailed once the two jobs were separated.

With the building of the new school in 1872 the need for a resident teacher was highlighted, so plans were put forward to raise money by public subscription. Mr. F. A. Argles, then the owner of the Burblethwaite estate, donated a piece of land, £37 was donated by a special Dioscesan Education fund and the rest came in from local benefactors. A modern house was completed in 1877 at a total cost of £360.

Isaac Robinson was probably the first teacher to live in the new house, with his wife Margaret and little daughter Elizabeth, but they had formerly rented Strawberry Cottage, next door to the Masons Arms.

In 1881, John White was living in Shanty Cottage, as the house was then known, the name taken from the little beck which tumbles past.* He was from Ulverston and only 23, sharing the house with his sister, who taught sewing, and their thirteen-year-old cousin Margaret Crewdson. John was still there in 1891, but by then married and with three small children. Emily and John who were six and four were already scholars, while baby William was two.

The long-serving Richard James Cragghill was installed by 1901, together with his wife, Mary

Amelia. Mr. Cragghill had been born in Tebay but spent most of his working life in Cartmel Fell, where a few old people still remember him kindly. As he was such a keen photographer, many of our archive pictures came from his camera, some portraits posed on the steps of Shanty Cottage, by the beck.

When the school became redundant in 1971, the house was sold and used intermittently as a holiday cottage, becoming more and more derelict and damp. Today it is modernised and looking proud of itself again, with permanent residents

* The Shenton family lived at Greenthorn in the 18th century and the house was known as 'Shenty's'. Presumably Shanty is a corruption.

Sow How

IT sounds as though this is the hill of the pig farm, although it is an exposed site and about 700 feet up the fell. There is a hill just to the south-west of the farm which helps to break the prevailing wind, and this may have been the how of the sows. Today there are conifers planted where mixed woodland would have prevailed, or rough heath and where four or five hundred years ago pigs could have rooted for acorns. In dialect, soo or sough means a murmuring, such as the wind makes in the trees, so that is a possibility also, but a third meaning is that of a simple lime kiln. Before the stone structures were built, such as one associates with lime-kilns in more recent times, depressions or deep furrows in the ground were used for burning lime. These were known as sows, and must have been the usual way of creating small quantities of lime for private use in mediaeval times.

The present farm-house looks as though it was rebuilt in the first half of the nineteenth century, with doll's house symmetry. There are nice little stone corbels to support the gutters and two larger ones to hold up the canopy over the front door. The windows are large compared with most farm-houses of an earlier date, but the barns are obviously much older than the house. The through-stones project from the walls of the outbuildings in massive courses of undressed stones, and this type of construction is believed to be seventeenth rather than eighteenth century.

The site was probably chosen originally because of a good spring, and this has been cleverly incorporated within the house so the need to draw water from an outside well was avoided. Frogs would occasionally surface in this well and alarm the children.

The earliest occupant to be found so far is Edward Robinson. He died in June 1606, and we know of him through his will and inventory. One can deduce that he had several strings to his bow, like most of his contemporaries on the fell. Most people farmed, but on varying scales, and a little cash might be generated with home industries. Edward Robinson had two oxen, which would have been draught animals, a cow and a heifer, and four 'troynter' beasts. These were cattle of three years, sometimes spelt thrunter and literally meaning three winters. Today, sheep are still called twinters when they have survived their second winter, but the terminology has died out in cattle usage. The other livestock mentioned without any quantity specified was 'Swyn'. Could these animals be the origin of the farm's name?

Edward Robinson had items in his inventory which related to the production of woollen goods. There was an unspecified amount of cloth, 'wolles' in the plural, and yarn. From the study of other inventories on the fell at this period, it seems that most farmsteads were producing small amounts of woollen cloth, and Sow How was no exception. The household goods were slightly up-market as brass and pewter are mentioned, not wooden vessels. Pewter is almost always spelt pewther, and one wonders if that is how it was pronounced.

The Robinsons were at Sow How for at least another half century, as their wills testify, until 1666 when Ann Robinson died, but only two years after that, William Harrison of Sow How left a long and complicated will. His wife Margaret was to have her widow-right according to the custom of the manor of Cartmel. He left three High Closes to his son Edward, and the two Wood Closes to his son Robert and his heirs. Edward was to have half the water corn mill and kilns called 'Nubie' (at Newby Bridge) and if Edward had no heirs, then Robert and his heirs should have the other half. There was a house at Staveley, maybe associated with the mill, and Robert was to have a meadow called Broad Meadow, and the property at Height. This presumably refers to Sow How as Height was then a large district of the upper fell. Out of the proceeds of his inheritance, Robert was to pay his sister Agnes fifteen shillings a year, 'to buy her cloathes withall'. Agnes was the wife of William Knipe, but the will does not reveal where they lived. There was plough gear and husbandry gear to be equally divided between the sons, the equivalent of a tractor and its appurtenances today. Despite the seemingly comfortable property holding, John Harrison left enormous debts. There were many sums of multiples of £11.4s. outstanding to fourteen people. It is hard to imagine what shares these sums represented, unless John had invested in a ship but there is no mention of this. Could the investors have had shares in the mill? The funeral was to be lavish, for £12.8s. was set aside for this, but the assets amounted to only £256.8s.4d., and the debts were around £366, (some of the figures are smudged and altered) so maybe his sons had to sell out to pay their father's debts. The livestock was more than double the number of Edward Robinson's, and there must have been several hundred sheep as the total value was £65. At this period one might get four or five sheep for £1.

A note of refinement comes at the end of the inventory in the form of sheets, napkins and other linen.

In 1695, William Crosfield of Sow How christened his daughter Mary at Cartmel. There was a family of Crosfields in Witherslack at this period, so the Cartmel Fell family may have been an offshoot.

The Cartmel Fell chapel warden's accounts for 1707 show a gift of £5 to the chapel from Anthony Knype of 'The Sow Howse'. This was a large amount for the time and indicates that Anthony might have been minor gentry, perhaps connected to the Knipes of Burblethwaite or Flodder, either of which might have been the family into which Agnes Harrison married. The many other names occurring at the same address are probably farm servants.

The following year, Edwin Briggs died at Sow How, and was described as husbandman. From his humble inventory, one could guess that he was perhaps a farm manager. There were only five items on the list, one of which was his wage in arrear, £2.10s. A little box was worth one shilling and he had £1.7s. in ready money. The last item was three sheep which altogether were only worth 3s.6d.

Sow How came into the ownership of James Backhouse of July Flowertree in Finsthwaite some time in the mid-eighteenth century. He had invested in all kinds of property, including two corn mills, so it is feasible that he had bought Newby Mill from the Harrisons, together with their shares in Sow How. James Backhouse died in 1762, leaving his many properties to his brother Richard and two nephews.

The name of Robinson crops up again in 1776. By this time, Cartmel Fell had its own licence for baptisms, and that is where Thomas and Elizabeth had their daughter christened for her mother.

For some reason, Sow How hardly features in the parish chapel wardens' accounts. Most yeomen served their turn as officers of the parish, but Sow How is not mentioned by name, so this might mean that it was tenanted continuously. From the 1814 land tax list we know that the estate was held by the trustees of John Dodson, late of Pattinson How. At that time, Ann Watson was the occupier, and an Ann Watson gave 4s.8d. to the curate's salary in 1821, but this cannot have been the same Ann Watson who was the farmer in the 1841 census. Her husband William had died in 1834 aged only 44, so if he had been the head of the household in 1821, it would probably have been his name as the contributor to the curate's stipend, not his wife's. Their youngest son was only eight-years-old when William died, so Ann must have had to struggle to bring up five sons and a daughter on her own. She died aged 53 in 1849 leaving her second son to continue farming. It is possible that the Watson's early deaths were from tuberculosis, as their oldest son John died in 1852 aged 34, and at that time he was farming at Fox field, just a mile or so down the fell track from Sow How.

James Watson was 26 and still unmarried when he took up the reins, and his younger brother William helped him. They had to have a housekeeper and a farm lad, and we see from the 1851 census that they farmed 147 acres. This acreage had decreased to 114 ten years later, and by then James had a wife Margaret (née Lund) and six children. The couple were able to employ a labourer, a house servant and a nurse, who was little more than a child herself. Young Mary Hewertson was only thirteen, but was no doubt heavily supervised. At the time of the 1861 census, Margaret was close to giving birth to Benjamin, so this may have been the reason for additional help with the other children. The parish register shows that Benjamin was baptised at home, usually a sign that the baby was not thriving, and he died the following year. Altogether, James and Margaret Watson had eleven children between 1853 and 1866, but two baby girls died in infancy. Although the Watsons were well used to early mortality, James lived until 1904, and died in retirement at Hawkshead aged 81.

The Watsons have a grave in St Anthony's Churchyard and from the gravestone we see that Margaret died in 1889, but their daughter, Mary Jackson, pre-deceased them. She was 28 when she died in 1884 and her two-year old son was living with his grandparents at Sow How in 1881, as was their widowed daughter Ann Hayton who was then 26. The family had known bereavement on a scale which was unusual even in Victorian times.

There may have been a change of ownership in the late nineteenth century. In 1871 J. Pearson granted his quarter share of the estate to H. Arnold and C. Webster of Kendal. This share was worth £300, so presumably the whole estate was worth £1,200. We know from the Finance Act of 1909 that by then Miles Higgin Birket of Birket Houses was the owner.

When the Watsons retired, their place was taken by the Allenbys. Like two earlier generations of Watsons, Rebecca Allenby was the widowed farmer, assisted by a labourer and her twin son and daughter, but they were only fifteen in 1891, and a younger son and daughter were still at school. They cannot have been at Sow How for very long, because by 1894 George and Emily Birkett were the farmers. Their daughter was baptised Emily May in that year.

In 1909 John Henry and Jane Downham were the tenants. They had three daughters while they were at Sow How, but later moved to Goswick Hall. Although John Downham was a farmer first, he was also a joiner, and a niece of his said that he helped to make the lych gate at the church in 1912, together with the family firm of Matthews.

Today, Sow How is part of the Ravensbarrow Lodge estate and was one of the first farms to be bought by the Bentley family. The farm manager Alan Foster is well-known for his success in training sheep dogs, winning countless awards in trials for nursery, national and international events, and he has a flock of 600 Swaledale ewes with which to educate his dogs. Ann Foster, his wife, is secretary to the Windermere Sheepdog Society. Besides the sheep, Sow How runs a herd of 60 suckler cows.

In the area which was anciently called Height, are artificial tarns for fish and wildfowl, and a nice stone boathouse. The dam and the boathouse were built from the stone of the ruined farm called Prentices. This homestead was sited on the edge of what is now conifer woodland just above the tarn, but was deserted by 1881. Swans frequently nest in the margins of the tarn and patrol the shoreline.

The beck which now runs out of the biggest tarn, dives down a steep gully at the bottom of which is an old sheep wash. The beck can easily be dammed at this point and a walled funnel runs down the fell from the southern side, straight into the pool. After storms, the dam is formed naturally from branches and vegetation washed down from above, so this useful attribute must have been noted at some earlier date and then enhanced.

Cartmel Fell

One artefact of bygone days is a large cheese press, now disintegrating. This is sited in a little building on the northern side of the house, especially built for the purpose. The front is open but the sun could not reach the cheese as it is shielded by the house. The Sow How press is not of a local pattern, but of the Wensleydale type. Only four cheese presses are known in the immediate district, one being at Hollins and the other two are represented by the weights only, one at the Hare and Hounds and the other incorporated in the wall of The Old Joiner's Shop, beween Bowland Bridge and Haycote.

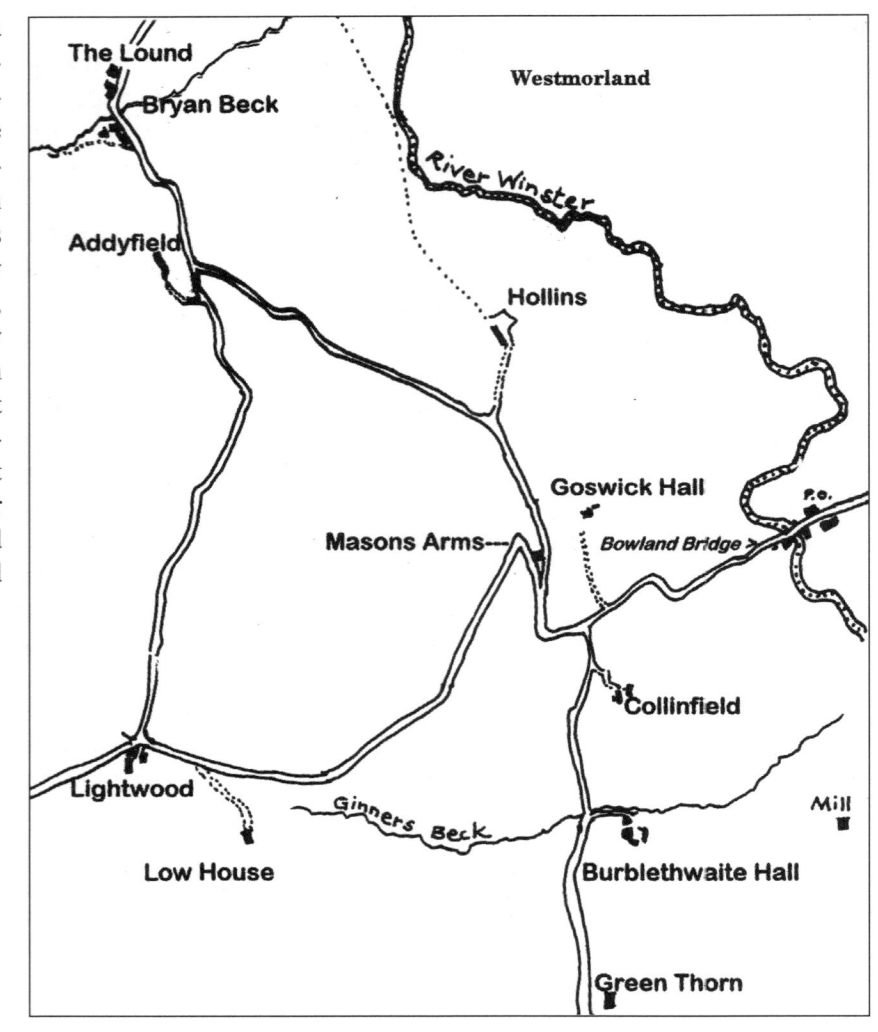

Greenthorn

THERE seems to be only one meaning for this little farmstead, which like Oaks, Ashes and Hollins, refers to the surrounding trees. Possibly it had a hawthorn hedge to separate it from the track which is now the road.

The earliest documentation so far found, is for January 1654, when Agnes, wife of Robert Harrison was buried. It would seem that this was yet another holding of that huge and widespread Harrison clan, who had been recorded on the fell since the 1300s. A generation later, in 1668, Lawrence Harrison of Greenthorn and Edward his son, sold for £10 an intack on the south side of an orchard called 'Anthony Wife'. Rowland Hodgson of The Green (Low Green?) was the purchaser. It might be relevant to give a brief comment here about the possessive 's', which was seldom used at this period. Nowadays we would expect the intack to be called 'Anthony's Wife's', but a parallel can be found at Height Meeting House, where the name of the field behind the house, 'Barrow Wife', has been taken for the new name of the dwelling.

Lawrence Harrison left a will which was dated 1678, and this shows that the Harrisons were typical small farmers of their day. It states that the property was held by inheritance from Thomas Knipe of Burblethwaite, gentleman, for the yearly rent of five shillings. Lawrence's two daughters, Mary and Margaret were his executrixes, but Mary was the heiress and had to pay her sister £10 out of the estate on the second Candlemas after their father's decease. There were the ordinary household goods in the inventory, including a spinning wheel, but only 12s. worth of sheep, which would have amounted to perhaps three or four in the orchard. When the outside chattels are listed, it becomes clear that this is only a smallholding and not a proper farm. A cow and a stirk are worth £3, and 'Beehives and other things' come to 5s.6d. There is no mention of poultry, and the crops include hay, straw, bracken and hemp. There were also peats and wool being stored and, rather surprisingly, 'potaties', the earliest so far to be found on the fell.

Following the Harrisons, came Richard Crewdson who died in 1681. He names no wife or children and had no stock in his inventory, but he had husbandry gear and he was was owed £22.14s.6d. Crewdson is not a surname associated with Cartmel Fell, and the Kendal branches of this family were mostly Quakers at this period.

In 1708, John Shenton of Greenthorn, yeoman, made his will. His wife was called Ruth, and their surname is probably the origin of 'Shanty' Beck. Apart from the very small amount of land which went with Greenthorn, John Shenton had Tom Parrock, adjoining Crosthwaite Fell. He had a cole-rake, so was evidently a charcoal-burner, and he had two spinning wheels together with hemp and wool. A genteel addition to his inventory were curtains and tablecloths, not everyday items at this period. Several generations of Shentons succeeded John and Ruth and it seems that the holding was nicknamed 'Shentys', as this appears in the chapel warden's accounts for 1746. The family seem to have been held in respect by their neighbours, and in 1764 William Gibson did duty as overseer of the poor for Mr Shenton of Greenthorn, 'Mr' implying a certain standing.

In 1772, Joseph and Agnes Crow christened their son Mark from Greenthorn. The Crows were birds of passage and four years later they were at Little Thorphinsty. The 1798 land tax return shows that Matthew Dodson of Oaks in Cartmel Fell owned both Greenthorn and Little Thorphinsty, so the Crows were obviously his tenants.

In 1806, the Rev. Thomas Thornborrow married Esther Dodgson. She was Matthew's daughter and had been born on the fell at Ludderburn, but although Thomas was the incumbent at Natland, and later curate of Kendal, Esther appears to have lived at Greenthorn before moving to her inheritance of Little Thorphinsty, left to her by her father. Thomas Thornborrow died in 1819, aged only 36, but they had a son Thomas and a daughter Selina.

After she moved out, Esther Thornborrow let Greenthorn to Thomas Hodgson. By 1851, Thomas was dead and his widow Margaret was left with five young children. It seems that she tried to make ends meet by taking in three boarders, and these ranged from 82-year-old James Swainson, a widowed tailor, to eleven-month-old Robert Huck. There was also Elizabeth Routledge who was eleven, but not entered as 'scholar'. Margaret lists her occupation as charwoman. By the next decade, the Hodgsons had left the parish entirely, and maybe Margaret returned to her native Crosthwaite.

A family of woodcutters came next as tenants, Thomas Nicholson and his father William. The Thorphinsty deeds refer to Nicholson wood-merchants at this period, but whether these were they is hard to say. There was a young family which included two step-children and Mary, their mother, made a bit of extra money by dress-making.

In 1881, the Winder family arrived at Greenthorn and were there for many decades. William Winder had been born in Liverpool as had Sarah his wife, but the children were born locally. Edwin was only twelve when the census was taken, and his sister Mary Ann was 22. There was also a six-month-old baby, James William Winder who was Mary Ann's son. William the elder was a hoop-maker, a fairly common trade at this period, and the hoops bound the dry barrels in which many foodstuffs were transported. Some of us who are less than youthful may remember new potatoes often came in such barrels, packed in peat. Edwin later followed his father's trade, making baskets and hurdles, and worked in the barn (now converted), which adjoins the house. He never married, but loved to talk and joke with the children on their way to and from school. He sold paraffin from a drum, and the children would take empty pop bottles to fill at 'Chippy' Winder's. In 1891, the Winders had a lodger who was described as 'Dog Trainer'. It seems somewhat baffling to have a professional trainer in an area where farmers were not wealthy and usually trained their own dogs, but that is what Alfred C. Bishop did, and he came from Biddlesden in Buckingham to do it.

After his parents died, Edwin continued his trade at Greenthorn, and young Mrs Batty from Burblethwaite Hall used to do a bit of baking for him from time to time and send up ginger biscuits with her daughters. He died in 1942 aged 74.

Today, the property has been modernised and a roof-top patio added above the kitchen. The barn is now an attractive dwelling and its dry stone walls contrast with the white render of the older house.

Burblethwaite Hall

THE earliest mention of this holding is in the Duchy of Lancaster Assize Rolls of 1351, when Roger, son of Simon de Knipe, held a plot of land in Broughton as appurtenant to his manor of Burblethwaite. There have been variations of the spelling down the ages, but all recognisable, burblek being a dialect name for burdock or coltsfoot. The very large leaves of this plant were used for wrapping butter or cheese in the days before paper was generally available. There must have been a clearing in the woodland where the common butterburr, *petasites vulgaris* grew, and this is where a favourable building site was developed. The hill above protects from the prevailing westerlies, a little beck runs close to the door and flood water drains past to the valley bottom. As with most of the long-established farmsteads, it faces the rising sun and benefits from an early thaw in winter, or the quicker evaporation of dew for drying hay in summer.

It is fortunate that many of the deeds relating to this property are still extant, at least, from 1561 onwards, and these early papers refer back to a pleading of 1532 in which it was disclosed that the property was held of the lord of Hampsfield, by knight service. Most of the following information has been taken from these documents.

Although Burblethwaite was called a manor in the first deed of 1561, it does not seem to have ever held manorial courts, whereas neighbouring Crosthwaite did. It extracted manorial service from many of the tenants in its immediate vicinity however, right up to the nineteenth century. These took the form of boon days, that is when free service was given to the manor by its tenants. For instance in 1812, Mary Greenwood, wife of Robert of Pool Garth Nook, gave boon service of leading six carts of peat and one day's shearing. A similar service was expected at Blewthwaite and Thorneythwaite. The curate of Kendal's wife, Esther Thornborrow, then living at Greenthorn, had to lead only three carts of peat and give one day's shearing, but also two ounces of pepper. These terms were all laid out in a document of 1812, when the Burblethwaite estate was sold to James Adam of Runcorn. The annual income from five properties and several fields was only 14s.10d., but, as with all manorial dues, the sting was in the tail. All householders were subject to a 'fine' or death duty. This applied to either the death of the lord of the manor, or of the householder himself. If a new tenant was an outsider and had not inherited the property, he paid an incoming fine as well. Even more of a blow to the family on the death of the head, they had to pay a heriot. This was the best article or beast that they possessed, or its equivalent in value.

On 13 March 1850, Tobias Atkinson, then owner of Burblethwaite, declared the estate and that of Collinfield to be henceforth free of tithes in the freehold inheritance of the said lands.

There was a dispute in 1561 between Anthony Knipe, the owner of Burblethwaite manor, and Miles Briggs of Brigg House which concerned the tenant right. Anyone who has followed family history back to Tudor times, will know how alarmingly eager the various land holders were to rush into litigation. It provides later historians with dates and facts, but it frequently bankrupted the litigants. It seems that in this case, the Knipes and Briggs had been warring for several generations, and had come to arbitration on 15 May 1533. The court awarded Thomas Briggs and his heirs-to-be their property for ever, according to the custom of tenant-right, but 30 years later, Anthony Knipe still claimed that Brigg House and its eight acres were part of the Burblethwaite demesne. Brigg House may have been on the site of the present cottage, now called Bridge House. From these snippets of information it would seem that the area claimed by the Burblethwaite demesne stretched along the lower flanks of Cartmel Fell, southwards to what is now the Newton to Kendal road.

In 1613, Anthony Knipe sold Burblethwaite for £1,500 and all his lands and tenements in Cartmel Fell and Cartmel to Myles Shaw of Cartmel Fell, yeoman. Myles Shaw was there for about 20 years, by which time he is titled 'gentlemen', and then he sold to another Knipe, Thomas, of Greenholme in Furness. This sale was for £450, but only included his messuage, tenement and farm called Burblethwaite Hall, consisting of one garden, three orchards, a water corn mill and kiln (for malting barley) and 30 acres of land, ten acres of meadow, twelve of pasture and twelve of woodland, with common rights in Cartmel and Cartmel Fell. In 1661 Thomas Knipe sold all the previously described property to his son Thomas, this time for £600. It would seem that the Knipes were shrewd businessmen.

The Philipsons bought Burblethwaite Hall in 1682 for £900. The agreement mentions the iron forge and corn mill, and tenements in several hands, yielding a yearly rent of 14s., so that sum stayed constant, inflating by only 10d. by 1812. The deed of conveyance between Thomas Knipe of Burblethwaite Hall and Sir Christopher Philipson of Crook Hall is dated 28 July 1682. This branch of Philipsons were always short of money, and their finances suffered severely during the Civil War, so possibly this was the reason for their needing to sell the property only ten years after they had acquired it.

In 1692, William Sandys, of Dale Park in Furness Fells became interested in Burblethwaite, but apparently did not have the necessary £1,000. He arranged a mortgage of £500 to be paid by James Grahme of Bagshott Park in Surrey and Francis Gwyn of Landsanner. These two had been at Oxford together and remained lifelong friends, James Grahme being then the owner of Levens Hall. A goldsmith, Robert Fowle of London was to lease the property at a peppercorn rent for 500 years if the mortgage was not paid off at the end of a year, but meanwhile, Sandys was to live there. Evidently his plans were not fulfilled, and on 11 May 1697, the money with £15 interest was due, but he was unable to pay. The property went to Fowle, but the 500 year lease passed to Francis Gwyn by payment of the £500 to James Grahme. The story behind these transactions was revealed in letters held at Levens Hall.

James Grahme and Francis Gwyn had been appointed joint trustees to the illegitimate daughter of James II, Lady Katherine Darnley. She caused them much anxiety by making a runaway marriage to the notorious Earl of Anglesey, and they knew that he had made the alliance to get his hands on her fortune when she came of age at eighteen. Grahme and Gwyn had real fears for Lady Katherine's life as apparently her husband was a violent man, and Lord Anglesey was bound over to keep the peace as an interim measure. Plans were laid for a more permanent solution however, and a dramatic rescue was effected when two men and four women in masks entered his lordship's house and spirited away the teenage wife.

Only ten years or so later, in or about 1700, a William Robinson of Staveley in Cartmel bought the estate. There were several inter-related families of this name in the vicinity, the most well-known being then at Fell Foot. A letter from Mr. Robinson's lawyers survives, advising caution while they investigated the Knipe original title, but all was well seemingly, and the sale went ahead.

The mill and the forge would have been valuable acquisitions, capable of producing more income than did the erratic fines. In his eagerness to improve the water supply to the mill, William Robinson overstepped the parish and county boundaries. He took in some land on the eastern bank of the river Winster, and also claimed common rights in Crosthwaite. The Crosthwaite parish clerk, Thomas Steele, together with others, objected strongly. They went in a body and tore down the new fences, and independent arbitrators were called in. These were Myles Sandys of Graythwaite and John Fletcher of Holker. Without knowing all the details of the case, the judgement seems fair and sensible. William Robinson was ordered to remove the fences at the south end, but he might re-erect the one at the north end of the ground between the two streams. The water fleak had to be restored to where it anciently stood, and the remainder of the land was to be enjoyed as Crosthwaite common. Mr Robinson might pasture his sheep and cattle upon the common, and take sods from it for repairing the mill dam as this was the ancient custom, and customary law had worked in an acceptable way for centuries. Finally, William Robinson was permitted to make a weir at the head of the west stream, between the mill and the disputed ground, so that the mill-wheel should not be in a backwater. The arbitrators decreed that the two parties should each pay their own costs.

The Robinson extended family inherited Burblethwaite when William died, and his nephew and great nephew John of Watermillock succeeded in turn. The younger John Robinson died on 23 June 1807, and at once there were family wrangles over the will. Evidently, the would-be inheritors tried to prove that the will was invalid because John was either senile or of otherwise unsound mind. It took two years for the final arbitration to be made, but the will was upheld, stating 'it being admitted and undisputed that the testator was of sound mind.'

The next document in sequence relates to the enclosure awards of 1809. The plans and awards were drawn up in 1797 for Cartmel Fell, but maybe the paperwork took a long time to catch up. John Robinson of Watermillock was awarded a parcel of ground near Burblethwaite Haw, (*sic*) containing 40 acres and one rood, bounded on the east by ancient enclosures and the Winster road, to the west by ancient enclosures and allotments awarded to James Barker (of Lightwood) and the Kendal Road. On the north, the bounds were an allotment awarded to William Gibson, (of Collinfield) and ancient enclosures, and on the south by ancient enclosures and an allotment awarded to Esther Dodson (of Greenthorn). John Robinson had to keep his boundary fences forever in repair.

In consequence of the disputed will, the whole Burblethwaite estate was sold at auction in September 1811. On this occasion, the estate realised £9,750 with another £1,100 for the woodland and timber. This very steep price rise, compared with the slow but steady inflation of previous centuries, was partly occasioned by the Napoleonic wars.

The new purchaser was James Adam, then of Brymbo Hall in Denbighshire. He was in some way involved in the iron and steel business, being an associate and trustee of John Wilkinson's, the owner of Brymbo Hall since 1792. Adam is an intriguing figure in the life of John Wilkinson, ever in the background but never far away. He was certainly involved in the Bersham ironworks at the latter end of the eighteenth century and also seems to have resided somewhere in the Warrington/Runcorn area, but his role is nowhere defined. At the Bersham Museum, Adam's signature is appended to posters advertising sales and so forth, and his address often coincides with that of the ironmaster. Towards the end of his life in 1822 he was living at Wilson House near Grange, another of John Wilkinson's properties. This evidence comes from the bishop's transcripts of the Cartmel parish register when James and Mary Adam's son James was baptised, and in the entry he is then described as 'gent.' The only other entry for this man in the Cartmel register is when he was witness at an unusual wedding in 1821, when William Legh Esq. of Winwick married Mary Anne Wilkinson, with the consent of the Lord High Chancellor of Great Britain. The other witnesses were both MPs, Thomas Legh and Thomas Claughton.

Mary Anne and her siblings had been the subject of a legal battle in the Court of Chancery in 1813. The case was brought as Wilkinson v. Adam, but this was John Wilkinson's nephew, Jones Wilkinson, who claimed his uncle's estate from James Adam, the latter being a trustee for the deceased ironmaster. Jones had lived and worked with his uncle for more than a decade, with little or no pay since he was 22, but, so he said, on the understanding that he would eventually inherit a substantial amount of his uncle's properties. When on business in London, John used to stay at Thavies Inn, and there he met Ann Lewis, a servant, and the two set up house together, although Mrs Wilkinson was still alive. The ironmaster was then 72 but he had three children by Ann, and the chancery case was to determine whether these children were legally the inheritors of their father's estates. The Lord Chancellor referred the case to judges in the three other principal courts, and eventually the decision was that the children were indeed 'clearly intended to be the object of his bounty.' Unfortunately, the lengthy legal wrangles absorbed much of John Wilkinson's fortune, then amounting to about £500,000, or the equivalent of about £15,000,000 today.

None of Adam's movements really explain why he bought the Burblethwaite estate, but it was clearly to do with his association with John Wilkinson, and he, like his friend, seemed to be permanently on the move. At one stage in 1819, he was living at Castlehead with Wilkinson's housekeeper and mistress, Ann Lewis. It seems that he had intended to stay at Burblethwaite until he died, as he wished to restore the Burblethwaite pew in St Anthony's and form a family burial place therein. A letter from

John Allonby, the curate in 1811, explains this in a letter to the bishop of Chester, but there is no burial record for this man in the Cartmel Bishop's Transcripts, and these cover the seven parishes attached to the Priory.

Possibly because of his association with the then famous John Wilkinson, Adam seems to have become influential in various other spheres in south Cumbria. He was responsible for drawing up the 'Order of the Constable's Office' for Witherslack in 1813, and his name was appended to a poster in 1819. This was produced by an association of gentlemen, lords of manors and men of property. These included Lord George Cavendish of Holker Hall and George Bigland of Bigland Hall, and offered a reward of £10 for information leading to the discovery and conviction of poachers.

It would seem that James Adam was a businessman who took risks. These were probably connected with innovations in steam power or the iron industry, but for whatever reason, in 1817 he borrowed the enormous sum of £35,000. This was lent by the commissioners appointed by an act in the reign of George III and for the repayment of which he gave a bond for £70,000. He had to apply for extra time to pay but when he died in 1823, he still owed £26,000, and so the Burblethwaite estate was ordered to be sold, Adam being the King's debtor.

The sale was at the King's Arms in Stricklandgate, Kendal, which used to occupy the site vacated by Marks and Spencer in 1994. The printed particulars list all the 21 lots with the occupying tenants, but not the rents paid. Thomas Atkinson of Brighton bought the hall, the mill and some of the land for a total of £7,700, and the map is of the area he acquired in 1827. Lot one was the hall with 131 acres and 15 perches. This land was occupied by James and Henry Mason who were yearly tenants. Lot two was the water corn mill and buildings, with about six and a half acres and occupied by George and William Jenkinson, whose lease expired in 1829. The rest of the lots were scattered as far afield as Greenodd, Meathop, Cartmel and Witherslack.

In the 1841 census, the Masons were still at the hall, with the Mounsey family at the mill, and so it was in the 1851 census too, James Mason being a farmer of 90 acres. It is hard to tell if this acreage had been reduced since the time of the sale, since it was then stated that 'most' of the land was in Mason's occupation, and 90 acres could be called most of 131. By 1861 the acreage had altered once more. Richard Barrow was the tenant and was farming 80 acres of old land and 30 acres of heath. Richard was 41 and he and his wife Jane had a ten-year-old son John. Three years later they had another boy and called him Richard James, and from the 1871 census we can see that father Richard was born in Cartmel Fell and his wife in Urswick. The acreage of Burblethwaite Hall had decreased to 90 acres by then, but ten years later it was increased again by ten acres. These mysterious changes in acreage may be accounted for by exchanges of land or sales of small parcels. The Argles family, descendants of the Atkinsons (see Burblethwaite Mill), owned several adjoining farm properties, so they may have, say, reserved a piece of woodland or moorland for their own field sports. Richard Barrow senior died in 1889 aged 71, but his widow continued to farm Burblethwaite with the help of her two bachelor sons. Her unmarried brother was living with her too, but as he described himself as

CARTMEL FELL

Burblethwaite, but before that he had begun married life at Goswick, so it was yet another case of families moving between farms to suit their individual circumstances. Bryan had made several moves in his early married life. He had farmed his father's properties at Sow How and Pattinson How, and also Thwaite Moss in Rusland, but with two school-age daughters at home, a more settled existence began.

Burblethwaite was still being farmed as it had been in the past centuries. Even in the 1930s there was no piped water, and the little Ginners beck which runs down the yard was the only source, from which it all had to be carried. When the Battys moved in, an ancient custom of the manor was re-enacted. Nine neighbours came, each with a pair of plough horses and a plough, and in no time at all the arable land was ready for sowing. A celebratory dinner for the hungry men followed at the end of the day.

Bryan's two girls were called Ella and Annie, and now they lived nearer the school they were able to get home for lunch if they were quick about it. As they grew older they appreciated being nearer the centre of life on the fell. There was occasional waitress work at the Mason's Arms if coach parties came for a meal, and they learned step-dancing from the Barrows in the farm where Ella had been born, Goswick Hall. The

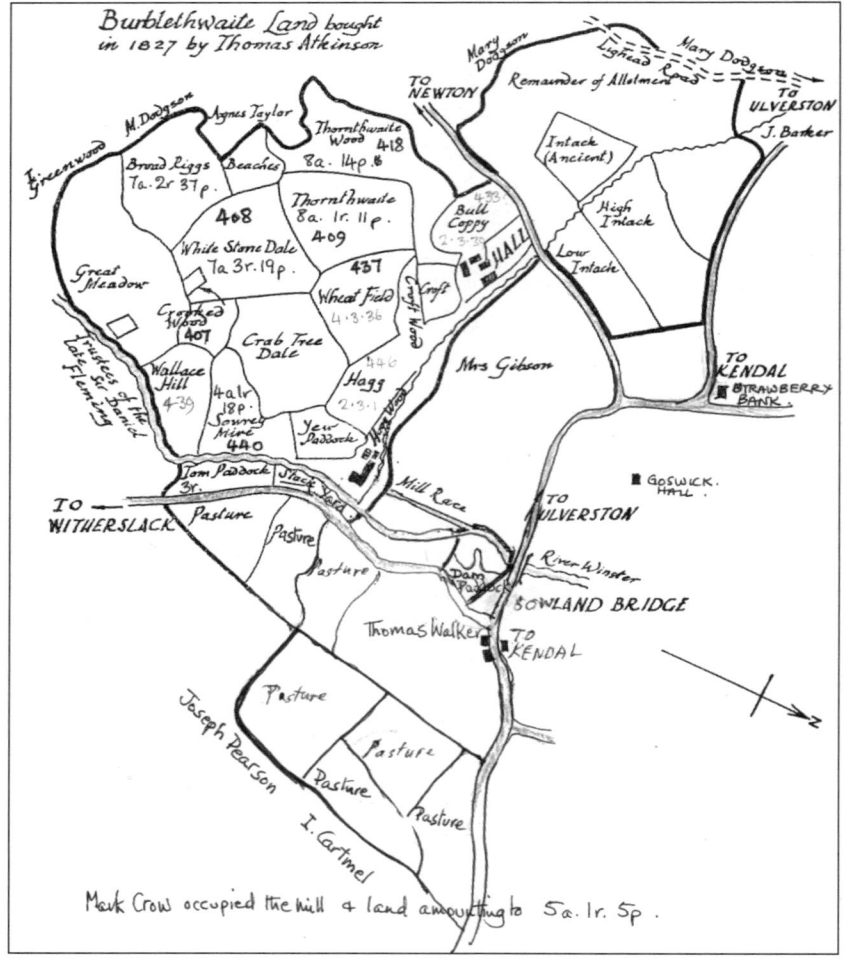

'retired farmer', he probably did not contribute very much to daily activities. In addition to her sons, Jane Barrow had a living-in farm servant, young John Churchman from Newton who was fourteen. Jane died in 1895 and at some time after 1909, the two sons moved to their own property at Goswick Hall.

By the 1920s, Bryan Batty junior was tenant at

only strict rule which Bryan imposed on his daughters was a ban on hunt balls, which were held in the school. He was not a kill-joy, but he was anxious for their safety. Apparently drink was always a problem, and violent fights were quite frequent. As we look back, we are inclined to think of a golden age when all was ordered and seemly, but it was not so.

Whilst the Battys farmed at Burblethwaite during the days of the depression, hiring fairs were still common. Ulverston was the nearest hiring centre, and the unemployed of Barrow-in-Furness sought farm work simply in order to have three good meals a day. Bryan used to go to Ulverston station to try and find his workers before they even got to the fair in the market place. His two girls used to take a day off and go in with him by train, but they took a mischievous delight in pretending to be for hire, turning down job offers with scorn. When their school days were over, Ella and Annie helped their parents at home. Among the many seasonal jobs was picking the damson crop. The work began very early in the morning when the dew was still heavy on the fruit, and Ella remembered the moisture running up their arms, cold and clammy. A firm from Barrow used to come twice a week for the fruit, but the Battys received only two pennies a pound for their crop.

In the second half of the twentieth century two generations of the Cleasby family have run Burblethwaite. A small close next to the farm was used to build a bungalow for 'Curly' Cleasby's sister and her husband, and they created a marvellous garden out of almost bare rock. Appropriately, they called their home 'Ginner's Burn'.

Burblethwaite Mill

THE association of a mill with a manor is commonplace, because it was another source of income for the lord. He supplied the capital outlay for the building and machinery, and then he leased it to the miller. The tenants of the manor were obliged to have their corn or oats ground there, and to desist from using their old hand querns. The miller ground the lord's grain without charge, also supplying him with malt for brewing. He might also keeps the poultry for the manor, or even provide eels from the mill dam. Payment depended on local arrangements, but we do not know what these were at Burblethwaite. By 1812, the customary tenants had to pay one shilling mill rent, so maybe this exempted them from mulcture, or 'mouter' as it was called in dialect. This form of payment to the miller was one scoop out of each sack which he ground, and in other parts of Cumbria it was called a toll-fat. The size of the scoop was not regulated, but was a matter of local custom. In Ambleside, this system was still in use in the 1830s.

In parallel with the Burblethwaite mill was the iron forge. Its existence is known from 1682 where it is mentioned in a sale to Sir Christopher Philipson, but it may have been in operation for a long time before that. The fuel would have been charcoal from the local woodlands and indeed, the adjoining property is called Collinfield, or the coaling field where the charcoal was made.

In 1696, the forge was lying idle, and a letter at

Levens Hall from Colonel Grahme's agent at the time, states this it ought to yield £10 a year. Even allowing for the very different monetary values of that time, this was only equal to about £85 today (2005), so it was not a major source of income. Myles Sands, who owned the Cunsey forge on his Graythwaite estate, had been instructed to manage it. This was the year in which the hall was mortgaged as an investment for Lady Katharine Darnley, and when William Robinson took up the reins in about 1700, he solved the problem of the forge by leasing it to the Backbarrow and Cunsey companies. This is the same William Robinson who bought the hall, though one document says 'of Staveley in Cartmel', and another says 'of Fell Foot'. In his will of 1759, William Robinson of Burblethwaite Hall named many of his relations, and from this it appears that he had no children of his own, and no wife. He had a nephew, John of Newby Bridge, to whom he left all his property in Staveley, but on the condition that he paid £200 to William's brother, John of Watermillock. In all, the bequest of money totalled over £4,000, which was wealth indeed on Cartmel Fell. Apart from owning land and premises, there is no clue as to how William Robinson amassed this fortune.

By that time Mr Robinson owned the forge; it was already old and in need of repair. This was done in 1713, and again in 1722 but was said to have ceased working by 1731. Edward Cranage or Cranege of Staffordshire had been brought in to manage it in the preceeding years, but the Backbarrow and Cunsey companies' lease did not expire until 1762. The Cranage family were well known around Coalbrookdale later in the eighteenth century, Thomas marrying a cousin of Abraham Darby II, and George his brother being foreman at Coalbrookdale, but it seems that the family links with the iron industry went further back. The ironmaster Isaac Wilkinson had moved from Backbarrow to Bersham near Wrexham. He had business connections with all the other ironmasters in the Severn area and it seems probable that by networking, he had recommended the appointment of Edward Cranage to Burblethwaite, but this is only supposition. The Cranages of the Severn valley were Methodists, but Edward had his five children were baptised at Crosthwaite parish church, one daughter and four sons, and a stillborn baby was buried in 1733. He died in 1737 when his oldest child, Elizabeth, was only ten.

The mill used the same water source as the forge, and an interesting link with the iron industry can be seen in the roof of what is now the garage, but was once the floor of the malt kiln. The ceiling is made of perforated iron tiles through which warm air could pass from underneath and a similar floor can be seen at the Heron corn mill at Beetham, but there the tiles are made of pottery. The iron floor must have been the very latest in technology at the time of its installation.

The folk who leased the mill and forge are not much in evidence in the Burblethwaite papers, and it is largely through parish registers and the censuses that we can glimpse their comings and goings. In 1769, there is an entry for baptism of Ann, daughter of James and Sarah Kelty of the mill. Kelty has a Scottish ring to it, but by 1777 the local name of Swainson was entered, when William and Katherine christened their daughter Dorothy. After this date, there is a big gap in available information for the millers, but a family of Crowes were in occupation in 1814.

When the property was auctioned in 1827, George

Jenkinson and his brother William were the tenants, with 20 years left of their lease. This was not renewed, but among the papers there is a receipt for £31.10s., for ten months rent of the mill up to 18 May 1828. Matters must have got out of hand because at the end of the Jenkinsons' tenure, £52 was spent on distraint. Their goods were sold and one of the Jenkinsons went to prison, but no christian name is given.

In 1833, Isabella and Henry Mason were at the mill and christened their daughter Jane in that year, then they had another daughter Frances in 1836, but their subsequent children were born at Goswick Hall. Isabella was related to the next tenants of the mill, and after six daughters, her son, born in 1849, was christened James Henry Mounsey. The 1841 and 1851 censuses enumerate the Mounsey family. George, aged 65 in 1851, calls himself a farmer, and his son Thomas is the corn miller. None of them was born in Lancashire, but there is much evidence that millers were a roving class, and bettered themselves by moving and negotiating milling terms. In fact, the Mounsey family came from the Bampton area, the first George having been born at Widewath in 1772, but by 1841, he had arrived at Burblethwaite Mill via Sedbergh, Wigton, Holm Cultram, Dumfries and Orton. We know this because of his children's birth-places. George was farming the mill lands at this date, though he was of retiring age as we might now think, that is 65 according to the census, but actually 68. His son Thomas was the miller, but ten years later, another son, John, had assumed that role.

The Mounseys spread out into the district for several generations as George the elder had at least seven children. Isabella, the sister of the two milling brothers and born in 1810, was living just up the fell at Goswick Hall. Their first-born, Jane, was living with her grandparents at the mill in 1841, a common practice when walls were bulging with younger children. There is photograph of John Mounsey's family, his wife Ellen being centre-stage, taken at the occasion of his granddaughter's wedding, after which she and her husband, Billy Blond, emigrated to Australia. John Mounsey, the younger son, eventually moved to Appleby, and the next tenant was George Hayton, who was described as 'farmer' in the 1871 census, with no mention of milling. He was born in Crook. By 1881 the Haytons had moved on, and the farmer/miller was Thomas Airey of Kirkby Lonsdale. He had two

Burblethwaite Mill, 1930s, by kind permission of the Armitt Library.

unmarried sons to help him, but when his wife died in 1888, he must have stayed on at the mill, because that was his address when he died, aged 83, in 1905. Probably, this was when the corn-mill became defunct. Large-scale industrial milling, together with transport by rail and steamship brought wheat from the New World. Cumbrian farmers had always faced an unequal struggle with the climate to grow good wheat, and Burblethwaite probably ground mostly oats, both for human and animal consumption.

The ownership of the whole estate passed to the Argles family, one of whom married a local girl, but their inheritance had been set in motion almost a century earlier. Thomas Atkinson purchased the property in 1828 and his address was then Brighton. He was not an off-comer however, having been born in Crosthwaite parish and then becoming a London merchant, but he invested his growing capital back in his home county. His sister Jane (probably of Spout House in Crosthwaite and Lyth), married Captain G. F. Argles, R.N., of Kent and they had two sons, Marsham and Frank. As Thomas Atkinson never married, his heirs were his Argles nephews and the children of his brother, John, whose daughter was called Susannah. Whether by family design or a happy coincidence, Frank Argles and Susannah Atkinson married, so the divided properties became united again.

The descendants of Susannah and Frank Argles built themselves a new house called Eversley at Leasgill near Heversham, and by 1910 they were living there, but they still held much property and land in Cartmel Fell, Crosthwaite and Lyth. Thomas Argles married Agnes Wakefield, sister of the more famous Mary, and the family association may have had some bearing on Mary's affectionate descriptions of the district.

Many people today have reason to be grateful to the Argles family, for they gave much to the local community, including Crosthwaite village hall. They also gave money and land to build a hall in Cartmel Fell, but although a collection was started, the Second World War intervened and the project had to be shelved. Inflation then overtook the fund, and it is now invested to provide maintenance for the present community hall, which is the former primary school.

The mill farmhouse and its buildings were bought with planning permission for conversions in 1972 by the Boothmans. The barns have been made into two attractive houses by their son, Tony Boothman who is an architect, the one nearer the road for his parents and the one behind for himself. The farmhouse behind was built for the miller some time around the end of the eighteenth or beginning of the nineteenth century. It has the neat appearance of a doll's house and is unlike the vernacular style of most homesteads on the fell. A drawing by another architect, Graham Hoggarth, perhaps dating from the 1930s, is in the Armitt Library at Ambleside. This shows the mill buildings and the picturesque pack-horse bridge, but the artist clearly had forgotten where he had made the drawing as the notes below it show.

A footpath used to go through the grounds of the mill complex, but it was inconvenient for the occupants as well as the walkers, who felt like intruders, so the path was diverted and a new bridge was built over the Winster to the south. At this point, a stile over the wall from the road affords a view of the old stack-yard, now a site for touring caravans. The bases of the stacks are raised humps in the adjoining field.

Collinfield

THIS farm is at a road junction, and just inside the boundary of old Lancashire. As is often the case, the house is tucked in under the hill, but faces towards the morning sun. 'Collin' is derived from coaling, i.e. the field where charcoal was made and in many early documents the spelling is Colling Field. As there was a forge below at Burblethwaite Hall, this arrangement for convenient charcoal must have been of mutual benefit. The forge was in decline in the seventeenth century, but in the sale of 1682, Burblethwaite still had an iron forge listed in its assets.

The first record of Collinfield we have found so far was in the Cartmel manorial records when in 1547 the entry was made: 'Willi Swaynson de Collinfield obit mortem at Cowmire.' Further information in this document shows that the son and heir was Robert Swainson, but one can only guess as to why his father died at Cowmire. Later that century, another William Swainson, yeoman, 'of Collingfield,' made his will in 1594. His son John was to have the tenement according to a marriage settlement, as his 'writtings' would show. His widow was called Isabel and he had at least three daughters, Janet, Agnes and Elizabeth. Janet was the wife of Christopher Atkinson, but Agnes was unmarried at the time of her father's death, so was given the free use of the back chamber during her lifetime. William Swainson may have been a charcoal burner, but he was also a farmer as his inventory discloses.

He had kye, (cattle) numbers unspecified, whies and a stott (heifers and a bullock). There were sheep, young and old, big and haver threshed and unthreshed (barley and oats) and hay. Amongst his implements was a churn and a fatt. This last item was a tub of some kind, and may have been for pickling meat such as salt beef or for brewing. The inventory was taken on 21 January, and rather disproves the theory that all cattle were slaughtered in the autumn, for lack of winter keep. Hay would have been the mainstay for foddering sheep, but barley and oat-straw could eke out the rations for cattle. The threshed grain would have been kept in the kist, which, the inventory tells us was in the firehouse, or living room. William Swainson was buried at Cartmel on 20 January, 1595.

The estate again descended to the oldest son, and the Cartmel parish register lists the burial of John Swainson senior of Collingfield on 6 May 1626. His son, John junior, was chapel warden for Cartmel Fell in 1634, and his accounts show that he travelled to Kendal (about eight miles) on parish business at a cost of 6d. In the previous year, John had sold half of the Collinfield acreage to his neighbour, Thomas Knipe of Burblethwaite Hall. This left the Swainsons with about 30 acres, the farmstead and the buildings, so the manorial rent was reduced to five shillings.

In the Cromwellian survey of 1650, John Swainson's rental for Collinfield was listed in two parts: '1s.5d. with 7d. Knowing silver, and 2s. 3d. with 9d. Knowing silver.'

John Swainson was buried on 18 December 1660 at Cartmel. His will expressed the wish that he be buried 'as near the aisle church door as conveniently may be.' His wife Frances was described as 'my now wife', implying former marriage, and she was to have her widow-right from the estate and the firehouse with all the rooms under that roof, with one half of all my houses, for life. After Frances's decease, the heir, George would inherit the estate, but within four years of his father's death, he had to pay a total of £75, divided between his brothers, Rowland and James, and his sisters, Agnes and Jane. It seems that the Swainsons were still charcoal burners at this period, as when John died, his inventory included coal-rakes and barrows, but there were small luxuries such as pewter dishes and linen sheets and the total value of his belongings was £81.10s., considerably more than a subsistence farmer of the day. His debts however amounted to £42.3s., £6.14s. of which was money belonging to the church, on which John paid five per cent interest.

George died in 1672, only twelve years after his father, and he left his wife Juliana with four young daughters under ten. She was granted administration of his goods and had to give a bond to the consistory court that she would bring up her husband's children. The parish accounts show that in 1696, she, like her father-in-law, had borrowed from the parish funds and held £8, on which she paid the interest. In that account, her name is spelt more or less as their Norse forebears might have written it - Swenson.

John Strickland of Rusland was the next owner. His first wife had died, leaving him with a son, Thomas, who was baptised at Colton in 1679. John married again in 1698 to Jennett Wilson at Colton and they had three more children, Timothy, Mary and James. The couple must have moved to Cartmel Fell soon after the marriage, because in 1701, John was churchwarden for his estate at Collinfield and in subsequent years was twice overseer of the poor. When he made his will, John was 68 and thought himself very aged, so in 1715 the estate went to Thomas, the oldest son, but he had to pay his siblings £175. If he refused, the estate was to be sold by the trustees and the legacies thus paid, but Thomas must have found the necessary sum, as he became the next owner.

As with many other single farms on the fell and elsewhere, Collinfield appears to have been more than one household in days gone by. In the Cromwellian survey of 1650, several names come under the Collinfield heading, and in 1664, James Harrison bought back the other half of Collinfield from the Knipes of Burblethwaite. Almost certainly they were part of the large clan which held many farms in Cartmel Fell in the sixteenth and seventeenth centuries, spreading out from Hartbarrow as the generations increased. Indeed, one of them witnessed William Swainson's will, so they may have been related. The Harrisons seem to have had two generations at least in Collinfield, as James christened his sons William and Thomas in 1668 and 1673 respectively, but James's first wife must have died, because in 1685, James Harrison of Collinfield married Elizabeth Barrow, widow of Ayside. The older children had been baptised at Cartmel, but this second wedding was at the Height Quaker meeting house. There had been Barrows at Height for generations, and the implication is that the Quaker influence had spread from there. James must have been a serious convert, because four years after marrying Elizabeth, he applied to have his house at Collinfield registered as a Quaker meeting house. This was duly confirmed as such at

Lancaster quarter sessions in 1689. It seems rather odd that the well established, custom-built Height meeting house had competition only three miles away, but the Quaker flame was sweeping through the area. James died about 1693 and his oldest surviving son, Rowland, inherited the estate.

Two sons were born to Rowland at Collinfield, James and his father's namesake, but for whatever reason, the estate was sold to John Gibson, a house carpenter. The transaction must have taken place before 1701, because in that year, John Gibson was listed in the parish records as chapel warden for his estate at Collinfield. The following year, John Gibson, yeoman, married Sarah Robinson. The couple had four children, Thomas (1703), John (1706), Elizabeth (1708) and William (1712). We learn the details from John Gibson's will of 1722, in which he states that he added to the holding by purchasing two closes called Back Corkerhow and others from Thomas Strickland, son of John, deceased, and also a house at Corkerhow. This is now one of the house names that has been lost, but a horseshoe shaped enclosure called Cawker How is shown on the 1888-1893 O.S. map, just to the north east of Lightwood and it contains several fields. Any buildings have long since been obliterated and were most likely used as a quarry for other buildings nearby. Another possibility is that this house was Gowk How, now called Goswick Hall.

The detailed inventories of the seventeenth and eighteenth centuries give us an insight into the worldly goods of the deceased, and these in turn can mirror a way of life. In John Gibson's assets were two separate lots of apples, indicating sizeable orchards. There was dried beef worth five shillings, a quantity of wool and eight hanks of spun yarn. Among the sacks was a window-cloth, used for winnowing the grain. The threshed oats or barley were tossed in the air from the cloth, and the draught from the open barn doors blew away the chaff. Many old barns have (or had) opposing double doors, so that when the wind was right, a through draught could be used to advantage. The farm animals included a horse valued at a guinea, a cow worth £2, two stirks and three heifers, fifteen hogs at two shillings apiece and 27 old sheep worth £5. This was approximately the same level of stocking as William Swainson's at the close of the sixteenth century.

John Gibson left his estate to the elder son, Thomas. A younger brother, William was to have £30 out of the estate, but if he died before reaching the age of 21, the money was to go to the poor of Cartmel Fell and chapel stock for apprentice money. Interestingly, one of the witnesses to the will was Jonas Barber, the great clockmaker, who lived at that time in Bowland Bridge. It would seem that William Gibson did not die before attaining his majority, as William of Collinfield appears in subsequent decades.

Sarah Gibson, widow of John of Collinfield was buried in 1751, but another Sarah Gibson, also widow of John was buried in 1759, so it would seem that several tiers of the family were living together. William Gibson was constable for Collinfield in 1734, and grave in 1735, and soon after this he bought back the other estate at Collinfield from the heirs of Thomas Strickland. He paid a surrogate, Rowland Rawlinson to take his turn as chapel warden in 1748 and 1749 but earlier, in 1740, he was chapel warden for Chapel House, and in 1741 was overseer of the poor for his estate at Lightwood. Although everyone had to take their allotted turn at these parish offices, substitutes could be arranged, and it might be that William Gibson was a literate and able man who shouldered other people's burdens. Alternatively, he was amassing his fortune in real estate. A quarter of a century later, he was overseer of the poor for his two estates at Collinfield, in 1766 and 1767.

William Gibson did not marry until October 1752 when he was nearly 40. His bride was Hannah Dawson, the daughter of John and Agnes of Warton, and their first son John was born nine months later. This child died of smallpox in 1766 aged thirteen and his sister Hannah had been buried two years earlier. The couple had two other sons, Robert and Thomas but bereavement struck the family again when Sarah died in 1782 and then Thomas died in 1786, aged only 28. William outlived them all and died in July 1795, aged 85.

The Gibsons must have had a number of cottages which were let to less affluent members of the community such as farm labourers, spinsters, widows and tradesmen. Their names crop up in parish registers and documents from the parish chest. One was Catherine, the widow of Robert Thompson of Winster and she died in 1800 at Collinfield. The Thompsons had been married at Cartmel in 1755 and seemed to be childless as Catherine's brother, Thomas Cloudsdale, was the administrator of her goods. Another such tenant was Agnes Crowe, spinster daughter of Joseph Crowe and Agnes Swainson. She had been baptised in 1774 when her parents were farming Little Thorphinsty, but her father had been born at Greenthorn, just along the road from Collinfield. Agnes died in 1850 leaving her clothes, £50 and all the household furniture 'now at Collinfield' to her sister, Nancy Dawes. The remainder of her belongings were to be divided equally between her brother Joseph, her sister Elizabeth and Nancy Dawes.

When the Burblethwaite estate was sold in 1827, an estate map was drawn up showing the ownership of neighbouring properties. Both parts of Collinfield were still in the hands of the Gibsons, but only one was farmed by them. The other half was let to Mary Hird, widow of William, who gave 1s.8d. as her half-yearly contribution to the curate's salary.

William Hird was the younger son of Henry and Margaret, formerly of Grasmere, but William was baptised at Crosthwaite in April 1766. He had a younger brother John who was born circa 1770 and a sister Agnes. His father ultimately inherited Moorhow from his cousin, William Harrison, the man who was tried for murdering his wife Alice in 1759. It seems that Henry had a musical bent and may have played some instrument akin to a penny whistle. A book of manuscript music with a martial flavour was found at the Post Office at Bowland Bridge, inscribed 'Henry Hird, Moorhow, 1815.' The arrangements were for a limited range of notes. This book must have arrived at Bowland Bridge from Collinfield, when the Walker family owned both properties.

William and Mary Hird had six children between 1797 and 1810, but four of them remained single, John and Agnes helping their widowed mother to run the farm after their father William died in 1818, aged only 51. Agnes was the dairymaid at Collinfield, and probably was grateful to receive only her keep, but she was the sole legatee of her cousin Betty of Moorhow in 1833, and when her uncle John died at Moorhow in 1843, he left her £50. Margaret, Agnes's sister, had gone to Moorhow to housekeep for their uncle, and she received £200 from his estate. Money was left in trust for his niece Mary Kitchen's daughters if they reached the age of 21 and were legitimate, and Mary herself had a bequest of £80. Dorothy, the third daughter, had married Christopher Birkett in 1835 and as they farmed Moorhow for their uncle, he bequeathed them the estate there. William junior died in 1823, aged only eighteen so he was not mentioned in the will.

Mary Hird had married William Kitchen of Kirkby Ireleth in 1828. William became the farm labourer at Collinfield, so the Hirds managed to find occupations for all their family around their various holdings. All seemed to be working out satisfactorily, but William died after only eleven years of marriage, leaving his wife with five daughters and no money. The census for 1841 labels Mary as 'Pauper', but at least she was living under the wing of her family with three of her daughters, Sarah aged twelve, Dorothy aged six and two-year-old Agnes. Her eight-year-old daughter Margaret was living up the fell at Moorhow with her uncle John Hird and her aunt Dorothy Birkett, so the family was taking care of their own. Mary Kitchen took on the role of housekeeper to her brother John Hird at Collinfield when their mother died, aged 84 in 1848, and by 1851, they had a farm servant, Edward Harrison living in with them. Although Mary Kitchen's unhappy life seemed to be settling down, it was not for long. In 1854, her oldest daughter Sarah died aged 25, followed by Agnes two years later when she was eighteen. In 1859, Dorothy had an illegitimate daughter whom she christened Sarah, then in 1865, poor Mary came to the end of her troublesome life, aged 57. The two surviving daughters married into the same family of Harrisons. Mary married William, the blacksmith at Strawberry Bank and Margaret married his brother Edward, who had been their farm labourer at Collinfield in 1851, but he too died young in 1865, aged only 34. The Hird history had an unpleasant way of repeating itself, as Margaret was left with five small children, just as her mother had been.

John Hird continued at Collinfield until his death, aged 72, in 1869. Then the tenancy was taken over by his nephew-in-law, Joseph Nicholson. In the 1871 census, Joseph Nicholson was the head of the household having been born in the neighbouring parish of Staveley. His wife Margaret was five years older, and it transpires that she was the widow of Edward Harrison, husbandman, returning to her birthplace when she married Joseph. Her first five children, had been born at Strawberry Bank in Cartmel Fell, but James, Edward and Isaac Nicholson, their younger half-brothers were born at Collinfield. Many photographs of this family and their descendants exist in the archive of the Cartmel Fell Local History Society. Margaret's daughter, Mary Harrison married Richard Walker of Bowland Bridge, and she ran the village shop for many years.

The farmhouse must have been bursting at the seams by 1881. The Nicholsons were still relatively young, he being 43 and she 48, and they had most of their joint families still living at home, that is four boys ranging from 24 to nine years, but also their daughter Mary Walker and her new husband Richard with their infant son Thomas, and John Nicholson, Joseph's bachelor brother. In addition to the family were two farm servants who lived in - a dairy maid and a farm lad of fifteen. Eventually, when they were in their fifties, the Nicholsons moved to Foxfield, taking their grandson David Walker with them. A young family of Hoggarths took over Collinfield some time before 1891, Lancelot and Sarah Jane, with three small children and a farm lad. Another daughter was born in 1892 and was given the unusual name of Annice, a first for Cartmel Fell.

A tombstone in St. Anthony's churchyard is dedicated to William and Sarah Jane Atkinson of Collinfield and their son Frank. The Inland Revenue survey of 1909-10 shows that the Atkinsons were already in residence at Collinfield. The house particulars were: 'Parlour, kitchen, back kitchen, dairy, pantry, 3 bedrooms, box room. Buildings, stone and slate, fair. Land fair to rough in places. 65 acres.' The owner was Thomas A. Argles of Eversley, Milnthorpe. William died in 1934 aged 71, and his wife in 1923 aged 67.

John and Lavinia Stott took the farm briefly between 1939 and 1945 and had two children in that time, then James and Jessie Wright followed them, moving from Thorphinsty Hall cottage. Whether they christened him for the farm or if it was coincidence, they called their son Collin in 1947.

Bowland Bridge

INSTEAD of separating the individual dwellings, it is more convenient to treat the hamlet as a whole. It is the nearest thing to a village that the township of Cartmel Fell can boast, and yet it is across the Winster, in another parish, and once in another county. Today, it is the centre for information and the 'Westminster Bridge', where folk meet at the shop or the pub and news is exchanged. This sort of social intercourse might once have taken place at the smithy.

The name of the hamlet could have several interpretations. The River Winster does a loop at this point, flowing west before turning south to go under the bridge, so this could be the bow. Bo is sometimes an element of a word describing cattle, or objects and places pertaining to cows, as in bovine, or bovate, which was the amount of land that could be ploughed by an ox in a year, or boskins, i.e. cattle stall divisions. If this course of reasoning is persued, in late mediaeval times maybe the cattle occupied the valley land, and the priory sheep took the rough grazing on the fell. Brierly's *Dictionary of Lakeland Place Names* suggests that Bowland was the name of the first bridge builder, perhaps from the trough of Bowland? *Place Names of Westmorland* suggests that the name could derive from *boga,* meaning an arched bridge or bend. The old Norse for a hut was *buo,* so perhaps there was an early settlement of Norsemen here. Lastly, and much more fancifully, could this have been the land of archers? We know how deep the grooves are on the church door jambs, where arrows were alleged to have been sharpened. Did they manufacture bows alongside the smithy where the arrows could be tipped? There was a bloom smithy at Burblethwaite to provide the iron, only a few minutes away - perhaps an archaeological clue will turn up one day to clarify matters.

There are three buildings of perhaps seventeenth century origin, all within a stone's-throw of the bridge. One of these was where the blacksmiths lived, conveniently close to the River Winster for tempering the iron. Once, the smith would have serviced the pack horses and the local farmers' many requirements, from shoeing oxen and horses, to making ploughshares, gate-hangings, nails or frying-pans. We know from the Crosthwaite registers that the smithy already existed in 1632. Christopher Garnett christened his daughter Annas in August of that year at Crosthwaite, and another daughter of his was baptised Janet in December 1635. On that occasion, his abode is called Bridge End, and was probably the cottage on the corner, now called Rose Cottage. Although the front of this house has been modernised and changed, the back is obviously of great age, with a piece of bottle glass in one of the windows. Almost twenty years later, in 1654, Christopher Garnett christened another daughter, Elizabeth, but this time his profession of smith is recorded, though not his dwelling. He may have had a son to follow him, because there is an Anthony Garnett who christened his son William in 1705, but no trade is given, and only Bowland Bridge as an address. Later in the century, the smith was John Thompson and rather unusually, when recording the baptism of John's first daughter Mally in 1786, the clerk has entered full particulars of his wife Mally, as daughter of Robert Mandle of Wythburn.

As was often the case, there were two blacksmiths at Bowland Bridge in John Thompson's time and very likely there was more than one in the Garnett's time too, but as there are no references in the parish registers, it is hard to check. On the opposite side of the road to the smithy, Corner Cottage as it is now called, may have housed the second family of smiths. Shoeing horses can be a one-man job, but for the manufacture of large objects, two are essential. Richard Robinson of Bowland was entered as 'smith' when he christened his son John at Crosthwaite in 1790 and he was contemporary with John Thompson so they must have been in business together.

Contemporary with Richard Robinson's family, James and Elizabeth Hodgson's children were growing up at the inn. When Betty was christened in 1790, her father was described as 'labourer', but four years later, when George was born, James was by this time called landlord. In 1798, his namesake was christened, but this time James is described as 'farmer', so he most likely combined all these occupations as did the Walkers who were owners of the inn, and they may well have all lived under the same roof. Little Betty Hodgson grew up at the inn, but married James Harrison who was the blacksmith from around the corner, so the Walkers were filling the hamlet with their extended families.

At the beginning of the eighteenth century, there were probably only three or four dwellings at Bowland Bridge, and there were only six until 2004. We can deduce where the smiths and the innkeeper lived, but which was the house occupied by Jonas Barber, the first of the great clockmakers in the Winster valley? The early clocks are inscribed 'Boulan Brig' and three of Jonas's children were christened at Crosthwaite, the last, Margaret, in 1727. After his removal to Bryan Houses at Winster, his life is fairly well documented, but little seems to be known about the years in which he worked at Bowland Bridge. He might have been a tenant or a lodger at Corner Cottage, or it is quite possible that he lodged with the smiths as a young man with little capital, and he could have shared a corner of the smithy as a workshop. The blacksmith in the early eighteenth century was Anthony Garnett, and though this was not Jonas's father-in-law of the same name, the two families may well have been related. The only other house where Barber could have lived is the shop, but when this was completely renovated by the present owner, not a single scrap of brass, a screw, or anything that could be linked to clock-making was found under the floorboards or anywhere else, and the house had to be virtually gutted. Although the Barber children were baptised in Crosthwaite, no address is given in the register, so there are no clues there. Whichever house the Barbers occupied, it must have had room for a modest timber store, as accounts found at Height show that Jonas occasionally dealt in wood. It is thought that the Barber family lived for about fourteen years at Bowland Bridge, before they moved up-river in 1727. Bryan Houses, their new home, cost £212, which might have been the equivalent of 85 long-case clocks of the period. Most inventories taken at the death of a farmer who owned such a timepiece, valued them at around £2.10s. in the first half of the eighteenth century.

The history of the Barber clockmakers has been written by Bryan Cave Brown Cave, a descendant of the Birkets of Birket Houses. He found that the family originated from the Skipton area, but that one, Jonas senior, had gone to London and become a member of the clockmakers' guild. Jonas the younger was his nephew, but the reason for his moving to Bowland Bridge in the early eighteenth century is undocumented. He had no local competition certainly. Until this period, very few clocks appear in local farmers' inventories, though Elizabeth Hutton of Thorphinsty Hall had one in 1690. Very little personal detail has come down to us about the Barbers, but when Jonas of Winster made his will in 1765, he wanted his wife to have one of his clocks for herself. If the one already at Bryan Houses was not suitable, then Jonas junior was to make her a new eight-day version. Mrs. Barber had been Elizabeth Garnett, daughter of Anthony of High Mill, Winster.

Today, the inn is the largest of the group of white buildings in the hamlet. It seems to have been built about 1740, after the marriage of Thomas Walker to Hartbarrow's heiress, Elizabeth Bigland and has probably been a place of refreshment since the Kendal to Ulverston turnpike was opened in the 1750s. It had enough land to provide the owners a certain self-sufficiency, and most of the earlier innkeepers were also small farmers, but today the farm buildings have been cleared, or incorporated into the public house.

It is possible that the Birket family of Birket Houses owned the land and buildings at Bowland Bridge in the eighteenth century, because when Thomas Walker was admitted as tenant on 6 February 1733 at the manorial court baron in

Kendal, it was by deed from Myles Birket, merchant of Lancaster and a member of the Cartmel Fell family of that name. This was to begin the Walkers' occupation and ownership of Bowland Bridge, which continued for over 200 years.

Thomas Walker married Elizabeth Bigland of Hartbarrow in 1727, and it was probably her money which enabled them to become the owners of Bowland Bridge. She had inherited £30 from her uncle, Anthony Strickland of Hartbarrow and a further £80 from her father two years after her marriage. Thomas was the youngest brother of George Walker, the curate of Cartmel Fell from 1715 to 1758, their family originating in the Hawkshead area. Thomas's trade was that of shoemaker when he was executor of his brother's will and he died two years later in 1760, but his son Thomas carried on the family name at Bowland Bridge. The middle child of seven, two of whom had died in childhood, Thomas junior married Tamar Nicholson of Grasmere in 1759 and they had six children, four girls and two boys, Thomas and George. Thomas was the heir, but he seems to have been a bachelor and willed the properties to his brother's son, another George, born in 1801. The younger George was a forgeman at Backbarrow when he inherited Bowland Bridge, his father being a farmer of Colton, but he moved across the Westmorland boundary to take up his inheritance and from then, his occupation was that of shoemaker. It would seem that when his mother was widowed, she came to live with her son and his wife Jane at Bowland Bridge. Her burial in 1854 at Crosthwaite was registered as 'of Bowland Bridge.'

The inn, now known as the Hare and Hounds, was well established and used as a meeting place for official business by 1801, which was when the trustees of the Bryan Beck charity met there to take the tenders for a fifteen year lease. The innkeeper was then James Hodgson. This same man christened his son James in 1798, and was described as 'farmer' in the Crosthwaite parish register. Reference to the marriage register shows that James was actually son-in-law to Thomas and Tamar Walker, having married their eldest daughter Elizabeth, so maybe she ran the inn, even if her husband was nominally the licensee.

George, the ex-forgeman, had six children, and his heir was another Thomas, his first born, who was christened at the family church, Colton, in 1854, and he too followed the trade of a shoemaker. His first marriage was to Ann Thexton of Underbarrow, but she died after only two years of marriage, leaving one son, yet another George who later became a master mariner.

Thomas was re-married four years later to

CORNER COTTAGE.

Elizabeth Mattinson, who though born in Selside, was a servant at Thorphinsty Hall in 1851, the year before she married Thomas. Elizabeth became the mother of seven more children, and was said to have been the ruler of the household and the inn. A family recollection was that she used to keep a whip behind the bar to wield on customers who drank more than three pints of beer. It seems a strange strategy for sales promotion, but maybe it was a very strong home-brew, and she may have felt vulnerable, because her husband became blind in later life. Another family memory was that of the Sunday visit. The grandchildren were spruced up and taken across the road from the shop to visit their grandmother. She would then give them a cup of beer as a treat, saying that a drop of beer never hurt anyone.

When Thomas died in 1902, he left all the property at Bowland Bridge to Elizabeth. As she grew older, she must have decided to take life more quietly and retired from active life at the inn. A survey made for the Inland Revenue about 1911 shows that Elizabeth was still the freehold owner of the Hare and Hounds, but that she had a tenant, Robert Pearson who was on a five-year tenancy. His annual rent for the house was £18, and the orchard was a further £6. Elizabeth lived for two more years after the survey, and she left her properties to her heir, Richard, but with a life interest for his wife Mary, after whose death all the properties were to be sold.

The pattern of the menfolk following their own trade whilst the wives ran the inn seems to have continued down the generations, though with variations. Elizabeth and Thomas's eldest son Richard had a team of horses and was a wagoner. He lived over the road at what is now the post office, and his wife Mary began to keep a shop on the premises. The improved roads allowed wheeled traffic, so supplies could easily be delivered to the door and passing trade increased. In the late eighteenth and early nineteenth centuries, two weekly carriers plied between Kendal and Ulverston, in all weathers, and William Pearson of Borderside recalled their white-sheeted wagons, adding that they both died insolvent.

Richard Walker married Mary Harrison of Collinfield and their first son, Thomas, was born in 1881. They had seven more sons and a daughter Violet, who was her mother's successor at the shop, and Heber Walker, their fifth son, became the landlord of the Hare and Hounds in the 1930s, after it had been tenanted for a while.

Violet married Arthur Parkinson, remembered by his daughter Connie as a kindly, mild-mannered man. Terrible tragedy struck the family during the Second World War; Arthur was directing the milk lorry which was backing up to the stand where the milk kits were waiting to be loaded. For once, the lorry was left-hand drive, and the driver was unable to see Arthur behind him, and though this was a daily manoeuvre, he backed into him, with fatal injury.

It seems that the Parkinsons had many enterprises in operation for the good of the community. Apart from the shop, Violet ran an insurance business, she financing her customers until their half-yearly payments became due. She also organised 'Mystery Tours' on Sundays, in a charabanc from Frank Parker's in Grange which arrived at 9am and returned at 7pm. The Parkinsons had two daughters, Connie and Doris, who used to help in the shop at all hours and even if they came home on their bikes from a dance at 2am, they still had to fill paraffin cans for late customers.

The public telephone was a new-fangled affair in the 1930s, and Connie remembers having to operate the dangerous machine for wary farmers. She also had her first paid job, that of telephone-box maintenance. This was a monthly contract with the G.P.O. and entailed disinfection of the telephone, floor-sweeping and window-cleaning inside and out. In those days, there were hundreds of corners to contend with as the windowpanes were very small to deter vandals, but five shillings of her very own was worth the effort to Connie. (In the 1990s, B.T. paid only 50 pence per telephone kiosk cleaned.)

Within living memory the inn was still a farm, and it was the only practical way of feeding the travellers and their horses. No doubt the folk who came to the shop would call in over the road for refreshment, having walked or ridden some miles to get there. Some of the older people remember the days when there was no such thing as closing time, either for the shop or the inn. If you felt the need for a packet of pins or a jar of ale at 2am, you could have it willingly, the Walkers seemed to need no sleep. Mrs Gladys Dunn remembers the shop counter at the beginning of the twentieth century. Mrs Walker had slits cut into the counter for silver and copper. The money fell into a drawer below, and she would closely watch the children push their sweetie pennies through the slots, counting each ha'penny. Dried fruit or sugar was weighed out scrupulously, to the last currant or grain.

When the Inland Revenue surveyed the Hare and Hounds in 1910, the inspector made some marginal notes: 'Free house, Trade varies, might be a barrel a week for twenty week average. Not much spirit trade. Buildings, pigsty, barn, henhouse, 4 stall stable with loft over used as bark store shared with Walker. House, 4 bedrooms with dancing room, separate entrance up steps over kitchen, 2 sitting rooms, beer storeroom, smoke room & kitchen across passage. Small cellar, dark, not used. Pump water.' His valuation of the property was £350 with the orchard an extra £35.

The 'dancing room' referred to was the forerunner of a parish hall. Many functions were held there including children's dancing classes. Mrs Airey of Lakeside has a photograph of herself and her brother and sister, taken about 1920 where they are all dressed up for the dancing class, the girls all in white, with white shoes and stockings. Their brother was wearing a type of Eton suit with a sailor hat. These children had to make their way from Pool Bank on the Crosthwaite-Witherslack border to Bowland Bridge, but since they walked to Cartmel Fell school every day, they were accustomed to that daily excercise.

The drinking water was supplied by the pump, referred to in the Inland Revenue report, but the inn had what was then a great luxury, an indoor W.C., and this was operated from a tank of rainwater on the roof of the bathroom. In times of drought, the family put their guests first, and would repair to the privy in the garden, still to be seen behind the large box tree.

After nearly 200 years of owning the hamlet of Bowland Bridge, the Walkers' sway ended before the end of the Second World War. When Mary Walker died in 1943, her son Heber, (said to have been named for bishop Heber, the hymn-writer,) had been her tenant at the Hare and Hounds for thirteen

THE POST OFFICE AND SHOP

years. By the terms of Elizabeth Walker's will, her oldest son was to inherit the inn for his lifetime and that of his widow, but after their decease, the whole hamlet was to be sold and the moneys divided between her descendants. The hamlet was bought by Harold Vennard, an uncle of the last incumbent of Cartmel Fell, but that fact came as a complete surprise to Canon Greetham when he arrived in the district. At the end of the war in August 1945, Mr. Vennard was living at The High, overlooking the Winster valley and he instructed Jackson Stops & Staff to auction the entire hamlet of Bowland Bridge. The Hare and Hounds was described as having an entrance hall, sitting room, dining room, store-room, tap room and kitchen, all the downstairs rooms being licensed. There was also a farm and orchard of sixteen acres, with four excellent cottages, a detached house and shop. The Vennards had leased the various properties whilst they lived at the High, and the net rental for the whole was £117.2s.6d. a year. The shop was let for £10.8s. as was Corner Cottage, Miss Willan paid £6.16s.6d. a year and and the other two cottages were let on a weekly terms of 3s. and 4s.6d. Heber Walker moved to Selside to run the Plough Inn and farm, with his daughter and son-in-law, John Dodgson Phizacklea.

The inn had several owners after the hamlet was sold, one of the most famous being Peter Thompson, the Liverpool footballer. He was capped for England thirteen times, and a showcase displaying the caps and photographs was a great attraction for aspiring young lads. Until this time, the Hare and Hounds had altered little internally, with small rooms on a domestic scale. Peter Thompson greatly enlarged the bar area and made a separate dining room out of two smaller ones. Ten letting bedrooms were added where the dancing room had been, but holiday patterns were altering and there was seldom full occupancy.

The Thompsons sold to Honeycombe Leisure who installed managers, several of which came and went, and then in 2003, Adrian Parr bought the business. The superfluous bedrooms and the long bar have been converted into self-contained apartments, with completely new building at the back for further housing. The pub has reverted to a modest sized hostelry, with good food. At a stroke, the hamlet has more than doubled in size, but most of the new apartments are for second homes.

When the county council decided that the old Bowland Bridge was in need of renovation in 1991, they proposed to iron out the hump and make a level road surface. There were protests from all quarters on several grounds and in the end the bridge was strengthened with a concrete arch underneath and replaced as before. The residents of the hamlet were relieved, because the hump provides a traffic-calming device which is far more picturesque than 'sleeping policemen', and the character of the little bridge is unchanged. The arch is so acute that on one occasion a very long tour bus became shipwrecked on the apex, see-sawing gently for four hours until a tug could tow it into calmer seas. This was another reason to be grateful for retaining the bridge's form, as large coaches cannot use it, and the roads are quite unsuited to such traffic. Whilst the excavations for new footings were taking place, a huge pile of oyster shells was unearthed, just beside the river. Without any dating techniques, it cannot be said how old they were, but their position is puzzling. If they were debris from the inn, why did they take them so far away to discard? Possibly because of the smell, but middens were much closer to the dwelling house than this tip. Were they then discarded long before the inn existed? Another question arises from this find. If the shells date from before the railways, where were the oyster beds? Was there perhaps an industry in the Kent estuary?

The bridge had undergone several renovations in its time. Originally it would have been a narrow pack-horse arch, probably with no parapet. With the coming of the turnpike, it had to be widened, and until the complete re-make in 1991 one could see the addition from underneath, as one can at the bridge over the Arndale beck, below Lobby Bridge. Bowland Bridge has carved stone tablets on either side, one naming the bridge itself, the other marking the parish boundaries, but it also divided Westmorland from Lancashire until 1974.

A little further up the Crosthwaite road is a field which floods very quickly after heavy rain. Sometimes there is a small lake for days, or even weeks in a wet season. According to William Pearson, writing at the beginning of the nineteenth century, this used to be a fully fledged tarn, and when he was a youth, he used to catch pike in there, using piebald mice as bait on night lines. He does not say where or how he caught the piebald mice. Apparently, decayed vegetable matter accumulated, and quite quickly the tarn silted up and became grazing land. However, two days of November rain can transform the landscape to how it looked 200 years ago, but the tarn's name is now forgotten.

Goswick Hall

THE element *Gos* usually refers to geese, but early indentures and wills show that this farm was originally called Gowk How, or Gowk Hall. Gowk, in dialect is a cuckoo or a horse collar, and How is a rounded hill, so there are several possibilities for the derivation. Possibly a saddler plied his trade up on the hill, or the little copse below was the haunt of cuckoos. The parish registers show Gowk and Gaulk How up to the last quarter of the eighteenth century, and in 1750, when James Bigland was chapel warden, he spelt it Goukhow.

The earliest reference to be found so far, is in the will of Robert Harrison of 'Gawckehow', dated 24 January 1587. His wife was already dead and he wished to buried nearby in Cartmel Church. Michael was his son and heir and was to inherit the firehouse and barn, all other housing and the orchard. The other sons, Christopher, Anthony and Richard were to have 6s.8d. apiece, but his daughter Isabel was to have £5 and enough beasts to set up a small farm. These included a little ox calf, a black stirk, a little bull calf, a brown cow, a great black cow, ten of the best gimmer sheep all to be in lamb, and hay and straw enough for her beasts and sheep. She also received his best cloak. The sons all had assorted bits of their father's best clothes assigned to them, and Michael's children were to have a gimmer sheep 'if they be spare.' Grandson Robert was to have three sheep and a little jacket. Isabel seems to have been especially favoured as she had in addition to money and stock, a great kettle, six pieces of pewter, two coverlets, two sheets and the best brass pot.

John Swainson was in residence some forty years later and he made his will in 1638. This yeoman was a considerable land-owner, and he bequeathed properties which were all within a short walk of each other. These included Haycote, Gowke How, Light Thwaite (Lightwood), Newhall (unidentified, but maybe at Staveley-in-Cartmel) and the 'tenement he dwells on', this last probably being Collinfield as other later Swainson wills relate to it. John Swainson's wife was pregnant when he made his will, so all kinds of provisos were made, according to the sex of the unborn child. If it were a boy, he should inherit the un-named tenement of his father's, if a girl, she would be heiress to Gookhow (*sic*). In the period before the daughter came of age, her mother Jenet was to have the 'Fyerhouse' at Gowk How and enough land to maintain a cow, summer and winter. She had to pay a rent however, but the amount was to be at the discretion of the supervisors of the will.

There are entries in the Cartmel registers for several families in later decades. Richard Crackell baptised his daughter Dianah in 1692, and then it was spelt Gookhaw. In 1705, the property was still known by its old name. Dorothy Bateman of Gaukehow was buried at Cartmel in November of that year, and subsequently, John Brittain had his children baptised between 1710 and 1721, and he buried his daughter Mabel.

The yeomen of the parish did their duties as constable, overseer of the poor, chapel warden, etc. in rotation, and if they owned more than one property, they had to do duty for each. In 1768, Martin

Harriman did duty as overseer of the poor for Gowk How, though he actually lived at Lightwood, so possibly these two farms were still in joint ownership as when John Swainson owned them 130 years earlier.

There were many different surnames of the occupants in fairly quick succession, so one might infer that these were tenant farmers rather than yeomen. In the second half of the eighteenth century, parish records show baptisms of Theckstons, Turners and Walkers, but by the 1790s the name changes to Goswick, though Cartmel bishops' transcripts still refer to Gouk How in 1799 when Christopher Turner was baptised. How or why the change occurred is now unfathomable.

The enclosure award shows that in 1814, a Miss Harrison was the owner of Goslick *(sic.)* and though she occupied the woodland, the family of Thornborrows (variously spelt) lived and farmed the estate throughout the first part of the 19th century. Anthony Thornborrow was the tenant of Miss Harrison and made frequent successful bids for charity lands on the fell. He seems to have been unable to sign his name to the various agreements, but must have been a clever business man to manage all his rented properties. His mother lived with them at Goswick, but Anthony, his wife Margaret and his mother Agnes all died between 1832 and 1837.

Henry and Isabella Mason then came to farm the 41 acres. Isabella was a sister to the Mounsey brothers at Burblethwaite mill, and she produced four daughters before the son and heir, James Henry Mounsey Mason, was born in 1849. Isabella died in 1864 aged 55, and Henry moved to the Lound where he died in 1875. Sadly, their only son died the year after his mother, aged only sixteen.

A family of Thwaites were in residence when the 1871 census was taken, but by the next census they had been succeeded by John Bowness who was a bachelor. In 1885 he purchased Blewthwaite, though continued to live at Goswick. This was the only son of John and Margaret Bowness who had formerly farmed Pool Garth. He died in 1901 aged 77 and was buried at Cartmel Fell. A fairly quick succession of young families passed through the farm in the early 20th century when John and Richard Barrow were the owners. Eventually, they and their sister went to live there and were famed for their pack of beagles. A hunting song was composed about the Goswick Hall beagles but few remember it now. The Barrows had no children of their own, but they adopted Rhoda Harrison who came from a family with thirteen children, and as times were very hard, Rhoda was lucky to find a home where food was regularly on the table. She became the whipper-in for the beagles and eventually, heiress to the estate.

After the Second World War, James and Jessie Wright became Rhoda's tenants and later bought the farm, dividing and enlarging the accommodation to house three generations. James was the caretaker at Gill Head for nineteen years before retiring, and he was also on the parish council.

Evidently, the old barn at Goswick was used for social events. A poster survives from 1913 which advertises a dance from 8pm to 4am with music by Cannon's Quadrille Band. Admission was 1s. and the proceeds were to be given to a fund for a parish room for Cartmel Fell. The fund never kept pace with inflation, and though land for a hall was given by the Argles family, the parish used the school when it became redundant.

Mason's Arms or Strawberry Bank

STRAWBERRY Bank is the hillside where the road from Bowness meets the turnpike from Kendal to Ulverston, and there have been several theories as to why the 'Masons' was so called. One is that this was where the members of Masonic Lodges met at a point equi-distant from Kendal, Ulverston and Bowness at a time when such meetings were prohibited. Another is that the Mason family of Goswick Hall may have either frequented or financed it in the mid-nineteenth century, but a very likely explanation is that the inn was tenanted and later owned by William Tyson, who was a stone mason, as the 1829 Parson and White Directory shows. The name 'Mason's Arms' seems to date from this time. The censuses and other documents merely refer to Strawberry Bank until around 1861, when both names are bracketed in the census. To many folk on the fell, their local is still simply 'The Strawberry'.

As with the Hare and Hounds in the valley below, it seems that the inn was established to cater for the needs of passing trade on the new turnpike road. Until the mid-eighteenth century, traffic going west from Kendal went via Witherslack, up Tow Top and then dropped down to High Newton. This was an alarming journey in a wheeled vehicle as the gradients are very steep and the corners sharp. The new road over Cartmel Fell via Gummers How must have seemed a slightly gentler route for nervous travellers.

The first evidence of a house at Strawberry Bank comes from the deeds. In a conveyance to Isaac Rawlinson, dated 1754, he was granted admittance on 31 December, so one imagines that there was a merry night that New Year's Eve. The fact that admittance was granted indicates an already extant building, but if this had previously passed from father to son, no deeds would have been generated.

In 1798 Isaac Rawlinson died and his will left the property to John Rawlinson, who conveyed it two years later to John Allenby, the curate of Cartmel Fell. It is unlikely that the Allenbys ever lived at Strawberry Bank, as they had their own house at Thorneythwaite. John Allenby's only son died in 1791, but he had several daughters and Charlotte seems to have been the heiress. Before she married George Williamson Reveley of Orton in 1832, she and her father had had a deed of feoffment drawn up for Strawberry Bank. The house was already licensed to sell liquor by this date, and the tenant was William Tyson. Public auctions and meetings had been held there at least since 1831, and William Tyson had to pay a peppercorn rent if demanded, to the Reveleys.

In 1838, the whole property was put up for auction on the premises, and the tenant became the owner, but only three years later he died, aged 67. William's widow Margaret Tyson was bequeathed the inn for her lifetime, and in the 1851 census she was described as innkeeper and grocer, probably with the first shop to trade on Cartmel Fell. When Margaret died in 1860, the business went to Betty Swainson, their niece who had lived with them as a servant for many years, their son having died in

1826, aged 25. The deed names the cottages occupied by Edward Harrison and Robert Atkinson, the inn with the barn, stable, garden, orchard and inclosure of land.

Two cottages are attached to the inn and one was occupied in 1851 by Robert Atkinson a hoop maker, and the other by James Swainson, a master tailor, who was by then aged 78. He was probably Betty's father. Earlier, in 1841, the schoolmaster had lived in one cottage and another had occupied it in 1871. In the census for 1861, the Atkinsons were still in one cottage with their son, who also made hoops, and their daughter was a dress-maker.

The inn was run by Betty Swainson and her elderly widowed aunt for close on twenty years, but they had living-in help from John Matthews who was their brewer and ostler. There must have been a great deal of passing trade, varying from coaches with horses, carts, traps and horsemen of all descriptions. A man to take care of the heavy brewing work and the horses' needs would have been vital to the womenfolk, who meanwhile had to cater for the passengers, riders and drivers. John was thirteen years younger than Betty, but whether for convenience or from a genuine attachment, when her aunt died in 1860, Betty married her brewer. She was then aged 56.

John Matthews was a member of the family of craftsmen from the Lound. They were master wallers, master masons and master carpenters, but since he and Betty had no family, the property was ultimately conveyed to Robert Matthews for £500 in January 1876, following Betty's death. He had previously been living at Haycote Cottage, now known as 'The Joiner's Shop', so he and his wife Alvarella moved up the hill to the inn, but later retired to their former home.

Robert combined his trades of joiner and innkeeper for some twenty years. His sons Robert Leighton and John James also followed in their father's footsteps as joiners, but John James took over the licence of The Mason's Arms in 1900, though Robert was still the owner. Several post cards exist from this time, showing coaches and horses outside. There must have been more changes to the trade in John James Matthews' time than in the past 150 years. Motor transport was slowly arriving and a taxi service was instigated from Barkbooth around 1914, but by the 1920s, charabancs were taking parties further than they had ever been in one day. Excursions of this kind needed extra staff, so girls from the parish could earn a little pocket money by waiting at table. The Inland Revenue survey of 1909 suggests that there was more tea drunk than beer, the latter of which amounted to 26 barrels a year and seven gallons of spirits. The comment from the inspector was 'Little drinking'. One of the cottages was used as a store by then and the other (one kitchen, two bedrooms) was let at a low rent. Outside there was a barn of twelve by eight yards, a two stall stable and three loose boxes, a cart shed and a hen-house. The whole was in good condition.

Elizabeth Matthews continued as licensee after her husband died in 1947, and then their daughter Nancy took over until 1966 when the family connection ended, though Nancy lived in the cottage adjoining until she died. Until her retirement, beer was still drawn from the barrel and served in jugs.

When the property was bought by the Dargues in 1977, unlike many publicans of the time they left all the old flagged floors, the ranges, tables and assorted chairs, which they bought lock, stock and (literally) barrel. There was no formica and no chrome, and for a while, a brew-house was in operation again, with their speciality of damson beer. Later, the pub gained a name for its huge range of beers from all over the world.

The painted notice of toll charges which was put up by the Dargues outside the door of the Mason's Arms comes from the Bannisdale toll-house. John Macadam is said to have stayed there whilst the Kendal/Penrith turnpike was being constructed. This board dates from 1823, one hundred years before William Dargue was born. Mrs. Blamire, who then lived in the toll-house, gave the board to William's mother for safe keeping at nearby Forest Hall. The charges displayed are probably very similar to the tolls levied on the Kendal to Ulverston turnpike, so it had a relevance to its new site. The board was repainted and restored when it was first installed at the Masons Arms, but is in a sorry state at the time of writing and has been removed, so is reproduced here:

BANNISDALE CHAIN. *Collector, Mrs. Blamire*
Table of Tolls payable at this gate.

For every horse, mule and other beast, drawing any coach, chariot, landau, landaulet, Barouche, Chaise, Phaeton, Curricle, Car, Chair, Gig, Hearse, or other such carriage, the sum of 6d.
For every carriage, fixed or fastened in any manner to any other carriage wagon, wain, drey or cart, the sum of 1.s. 0d.
For every horse, mule or other beast drawing any wagon, wain, cart or caravan or other such carriage if drawn by one horse, mule or other beast; 4d. And for any ass drawing any such carriage, the sum of 2d.
If such tyres are of breadth of not more than 4½ inches, the sum of 5d.
For every horse, mule or other beast drawing any wagon, wain cart, caravan or other such carriage NOT laden with coal, cannel or cinders; 2d.
For every drove of oxen, cows or neat cattle, the sum of tenpence per score and so in proportion for any greater or lesser number.
For every drove of calves, sheep, lambs or swine, the sum of fivepence per score.
                    Roger Moser, Clerk.

Roger Moser was an ancestor of the firm of Milne Moser, solicitors in Kendal.

Lightwood

THE earliest documentary evidence for this farm comes from a Cartmel manor rental of 1590 when it is referred to as 'Lightwhaite', and the names of Thomas Brigg and William Barwick are the recorded owners. This infers a colloquial spelling of 'thwaite', which is of course the very opposite of Wood, and means a clearing. The men who first cleared the land for farming may have been dealing with dense woodland, letting in the light.

The farm was not mentioned in Cromwell's land survey of 1650, but perhaps it was too remote to be noticed, the turnpike road to Ulverston being not even dreamed of until a hundred years later. The first reference to people at Lightwood comes from the parish register of Cartmel for 13 October 1656, when an un-named baby was baptised as the son of George Garnett of Lightwood. The next entry is in the same register, when another George, this time Barker, christened a namesake on 25 November 1669.

In 1709, the Quaker, George Knipe of Monk Coniston, bequeathed moneys to various good causes which were to benefit the Friends. Lightwood estate was purchased in 1713 for £110 and leased for £6 a year to Thomas Garnett, no doubt a descendant of George. The rent was paid to James Birket of The Wood and, it would seem, invested by him for the good of the Quaker community. Unfortunately, James became bankrupt in 1733, so the rents for 1729 until the half-year of 1733 were lost. After that, rents were paid twice yearly to a Colthouse Meeting member at Newby Bridge. Thomas Garnett had trouble paying his rent from time to time, but the Quakers made allowances for drought, the death of a horse or storm damage.

Thomas Garnett is mentioned in the Colthouse Meeting minutes of 1751 as 'now grown aged and not able to manage the estate.' He retired, and the ten ewes and lambs were bought from him, which covered his rent arrears. The farm was then sold for £200.11s.6d.

The farm was owned by the Garnett family until 1792, but they do not seem to have lived there continuously, from the evidence of various documents, so George Barker was either a tenant or a farm servant, and over a hundred years later, a family of Barkers became the owners of Lightwood, but whether or not they were directly related to the former occupants has not been traced. The 1662 hearth tax names George Barker as being liable for just one hearth, but the Quaker accounts mention repairs at Lightwood to 'an old Dwelling House', so there were at least two on the site.

The Addison family seem to have been the occupants at the beginning of the eighteenth century. Wills of Anthony in 1713 and John in 1721 were of Lightwood, and letters of administration were granted for Thomas Addison in 1737. This family were probably related to the Addisons of Kitcrag and Tower Wood as the three christian names were family favourites. In his book *Quakers in Hawkshead and Langdale*, Rob Mckeever has traced the Quaker accounts at Barrow Record Office, detailing the costs of what was possibly a re-building of the homestead in 1726. Robert

Sharpe was paid £2.8s. towards the cost of the house building, and further costs are shown for the roof and the rearing. The present house has a slated roof, but before the re-build of 1726, in 1722, accounts are for a thatcher and thatch, and again in 1749. It has to be said that the appearance of Lightwood today is that of an eighteenth century house, not a sixteenth century one, so this account of 1726 is the likely date of the present house, but there would have been much re-cycling of the original dwelling or dwellings and parts may be embedded within the newer shell.

William Gibson was chapel warden for Lightwood in 1727, and the Cartmel manorial records show him as tenant, together with Thomas Garnett in 1739. Tenant, in this case meant that they paid manorial tithes and fines to Cartmel even though the farm was owned by Quakers., but were in fact owners of the property. At this period, the chapel warden's accounts for 1728 show a payment to Lightwood for 1s.6d. for housing an un-named body overnight. Martin Harriman and then William Harriman were living there in the period 1750-1770. Martin's wife Isabel was buried in 1766, and two years later she was followed to the grave by her husband.

There may have been a period after this when the overseers of the poor paid the rent of Lightwood. George Bennett christened three children between 1787 and 1790 and is described in the bishop's transcripts for Cartmel as 'pauper'. In 1790, Betty Gosling christened her daughter Jane from Lightwood. This child appears in the accounts of the overseer of the poor for 1792, when five shillings was paid to Dr. Coward for inoculating her against smallpox, and her mother was costing the parish one shilling a week.

The Garnett family continued to own the farm until 1792 when James Barker married Mary Seward at St Anthony's. Mary had been living at Foxfield prior to her wedding in 1790. After she and James had bought Lightwood, they produced a family of seven children. Tragedy struck in 1807 when James died, leaving Mary to run the farm of over 100 acres with her young family. She was not able to inherit her husband's estate immediately, but in the following years, Mary and her eldest son James seem to have managed the farm successfully together with a servant named James Seward, a relation of Mary's. It was not until 1825 that she succeeded in obtaining £246.13s.4d. from her late husband's estate, being five ninths of the residue. Two of the younger sons died in childhood, but the 1841 census shows that two brothers and their sister Margaret were all living with their mother and employing two farm servants. Mary, James and William Barker were said to be of independent means, but their sister was a farm servant, together with fifteen-year-old Elizabeth Pearson. James Seward was described as 'agricultural labourer.'

Mary Barker died in 1852 at the age of 88. She must have had some kind of circulatory disease as her death certificate gave the cause as 'mortification of the foot', and during her last days she was tended by Ellen (or Eleanor) Robinson of School House, then used to house the poor of the parish. The censuses show that Ellen, a widow, eventually became part of the household and after Mary's death was housekeeper to the family. It is nice to know that after a hard life as a pauper, Ellen had a comfortable home in her later years. Previously, the family had been housed in any building that was dilapidated and uninhabited. The school house in which the family lived was not the custom-built one, but a ruin near the church, long since demolished.

The Barker family continued to manage Lightwood with increasing numbers of servants until James junior died in 1865, aged 69. James Seward had been living at Lightwood as an unmarried servant for thirty years or so, and from James Barker junior's will we find that he was a cousin. Neither of the Barker brothers had married, so the estate was left to James Seward who then married his housekeeper, Mary Ann Dickinson. She was the daughter of Edward Dickinson, a waller of Addyfield and she was twenty years younger than James. They had one daughter, Mary, born in 1871 when her mother was 40. James, then in his 60s, leased the farm and went to live in Lightwood Cottage just below, but both of young Mary's parents died within months of each other and so she went to live with a governess in Ulverston until she was 21. She worked at the Temperance Hotel in Ulverston as a trainee confectioner, and in 1893 she married Benjamin Pennington at the parish church in Ulverston. He was the son of Christopher Pennington of the well-known ironmongers in Cavendish Street, and together they had seven children and lived a happy life in Braddyll Terrace, but, as with the previous two generations, Mary's family was bereaved in 1903, when their father died aged only 41. She still owned Lightwood and paid land tax for it of 8s.8d in 1886, the same amount as her ancestor paid 100 years before. George Cowperthwaite had signed a seven year tenancy agreement for Lightwood in 1894, and the arrangement must have suited both parties as he was still there in 1910, according to the finance act of that year. The gross valuation of the farm at that time was £2,084, but the buildings were in poor condition.

In 1921, Mary Pennington was re-married at Bootle in Cumberland, this time to a widowed farmer, Bryan Batty of Cartmel Fell. The large Batty family were from Hare Hill and the sons spread out to find farms of their own, but Bryan built Silver Birch for his new bride, on a corner of the Hare Hill land. The couple had sixteen years together, but Mary died in 1937 and Lightwood was sold for the first time since 1792. The estate went to auction on 5 November of that year, together with Silver Birch and Lightwood Cottage.

The next owner of the farm was Wilfred Bentley and he made considerable improvements to the house, including the installation of a bathroom in a small harness area over the entrance hall. He rented the farm to the Park family who were there throughout the war, but left on V.E. day.

The government carried out farm surveys during World War Two for the War Agricultural Committee. Lightwood had well-water, no electricity and the buildings were in good condition. The crops grown were potatoes, turnips and swedes for fodder, mangolds, kale and grass. They had eight cows and heifers, five of them in calf, eight calves, 61 ewes, ten lambs, a sow for breeding, four other pigs and nine piglets. The poultry consisted of 65 hens and fifteen turkeys, and there were two workhorses.

The very day after V.E. day, Tom Newton and his family moved into Lightwood, and his descendants are still there to this day. Tom played the organ at St Anthony's on Sundays and bred turkeys on a larger scale than his pre-decessor. Diversification is nothing new in the farming world, and the womenfolk of the Newton family used to provide renowned ham-and-egg teas after the war, and it was a favourite weekend destination for people of South Cumbria and beyond. In more recent times, some of the farm buildings were converted into holiday cottages, and a bed and breakfast business was successful for many years. The old shippons have been converted into a modern dwelling for Evelyn Cervetti, Tom Newton's daughter, and her husband Fideo. The work was largely done by Fideo and their son Stephen.

Hollins

THIS farm is on an ancient track, possibly a drovers' route. It has been suggested that many farms with the name of Hollins could have been wayside inns, since the holly bush or branch indicated a beer house. There are many recorded instances of bushes being hung up as inn signs, and holly retains its leaves long after being cut, so it would be a good choice. An old table at Burneside has a painting of a holly bush underneath, and has obviously been made from an inn sign. On the other hand, the land above the farm on the western side of the road, is covered with holly trees. This was once unenclosed common, and the sheep would nibble the softer growth of the hollies when no other fodder was available. Holly was actually harvested and crushed, sometimes with gorse, to provide winter feed in times of scarcity, so maybe the farm utilised what nature had provided.

This farmstead was one of some standing in the parish, for its occupants were constantly appearing in documents of their day. In 1662 Thomas Hodgson of Hollins, yeoman, was the purchaser of Bryan Beck estate for the sum of nine score pounds. It was bought from William Knipe, using the old form of symbolic conveyance, the delivery of the 'Key of the door, a clod of earth and a twig, together with this perfect deed'. Bryan Beck later became parish property, the rent of which provided income, but the deed to the estate is the earliest title we know of. We do not know if Thomas Hodgson then moved to Bryan Beck, or if he continued to live at Hollins.

It seems that a Quaker family were in residence soon after the Friends Meeting House was built at Height in 1677. In the Quaker records, a birth is entered on the 18th of the 2nd month (i.e. April) for Jane, daughter of Brian Braithwaite of Hollins. The Quaker incursion was short, as in the Cartmel Fell chapel warden's accounts of 1707, a list of donors of 'Monie to the good of this Chappell' shows that John Swainson of the Hollins gave ten shillings. The Swainson clan were prominent members of the community in the seventeenth and eighteenth century, and three other members were listed as having donated to St Anthony's. Later, in 1731, William Garnett was chapel warden, but it is possible that the house was in two units, as many were, because there seems to be an overlap with family names in various records.

William Gibson arrived at Hollins some time in the first half of the eighteenth century. He was a most remarkable man and we know of his early life from his obituary in *The Gentleman's Magazine* of October 1791, by which time he was internationally famous. Apparently he was born in Bolton, near Appleby in 1720, and was orphaned early in life. He apprenticed himself to a farmer to learn all he could, but his real bent was mathematics. He read all the books and journals he could find on mathematical topics, and corresponded with universities in Europe, posing and answering questions. Whenever he discovered a gap in his education, he set about rectifying the matter by reading widely. Astronomy fascinated him, and he was said to have calculated the forces which hold the universe together. In times of perplexity, William would take a piece of chalk from his pocket and scribble his calculations on the leg of his breeches or on the barn door. Sadly, no traces of these reckonings remain.

It would seem that Hollins was his first abode and perhaps his favourite, for even after he had left and was living at Tarn Green at the foot of the fell, he used the pseudonym of 'Willy o' the Hollins' in the journals for which he wrote. It is possible that there was a family connection between the long-established family of Gibsons at Height Farm and William, and that is why he came to Cartmel Fell from Appleby. Certainly, both families had clerical connections; William's forebear, Edmund, had been Bishop of London, and Edmund of Height had a brother who was vicar of Biggleswade. In the Height account books, Edmund sells a parcel of spring wood (coppice) to William, but none of these facts actually proves a relationship, but there is an echo in the somewhat unusual name of Edmund.

A marriage bond of 1745 exists for Isabel German of Cartmel Fell and William Gibson. The Germans farmed at Addyfield, the estate just above Hollins, so William married the girl next door. Probably Hollins was not owned by the Gibsons, and later they moved to (High) Tarn Green where some of their children were born. For 40 years he ran a gentleman's school in Cartmel, said the obituary, but one wonders if Cartmel Fell is meant. During his last years, Willy was one of the surveyors for the enclosures, a job for which he was eminently suited, with his farming background and brilliant mathematical mind. At his death, William Gibson left 'A disconsolate widow and ten children', according to the *Gentleman's Magazine*. He died, following a fall from his horse in Eggerslack woods near Grange-over-Sands, and although a forebear was Bishop of London, Willy seems not to have been buried by the Church of England, or at least not within the parishes of Cartmel.

Two tombstones in Cartmel Fell churchyard show that the Robinsons were the next inhabitants of Hollins. This family had very old associations with the parish, and were relatively wealthy yeomen. They had held lands at Fell Foot, Tower Wood, Burblethwaite Hall and Moor How in Cartmel Fell, together with other estates in the Lyth valley, but the land tax returns for 1799 and 1814 show that Myles Sandys of Graythwaite was the owner of Hollins. In 1841, William Robinson was the farmer and his daughter Elizabeth and son Thomas were farm servants, with the help of little Henry Matthews, aged eleven. William Robinson of Hollins died on 21 December 1850, aged 90, and in the following year's census, Thomas Bennet, aged 46, and his wife Betty, aged 58, were farming 73 acres at Hollins, and living with them was Thomas Robinson, brother-in-law, unmarried and an annuitant, i.e. in receipt of a pension. From this information we may deduce that Elizabeth was formerly a Robinson and the farm's tenancy continued through her. The somewhat elderly Bennetts continued to farm Hollins for the next twenty years, assisted by a farm lad. Betty Bennett was 78 when the 1871 census was taken, and by then she had the help of a domestic servant, young Mary Eleanor Matthews who was born on the fell, so the tradition of employing one of the Matthews family continued. Betty died in 1875, aged 82, and her husband followed her four years later, aged 74.

An oddity concerning Hollins is that throughout the period of the 'new' baptismal register for

The old cheese press at Hollins.

Cartmel Fell, that is from 1836 to the present day, only one birth is recorded for Hollins, and the deaths are for the really old, ranging from Thomas Bennett and William Robinson, to William's wife Anne, née Kilner, who was 83 when she died in 1840.

A branch of the widespread Crowe family followed the Bennetts. Mark had been born on the fell, but he and his wife Elizabeth had moved to Broughton and then to Allithwaite before arriving at Hollins, which had 74 acres by the time the 1881 census was taken. Two daughters and a son were helping on the farm, two younger children were scholars, as was their nine-year-old grand-daughter,

Elizabeth Rowlandson who lived with them and was the same age as her aunt Jane. Ten years later, Mark and Elizabeth were 65 and 64, but they still had a son and a daughter helping on the farm, and they continued to live at Hollins until Mark died in 1904, and Betty in 1908. The survey was made for the Inland Revenue in the years preceeding 1909, and descriptions of every farm and its land are detailed. In the case of Hollins, T. M. Sandys, (deceased) was the owner, but the house was in poor condition, with two kitchens, a parlour, dairy, wash-house and four bedrooms. Jacob Crowe was the occupier, no doubt related in some way to Mark and Elizabeth.

The baby who was baptised at Cartmel Fell from Hollins in the twentieth century was Frances Margaret Scott. She was born in December 1930, and her parents were Annie and farmer Samuel Edward.

Today, an interesting relic of the local dairy industry is a massive cheese press, standing outside the barn. Several are still to be found on the fell, but none in such good condition, or so large.

The track which passes through the farmyard is now merely a footpath, but this must have been the type of road which served all the other areas of Cartmel Fell in the past. Just below the farm on this path, one can see the simple but effective type of gateway. Opposing gate-stoups have on one side square holes and on the other, round ones. A coppice-wood pole could be fed through the square hole and wedged, with the slender end locating in the round hole. It was effective in barring cattle but could be removed easily or replaced when rotten.

Addyfield

THE name of this farmstead derives from an enclosure made by some distant would-be yeoman. Addy is sometimes a diminutive of Adam, but can also be the old English personal name of Aedi or Adda. An early surname recorded in a Cartmel Priory rental of 1508 is William Addison of Cartmel Fell, so it might not be too fanciful to think that this might be Addison's field. The present house was probably built in the seventeenth century, but there are good reasons to believe that it is on or near a much older farmstead, once called Wayridding or Warridding, possibly where the way or track divides in three directions, or where the land was cleared there.

The house is set around the 400 foot contour, looking east over the valley towards Whitbarrow Scar. If this were an early settlement, it might have looked down on an ill-drained valley bottom, filled with birch and alder scrub. Higher land would be easier to drain, and because of its aspect, would warm up more quickly on a winter's morning. Our forefathers were canny in choosing building sites, and as a general rule, one might say that the best sites were the earliest to be settled. Late-comers had to take second best or work harder to improve their land.

For whatever reason, Addyfield does not often appear in documents relating to the parish, maybe because it changed its name, and our earliest documentation so far comes from the Cartmel Priory registers. In October 1669, John Strickland of Addyfield christened his daughter Isabel, and in 1673, his son Nicholas was baptised. An entry such as this does not give any clue as to the status of the family, that is whether they were tenants, owners or labourers. Six years later there is another entry at Cartmel for the baptism of James Hodgson's son Christopher, and in 1697 the daughter of Rowland Park was baptised Anne.

Addyfield appears to have been a farm let to tenants who moved on for various reasons, and the first piece of firm evidence for this supposition comes in 1703. Then, Rowland Briggs of Swallowmire left a detailed will, the best-known bequest of which were the loaves of bread for the poor of Cartmel. These were, and still are placed every week on a shelf in the priory. The will reveals that Rowland Briggs was also the owner of Addyfield. He inherited the three properties of Swallowmire, Kitcragg and Addyfield from his father in 1688, so this would seem to be a further pointer to tenants or farm managers at Addyfield. The Briggses' tenants must have been relatively prosperous, because Elizabeth Garnett, widow of Thomas of Addyfield, left £20 to the poor of Cartmel Fell in 1707, the equivalent of about £1,500 today.

In the year 2000, Larry Crowe, the present owner of Addyfield, produced a large bundle of documents, many on parchment, and all relating to this farm's history. The suppositions were clarified and the pattern of ownership identified.

In 1701, in a document of lease and release, Roland's heir, Thomas Briggs and his wife Roberta sold the Addyfield estate to James Wayles and his heirs. James died in 1741, and was then living at his other estate of Roper Ford in Winster, and as he had no heir, he left Addyfield to his brother Thomas. Another generation of Wayleses must have ensued before a Thomas Wayles of Ayside made his will in 1768, in which he left Addyfield to his niece Mary, the wife of John Bramwell of Allithwaite. Out of the estate, Mary was to pay her sister Elizabeth Towers £2.10s. a year.

Towards the end of the eighteenth century John Bramwell moved to Wigan and was in need of substantial cash. He already owed Robert Atkinson of Longlands in Cartmel the sum of £600, half of which, plus interest, was due in 1793. He therefore mortgaged Addyfield to Robert Atkinson who died the following year and his widow Agnes inherited the estate from her husband, so it was to her that the repayments were due. John Bramwell still had money problems and he requested a further mortgage of £250 from Agnes, but at this stage he must have realised that repayment was becoming quite impossible, so he sold the somewhat diminished estate of 57 acres at Addyfield to John Newby in 1807, for the sum of £1,210 and that settled all his outstanding debts. John Bramwell seems to have been an honourable man, and a letter survives which he wrote in Liverpool in 1798. In reply to his Ulverston solicitor Mr Robinson, John Bramwell clearly wants to do the right thing with regard to 'fines' or local taxes. His letter is imaginative in spelling:

'Dere Ser... I have Inclosed Mr. Richardson Recept for Thouse tow fines wich you plase Axe Aske him what more is deu.' There is more, indicating his willingness to settle any outstanding debts, but hoping to receive something for the wood.

The 1814 land tax document shows that the

owner and occupier at that time was still John Newby. This document shows the field names and acreages, the total of which was 82 acres and 9 perches. The field names are not very revealing, but Corn Close was only just over an acre and Whag was about the same size. The map, which relates to a later sale, provides a clue however to the 'missing' farm of Wayridding in one of the Addyfield wood names. The name of this old farm disappears from wills and inventories at the end of the sixteenth century, but these give no clue as to its whereabouts. Number 518 on the land tax schedule is 'Wood in Wayrudding, 3 acres, 2 roods & 3 perches.' Could Addyfield have been built from the ruins of Wayridding, or did it just change its name? A pile of stones in the area called Warudding might be the remains of a farmhouse. A cottage on the site is also mentioned in 1814, and that was occupied by Arthur Copplethwaite.

Throughout the mid-nineteenth century, the Dickinson family farmed at Addyfield, and had probably been there even earlier. When the 1841 census was taken, old Jane Dickinson was the head of the household, assisted by her son Edward and daughter Sarah who were the working team, helped by a farm hand, John Matthews. Ten years later, when the census gives more detail, we can see that the farm had only 40 acres, and the matriarch, Jane, is still with the family, aged 92. Mary Ellen is Edward's daughter and aged 20, so he must have been widowed early since his wife was already dead in 1841 when he was 30. A search of the Cartmel Fell baptismal register disclosed that Edward and his wife were living at Old House Beck when their daughter was born in 1830, and Edward's trade was walling. The 1851 Mannex directory has an entry for Addyfield indicating Edward as the farmer.

The Dickinsons continued farming at Addyfield until some time in the 1870s, and had acquired another five acres by 1871. Edward was then 70, and his sister Sarah had taken over as housekeeper to her widowed brother, but she was 75, so they must have been ready to retire. A grandson George was living with them, and at fifteen he would have provided some useful muscle. There was another farm servant living in, but he was 72 and no doubt glad of some young help.

By 1881 there was a new family at Addyfield. The young Pearsons were both 28 and had come from a bit further east. Daniel was from Old Hutton and Mary Ellen from Sedbergh. The family must have arrived at Addyfield before that, because their son Robert was baptised at Cartmel Fell in 1877 and by 1891 they had three boys and two girls, but the acreage had shrunk to 35.

At around the turn of the twentieth century, the holding was farmed by the Kelletts who were also builders. Mentioned elsewhere, they helped in the construction of Hare Hill and Hodge Hill new barn and helped to modernise the vicarage. One of the daughters married the present owner, so for most of the twentieth century their association with Addyfield was maintained.

Today, the old farm and barns have been converted by the owner into delightful holiday houses, and he built himself a modern bungalow called Addy Vale alongside, which has the same superb view over the valley. A nicely carved oak chest of drawers is a family heirloom, commemorating the wedding of Elizabeth Lawrence to Mark Crowe in 1864. The bride was from Raven Winder, and her husband was then a game-keeper at Holker, but the Crowes had been on Cartmel Fell for centuries. Elizabeth Lawrence's surname has been preserved as the fore-name of her descendant, the present owner.

There is a well-known photograph taken during the 1950s of Allhallows Lane in Kendal, filled with sheep. These were Swaledale hogs being driven back to the Haws district of Yorkshire after wintering on the slopes of Cartmel Fell where the climate was milder than that of the Dales. The farms from which these sheep came were Hardraw and Pry House. Today, the heathland behind Addyfield is largely afforested, but once it offered winter grazing which was worth the forty or fifty mile trek. The winters were often harsh in the early twentieth century, and the dales were quickly snow-bound. Many farms in this gentler near-coastal climate of Cartmel Fell used to take hogs for wintering, and usually the drovers were accompanied by a horse and light cart for picking up stragglers that were getting weary, or even to give the sheepdogs a break.

Bryan Beck

THIS farm, spelt sometimes as Brine Beck in earlier days, has deeds which date back to 1662, though the farmholding is much older. A small beck tumbles away behind the property to the north, and this may have been associated with some long-dead occupant called Bryan, or it may be that 'Brine' is the more accurate spelling, for this area was long associated with tanning. Any seepage from the tan-pits could have polluted the beck, and so could the subsequent washing of the hides. Until 1994, a roadside well was evidence that the beck water was not used for drinking.

Most of the documents relating to this holding have kindly been lent by the present owner, and the first is a conveyance between William Knipe of Cartmel and Thomas Hodgson of Hollins in Cartmel Fell. Even earlier however is a will, dated 1590, in which Hugh Barrowe of Bryan Becke disposes of his house and farm to his heirs.

In this will and inventory, we can learn quite a bit about the Barrowe family who were farmers. Hugh's wife was Margaret, usually spelt Mergeret, so we can hear the pronunciation, and he had sons William, Robert and Edward. There was a daughter Genet, and an unmarried sister Isabell Barrowe. Genet or Jenett was a very popular local name in the sixteenth and seventeenth centuries, and is the old spelling of Janet. At this period, the widow's right was a third share of the property, but here she is to have half, 'so long as she kepes my name and is unmarried with anie other man.' Hugh bequeaths certain useful items to Margaret: 'The chest that stands in the chamber, a brass pott that came from Winster, a frying pane, a rackencrook, a spitt and a litle caldron.' Hugh must have been comfortably off by the standards of the day. He bequeathed actual money to his children, £30 to be paid to Robert, and £10 to Edward and Genet. His sister Isabell got two shillings. The inventory was taken on the day of Hugh's death, as was the custom. At a later period, the order of the stocktaking gained a pattern, usually starting with the purse and apparel, but this one is rather random. It begins with the stock, a cow and calf, a young cow and two other kye, all amounting to just over three pounds. An old horse and all its gear is worth sixteen shillings and the seventeen sheep have an unreadable value. Two hives of bees are worth 6s.8d, the inventory being taken in April. As with most households at this time they brewed their own beer, so there is malt and a gile-fatt or wort-tub for this purpose, but also a flesh tub for pickling meat. Two items lumped together were 'three hens and a little flesh,' but no further description. The hens could have been live and the flesh 'hung', smoked or salted.

The furniture listed was very basic. Only two pairs of bedstocks, but the children may not have been living at home, 'a Meatboard, chares, stules and formes,' and the item following was 'Whilles and cards,' i.e. spinning wheels and the combs for carding the wool. Another interesting item is 'studdles', the upright parts of a loom, so the Barrowes were producing cloth. Though wheels are quite often found in inventories of the seventeenth century on the fell, weaving equipment is less common. In the debts column, he owed Robert Swaynson 2s.6d. for 'a seare cloth of wole,' and another debt for 'Half a seare cloth of wole,' so maybe they were dealers of a sort, as well as producers. We tend to think of burial clubs as being a nineteenth century idea, but the next to last item in the debt column is provision for the funeral, 'Laid forth a bond, buriall, 8s.' This was to be a good funeral. The last items are for the priest and clerk, 1d. and 4d. After this will, Bryan Beck must ultimately have passed or been sold to the Knipe family. Hugh Barrowe willed that his son William should not sell or rent the farm as long as his brothers might want it, or their heirs, but seventy years later, all the names had changed.

The 1662 indenture is beautifully written on parchment, and on the outside fold it summarises the contents, and uses the customary seventeenth century form of property conveyance in words, which echoed the deed, by the delivery of the key of the door, a clod of earth and a twig. This signified the house, the land and (importantly in this area) the woods. The price was nine score pounds of lawful English money, but there was also an annual fee farm rent of 7s.9d., as well as 5s.9d. knowing rent. As in the other cases we find on the fell, this 'knowing' was paid every two and a half years. The fee farm rent was payable yearly to 'the King's majesty, his heirs and successors'. This first deed was an agreement between William Knipe of Broughton in Cartmel, gentleman, the vendor, and Thomas Hodgson of Hollins in Cartmel Fell, the purchaser. The Hodgson family may have been tanners at this time, and had scattered properties on the fell between Blewthwaite and Bryan Beck. A Rowland Hodgson died at Oaks in 1703, at the home of the Harrisons who were curriers, and there is evidence for a partnership of some kind between the tanners of Bryan Beck and the curriers of Oaks in the seventeenth and eighteenth centuries.

The next deed in sequence is dated 28 June 1714 and it registers the sale by Samuell Matson, tanner, to a newly formed trust. This time, it changed hands for £220 with again 7s.9d. fee farm rent, but only 2s.9d. for the knowing, still to be paid at two and a half year intervals.

One of the enlightening facets of these documents of conveyance, is that they usually have neighbours as witnesses, so it is possible to build up a picture of most of the local families at a given time. For the 1714 indenture, Richard Hutton of Thorphinsty is one party, but by 1727 he and his fellow trustees, Brian Philipson of Hodge Hill and Anthony Strickland of Hartbarrow, yeomen, were all dead.

The second document is an important one from the historical point of view, because it marks the change in status of Bryan Beck from farm to charity. A number of influential landowners formed a trust with numerous bequests, and the money was invested in Bryan Beck farm to provide income for the parish. In this case, there are numerous trustees, for the estate was bought with amalgamated bequests. On the outside of the 1743 parchment, it lists the various bequests and gifts to specified charities by named individuals, though many were in place earlier. For example, 'The gift of Benjamin Fletcher for the use of the curate, being fifty pounds. The gift (no donor named) of seventy seven pounds, the interest to go to the poor.' Lawrence Harrison left three different sums; £10 for administering the Easter Sacrament, £2 for road repairs, and £10 for the use of a curate, teaching.

The overall total was £179, but some generous soul must have thrown in the extra pound to make it a round number, because the inside of the 1727 indenture quotes £180. The reason for the trustees' purchase of Bryan Beck was to secure the various moneys, given or bequeathed, in the days before building societies or banks. The income derived from letting the estate would be divided proportionately between the poor, the minister, the church and the roads. In later years, with the advent of banks in Kendal, money from the rent and the underwood was invested. An H.M.S.O. booklet of 1900 states that Messrs Wakefield's bank had £25, and Messrs Wilson's had £50, both sums from the sale of the underwood. This produced £3 per annum for poor relief. Looking at the effort involved from our perspective of a hundred years later, the amounts realised were hard won. A reference to an 1820 document mentions the sums in the Kendal banks, but says that part was to be applied 'to build a new house on the estate'. The reprint was in 1852, and it is not clear from the wording, when they say 'eighteen years ago an allotment of mountain land was given to the charity,' does it mean 1802 or 1834? The latter seems probable, as Anthony Thornborrow was the successful bidder, and he was at Bryan Beck at the time of the 1831 lease agreement.

The present house at Bryan Beck is thought to be eighteenth century, but it could be the above quoted 'new' house on the estate. Behind it is a much earlier dwelling, now reduced to barn status, but it has obviously been a substantially-built house, with the windows now walled up. The form of the relieving arches over these windows is a local speciality, and can be seen in other old houses, or one-time houses.

A conclusive bit of evidence for the Bryan Beck barn having been a dwelling is the upstairs room, now a bay of the barn, which has a moulded plaster frieze at about head height. This seems to be seventeenth-century work. The beam in the room below is one of quality with some chamfering, but there is no obvious provision of a chimney. A square recess in the far wall might have accommodated a box-bed or possibly a charcoal brazier, but not a fireplace.

The use of the lands and the buildings was carefully regulated by the trustees of the charity, and many of the nineteenth-century papers relating to the letting are still in good condition. Written on flimsy paper in a free bold hand, are the conditions for the 1801 letting. The meeting was held at Bowland Bridge, at James Hodgson's, innkeeper, on 8 October. The conditions were as follows: 'It is hereinafter mentioned that the tenant is required to plough no more out of leay in one year than one acre, and to sow the same with big or barley the second year, manuring the same in an husbandly like manner, according to the customs of the country.' The next clauses are similar to the 1831 deed and subsequent ones, but in them there is no mention of the springs, i.e. the newly sprung coppice-wood. In 1801: 'The tenant not to have any liberty in the springs called Great Spring and Two Gill Woods.' He was also not at liberty to keep any sheep upon the premises. This seems an odd exclusion for Cartmel Fell, where sheep figure largely on every farm, but they nibble newly-sprung coppice growth. In this letting, he was allowed three days graving of peats upon Ludderburn moss, each and every year, but none upon the premises. This mention of peat cutting is omitted in future documents, so perhaps the enclosures put an end to it. The successful bidder in 1801 was James Dickinson senior of Ludderburn, and he offered £25 per annum.

In the 1831 letting, the document is easy to read and more comprehensive. Anthony Thornborrow of Goswick Hall was in occupation, except for the game and the coppice wood. The term was to commence on 14 February for ploughing and garden grounds, 25 April as to the residue, and the house from 12 May, for a full term of seven years. Anthony Thornborrow was to pay £28 each and every year, in two equal instalments, plus his own parliamentary and parochial taxes. He also had to leave all the slates, windows, doors, gates, rails, stiles, hedges, ditches, drains and rails in good repair. Whoever purchased the coppice wood was to have the use of the outhouses for storing bark (for tanning) and for manufacturing hoops. These last two activities were allowed until the buildings were needed for wintering the cattle. The next clause concerns fodder: 'To consume upon the said premises, all the hay, straw and other vestures, and ashes which shall be produced thereon, and at the end of the term, to leave the same in the usual and convenient places.' The reference to ashes is probably the old custom of zero grazing, where young ash branches were fed to cattle when pasture was scarce. This could be in a dry spring, or when the meadows were shut up for hay. The custom still persists in the Auvergne, and is the reason for so many men leaving the villages there with ladders in the mornings. Their method of cropping reducing the trees to something akin to telegraph poles, but in this country, we favoured the pollarding method, and many such cropped trees can still be seen.

The next clause in the agreement is to do with

land management. This was to be according to 'the best and most approved mode of husbandry.' No soil was to be burned, and no ploughing of meadows which had not hitherto been tilled, nor to plough more than two acres of arable ground, and that in a regular course, and only three years in succession, but in the third year, to lay down the same in seeds and barley stubble in a proper manner. Every third or fourth year, to well top dress the meadows with manure or compost, and yearly and every year, to lay upon the said premises, at his own expense, one hundred bushels of good lime. Also, to preserve the coppice woods from being depastured by sheep or cattle and maintain the fencing thereof. If any of the terms were contravened, then the tenancy should cease. Among the trustees who signed, was John Poole of Gill Head, to whom the rent was to be paid. The tenant, Anthony Thornburrow, (spelt variously) probably could not write, and signed this and other documents with a cross.

A separate document of conditions was drawn up for the coppice woods, which, as mentioned, were to finance the poor. There were provisions and exclusions at this date, which were gradually whittled away as the century wore on. One was the lessors' right to shoot the game on the land. The trustees were almost always landed yeomen or gentry, presumably with sporting rights on their own properties, so one can imagine the lessee feeling irritated by this clause. The terms are just as precise, and ensure that conservation is strictly controlled:

1. That all the coppice wood except the oak, be spring felled in a workmanlike manner before the first day of April, and all the oaks before the twentieth day of June, now severally next ensuing, otherwise all such unfelled coppice shall be forfeit to the vendors.

2. That the vendors will provide proper places wherein to house the bark until the usual season when such places will be required to be given up to the vendors for cattle or agricultural produce.

3. If the purchaser (lessee) shall make charcoal, he shall be confined to make it in the accustomed pitsteads, and be confined to the coppice woods for cover of the pits.

4. If any damage be done to the said coppice woods or to any lands or grounds through which the same may be led or carried away, or to any walls gates hedges or other fences, or to any other trees not hereby intended to be sold, or by improperly felling any oak below the cutting, or by permitting any horses employed in carting to eat the scions or herbage, such damage upon demand shall be immediately compensated for. That the purchasers shall immediately after the sale, if required, sign these conditions, and shall upon demand, produce sufficient sureties to the satisfaction of the vendors as they shall require for the due payment of the purchase money at the time above specified, and for the felling, cutting and peeling of the wood, according to the true intent and meaning of these conditions.

In this instance, the coppice wood was purchased for £68 by William Birket of Hodge Hill, and John Poole of Tower Wood. A footnote to the coppice agreement states: 'According to the foregoing conditions, the wood in the Poor House field was sold to us for the price of £12. As witness our hands, James Hunter, James Robinson.' The land referred to was bought with Richard Hutton's charity of £40, and it bought the field then known as Low House field, of around two acres. At the enclosures, another three acres was added to this, and yet again let to Anthony Thornborrow. He seems to have been a charity baron.

One problem with the enclosures was the cost of fencing or walling. It was therefore necessary to borrow what was then the enormous sum of £53 to separate the Bryan Beck lands. The money was borrowed from the trustees in the township, and secured on the estate, 10d. in the pound being repaid as interest.

On 4 November 1836, a meeting and auction was held at the house of Mr Robert Long of The Oaks farm, the property having common boundaries with Bryan Beck. Evidently, the trustees had acquired some more woodland, called Birch Hill. Sufficient wood to enclose the coppice was excluded from the auction, also the coppice trees marked with red paint, also the trees which were older than the coppice woods. All the previous terms were applied, and in a different hand at the end of the document it says: 'Be it remembered that Henry Railton and Thomas Bateman were the purchasers of the aforementioned wood at the sum of thirty pounds.' The 1862 conditions are very similar to the 1831, with an additional restraint on the tenant i.e. 'that he shall not sell off any hay or straw or other vestures, but that he shall convert them into manure.' Had someone been caught not following the guidelines of good husbandry? The Low House allotment had been added to the estate also, but in three places in this agreement, the terms relating to sporting rights have been firmly ruled out. 'The lessors further reserve all game upon the Premises, and full liberty for themselves, and all persons in their company, or by their appointment, or permission to hunt, course, shoot, fish, and follow all field amusements through and over the same.' It is pointless to speculate whether an actual incident had brought this matter to a head, but it is easy to imagine the indignation of the tenant if the Hooray Henrys of the day had, for instance, gone hare coursing around lambing time. Land prices were dropping, so the trustees must have had to give some leeway.

As well as the formal documents relating to the letting of Bryan Beck, there are odd slips of paper in the collection with scrawled notes, letters from one trustee to another, and public notices. There are also the actual sealed bids of some of the would-be tenants. There is an interesting interpretation of the 1861 bids from Ailna Martin, regarding the bid of John Lishman. She has researched her branch of the Lishman family, and says that John had a firm, vigorous hand in earlier life when he wrote in the family Bible. She conjectures that his was a token bid, made for the farm alone, not the three lots, so that his prospective son-in-law, Henry Matthews, would get the estate (which he did) although his bids were not the highest. A William Geldart of Ealinghearth made bids of £32, £34 and £35 and was approved, but maybe his sureties did not come up to scratch. Henry Matthews got the estate for £31, £32 and £33.10s.

In the 1851 census, John Lishman was listed as a farmer of 57 acres and he was 57 years old. He was a widower living with two daughters, a son and a grandson. By 1861, he would have been reluctant to take up a long lease, and amongst the letters in the Bryan Beck collection, is one from Thomas Pearson of Pool Bank, giving the old man notice to quit, according to the trustees resolution of 29 May.

John Lishman died 'Of Senile Decay' as it said on the death certificate, in 1868.

Henry Matthews negotiated a fourteen year tenure, and was feeling secure enough to make an offer to the trustees to re-slate the barn roof. In a confident, decorative hand, he writes to William Wakefield Esq. Birklands, near Kendal:

'Sir, I have seen Mr. Pearson, and I agree to give £34 a year for a term of fourteen years for the Bryan Beck Farm and also to slate the barn for nothing, upon condition that the Trustees (yourself being one,) find the slate and other Materials. I will sign the lease at any time if you will be kind enough to let me know when its ready, and also let me know if it is necessary for me to provide witnesses to attest it. Believe me, your Obedient Servant, Henry Matthews.'

The address on the letter is already Bryan Beck, so the Trustees must have had faith in Henry to allow him to move in before signing the agreement. William Matthews, Henry's grandson, recalls that his grandfather was very much addicted to cock-fighting, and on one occasion lost £40 on an 'unbeatable' bird. That was more than the year's rent for Bryan Beck.

Quite a number of anecdotes involving gambling have come to light during this compilation, as told by the families' descendants, not just in general folk memory. An element of excitement must have been injected into an otherwise routine round of daily chores. Today's equivalent might be a flutter on the National Lottery?

Henry Matthews continued to live at Bryan Beck into the twentieth century, surrounded by various degrees of relatives. There seemed to be an ever-shifting pattern of nieces, nephews and in-laws living either with him or in the surrounding cottages. He describes his occupation as farmer in all the censuses, but the acreage varies between 20 and 29.

After this time, information is harder to come by in documentary form. Census returns only become available after a hundred years has elapsed, but the Lishman family still retain Bryan Beck, having purchased the farm and the woodland in the early part of the Second World War. They used to get a special petrol allowance during the war, because the coppice woods provided besoms, not to sweep the floor, but for ships' fenders. A load was transported regularly up to Clydeside.

Mrs Gladys Lishman relates that her father-in-law and his family were charcoal burners in Hodge Hill woods, and her husband remembered going to stay in the sod-houses when he was a boy, before the Second World War. He used to come home black, and reeking of smoke, but it must have been fun for a child who had no other holiday. A film company wanted to shoot them at work, but they could not be bothered with such nonsense whilst they were burning, and sadly for us, the film was not made, though there are a number of photographs, taken about the beginning of the twentieth century.

The Lishmans were always keen supporters of the hunt, and during the week when the Coniston pack are hunting on the fell, they are kennelled at Bryan Beck in what was the old house.

The Lound

IN dialect, *lound* means a quiet or sheltered place and this area is certainly in an elbow of the hill, sheltered from the west and north. The late William Rollinson found a specialised variant in the Cartmel area, *loand*, meaning quiet weather. The little hamlet in this corner consists of five dwellings, Bryan Beck being by far the oldest, but somewhat apart from the others. The names of the newer houses have mutated, so that the house which is today known as Summer Hill was the original Lound Cottage. The nineteenth century censuses show that this title was a generic term for the hamlet, but every ten years or so, a new name crops up and then sinks without trace. In 1841 there were only Lound Cottages (plural) but in subsequent years there was a Plane Tree Cottage, Ashes Cottage and Lane Cottage, then in 1871 there were just three Lound Cottages again.

The group is not very old, compared with many on the fell, and seems to have grown up in the very early nineteenth century. The first reference found so far, is in the 1814 land tax, when William Matthews was the owner/occupier of a homestead and orchard, valued at £2.10s. The acreage has not been filled in. The Matthews family were there throughout the first half of the nineteenth century. In the 1841 census, the head of the family is William, 50-years-old and a waller. Ten years later, the more detailed census tells us he was a master waller, born in Westmorland. His wife Mary was born in Lowick and was the same age. Living at home in 1841 were daughter Jane, 25, twins Edward and Thomas aged 20, one an agricultural labourer, the other a waller like his father, and another set of twins, Sarah and Elizabeth who were fifteen, and lastly Eleanor who was nine. A child of seven, Matthew Bevins, is an extra member of the household, but his relationship is not explained.

The parish registers tell us that the Matthews family had previously lived at Addyfield, and had christened two of their children from there in the 1830s. Maybe this family inherited Lound Cottage (alias Summer Hill, named for the land behind) from William, who was probably the original builder of the property.

By 1851, this large household contained the old couple and unmarried Thomas, then described as a journeyman waller, born in Cartmel. The term 'journeyman' crops up frequently in the censuses. It does not mean that the craftsman travelled, though no doubt he did; it meant that he had served an apprenticeship and was paid a daily rate by his master. In addition, there were two more unmarried sons, Robert who was a master waller and Henry, a journeyman waller. Two unmarried daughters were still at home and a grand-daughter, Mary Crake, who had been born in Liverpool. There was also room for a lodger, seven-year-old John Holme from Ulverston who stayed on in the household, later becoming an apprentice waller.

The master wallers must have been busy in the next ten years, because by 1861, two more houses appeared at the Lound. In the one nearest Bryan Beck, called Lane Cottage, was the family of Robert Matthews and his wife Alvarella. By now, Robert was employing a man and two boys and was

Summer Hill

supporting a family of four little girls. Living in was a niece, Mary Bevins (thereby explaining the relationship to Matthew), and two lodger apprentices, plus a boarder who was a journeyman joiner.

The old couple were both 71 by 1861, and had unmarried Henry still at home, and a grandson, John Thornhill, who was ten. John Holme was lodging there still, and next door in the other new house (Ashes Cottage) was Thomas Matthews, the younger son. Thomas was a stone-mason and had a young family of a son and two daughters.

The Matthews family needed to spread out, and by 1871, Henry Matthews and his wife Jane were farming Bryan Beck. The farm had only 29 acres, but nonetheless, they employed two servants and also had a lodger. For a while, this corner of the fell became a kingdom of wallers.

All the cottages were called 'Lound' by 1871. Old Mary Matthews was by then 81 and a widow, but she had contemporaries living with her, Joseph and Mary Robinson. It seemed that Joseph was still active as he declared himself to be a wood-cutter. Next door was Birkett Francis Lishman with his wife Nancy and two small children, together with Nancy's father and her sister. The Lishmans had been living at Bryan Beck, so there had been a re-shuffle of families. Not only the names of the houses changed, but the families which moved around them. Birkett progressed from being a labourer in 1871 to a wood-merchant twenty years later. He and his family seem to have lived in the first house next to Bryan Beck, by that time called Plane Tree Cottage. Next door in 1891 was the Kellett family who were builders and wallers, and as was then the custom their nineteen-year-old apprentice, James Crow, was living with them. Although some of the surnames had changed at the Lound, this was only through marriage, the Matthews daughters very fortunately choosing husbands who could work as a building team. If anyone on the fell needed a new building or house repairs, they needed to look no further than the Lound. Some of the buildings erected in that era include Hare Hill, the new barn at Hodge Hill, the church lych gates and the modernisation of the vicarage. There was much new building at High Newton in the first half of the nineteenth century, by George Gibson of the Height, and surviving accounts show that the Matthews team were involved here too. Earlier in the century, Ravensbarrow Lodge was built.

There is a family of Masons of Lound Cottage who are commemorated in Cartmel Fell churchyard. Henry died in 1875, aged 79, but his wife Isabella had died eleven years earlier at Goswick Hall, and on referring to the relevant censuses, we can see that the Masons farmed Goswick in 1841 and 1851. Probably, the widowed Henry lived in the small cottage fronting the road, then called Plane Tree Cottage.

An Inland Revenue survey of land and dwellings in 1910 indicates ownership and tenant. John Lishman occupied Summer Hill, and the owner was John Coward of Hartbarrow. John Lishman had gone down to Liverpool to become a schoolmaster, but his family used to return to Cartmel Fell during the holidays, coming up from Liverpool by train. The children slept at the back of the house, where they could escape through the window onto a tin roof, and thereby onto Summer Hill. One of these children was Gladys, now Mrs Dunn, a child in the first decade of the twentieth century and she remembers going to a wedding feast at Summer Hill. At the gateway was a huge topiary armchair, part of the hedge, but it was more than your life was worth if you dared to try it for size. The day was so hot that none of the jellies would set, and the date of this event was mentioned in the diary of Thomas Price, then the new curate; it was 11 July 1910. The pull of the fell was so strong that generations of Lishmans returned regularly, and one of John Lishman's grand-daughters and her husband bought their own holiday home on the fell, Heightside, which is shared with their children and grandchildren.

Until the 1990s, there were still descendants of the Kellets and Matthews living at the Lound, but the twenty-first century has produced many changes. There is still a builder, Derek O'Loughlin, who owns the cottage next to Bryan Beck, and the building has been extended and modernised extensively; others in the hamlet have become holiday homes.

The well at the corner of the road used to serve all the properties, but that was demolished in the mid-1990s. It has to be said however, that a hundred years earlier, the Lishman children were forbidden to drink from the well, and drank buttermilk instead, but mains water on the fell is still a dream.

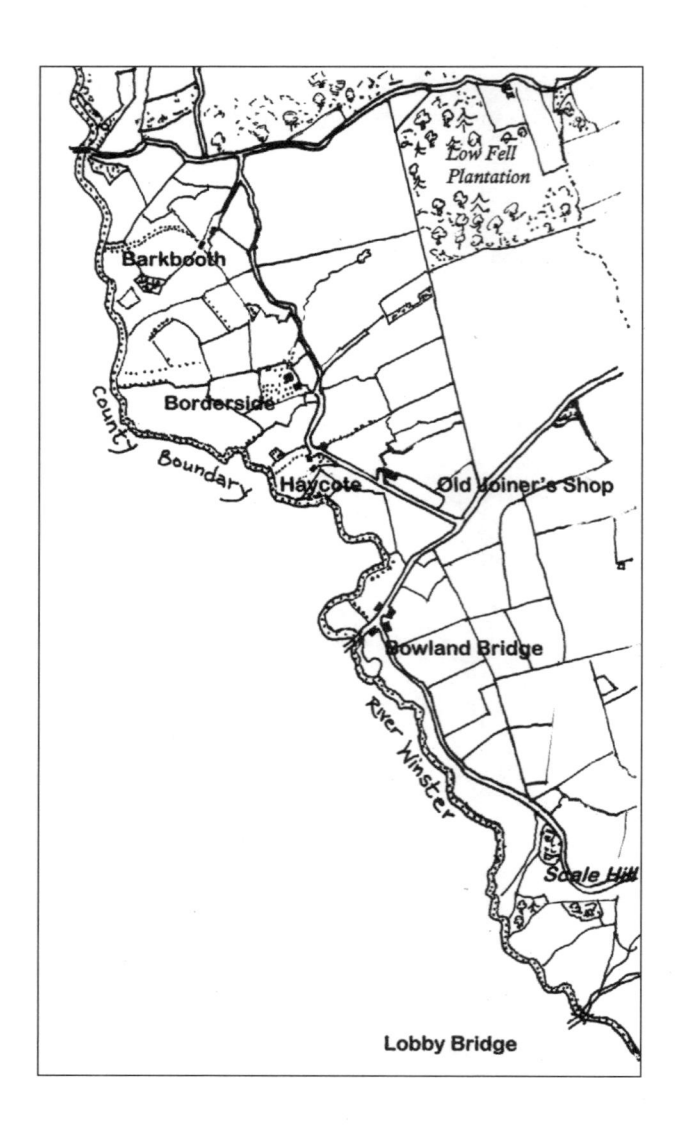

Haycote

ALTHOUGH not actually in the parish of Cartmel Fell but in Crosthwaite, Haycote is closer in spirit to the fell, as its lands go down to the river Winster. This old farm has undergone extensive re-furbishment in 2004, extending the floor area considerably. The core of the house is of sixteenth or seventeenth-century origin, with timber-framed walls, and the associated barn is nearly twice the area of the house. The barn is also undergoing conversion to housing, as is a small two-storey bothy in front of the house.

The cote element of the name means a cottage or shelter (such as dove-cot) but *hay* is often associated with an enclosure, from the French *haie,* a hedge. The farm is however in the lusher valley land, and ideal for hay-making.

We know that the farm was in existence in 1638, for at that date, John Swainson made his will, leaving his tenement at Haycote to his wife Elizabeth, and 'the tenement she dwells on.' At that time, Elizabeth was pregnant, and John wished the child, if a boy, to inherit all his tenements, and these were considerable. Apart from Haycote, they included Gook How (now Goswick Hall), Light Thwaite (now Lightwood), and New Hall, which cannot positively be identified. If the child was a girl, she was to have Haycote, Gook How and Light Thwaite, whilst his daughter Ann was to have 'the tenement he dwells on,' which is not named, and New Hall. She was also to receive £200 within two years of the yet unborn brother inheriting the tenements. This was wealth indeed at the beginning of the seventeenth century, but the Swainsons were then influential and well connected. The testator's uncle was Robert Curwen, gentleman, to whom was owed £10, and also another £32.8s. upon specialty. Unfortunately, John's debts were more than his assets, totalling £188.7s.10d., but the difference was only £10 and that was mostly the cost of his funeral.

Apart from his tenements, John Swainson had intakes at Moor How, and he acknowledges that these may have to be sold by his executors, so he was aware of his financial state, and maybe part of his flock of 268 sheep would have to be sold too. The livestock included a team of four oxen, fourteen head of cattle and seven calves, and refinements indoors were tablecloths and napkins, together with woollen table-covers and silver spoons. He was obviously fond of his mother Jenet, and made sure her wants were taken care of. Her funeral expenses were set aside (£8), and she was to have the 'fyer house' at Gowk How for her lifetime, and sufficient land for a cow in summer and winter, with sufficient for fire. Other beneficiaries of the will were godchildren and 'ould Isabell', who was to have a house to dwell in during her life. Anthony Pull was to have the testator's worst suit of clothes but one.

Forty years later, the Harrison family were ensconced at Haycote. There is a receipt of 1682 from Thomas, son of Edward Harrison, cordwainer, for £2, being a gift from the legacy of Lawrence Newton of Height. This might imply that the Harrisons were Quakers at the time, as it was Lawrence Newton who endowed the Meeting House at Height, but twenty years later, the Harrisons were baptising their children at Crosthwaite parish church. In 1703 and 1704, Thomas Harrison had his children baptised Frances and William. Another Thomas christened his daughter Elizabeth in 1737 and this child later married George Theckston, linsey weaver of Crosthwaite.

It seems that the later Harrisons were all linen weavers by trade. Father Thomas and his three sons all carried on the business, probably in Crosthwaite village. At their father's death, Thomas, the heir, was expected to inherit the farmhold, but he was already of Crosthwaite Churchtown. His father Thomas had made a will and had it witnessed by three people, but he had forgotten to sign it himself. Evidently he wished his younger son James to inherit Haycote, and the other members of the family were in agreement, providing they received their shares. Their solicitor advised them to settle it quietly between them instead of going to court, and that is what happened. Sarah, the widowed mother was to receive an annuity of £3 a year out of the estate and James had to pay his brother William £40 and a further £30 to his sister Elizabeth. This money was not readily available, so James took a mortgage for £70 from Richard Moorcroft, blacksmith of Crosthwaite, and then went up to London and became a woollen draper in Ludgate Street. His brother William was in business in Southwark already, though all were linen weavers at their father's death.

For whatever reason, James decided to sell Haycote in 1794, and the auction was to be at Thomas Harrison's, innkeeper of Crosthwaite. One wonders if the landlord was another relation or even his elder brother, returned from the big city. The purchaser was George Lucas, a house-carpenter, late of Burblethwaite, and the change of ownership had to be ratified in the manor court of Crosthwaite, part of Lord Lonsdale's domain.

John Lucas inherited Haycote from his father, and in 1850 he signed a deed agreeing to the commutation of his tithes of corn and grain. The 1851 census shows him in residence, aged 43, a bachelor and farming 20 acres. Whether he eventually married and had a family is unclear, but someone in the Lucas family continued to own the farm and let it, because by 1885, the Bulmer's directory advertises Thomas Nicholson at Haycote, farmer and timber merchant, probably the same man who had previously lived at Greenthorn. Yet another George Lucas was the owner in 1922, but he also had a tenant, John Titterington Bownass. By then George Lucas had moved to Meltham, near Huddersfield, and wanted to sell Haycote.

The new owner was Harry Hargreaves, a master baker from Horncastle, Lincolnshire, and he paid £1,075 for the property, a cottage and a little over 27 acres. Here was another absentee landlord however, and the farm was tenanted by Ernest Lodge Fleming and his wife Elizabeth. The Crosthwaite parish register shows that they christened their daughter Margaret in 1921.

In the latter part of the twentieth century, Haycote farm was the home of Joy Millburn. She was a familiar figure locally, sometimes taking one of her donkeys or Shetland ponies out with a flat cart. When she died, quite unexpectedly, in 2002, a seat was installed in her memory, opposite the Hare and Hounds, but looking towards Haycote. Two tubs of plants are maintained by her friends from Borderside on either side of the seat.

The small building in front of Haycote farm had a fireplace inside, and was said to have been occupied by a shoemaker as both shop and dwelling, but his name has been lost. There were no fewer than three Haycote Cottages, apart from the farm, in the 1851 census, and one was occupied by Ann Otley, then 92, and her daughter Jane. Ann had an obituary in the *Westmorland Gazette* later that year which disclosed that she was born near Coniston.

In 1851, another of the Haycote cottages was inhabited by William Harrison and his family. William was 56 and a journeyman blacksmith, born in Heversham. He was almost certainly the brother of James Harrison who was the blacksmith up the road in Bowland Bridge, but whereas James' son was already following his father's trade, William's wife was 23 years younger than he, and they had three small children aged one, three and four.

Haycote Cottage

EARLIER in the twentieth century, another family nearby christened their baby Elsie. They lived in the dwelling across the road which was called Haycote Cottage, and it was here that the Matthews family lived. Robert Matthews was a joiner by trade, following in his father Robert's footsteps. The older man was a master carpenter who had served his time with a firm at Grange-over-Sands. Here he had also been instructed in undertaking, and this business he brought back to Crosthwaite and Cartmel Fell. He and his wife Alvarella lived at the Lound for a while, then bought Haycote Cottage, adding a joiner's shop to it, including a saw-pit in which they could saw trees and baulks of timber by hand. In later life, the older couple moved up the hill to the Mason's Arms with their daughter Nancy, but she married the apprentice John Hodgson and the young couple went to live at Haycote, keeping an eye on the business as it were. Eventually, John and Nancy moved to Witherslack to set up business there, and young Robert Matthews moved into the premises. The whole complex had been built by the family's forebears in the nineteenth century, some of whom were master wallers and others joiners, so the house should have been very well built.

At the end of the nineteenth and beginning of the twentieth century there were some large building works in progress on the fell. One instance is the complete re-build of Hare Hill for the Robinsons, and the Matthews were responsible for the superb joinery in the house and barns. Another project was the new barn at Hodge Hill, but apart from house carpentry, the Matthews did everyday repairs to farm carts, and made items which varied from farm gates to ladders. They were wheelwrights also, but had to take the wheels to the blacksmith in Crosthwaite to have the iron tyres fitted, as by that time the smithy at Bowland Bridge was defunct. Coffins were bespoke in those days, so the Matthews offered the extra service of undertaking. Horse-drawn carriages with black plumes were still in use in the early 1900s, but the day came when clients could choose between the traditional horse-drawn hearse or a new-fangled motor vehicle.

Next to the house was the workshop, largely built of wood and containing the saw-pit. One night in December 1925, when the frost was intense, the 'shop' caught fire. The cause was unknown, but because of the nature of the contents, the fire was intense. A fire engine was summoned, but the roads were in such a poor state that it did not arrive until 7am the next day. The hoses froze when they tried to pump from the river, but friends and neighbours saved the house by passing buckets along a human chain, though the workshop was totally destroyed with all its contents. William Matthews was a young boy when this dramatic event occurred, but when he grew up, he too lived in what is now called 'The Joiner's Shop,' following his father's trade. When he retired, he built his own house on the fell with commanding views over the Winster valley to Whitbarrow, and called it 'Rockway', now re-named 'Heron Syke.' In 2004, the business still survives, but in another name, that of William's apprentice, Anthony Clarke of Ashes.

Borderside

THE name says it all. This farmstead is on the very border of the former county of Westmorland, and as such is part of Crosthwaite rather than Cartmel Fell parish. The river Winster which is the boundary, could be jumped at this point, at least by an athlete. Although the present farmhouse is only about 150 years old, there was a much older house on the estate which had a moulded plaster lozenge on the chimney breast with the initials, J. P. and the date 1686. This old house was demolished in the mid-1970s, but was recorded photographically before demolition. It is tempting to think that the P stands for Pearson, since the farm has belonged to Pearsons for about 150 years, and they held land extensively in Crosthwaite for centuries, but evidence is hard to come by.

The site is probably very old indeed, for this farm takes in the relatively flat valley land of the Winster, and would have been easier to cultivate with primitive implements than the stonier uplands, but oddly, it is not often mentioned by name in early Crosthwaite records.

As far as local historians are concerned, the most illustrious owner was William Pearson, and he was the builder of the present house. William was born at the Yews in Crosthwaite in 1780, the oldest son of a traditional 'statesman,' that is the owner and occupier of his small estate, and from boyhood was a keen observer of local life, natural history and farming practices. His father was a great reader, and belonged to a book club in Kendal, favouring medical and veterinary subjects. Probably William absorbed his father's scientific interests at an early age, and must have dipped into the library books on many occasions. He was educated at Crosthwaite and Underbarrow to a very high standard, and it was at Underbarrow that he learned shorthand from the teacher, the Rev. Thomas Hervey. In the summer, during the dinner hour, the pupils learned to swim in the pool by Gregg Hall.

When he left school, William taught at Winster School for a while, but then became private tutor to the widowed Mrs Dodson's children at Swallowmire in Cartmel Fell. Fortunately for us, in later life he wrote many letters and articles which his widow preserved and published, many of his articles were for journals or societies of the day, and had already been in print. A great deal of what we know of the day-to-day life in the Winster valley in the eighteenth and nineteenth centuries is by courtesy of William Pearson. Because he was interested in so many local issues, he enlightens us on folklore, weights and measures, the enclosures and their effects, children's games, turnpikes and highways, the game laws and many aspects of natural history.

I have drawn on his writings in other sections and

OLD BORDERSIDE. CHIMNEY BREAST.

find that his social comments show his compassion and understanding of his neighbours, all of whom were brought up in the same hard-working tradition as the Pearsons. Two of the causes he espoused were the repeal of the corn laws and the repeal of the Married Women's Property Act. One of his greatest crusades was against the game laws, some of which were amended in 1831. Up until then, the only people who were allowed a gun were wealthy landed gentry and their heirs, and of course, gamekeepers. The penalties for poaching were savage, ranging from fines and imprisonment to deportation. The unfairness of this state of affairs must have rankled with every small farmer in the country, but William Pearson used his gun without the necessary qualifications and then his pen to vent his wrath. He wrote to a local paper in 1808, deploring the malpractices which the game laws engendered, such as employing informers to tempt suspected persons and then to betray them. Apparently, the Ulverston carrier had been dogged at night by searchers on the lonely heights of Cartmel Fell, and William wrote to what was probably *The Kendal Mercury* (though a copy has not survived in the Kendal Library) protesting against the malpractices of one class, whilst pleading the cause of the other. Fishing also came under the umbrella of respectable poaching in William Pearson's book, and he made no bones about the fact that he often fished becks other than his own.

For many years in the early nineteenth century, from 1803 until 1820, William worked in the Manchester bank of Messrs. Jones, Fox & Co., one of only two banks in the city at the time. Whether he mistrusted the bankers of the big town, or whether he was more inclined to support home industries, all his earnings were invested in a Kendal bank, and his first year's savings were £75. Eventually, in 1822, he was able to buy Borderside, but it seems that he installed a tenant farmer there who did not pay his rent. This led to the seizure of the barley crop which was duly thrashed and sold to cover the amount due. The tenant brought the case to trial at Appleby, after which he was ready to give up and leave the neighbourhood. The way in which the widowed Mrs Pearson related the tale makes the jury's verdict unclear, but at least the outcome was what they desired.

When William first acquired Borderside, the place was very run down, with all the buildings needing attention. The fields were badly drained, and with too many small ones, so that boundaries had to be removed to lay one or two together, and as the journal comments picturesquely, 'they were sown with boulders.'

Before the arrival of the railway, the farmers in the Crosthwaite area depended greatly on their orchards for cash, making perhaps £40 to £50 in a season at Kendal market. The old panniers which were slung across the back of a pony were sold by volume, each being sixteen quarts. William Pearson helped to get this changed to a sale by weight, which came into force in 1832-3. He was very interested in fruit, and grubbed up land at Borderside to plant three new orchards, one of 300 trees, and two smaller ones with about twenty trees apiece. Apart from the main crop of apples, the trees included pears and plums, but oddly for this area, there is no mention of damsons. The young trees were screened by a shelter-belt of oaks, with hazel undergrowth. He kept abreast with new varieties, and proudly wrote in 1832 that his Mary Oldhams were tall slender trees, about to produce the first fruit of their kind in Westmorland. Does anyone know this variety in the region today?

Through his papers written for the Kendal Natural History Society, and through the Unitarian Chapel there, William became friendly with the Wordsworths, and became a sort of unofficial agent for them in farming affairs. He found them hay and straw for their pony, fruit of all kinds in season, potatoes and even a dog, and he accompanied them on fell walks around Rydal. Letters flew to and fro regarding these topics, but also on poetry, natural history and planned excursions. When the new Borderside was built in 1848, William Wordsworth's liking for the old style of tall round chimneys on a square base was not forgotten, and in a letter of December 1849, William Pearson wrote to invite the ageing poet to inspect his fine new house, chimneys and all. The visit probably never took place, as Wordsworth died in April of the following spring.

From 1824, until a year before his late marriage in 1842 when he was past 60, the old Borderside farm was home to William Pearson. He wrote to his old friend Thomas Smith in April 1841: 'I think I told you I was going to give up farming. The sale is fixed for Monday next but one.' He goes on to say that he dislikes change, so that it seems odd that he should even think of marrying, and he continues, 'This disruption of old habits and great change consequent on it, I can assure you, puts me in a state of mind ill-befitting a joyous bridegroom.' His bride was Ann Greenhow, some seventeen years his junior, and they began their extended honeymoon on ponies, visiting the Duddon valley. That was just a preliminary jaunt, for the newly-weds spent the following year exploring Europe, keeping closely to recommendations for an itinerary made by the Wordsworths. When the couple returned to England, with feelings of relief at seeing familiar hills, they did not go back to the old Borderside. Maybe William thought it too old and delapidated for his bride, and they took rented accommodation in Winster, Cartmel Fell and Underbarrow until finally building a new house, just up the road from his new barn at old Borderside. Mr and Mrs Pearson moved in on 31 July 1848, 'with a feeling of measureless content.' One of the features they valued greatly was 'the well in the rock', a spring which never gave out in times of drought, and William built a fishpool nearby, fed by the beck. The ice-cold spring is still there, and when its water was tested for use in the milking parlour some years ago, it was found to need no treatment of any kind from the point of view of purity.

The Pearsons were very much attached to their pets, whether tame fish or robins, but their ponies get especial mention in the memoirs. Old Nep was over 30 in 1862, a Welsh pony born at Borderside, and she had a daughter, Camel, who drew a gig in William's old age. Nep was wintered at Yews or Pool Bank, but would escape and make her way home again. She is honoured by her own gravestone at Borderside.

The 1851 census shows that the old house was still inhabited, the tenant being Isaac Taylor who was the farmer of 21 acres and aged 48. We know from Ann Pearson's memoirs that the Taylors' horses were called Charlie and Blithe - not the sort of information to be gleaned from a census form. William Pearson was then aged 70, and his wife 53. William was described as a landed proprietor and

OLD BORDERSIDE BEFORE DEMOLITION.

fund holder. His early letters revealed that he had put money into South American stock which had been a disastrous investment as it had produced no dividends for 30 years or more. Unexpectedly, they began to yield in William's late middle age, so he must have been comfortably off, living in his airy new home. At this time, they had a nephew, Thomas Pearson, a scholar of fifteen living with them, and a great niece, Fanny Robinson who was a servant of 20 years and married.

By 1891, the census shows that Pearsons still reigned at the new Borderside; Thomas, a farmer aged 55, his wife Margaret, aged 46, and their nine children, plus Thomas's father, William who was a widower of 86 and a retired joiner. The age of Thomas makes it seem likely that he is the same scholar of 1851, so probably William's heir. At the old house were Margaret Atkinson, widow, a retired farmer of 78, and a boarder of 58, Robert Nicholson, a widowed woodcutter.

A story which relates to Borderside comes from a private selection of dialect readings of *What Used To Be, Lang Sen,* collected by Harold Pattinson of Bowness. The date is around the turn of the twentieth century: 'When Fenton Pearson of Crosthwaite Borderside threw t'dog cart ower, he crept fra' under it. They ext him if he was any warse. Fenton sed "I'se neeah better."

During the Second World War, Borderside had assistance on the farm from local prisoners of war. At first, these workers were delivered daily to farms from the Bela camp near Milnthorpe, but later in the war they were trusted to live in. Fritz, who was the last farm labourer at Borderside stayed on until 1966. His family were in East Germany so he could not join them after the war was over, and he went to work in the boiler house of K Shoes after his farming days were done.

Borderside is still owned by the Pearson family today, but they have introduced a summer crop which old William would not have recognised, that of the touring caravan.

Barkbooth

LIKE Haycote, this is another farm which is just beyond the boundary of Cartmel Fell, on the Crosthwaite side of the river Winster. Nonetheless, it has more connection to the parish of Cartmel Fell because of its location, Crosthwaite village being a mile or two away.

The name indicates a place where bark was stored in a dry place, ready for use by tanners. On the fell above are the farmsteads of Bryan Beck and Oaks, both being documented as having been connected to the tanning and currier's trades. There are still mixed woodlands around the area today, which contain many oaks.

The Crosthwaite parish registers are helpful in naming some of the occupants of Barkbooth, but the spelling of the farm is often wayward and may reflect local pronunciation. In 1781 and 1816 it was recorded as Barkbore in the Cartmel Bishop's Transcripts, but that might be the result of copying poor handwriting. In other instances it was spelt Barkbough or Barkbouth.

The farmstead is undoubtedly ancient, but most of the present house was completed in 1903 in a typically Edwardian gentleman's style. It is a little removed from the original site and was probably built with stone from its predecessor. At the back, contemporary with the 'new' house, was a two-storey coach-house with stabling, shippons and useful outbuildings, now converted into another dwelling. The large barn has the appearance of an eighteenth century building and may have been added to the old farm buildings at a time of increased prosperity. A decorative feature in the great barn door is a smaller inset door with an ogee-arched head. An indication of ancient agricultural activity on the estate are the ghosts of rigg-and-furrow arable field systems, visible in frost, snow or low light.

The farm would seem to have been held by the Strickland family at least since 1632 when James Strickland buried his wife Christabel (née Walker) at Crosthwaite. His son John married Agnes Jackson of Lyth two years later and had a son John who was baptized in 1635. A Matthew Strickland of Barkbooth, probably John's brother, christened his daughter Ellen in 1633, so it would seem that there were at least two households living side by side, but maybe the house was divided, or there was more than one dwelling on the site, as at Foxfield and Moor How. In 1637, Miles Birket married Margaret Strickland and they also seem to have lived at Barkbooth, at least for a while, as their daughter Elizabeth was christened from there in 1641. The pedigree of the Birkets of Birket Houses does not show this Miles, but it was a family christian name and later that century, in 1678, Anthony Strickland of Barkbooth was a supervisor of the will of William Birket of Birket Houses. He also bought Hartbarrow from Thomas Strickland of Kendal, cordwainer.

The household must have had many farm servants over the centuries, and other names occur concurrently in the parish registers, but living-in servants were usually single and there were many married couples who appeared in the parish registers. Within ten years between 1653 and 1663, children from

Barkbooth were brought to Crosthwaite for baptism with the surnames of Garnet, Suert and Phillipson, this again implying more than one household as the Stricklands seem to have been in continuous occupation until the eighteenth century. Alongside the Stricklands, the Crosthwaite registers from 1653 until 1742 place Garnets at Barkbooth, both in burials and baptisms, but not marriages.

When James Strickland died in 1708, he left the farmholding to his nephew, John Bigland, the oldest son of his sister Elizabeth. The will names 'Edward Willson, my farmer', who was allowed ten shillings rebate from his rent, and Edward's children of Barkbooth were christened in the early years of the eighteenth century, his wife Ellen dying in 1708. John Bigland was also the heir to his uncle Anthony Strickland's estate at Hartbarrow. It did not necessarily follow that the owner of an estate also lived in the homestead, and it seems that John Bigland chose Hartbarrow for his home. He died in 1729, leaving Hartbarrow to his heir, James, and his younger son Anthony lived at Barkbooth.

It appears that two households were living at the homestead throughout the eighteenth century, again implying either a large house or two separate dwellings. Whereas the Stricklands and the Biglands were undoubtedly the owners, there were farmers living at the same address. After the Willsons, the Garnet family appear in the parish registers. George Garnet died in 1726, but his widow Ellen continued to live at Barkbooth until her death in 1742. The families which followed, at roughly ten-year intervals, were the Rockcliffs, Gravesons, Ellerays and Sedgwicks.

The Crosthwaite marriage register poses a question in 1879. William Fleming, a basket-maker,

Barn door at Barkbooth

married Margaret Ann Davison, spinster. The bridegroom's residence was 'Bobbin-mill at Barkbooth' and his father was a bobbin manufacturer. There has not been any evidence for a mill on this site, and the 1881 census shows William Fleming, wisket-maker, and Margaret his wife at Bobbin Mill Cottages, Crosthwaite and Lyth, where there were apparently four cottages, two of them uninhabited. The other occupied cottage housed John Fleming, a bobbin manufacturer, employing eight men. These dwellings were at Starnthwaite, so it seems that the register might have been carelessly written, as it was the bride's parents who were living at Barkbooth in 1881.

Cartmel Fell

By the nineteenth century, the censuses are able to give us more detail of the occupants. There are separate households at the same address, but no known photographs of the house or houses. Three generations of Davisons were in residence in 1881, the grandparents living apart. This family had moved a lot, as whereas the old man had been born in Middleton, Westmorland, and his wife in Longsleddale, their descendants were born in Kendal, Distington, Workington, Beetham and Crosthwaite.

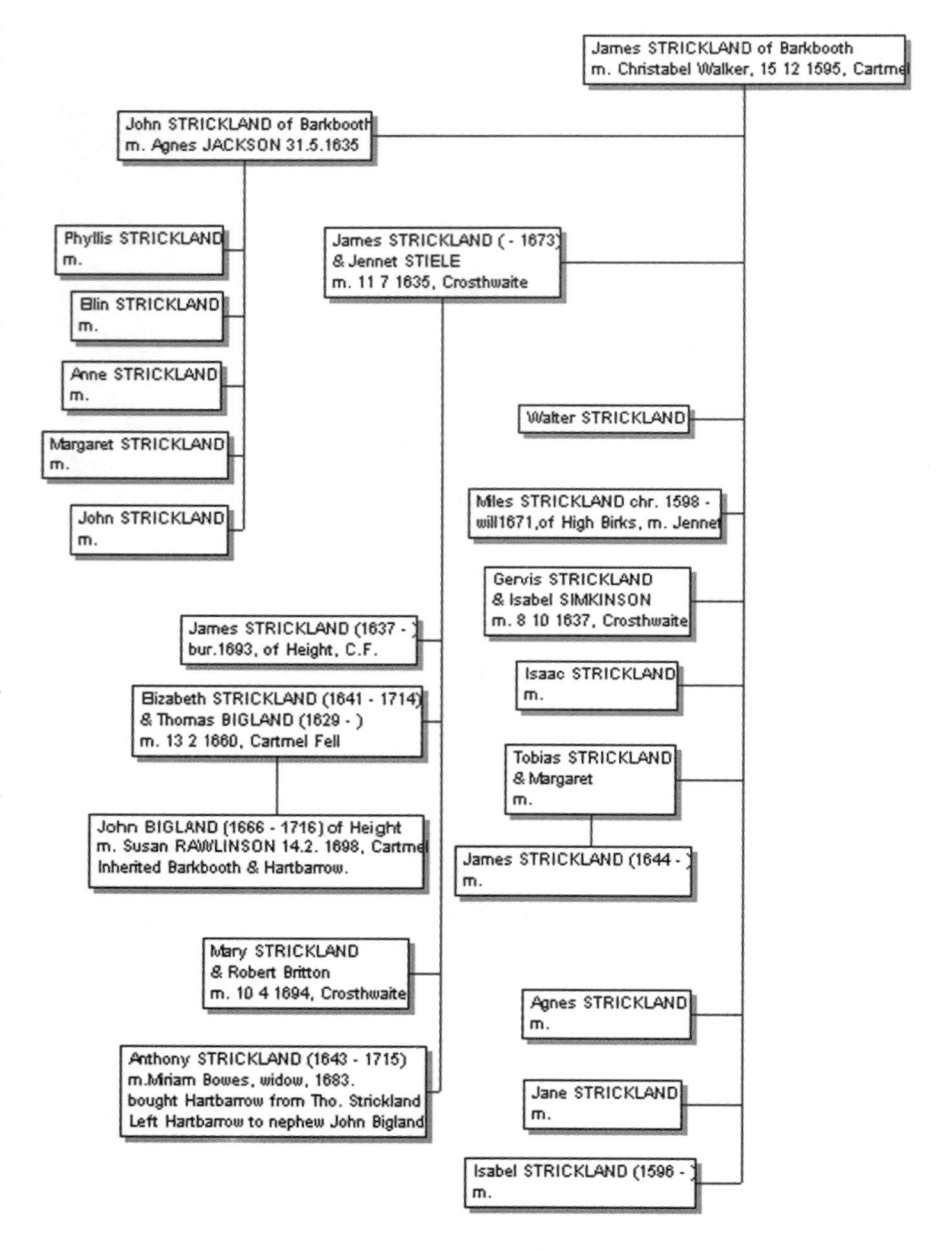

In 1873, Richard Frederick Matthews christened his son at Cartmel Fell and styled himself 'Yeoman of Hartbarrow.' The son was named after his father, with the extra family name of Bigland. The family had left Hartbarrow some time towards the end of the nineteenth century and had gone to live in Barrow-in-Furness where father Richard was described as a brickmaker. This was a time when Barrow was expanding rapidly, so bricks were in great demand. This may have been the means by which the family fortunes increased, because Richard Frederick Bigland Matthews (the younger) built the new house at Barkbooth, finishing it in 1903, but the farm possibly already belonged to his father. The new building probably utilized stone from the old one, but there is a quarry in nearby 'Rocky Field' so new stone was readily available. This smaller house was the core of the present-day building, which had additions east and west added around 1909/10, making six more rooms and a conservatory. Sadly, Richard Frederick had only a few years left to enjoy his fine new house, because he died on Christmas Eve 1908, aged only 35, whereas his father lived until 1942 and died aged 88. A memorial tablet in Cartmel Fell Church confirms the details of the younger man's birth and death.

In 1891, James Dixon and his family were farming Barkbooth. They had seven children, ranging from ten-month-old Etta to fifteen-year-old Hannah, but only one son, Thomas. Also in the household was Agnes Kitchen who was James Dixon's mother-in-law of 84, living on her own means. It would seem that the farm still belonged the owners of Hartbarrow, so the Dixons were either tenants or farm managers.

The parish register traces the connection to the Biglands, who were still keeping a toe-hold at Barkbooth but through the female line. Archibald Kendall, a motor engineer of Barkbooth and his wife Martha Elizabeth, inserted the family name of Bigland when their children were christened at Cartmel Fell. Mary Bigland Kendall was born in 1915, John Bigland Kendall in 1917 and Richard Bigland Kendall in 1920, though by that time the family had moved to Walney. Archibald Kendall had one of the first taxi services in the district, and in 1913, Thomas Price, then the curate of Cartmel Fell, noted in his diary that the family ordered a motor from Barkbooth to go to Keswick. The journey took one and a half hours each way.

In 1925, Colonel Kelsall brought his family to live at Barkbooth. Here he created a market garden and became a friend and fishing companion of Arthur Ransome who visited Barkbooth frequently from his home at Low Ludderburn, just above on the fell. The two men devised a system of signaling from one house to the other, as no telephones were yet in private homes on the fell, and photographs of the symbols they hoisted formed the basis of Ransome's drawings in *Winter Holiday*. The signaling devices have recently been re-created for the enjoyment of members of the local Arthur Ransome Society, which meets several times a year and occasionally visits Barkbooth.

Sir Charles Craven.

Ownership of the property passed to the Craven family in the late 1930s. Sir Charles Craven was the Chairman and Managing Director of Vickers-Armstrong. During their occupancy, the Cravens enjoyed field sports, and they had a clay pigeon shoot in Rocky Field, and a well-stocked fishing tarn with a boat on Barkbooth Lot. Sir Charles died in 1944 and his son, Derek, was killed in a car accident two years later when he was returning to Barkbooth.

In 1946, Dr John Caldwell retired from his medical practice in Milnthorpe and moved to Barkbooth, later buying the property, where he lived until his death in 1967. His widow Sheila gave Barkbooth Lot to the Cumbria Wildlife Trust in 1975 and they manage the nature reserve, home to medicinal leeches, High Brown Fritillaries and Dark Green Fritillaries. Ownership of Barkbooth passed to Dr. Caldwell's younger son John and his wife Jean in 1991. There was an echo of the Cravens' occupancy in this move, as John Caldwell had served a ship-building apprenticeship with Vickers Armstrong at Barrow in the 1940s. Later, he had appointments with the Admiralty and at various universities and then, for 25 years, was Professor of Naval Architecture at Newcastle University. Jean graduated from Bristol University and trained as a teacher. Her spare time is consumed by garden-related activities and societies. The Caldwells continue to enhance their mature garden, also having built new garages, restored the barn and converted the former coach house and two shippons into residential accommodation.

Hartbarrow

THE name probably derives from the old Norse, *Hjorta*, a hart, but it could be the personal name of *Hardr* in the same tongue. Barrow is either the old English *beorg*, a hill, or barrow as in burial ground or mound. Whichever is the case, Hartbarrow is certainly very ancient in terms of a continuous dwelling place, the first documentary evidence being in 1332.

Today, there are three houses to carry the name, with distinguishing adjectives of Great and Little, and the third being 'Cottage'. Unfortunately, most historical documents do not show such distinctions, and possibly Great and Little Hartbarrow were Harrison family holdings originally.

An exchequer lay subsidy roll for North Lonsdale hundred in 1332 names Adam de Hertbergh and his tax liability assessment of 3s.11d. This was to finance King Edward III in his continuing Scottish wars, and as Cartmel and district had been devastated twice in the previous two decades, the need for controlling border raids must have been well-recognised locally. So much pillage, destruction and slaughter was caused by Robert the Bruce's men in 1322, that Cartmel priory's ecclesiastical tax was reduced from £46.13s.4d. to a mere £8. Cattle were driven off the farms, and even from the priory's lands. It is not very likely that the Scots penetrated the woodlands of Cartmel Fell, but the tales of horrendous doings would soon be passed on, so perhaps the heavy taxes were borne with resignation and hope of quieter times.

A Patchwork History

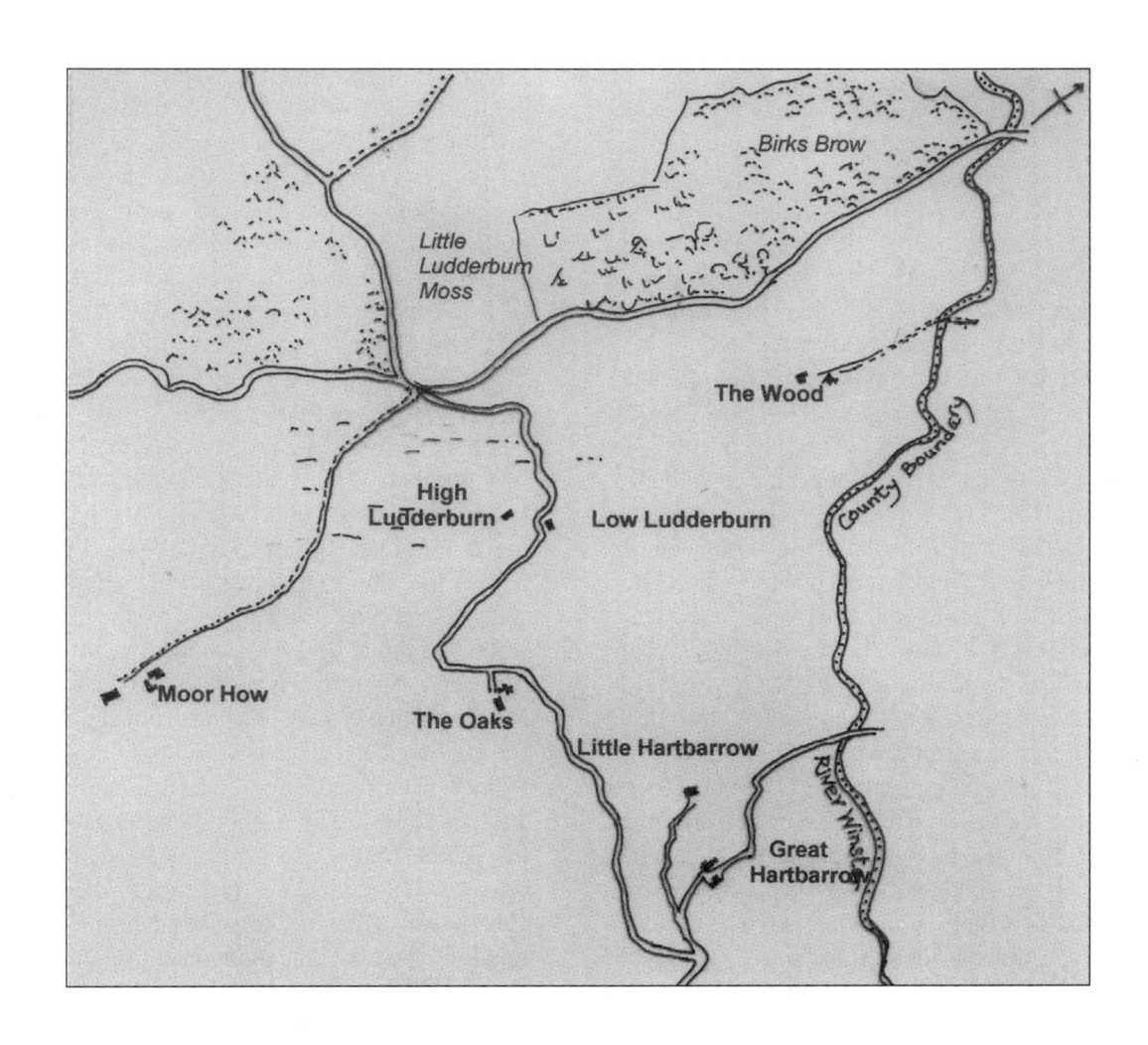

The next mention of Hartbarrow comes in a Duchy of Lancaster rental of 1508, in which the Harrison family are named and twenty years later, the same family were involved in a lawsuit. By this time, surnames had come into general use, so possibly the Harrisons were descended from Adam de Hertbergh, who could have had a brother or a son called Harry. As will be seen from the lawsuit, the Harrisons were prepared to go to great lengths to keep their holding by fair means or foul.

In 1508 there were three Harrisons of Hartbarrow - Robert, Michael or Mitchell and William. The widow of one Thomas Harrison took tenements on Cartmel Fell at this time, but her relationship with the Hartbarrow family is not revealed. A dispute arose in 1529 between Harrison cousins. Robert was in occupation, having inherited the property from his father John, but he was only six-years-old at his father's death. His appointed guardian was his father's brother for whom he had been named, but it would seem that Uncle Robert must have died at about the time of his nephew's majority, and his two sons, Christopher and Richard had other ideas about inheritance. One assumes that first they tried to oust their cousin by verbal persuasion. This cannot have worked, so the next method was much more primitive. Young Robert was besieged by his cousins and seven other men, armed with 'clubys, bowys and bylles'. It was an unequal struggle, and Robert was ejected. As a young man, deprived of parents' or a guardian's advice, the Harrison heir must have wondered where to turn for help. Six years elapsed before his first appeal was made to the Chancellor of the Duchy of Lancaster, and this is where we learn the details of the case. Uncle Robert, it was alleged, had 'brent' (burned) the will, thus making the title to Hartbarrow unclear. The cousins Christopher and Richard and Johane his wife were summoned to attend the court of the Duchy at Westminster, but chose to ignore the summons. The tactic paid off, for Sir William Fitzwilliam, the Duchy Chancellor, decided to submit the case to local arbitration. We do not know who the arbitrators were, or what means of persuasion were used, but they found for the usurpers and awarded Robert a cash settlement only, together with one acre of land. It is tempting to think that perhaps this acre was the site for Little Hartbarrow, but of course there is no proof. He later complained that no account had been taken of the crops of which he had been deprived over the years, and had no recompense for bringing the suit.

There is a will in Preston Record Office, which was made in 1619 by Robert Wallas of Hartbarrow, but again, there is no defining adjective to pinpoint the farm. This Robert may have died prematurely, for his five children appear to be under age, and his wife Jane is instructed to bring up the children within his tenement and houses, until such time as they can serve themselves. It is hard to deduce the source of the Wallas income from the inventory of this will, as his livestock is that of a very small farmer, four cows and a heifer and one wether sheep. There are axes, wombles, saws and 'other of his worke toyles,' so probably he was a carpenter with a few acres, and therefore of Little Hartbarrow. His debtors owed him £22.11s.10d., maybe for work done and as yet unpaid. He had no debts of his own.

The Harrison tribe continued at Hartbarrow, and their increasing numbers began to colonise other sites in the vicinity. In the sixteenth and seventeenth centuries there were Harrisons at Moor How, Ludderburn, Oaks, Collinfield and Sow How. The Hartbarrow branch must have been farmers with a larger than average holding of land from Tudor times, for when Bryan Harrison died in 1593 his inventory included 104 old sheep worth £20.16s. and 36 lambs worth £4.14s. He also had '12 olde yewes of the worst shepe, and 29 stonne of wolle'. This was a valuable commodity worth £14.2s, and there was also two stones of woollen yarn, which added greatly to the value of raw wool, being assessed at £1.4s.

We can see further on in the inventory that Brian had a tenement in Winster, un-named, and as the list was compiled in August, the standing crops of bigg and haver are mentioned there, together with an arke and a ladder. Some of the items were held jointly with another person, as Brian left half a cow, half a calf and half of three hives of bees. Many people owed him money, totalling £94.10s.8d. His only debts seem to have been ten shillings to each of three of his brothers, and to Nicholas Fisher of Beardleyfield (Bradleyfield) for a bushel of bigg. Apart from fairly extensive farming activities, we could make the inference that the Harrisons were dealing in, or even manufacturing woollen products. Apart from the yarn, already spun, Brian was owed money by William Atkinson of Winster for '4 Whittes at 13s. a pace, and more at 6s.' Whites were probably double and single blankets, and some forty years later, we find that Margaret and Christopher Harrison paid a tax of 2s.8d. in respect of a fulling mill 'long since in decay.' The site of this mill has not yet been identified, but there is no shortage of water sources in the area, and a small beck runs quite close to the front of the house. A fulling mill did not need a large water supply, but would have a dammed area to make a mill pond. The mill itself was like a cross between a washing machine and a beater. Soap was made from bracken potash, then the cloth was pounded with paddles like sections of a cartwheel until it was clean and partially felted. The northern breeds of sheep tend to have a wiry, kempy fleece which when woven is open and draughty. Fulling improves the density and body of the fabric, and also pre-shrinks it.

The source of the Harrisons' wealth must have been in part from their cloth production, but obviously that money was made to work by lending it to neighbours and family. When Edward Harrison of Hartbarrow died in 1630, he bequeathed his loans to his brother-in-law James Dickinson. These totalled £53.16s.11d. He too had wool and yarn, and also wheels and cards for spinning.

Reading the bequests of another age can cause a few wry smiles. This Edward Harrison, a man of some wealth and standing, had apparel worth 36s. and that was valued as part of his estate, but he left a lot of old clothes to friends and family. His goddaughter, Michael Powe's (Poole's) wife was to have an old hat and a pair of old stockings, and Christopher Harrison's daughter was to have an old waistcoat.

Because of its position on the fell, it was easier for Hartbarrow folk to go to Crosthwaite Church for major occasions before St Anthony's was licensed, and many marriages, burials and baptisms took place there instead of at Cartmel Priory. From evidence in the Crosthwaite parish registers, it would seem that the Harrison era was drawing to a close at Hartbarrow in the mid-seventeenth century. The daughter of Christopher Harrison was buried in

1631, but the next entry specifically naming the farm is a new surname in 1652, that of Strickland, when James buried a stillborn child. Nine years later he christened a daughter Frances. We know from an earlier will that the Stricklands were in residence by 1642, when William mentions the 'Knowing Rent' of 6s.2d. There is a farm in Witherslack called Strickland Hill, possibly the original seat of this family, and the letter-writing Brockbanks of Witherslack mention that in 1690, Anthony Strickland had returned to his own house at Hartbarrow from Low Wood, this being the farm adjoining Strickland Hill. That area of Witherslack was a Quaker stronghold, and it seems that the Stricklands had dissenting tendencies at this period.

In 1684, Hartbarrow became the temporary home and academy of the renowned Richard Frankland. The attractive datestone on the front of Hartbarrow bears this date, with intertwined initials for Anthony and Susannah Strickland. If the house had been newly renovated, perhaps for newly-weds, why did they move to Low Wood? There are no ready-made answers, but possibly the Stricklands were sympathetic to Frankland's persecution as a nonconformist who was banned from his very successful academy at Natland owing to the Five Mile Act limitation. No dissenter could be permitted to live or preach within five miles of a market town, according to this Act, though Kendal corporation were slow in implementing Frankland's removal.

Richard Frankland was an interesting man of high principles. He was born at Rathmell, near Giggleswick and first went to Giggleswick School. From there he went up to Christ's College, Cambridge, where the master, Samuel Bolton was a cultured Puritan. This may have influenced Frankland in his steadfast Presbyterianism in the years to come. He gained a B.A. in 1651, and an M.A. three years later when he became chaplain to John Brooke, who was twice Lord Mayor of York, and also a Presbyterian. In 1658 he married Elizabeth Sanderson and took the cure of Lanchester, Co. Durham, and seemed to settle down until the Restoration. Then the trouble began. From all accounts, Frankland was a mild-mannered man and did not seek out conflict, but in matters of conscience he was unyielding. He was asked if he would conform by an attorney of his parish, and his reply was that he hoped the King's proclamation for quiet possession would secure him. To Mr Bouster, the attorney, this was sheer evasion, and he took the key of the church to debar the minister. The matter went to law, and to appeal, but Frankland lost. The Bishop of Durham seemed particularly to want Frankland's conformity, and offered to re-ordain him secretly. This would have meant swearing an oath, which was against nonconformist principles, so Frankland thanked the bishop, and said 'It was Conscience, not Obstinacy which hindered his compliance.' He was ejected from the living and returned to Rathmell.

Possibly this was the break which gave Frankland time to review his life, for in 1669 he set up the first nonconformist academy at Rathmell, though there were many others later. These colleges provided substitutes for the degree courses of Oxford and Cambridge for dissenters, as no degree could be conferred without the swearing of an oath of allegiance. This meant that there was no place in the ministry for would-be nonconformist preachers.

In 1672, Richard Frankland took out a licence to teach, i.e. preach, under a special indulgence of that year. This was for use in his own house at Rathmell, but a call came from Natland for him to go and preach there. This was actually less than five miles from Kendal, and for a while the magistrates turned a blind eye, being unusually tolerant for the times. Eventually they were forced to act, but gave the academy until Michaelmas to find new premises. By this time there were many pupils, and over 300 had passed through to take degrees in Scotland, where the laws were different. It was not easy to find new accommodation, and Kendal magistrates did not harry the academy and its master, but around 1682, the government were pressing corporations to enforce the Five Mile Act. For a brief period, the establishment moved to Kirkby Malham in the Yorkshire Dales, but then found a home at Dawson Fold in the Lyth valley, which was then in Westmorland.

The moves had greatly affected the health of the institution, and between 1682 and 1686 only thirteen scholars had been admitted. Crosthwaite and Lyth parish came under the greater parish of Heversham, and the Franklands were amongst several who were cited at the Consistory Court of York as not having attended church. This was denied by the Crosthwaite parish wardens, and they signed a declaration testifying to Mr. Frankland's good behaviour, 'his wife and Family keeping due and Constant Communion with us in god's publick worship.' In all the instances where Richard Frankland came up against laws or decrees, it seemed that his own honesty and personality were his greatest defence. No-one seemed eager to persecute him for the sake of bigotry, from the Bishop of Durham to the Kendal magistrates, and now, his neighbours, the church wardens of Crosthwaite.

It is thought that the family moved to Hartbarrow some time in 1685, but may have been travelling in between. A letter dated 24 November 1685, from Richard Frankland junior to a friend, says: 'We could not possibly write sooner, for we were longer on our journey than expected.'

The following year brought the Act of Toleration, and though it was principally to allow free worship for Catholics, the nonconformists gained equally. The Frankland family moved yet again, to Attercliffe, near Sheffield, and with his high reputation, Richard had twenty pupils in the first year. It seemed that a return to Westmorland was envisaged, as James Garnett's house, Moss Side in Crosthwaite, was licenced in 1691 for Frankland to preach in, but it did not happen. Richard junior, his father's right-hand man had died two years previously, so maybe the effort was too much for the ageing father, and he ended his days in his birthplace of Rathmell.

As mentioned earlier, the Stricklands moved back to Great Hartbarrow in 1690, six years after the date stone with their initials was erected. Anthony was a signatory of the Bryan Beck rental agreement in 1714, as a trustee, but he and his wife must have been victims of accident or epidemic, for they had a joint burial at Crosthwaite on 24 September 1729.

In 1727, John Bigland, yeoman of Hartbarrow, was a trustee of Bryan Beck, and this is another instance of there being no differentiation between the Hartbarrows. Yeoman, implies ownership, but Anthony Strickland was also a yeoman, so either the farm and house was divided at Great Hartbarrow, or else one was the owner of Little Hartbarrow. The Strickland initials on the 1684 date stone show their ownership, but we know that the Biglands were of Great Hartbarrow in the nineteenth century, though they could have moved down the hill.

In 1743, Thomas Strickland and James Bigland, both of Hartbarrow, signed another Bryan Beck indenture, but their status as yeomen is not mentioned, and we know from later census returns that the Biglands were in residence throughout the nineteenth century, though there is evidence of a Bownass family being owners. In 1812, John Bownass of Townend House, Witherslack, made his will. He left all his property at Hartbarrow to his son, John Fletcher Bownass, and this is born out by the land tax copy of 1814, when William Bownass was the owner/occupier. Yet again, however, neither document reveals whether this is Great or Little Hartbarrow. If any of the field names listed in the land tax could be identified today, this might clarify matters. Apple trees figure largely, such as Near Apple Tree Field, and Apple Tree Field Wood.

The story of the later branch of Biglands can be pieced together through the parish registers, the tombstones and the census details. In 1841, John and Richard were described as 'independent,' that is with a private income, whereas William Goss at Little Hartbarrow was 'farmer.' The Bigland brothers were 65 and 60 and they had four farm servants living in, two young men and a girl of thirteen. The fourth was Martha Bell, aged 30. John Bigland died in the year of the census, and although he was there listed as 65, his burial record says that he was 60 when he died, so the census enumerator probably got the brothers' ages confused. Brother Richard must have married Martha Bell the servant fairly soon after John's death, because he died in October 1847 aged 70, and in the next census, widowed Martha was the head of the family with a four-year-old daughter, Hannah. She was farming 49 acres (one less than there was at Little Hartbarrow at that time) and had two farm servants, one of whom was her younger bachelor brother, Isaac, and he remained as her right-hand man for the next twenty years. The farm expanded to 80 acres of old land in 1861, plus 50 acres of heathland. Martha died in 1880, aged 71, and the family grave continued to be used until her grandsons' time. The last to be buried there was Richard Frederick Bigland Matthews who died on Christmas Eve, 1908. He was the son of Hannah, Martha's only daughter who had married Richard Frederick Matthews. A tablet in St Anthony's commemorates Richard Frederick Bigland Matthews' death at the newly-built Barkbooth, just in the valley bottom.

One can see from the parish register that a family of Cowards was in residence at Hartbarrow at the end of the nineteenth century and the beginning of the twentieth, and several burials took place from there. Isabella Coward died in 1898 aged 83, and John in 1911, but on reference to the censuses, it is apparent that this family had been at Little Hartbarrow for at least 60 years, though the parish register does not make that clear. Edward and Isabella Coward christened their son Edward in 1847. He had been born in Langdale, and she in Claife, and when they christened Edward, they already had an older boy, John. It was not a big farm, 23 acres of old land and 27 of heath, but they must have kept some cattle, because in 1881, Isabella's grand-daughter, Isabella Barclay was their dairymaid, aged fifteen. Little Hartbarrow was farmed by Christopher and Helena Tugman for at least four years between 1888 and 1892, as their children appear in the baptismal records. Helena was the daughter of Simon Bathgate, a gamekeeper who had lived at High Ludderburn and a Scot. Her brother John was living with them as a farm servant when the 1891 census was taken.

The regular ten-yearly census returns are of great value when it comes to tracking family patterns and farm occupation. If a house was falling into decay, it might be tenanted by agricultural labourers or even used to house paupers, as was the case with the ruinous school-house in the early nineteenth century. The census returns for most of the nineteenth century make no mention of Hartbarrow Cottage, and it first appears in 1881 when William and Elizabeth Davison are in occupation, he being described as a labourer. Houses change their names at times, but there is no other dwelling in previous decades which would fit into the Hartbarrow Cottage location, so presumably it was built between 1871 and 1881, maybe to house workers at Great Hartbarrow farm. When the 1909/10 Inland Revenue survey was made, surprisingly, Hartbarrow Cottage is said to be 'fairly old'. The parish registers show baptisms for several families of labourers early in the twentieth century. In the 1920s and 1930s, a branch of the old family of Thornburrows was at Little Hartbarrow. Frederick was a policeman when he christened his daughter Freda Margaret in 1921, but sixteen years later, Anthony Thornborrow was the farmer, and his daughter was christened Thelma Elizabeth in 1937. Thelma was a new name in the Cartmel Fell baptismal register, and a sign of outside influences infiltrating into the traditional names of grandparents, aunts and uncles. Surnames from the maternal side of a family had long been used as christian names, keeping a thread of visible descent, but from the 1930s onward, a whole series of names derived from films, radio, books, and later, television, occur in the register. The traditional names remain however, and far outnumber the new ones.

There must have been increasingly hard times for the farmers on the fell in the nineteenth century. So many have come to light that were in need of a mortgage to keep going, and one of the principal lenders was the Birket family of Birket Houses. If the mortgage payments could not be maintained, or the mortgagee died, the Birkets acquired the property, and in this way, they gradually accumulated about one third of the farms on the fell. Apparently, the same thing must have happened at Hartbarrow, for older people remember Major Birket as having been the landlord in the 1930s. The 1909/10 Inland Revenue survey reveals that Myles Higgin Birket was the owner of Little Hartbarrow at that time, and the occupier was Matt Dobson. Great Hartbarrow was still owned by Richard Frederick Matthews of Barkbooth, and he also owned Hartbarrow Cottage.

Herbert and Agnes Moon arrived at Great Hartbarrow before the Second World War, and raised a family there. Wartime photographs show their harvest fields which helped to feed Britons with home-grown produce. Their family expanded during the war years, but another name appeared in the baptismal register, also at Hartbarrow. Edward Thomas and Annie Irene Vinall christened their son Martin in 1945, and the father's occupation was motor engineer and farmer. John Bigland of Barkbooth was one of the first motor engineers on the fell during the First World War, but most fathers were still involved in agriculture or forestry until after World War Two.

At the beginning of the twenty-first century, the old barns opposite the farmhouse were converted into dwellings by Robert Hughes & Co., and the three Hartbarrows have become a hamlet of seven houses. In the woods below the farms, evidence of ancient gardens can be seen in the wild gooseberries and raspberries which have colonised the area.

Oaks

OAKS abound on Cartmel Fell, so it is hard to imagine what engendered this particular farm name. Perhaps other trees were eliminated so that the tanning trade could flourish, for this area was a centre for tanning in the seventeenth and eighteenth centuries and possibly earlier.

The earliest documentation found for Oaks so far, is a will of Richard Harrison, yeoman, in 1611, and in this case the farm is spelled Akes. The Harrison clan had colonised the northern end of the fell for at least 200 years prior to this, and had many strings to their bow. Some had had fulling mills, (Hartbarrow) some had corn mills (William of Sow How, 1726) and all were relatively large-scale farmers as their inventories attest. This Richard Harrison mentions the right of his widow to half the tenement and thirds of the goods and chattels during her lifetime. Like many other local inventories of the period, this one lists the equipment for processing wool; cards for teasing out the strands, wheels, and in this household, studdles, the upright members of a loom. The Harrisons appear to have been either supplying coopers or manufacturing barrels themselves, as there was a quantity of coopering timber listed among Richard's belongings at his death. The oaks of the estate could have been used for cask making. Katherine, Richard's widow, was to have half the estate and an extra little close called 'Klarmer' (maybe the same close called Ellmer at a later date), except the end half of the meadow, and the gate for one cow in foggtime, the access to grass which follows the hay harvest. Christopher, the elder son, was to work the farm for his mother, but if he did not comply with the terms of the will, then James his younger brother should inherit all. When reading these ancient clauses, it is difficult not to fantasise about family relationships. Was Christopher a rebellious customer? Was his father overbearing? Did the person drawing up the will suggest caution?

The inventory was appraised by three more Harrisons and Edward Swainson, 'beinge bodilye booke sworne.' There must have been quite a lot of plough land, as the Harrisons had a team of oxen, two being worth £5.13s.4d. Smaller farmers would borrow oxen to work their land. Two horses were of equal value to the oxen, but 'towe alde kye' were valued at £4.13s.4d. In addition to the old cows, there were four young ones, described as 'towe stots and towe stirkes, a cow and a halt (lame) cow. Sheep, as was usual, are not enumerated, but since their worth was £8.12s.0d., one can estimate that there might have been between 60 and 70, depending on age and quality. There were sizeable crops in the barn and as this was October, haver and bigg combined were worth over £12, but there was twice the value of oats or haver, so probably about twice the amount was grown. Hay, fruit and wool comprised the rest of the harvest, and bees and honey were worth £1, the equivalent of eight sheep or thereabouts. The Harrisons must have had many skeps of bees and enjoyed a good summer in 1611. Although the total of Richard Harrison's estate came to £59.1s.2d, unfortunately he had debts which amounted to £49.5s.1d. Eight of his creditors were Harrisons, and the other ten were all local names of the day - Swainson, Kilner, Briggs and Knipe.

Eight years later, in 1619, Robert Pull of Prentices bequeathed his property at Oaks to his son Rowland. Possibly he had bought the estate from the Harrison family, as we have seen that Richard was barely solvent, or else there was more than one estate there.

In 1673, two family names appear, and the parish clerk at Cartmel had a real struggle to spell the farm name. In the first instance it is Oaxes, and in the second, Oaxe. Edward Harrison's daughter was christened Elizabeth and John Caton christened his son John a month earlier in June. This latter could have been a farm servant, but it could have been a separate household. The fact that the Harrison name is still in evidence seems to point to a customary tenure, that is by paying a ground rent known as a fine to the owner or lord of the manor, the occupier could pass on the holding to his heirs. He could still be called a yeoman, as to all intents and purposes, the estate was his.

In March 1678, Michael Harrison's daughter Agnes was christened at Cartmel. From that end of the fell it must have been a journey of nearly three hours on foot, and even on horseback maybe two, as one could hardly gallop with a small baby aboard. The mother might have ridden pillion behind her husband, but she would find it difficult to hold the babe and cling on to her man. There would be little possibility to shift her burden either, so we would expect the family to choose a fine day for the round trip. The roads at this period were only narrow rutted tracks, so there was no possibility of wheeled transport.

The Harrisons were still at Oaks a century later,

but in between, the name of Hodgson crops up, so the likelihood of two dwellings on the site at this time seems to be strengthened, but maybe the Harrisons took a lodger. Whatever the arrangements were, a Rowland Hodgson of Oaks made his will in 1702. He left his property at Blewet (Blewthwaite today) to his daughter Agnes, she paying the annual rent of six shillings to Burblethwaite Hall, plus two pence for a little close. Another married daughter, Dorothy Archbold, was to have twenty shillings, and her two daughters £2 apiece when they were 21. Thomas Hodgson, Rowland's son was to have £15 on the Candlemas following his father's decease. We know from the Blewthwaite papers that Thomas was a mariner, and that Agnes later married George Lindow, a grocer or importer.

Apart from his Blewthwaite property, Rowland had a modest inventory. Most of his personal belongings were worth only a few shillings, but an unusual item was 'A pair of spectills and books.' The appraisers were obviously unfamiliar with the word spectacles, and got around it as best they could. Books were very uncommon at this period in local inventories, Brian Philipson of Hodge Hill and Miles Birket of Birket Houses being the only other book owners to have been found so far. Both were roughly contemporary with Rowland Hodgson. No cattle or other stock appear in this inventory, but there is a dung hill, worth six pence, so perhaps Rowland had a vegetable garden. There are no clues in his will as to how he made his money, but since his son was described as mariner, possibly he was following in his father's footsteps.

In the miscellaneous accounts of the chapel, we learn that William Harrison of Oaks was currier to Samuel Matson of Bryan Beck in 1714. The document relates to the trustees at the sale of Bryan Beck, and that it was the property of Samuel Matson, tanner. The two trades were intermeshed and used to be in close proximity. There must have been tan-pits somewhere in the area between Oaks and Bryan Beck, if not at each site, but they have not so far been located. Almost directly below Oaks, in the valley bottom, is the estate of Bark Booth, and this may have been where the stripped oak bark was stored, to keep it dry until needed for tanning.

The Cartmel Fell parish church documents list the constables, graves and overseers of the poor for much of the eighteenth century. William Harrison of Oaks was overseer of the poor for the year 1725, and Christopher Harrison was constable in 1734, followed by a year as grave, a sort of deputy or clerk to the constable. Unfortunately, no farm name is given, but since it comes between the entries for Hartbarrow and Moor How, it probably refers to Oaks. At some period in the mid-eighteenth century, the Harrisons gave way to the Dodsons or Dodgsons at Oaks, but were still widely scattered in other farms about the parish. William Dodson did his duty as a chapel warden in 1755 and 1756, but when he went to Oaks is not known. Two families of Dodsons arrived on the fell at this period, and seem to have been wealthy. John went from Wilson House to Pattinson How in 1741, and William went to Oaks at about the same time. We know that William was the father of Matthew Dodson, since Oaks was one of the many estates that Matthew listed in his will of 1800. It would be interesting to know the source of their wealth, but apart from the fact that John was 'of Wilson House' when he bought Pattinson How on a 99-year lease, there is no other evidence to show whether they were connected with John Wilkinson's iron industry. Alice Dodgson, wife of Matthew, was buried from Oaks in 1778, and from evidence of wills and property, we know that this is the same Matthew who died at Poolgarth where he made his will in 1800, 'being very far advanced in years,' as he says in his will. He must have re-married fairly soon after his first wife died, as he left a young family, all under 21 - five daughters and a son. Close to extinction in 1778, this Dodson line had seven children by 1802.

The 1814 land tax list gives the next clue as to the owner and occupier of Oaks. The owner was John Dodson, Matthew's heir, or rather his trustees, as he was still under age. The tenant was Thomas Strickland who might have been connected to the Stricklands then at Hartbarrow. The 1785 land tax return has the names of the assessors and collectors of the tax, and one of the collectors was this same Matthew Dodson. His own payment was 15s., which was one of the highest on the fell, plus smaller amounts for his other properties. As a comparison, Myles Sandys paid 14s.4d. for Burblethwaite. The land was assessed in proportions of £1 per acre, and the tax was collected at the rate of four shillings in the pound at that date.

By 1829 the tenant had been replaced by John Dixon, as the Parson & White directory shows, but there are no details of this man and no asterisk to denote a yeoman. Twelve years later we can get fuller details of the occupants from the census of 1841, and by this time the Long family were in residence. From an existing tenancy agreement for Bryan Beck, we know the meeting of the trustees was held at Oaks in 1836. Robert Long was the host, and more of his family is revealed in the 1841 census. Robert, aged 50, was born in Crosthwaite and was termed 'farmer.' No detail is given of family relationships, but if one reads between the lines, we could guess that Jane, aged thirty, is his second wife, as the five children range from nineteen to one year, with a big gap between Robert, the oldest, to Nicholas who was only seven. All the younger children were born on the fell, as we see in the next census. The 1841 census can be misleading, as it rounds all adult ages down to the nearest five years, but by 1851 the true ages emerge. Robert is now 66, and Jane 43. Ten years later, Robert is 76 and still farming 100 acres plus upwards of 100 acres of what is termed heath. His son Nicholas has married and is living at Oaks, pursuing a career of woodmonger, and he has three small children. Rather surprisingly, grandfather Robert has a son of twelve still at school, young George Long. As well as the extended family, two unmarried farm workers are living in, Thomas Strickland aged 50, and Henry Dickinson aged 25. The parish register shows that Robert Long died in 1862 aged 79.

By 1871, the Pearsons of Crosthwaite were farming 130 acres at Oaks, with four hired hands. George and Nancy had five children at home, three of them at school, but the younger two were only two years and ten months old. These last were born in Cartmel Fell, presumably at Oaks, but all the rest of the family were born in Crosthwaite. From that knowledge, one could assume that the Pearsons arrived on the fell in 1868 or thereabouts. From deeds in private hands which refer to Oaks, there is a section which shows that T. Pearson granted his quarter share to C. Webster of Kendal in 1871. This was subject to a redemption of £250 plus the interest. Evidently the

THE OAKS, BARN

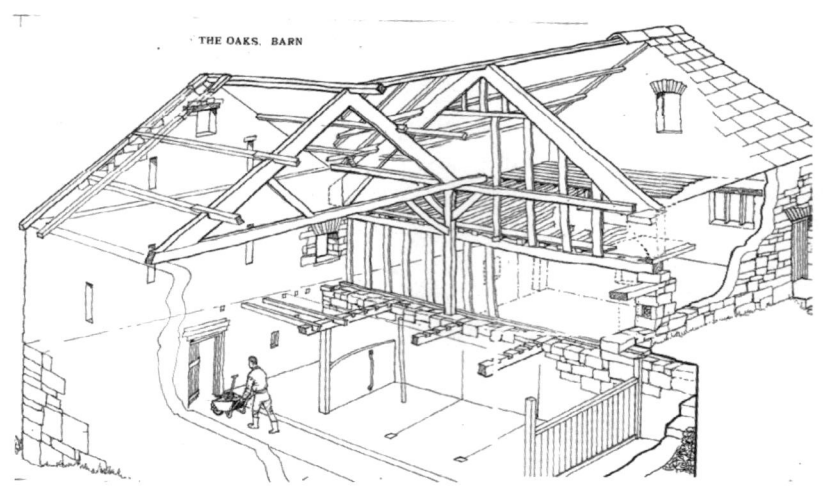

property had been mortgaged privately at some stage, but we do not know the relationship of T. Pearson to George Pearson. By 1881, the acreage has risen to 170, but as the elder two boys were now in their late teens, only one hired man was needed, though there were still two domestic servant girls. The Pearsons continued their occupation throughout the next decade, but by 1891 they had departed.

The newcomers were from Kendal, Nathan Burton and his wife Margaret, who was born in Kirkby Stephen. Obviously, the family had moved considerable distances in the past, as their daughter had been born at Kirkby Stephen also, the elder son at Rawtenstall and the younger in Kendal. George Birket was the occupier in 1910, and the owner Myles Higgin Birket. In the years between the world wars, John and Edith Ellis were farming at Oaks. The parish register records the baptisms of four children between 1919 and 1931.

The present house at Oaks is probably well over 300-years-old, but when photographs were taken in December 1993, Mrs Smith pointed out the filled-in windows at one end of the old barn. It had obviously been a house at some stage, so further investigation was needed. Alan Forsyth went back to do a detailed drawing when the weather warmed up. (see plate) This dwelling could be contemporary with the present house, with very complicated timber work where the barn adjoins at right angles. The remaining lath and plaster walls on the inside are of good quality, the riven oak laths being thick and almost touching. An old plasterer who had served his time in the 1920s, showed me how he used to measure the distance between the laths when nailing them up. He just used his first and second finger as a spacing gauge, so every plasterer had his individual spacing, those with small fingers using more laths. These at Oaks are a finger-nail apart and it must

Oaks Barn windows.

have been a quality partition, meant to last. This older building has the windows in the gable end of the wall, which seems to be the pattern of the oldest houses locally, and it seems to have been two rooms only, one above the other, with possibly a loft above. No chimney can be detected, but this again may be a sign of great antiquity, since even in the south of England only the grand houses had chimneys until the fifteenth century. A charcoal brazier may have served for warmth and cooking, or perhaps there was a separate cookhouse as an adjoining hay barn was a fire risk. The windows do not have lintels, but have the same massive relieving arches as at old Bryan Beck, old Ludderburn and High Old House Beck. It could be that such stark accommodation was for the farm hands; they would take their meals in the main house and retire to their barn lofts at night. Probably it would be no colder in the winter than the bedrooms in the house. Until the eighteenth century, most upper rooms had no ceilings and were open to the roof, and such rooms can still be seen at The Wood and Thorphinsty South Cottage. The warmth from the beasts below would be at least as much as that from a peat fire in the house.

The main farmhouse was completely renovated just before the millennium. The plaster was removed from the inside walls and many earlier features were then disclosed. There was a bricked-up fireplace which extended into an upstairs room, and there tapered off. This looked like the remains of a smoke-hood which would have protruded into the upper floor. When peat was the only fuel, a wattle hood was perfectly adequate to carry away the smoke, and the smouldering fire was no danger. In later times, when coal and wood became the usual fuels, the smoke-hood was a positive hazard, and this was seen at Oaks in the blackened floor timbers above the fireplace. After such a fire, they probably decided to make a proper chimney.

Another find beneath the plaster were two little recesses, perhaps six inches square. In one of these was an iron shackle with a lock, almost identical to the one displayed at Town End, the National Trust property at Troutbeck. There, it is pointed out that Benjamin Browne was high constable of the Kendal Ward, and these were his tools of the trade. If the fetter found at Oaks was the property of a one-time constable of Cartmel Fell, why was it walled up? Another revelation beneath the plaster was where many more windows had been filled in, probably to avoid paying one of the window taxes.

In the same tradition of owners past, there is a new dwelling at Oaks today, built by the elder son for his family. The elder of his two sons moved into 'L'ile Yaks' when he got married and is the third generation of Smiths to farm at Oaks. A decorative path made of old gate stoups links the old house to the new one. However, this time the old house is not destined to become the barn.

Ludderburn

THIS place name first occurs in 1537, and was then spelt Litterburne. The name comes from the old English *hluttor*, meaning clear or pure. There is a local belief that the well for Low Ludderburn is Roman in origin, but it must be said that there is no actual evidence for this, though the steading is undoubtedly very old.

There are several holdings of this name, now differentiated by the prefix High or Low, and one could almost call the Ludderburns a hamlet but the early documents make no such distinctions. The spellings vary from Ludder (1593), Loder (1683), Louther (1721), Luther (1727) and also in the nineteenth century census records, and back to Ludderburn today. There are many instances in Cumbrian dialect of *th* and *dd* being interchangeable, such as in fodder or father, and one wonders if this is a relic of the old Cambrian speech, i.e. Welsh.

Dating any building is only an approximation of the oldest remaining parts, but parallels can sometimes be drawn. The barn at Low Ludderburn was altered by Arthur Ransome when he lived there during the 1930s, and although he put in windows in the upper floor, the lower level is substantially unaltered. Here the flooring is of small slates set on edge vertically. Another place in which such treatment can be seen is in Kendal's Castle Dairy, which is said to date back to the fourteenth century. If this was then the local method of producing non-slip flooring and given that it is uncommon in later times, one could assume that Low Ludderburn is the oldest of the dwellings, and therefore the one to which early documents relate. The present owner suggests that in a group of the same name, the first dwelling is the one with the most sheltered position, and the logic of this idea is attractive.

The first mention of Ludderburn's owner or occupier is in the will of George Marshall, dated 18 January 1575. From this document we learn that when his son-in-law, Robert Harrison, married into the family, a covenant was made that Ludderburn farmhold, with all its appurtenances, should become his on his father-in-law's death. George's grandsons, John and Robert Harrison, were to have a sheep and a ewe and a lamb. All the family inherited the bedding and raiment. Daughter Anne was yet unmarried, and she was to receive useful household equipment of two arks, a cauldron, a spit and a rackencrook, but also a total of £20 in three instalments, the first on her wedding day, a very handsome portion in 1575. There was also an absent son-in-law, Robert Allay(r?)e, who might receive 13s.4d. 'if he come into the country.' Another daughter, Catheren, was to have 40s.

There may have been two Ludderburns even at this point of the sixteenth century. From George Marshall's will it seems that he had no direct male heirs, but Richard Marshall of Ludderburn was mentioned in an inventory of Bryan Harrison of Hartbarrow in 1593. The Harrisons were substantial farmers and fulling-mill owners, and obviously money-lenders too, for about two dozen debtors were named, one of whom was his father-in-law, Richard Marshall (or Mershall) of Ludderburn, whose debt of a mark he 'forgave'. William

Marshall of Ludderburn owed £1.12s.4d. and another of the same family, Anthony, owed fourteen shillings. The likelihood is that all these Marshalls were related, but this has not been substantiated. Five years later, in 1598, there is an entry in the Cartmel parish records concerning monies belonging to the grammar school. Some concern was expressed about the safety of these sums in the hands of the men from Cartmel Fell, one of these being Robert Harrison of Ludderburn, 'And for which hee hath laid a gaidge, 40s.'

It seems from Bryan Harrison's will that the Harrisons were farming Ludderburn, and that William Marshall was a widower living in his married daughter's household. Another William Marshall of Ludderburn was buried at Crosthwaite, almost a hundred years later, in November 1692.

A document in Kendal Record Office dated 1673 concerns the feoffment of Ludderburn. The first party was Robert Philipson of Calgarth, Esq. and the second Robert Wallas of Ludderburn, Cartmel Fell, carpenter. There was a yearly rent of 4s.6d. and a fine of £1.16s. The consideration was £43.10s. to include a parcel called 'Old Ridding'. This last mentioned might just possibly be part of the 'lost' farm of Wayridding.

The Harrisons were still at Ludderburn some fifty years later, when in 1715, John made payments to George Fleming of Hilltop in Crosthwaite. Four years after that he made his will, naming his wife,

Low Ludderburn

Margaret as executrix and his daughters Elizabeth Moon and Margaret Lickbarrow. Margaret, daughter of John Harrison of Ludderburn was christened at Cartmel in May 1677. There is nothing unusual about the items in the inventory. He had £5.12s.9d. in his purse, two beds and a chest with some malt, a pack saddle and other lumber (another reminder of the lack of good roads), and 'the seed and Plowing of the big (barley) and oats and hemp upon the ground.' John was buried at Crosthwaite.

Towards the end of the seventeenth century and into the eighteenth, many names appear on various documents, all with the Ludderburn address, so it seems likely that High Ludderburn had been built by then, and here we come across another puzzle. There are two higher houses, one of which is reputed to have been a drovers' inn. This house is obviously older than the Georgian one opposite, but beyond them both is a truly massive barn. This, on closer inspection, has in earlier times been a sizeable dwelling house with a barn attached. Some of the windows have their original wooden mullions still in place, and the relieving arches over the windows display the very characteristic local style, which is something like a double fan. Usually, this style of relieving arch goes hand in hand with massive stepped foundations, visible for two or three feet above ground level, and this is the case here. Although there is no provision for a chimney in this derelict building, the upper room is nicely plastered, unlike the rough render of a barn. A very similar outbuilding can be seen at Oaks and another at Bryan Beck. Although granaries were usually on an upper floor and plastered so as to keep out vermin, usually they are windowless and no effort was wasted on plaster mouldings. Possibly, these were dwellings for agricultural workers who took their meals with the family, but slept elsewhere.

To return to all the families - between 1683 and 1729, eight different family names occur at Ludderburn, and clearly not in the same household. In 1683, Edward Myles paid a fine of 4s.6d. for attending a meeting of the Friends. This name occurs only twice in our file of fell-folk, so maybe he was a lodger or farm servant. A schoolmaster, William Myles, was appointed in 1697, but no relationship has been discovered. William Allerson of Ludderburn was buried in 1705 at Crosthwaite, which seems to have been the preferred church for this end of the parish, and this seems odd at a period when seating was allotted to parishioners according to their dwelling-place within the parish. Maybe some were the descendants of Crosthwaite folk who were allowed to take their former seats and to use family graves. A new name appears in 1721 - that of John Taylor. He is mentioned in a Quaker will of Thomas Braithwaite of Rosthwaite, also in the parish of Cartmel Fell. Apparently, John Taylor had lent money for a mortgage, probably for Rosthwaite, but the will does not make this absolutely clear. The Braithwaites held lands and tenements for miles around so this mortgage cannot be pinpointed.

It seems that the Ludderburn end of the fell was a centre of dissent, neighbouring Hartbarrow being a nonconformist academy in 1684-6, and Thomas Brockbank who was the vicar of Cartmel in 1706 expressed concern about the Presbyterians, 'Who are nestled only in this corner of the parish.' There were many Quakers nearby too, including the influential James Birket of the Wood, which was within a short walk down into the valley. Some of the Harrisons may have had Quaker leanings at this period as James Birkett was a supervisor of the will of John Harrison in 1719.

In 1727, the will of James Hodgson of

Barn at High Ludderburn

Ludderburn was proved. Later that century, there were Wilkinsons and Parks in the parish registers, also of that address and in 1801 James Dickinson senior of Ludderburn rented Bryan Beck.

By the time of the 1841 census, two of the three houses were uninhabited, but it does not say which. Presumably the highest house was by then a barn, or the Georgian-style house had not been built. William Stewardson was living at one of the houses as head of the household, aged 65, together with (one guesses) his son aged 40, and a daughter-in-law of 30. There were also two boys, William and Matthew aged eleven and two. Both men were accounted for as 'agricultural labourers'. Martha Stewardson of Ludderburn had been buried at St Anthony's in 1839 aged 66 and may well have been William's wife. William died in 1848 aged 75, and by 1851, Matthew's sister Agnes had become his housekeeper. There was also Martha, his niece aged five months, and his nephew Matthew junior was a scholar of twelve years. At last, in the 1861 census, the Stewardsons are identified as living at Low Luther Burn, (as it was then spelt,) the Stricklands at High Luther Burn and the Prestons at Middle Luther Burn. None of the families' heads were classified as farmer, but all as labourer, whereas in the past, most had been yeomen who owned their farmholdings.

The second half of the nineteenth century was a difficult time for small farmers, and many ailing farms became derelict. This was when the wealthier yeomen bought up estates or lent money for private mortgages, many of which failed. In 1872, James Birket of Birket Houses bought several quarter shares of local estates, including the Ludderburns. By the end of the nineteenth century, Myles Higgin Birket also of Birket Houses had acquired all the Ludderburns by this means, and many other estates as well.

By the time the 1881 census was taken, the enumerator reverted to calling all the houses merely Lutherburn, but as the Stewardsons were still there, and Matthew was by then 81, we can deduce that the Scottish family of Bathgates was at High Ludderburn. Simon Bathgate was a gamekeeper of 37, and had two children at home. Unusually for the times, Helena was still a scholar at sixteen, but the Scots were always keen on education. The whole family were born in Scotland, but no town is given. The nearest estate where Simon might have been keeper is Gill Head, but it is more likely that he worked for the Birkets of Birket Houses since they owned the Ludderburns by this time. Jessie Bathgate must have been away from home when the 1881 census was taken, but she appears ten years later, the year in which she married Robert Leighton Matthews, joiner, of the Mason's Arms. The Matthews family dynasty of master craftsmen was about to renew itself.

Middle Ludderburn in 1881 was occupied by the aged Sarah Dickinson, an annuitant of 86, and her unmarried nephew of 25. She may have been a descendant of the Bryan Beck Dickinsons who were tenants in 1801. In a time before old age pensions, Matthew Stewardson at 81 was still working as a labourer in this census year, but had given up wood-cutting. He and his sister still lived at Low Ludderburn, and although ten years younger, she died in 1885. Matthew lived to be 90, dying in 1890, but one more Stewardson followed him at Low Ludderburn, Fanny, a spinster of 89 at the time of the 1891 census and probably Matthew's sister.

She was of independent means and lived with a widowed servant, Mary Blamire, who was a mere 64.

In the twentieth century, the most celebrated owner of Low Ludderburn was Arthur Ransome. In his day, the road was still unmade and gated, as an old photograph shows. The days of refuse collection were still in the future when the author lived on the fell, and the old rubbish tip has yielded some souvenirs of his occupation. One of these was a Russian typewriter with Cyrillic letters, and a Russian samovar or teapot. The second Mrs. Ransome had been Trotsky's secretary, and met Arthur in Moscow when he was foreign correspondent for *The Manchester Guardian*. Her name was Evgenia Petrovna Shelyepina, but Arthur Ransome called her Genia. The couple were married in Lithuania in 1924 and arrived on Cartmel Fell the following year. Arthur had digestive problems, probably a peptic ulcer, and Milk of Magnesia bottles were also amongst the debris of the rubbish heap.

Fortunately for posterity, Arthur Ransome was a good correspondent, and we can read of his enthusiasm for Low Ludderburn in his published letters. He wrote to his mother, the elder Mrs. Ransome: 'We are so overcome by finding ourselves in the loveliest spot in the whole of the Lake District, with a very small house that wants a lot doing to it to make it really nice and comfortable.' The state of the house at that time must have been a bargaining point, because instead of paying the asking price of £650, Arthur talked to the owner and not the agent, and managed to get the property for £550. Completion was to be on 12 May 1925, but while renovations were under way, Arthur and Genia lived at Hartbarrow. On 27 May, Arthur wrote to his mother to tell her that the move had been accomplished in two journeys with their 'perambulating biscuit tin,' a 'Trojan' motor car. After their effects were installed, they had to drive to Windermere to buy a looking glass, since they had not even a shaving mirror.

Before looking after the bare essentials, Arthur Ransome had negotiated the most important hurdle, that of getting fishing in the vicinity. The previous owner of Low Ludderburn, Major Birket of Birket Houses, gave him permission to fish the upper Winster, and two days before moving in, Arthur had caught a nice bag of eight trout. In the same letter which described these activities, Mrs. Ransome senior was told that the house, furnishing, barn conversion and motor car would all come within her son's £1,000 budget. He had a friend, Colonel

Arthur Ransome's Trojan driven by his nephew.

Amy Johnson

Kelsall, who lived across the valley at Barkbooth, and before the telephone arrived on the fell, they used to send signalled messages to each other with a system of geometric shapes hoisted up the walls. The friends were keen fishermen, and the communications were usually on the state of the river, or the mayfly hatch, followed by a time and place for rendezvous. This system of coded messages was used in *Winter Holiday,* which was published in 1933. The first of his children's books *Swallows and Amazons,* was written in the partially converted barn at Low Ludderburn and published in 1930. The upper floor of the barn was originally without windows, but electricity was still 35 years away, so plenty of light was necessary for a writer to earn his living, and a large window was installed, together with a new floor to quell the updraught from the shippons below. After the success of *Swallows and Amazons,* other books followed, with permutations on the original cast; *Swallowdale, Peter Duck, Winter Holiday* and *Coot Club,* and as Ransome illustrated the later books himself, he used the Kelsall boys at Barkbooth as models, first posing them for photographs.

It may have been that working as a foreign correspondent had given Arthur itchy feet. He seemed to like change and moved house many times, but his stay at Low Ludderburn was one of the longest. He left for the south in 1935, but later returned to the Lake District.

Most people know of Amy Johnson's exploits as an aviator, but it is less well known that she used to come and stay with her aunt, Ethel Rubina Johnson, who bought Low Ludderburn from the Ransomes.

High Ludderburn farm was renovated in the 1990s, but until that time, it still had its old peat burning hearth, open almost to the ceiling, with a fire-hood above, now a shallow alcove.

Moor How

THE name is self-explanatory, for these farms can be seen from miles away on the high north eastern end of the fell. Behind them to the west, the land could still be described as moor, but improvements must have been carried out over many centuries to make the rocky grazing which surrounds the two holdings. Unfortunately, in the past, these farms were not differentiated by their prefix of High or Low, so it is often difficult to unravel the threads of their occupants, but as there is a dated cupboard inside High Moor How with the initials W P A and the date 1693, it is possible to make informed guesses. The Cartmel parish registers show that William Pull (the surname was later spelt Poole) of Moor How christened two sons in 1694 and 1696. The date on the cupboard might therefore be to commemorate the wedding of William and Agnes. Agnes Pool, wife of William, was buried at Cartmel on 1 July 1712.

The farms at Moor How are very old settlements, the earliest mention found being in 1588, when Michael Pull's inventory mentions Elizabeth, daughter of Rolland Wallas of Moor How. A few years later, in 1593, Robert Wallas of Moor How owed a debt of £2.7s. at the death of his neighbour, Brian Harrison of Hartbarrow. In 1590, a Duchy of Lancaster rental for Moor How mentions three families, indicating three separate holdings. The tenants' names were Brian Harrison, George Garnett and Robert Walles.

A will in Preston Record Office was that of an earlier William Pull of Moor How, written in 1630. It appears that his son Michael was dead, and that he mistrusted Dorothy, his daughter-in-law, as there was an undischarged marriage settlement which William was prepared to waive 'if she and her children be content to claim no part of my goods. And if they claim any, then I give this parte unto my two daughters, Elizabeth and Anne to be equally divided between them.' Other rather uneasy relationships are suggested in the will: 'Item, I give unto my brother John Pull if he stay untill I die, my best Cowe. Item, I give unto Elizabeth Dixon my tenant 6s.8d. if she stay untill I die.' Various grandchildren were bequeathed a lamb apiece and the supervisors of the will received two shillings each, his daughters being joint executrixes. Particularly interesting is the inventory which is attached to the will. It is about three inches wide and shows what a yeoman's household was like in the early seventeenth century. Although the will was made on 30 June, the inventory was made in December, and William Pull had 30 head of cattle at that time, a surprisingly large number for such a high farm. Perhaps he had good hay meadows lower down the slopes of the fell, as his hay was worth £2. Two pack-saddles tell us of the state of the tracks in those days, and maybe his daughters used the 'Syd sadle'.

The Poole dynasty colonised the northern end of the fell and down to the lake as well. At different periods they owned property at Tower Wood, Spooner Close, Gill Head, Moor How and Prentices.

In the mid-seventeenth century, Quaker influences began to spread along the fell, and Spooner

Close was at one stage used for meetings, so maybe this was where some of the Pooles were converted. A family of Garnetts were still living at one of the Moor Hows, whilst another branch of their family lived at Spooner Close and they were all buried or married at Height Meeting House. A William Poole of Moor How was buried at Height on 4 October 1698.

As High Moor How was home to the Pooles, it therefore follows that the Harrisons of Moor How lived in one of the other farms. Cartmel Priory registers show Harrisons of Moor How from 1695, and the names of Garnett and Poole march side by side with them through the registers for generations. They probably shared or let their dwellings also, since many other names occur at Moor How, and it is very likely that a number of farmsteads had other dwellings attached, constituting small hamlets.

Moor How is the given address of both Pooles and Harrisons throughout the seventeenth and eighteenth centuries, and the parish records show them serving their terms as constable, overseer of the poor, chapel warden and grave. The Garnett family feature at Moor How in Quaker registers from 1688 to 1734, but they did not serve as officers for the parish since they were not members of the Church of England. In 1758, Robert Harrison served his year as chapel warden for one estate at Moor How, followed by his son William in 1759, again for one estate. This implies two separate estates, and papers from the Robinson family who succeeded to Low Moor How prove the point. The Robinsons were first tenants, and then bought the estate in 1758.

In the chapel warden's accounts for 1759, a line jumps from the page: 'Paid to Thomas Atkinson for costs on account of William Harrison's tryal for murder of his wife Alice.'

The documents relating to this case are at Kew and make startling reading. Alice Harrison's battered body had been found by two of their farm labourers. She was hanging from a beam in the house, and at first, it appeared to be suicide. There was an inquest, and depositions were made. The two men who found the body were William German and George Hudson, employees of the Harrisons, who had lived in the household for about eight months. They gave Alice a mild character, but said 'she complaines bitterly of her hard usage.' She had run away soon after Whitsun, but had returned. Her mother and father-in-law had refused her entry to the house, but put her in a ruinous building, where she stayed three weeks or more and then went away again. She sought refuge at the house of Roland Rawlinson, overseer of the poor for that year, and he declared that she had several times told him she was afraid her husband would kill her. William Harrison had come for his wife with a peat cart, and because she was legally his property at that time, Alice had submitted. Roland Rawlinson was one of the fifteen jurors who unanimously charged William Harrison with Alice's murder.

William Robinson of (Low) Moor How, one of the deponents, said that Alice had told him that whilst she was in the ruined granary, her husband and mother-in-law had come to the door and had it not been fastened, she believed she would have been murdered. After this episode, she was chained to a bed at Moor How, the chain so tightly fastened that she could not get out of bed. On 15 July, after dinner, she complained of a pain in her back, so William loosened the chain somewhat, and his father went into the barn to chop bark. The two husbandmen were sent to burn brackens (for potash), but it soon began to rain so they returned to the farm. Old Robert Harrison was still chopping bark in the barn, and gave them the key to the house whilst he went to see what a heap of ashes they had got. There they made the shocking discovery.

The indictment is strange. It describes the appalling battering which Alice had endured on every part of her body, 'of which mortal wounds, bruises (etc.) the said Alice instantly died.' Towards the end of the account when the cord around her neck is described, the conclusion becomes: 'of which strangling, the said Alice instantly died.'

The case seemed so clear cut, with all the Harrisons' neighbours testifying against William, that hanging seemed inevitable. A search at Lancaster found nothing, but a will was another surprise.

William Harrison made his will on 23 March 1777, and was buried on 6 April. He must have appealed successfully, if indeed he was ever sentenced, but these papers are missing. The will mentions two freehold messuages in Cartmel Fell, commonly known by the name of Moor How. This implication of a third house crops up again, but evidence on the ground is unreadable after so much time has passed. Also the will discloses that William had bought the piscary or fishery in the lowest couble (division) of the lake, and owned Burrow House near Tower Wood. This last piece of information may be a clue as to how he became associated with his wife Alice. A marriage bond exists of 1742 for William Harrison of Moor How, yeoman, and Alice Bulfield of Spooner Close.

Burrow House is quite close to Spooner Close, and as previously mentioned, the Garnett family were of both Moor How and Spooner Close. Possibly, Alice was either related to or in service with the Garnetts.

After this episode one would expect the Harrisons to keep a low profile locally, but when his parents died, William erected a tombstone, inside the church, on which was a pedigree of his mother. Was this a defiant gesture or one of contrition? The inscription on the stone is as follows:

Near this place lie the remains of Elizabeth the daughter of John and Frances Borrow of Beathem and wife of Robert Harrison of Moorhow in Cartmel Fell who departed this life the jj day of February 1762 aged 73. Here also lie the remains of the aforesaid Robert Harrison who Died the jj day of September 1768 aged 79.

Robert's will left his two properties at Moor How to his son and his only items of value were his 140 sheep worth £30. He left £20 to Henry Herd, described by William in his own will as 'my relation,' and who inherited Moor How eventually. He was living there at the time of William's death, though when Robert died, was of Pool Bank in Crosthwaite. Margaret Herd, Henry's wife or daughter, was the sole executrix of William's will and Henry was buried at Cartmel Fell in August 1801.

The Herds (or Hirds as it was later spelt) continued at Moor How for at least another generation. The 1814 Land Tax list shows that John Hird had approximately 100 acres of pasture, and another 70 acres of allotment from the enclosure awards. A manuscript music book of theirs was found at the Post Office at Bowland Bridge in the 1940s, and contains music with unusual notation, perhaps suitable for a penny whistle, many tunes having a martial flavour.

By 1841, the first census to disclose household detail shows the Hirds at one of the Moor Hows and the Robinsons at the second. A descendant of the Robinsons has evidence that the family bought Low Moor How in 1757, the year of the murder, and their initials and 1758 can be seen on the front wall. This date commemorates the wedding of Margaret Blades and William Robinson. The marriage was a fruitful one with ten children surviving, some to a great age, but very few were inclined to marry. Seven of the brothers and sisters remained single, and it is surely three of these brothers that William Pearson recalls in his memoirs, though he does not name them individually. In an account of the three Robinson brothers' prowess, William Pearson defended them fiercely in the press when they were fined for poaching. On snowy moonlit nights, these three would hunt hares, merely by running and directing each other with shouts. No dogs or guns were involved, and they enjoyed the sport for its exhilaration, not for monetary gain, as they left the hare on the doorstep of the farmer on whose land they made their catch. No subterfuge was involved either, as William Pearson said their shouts could be heard echoing back from Gummers How. The fine was £3.13s.6d., about one week's wage each, but William Pearson declared that the Ancient Greeks would have crowned them with laurels. He also added darkly, 'But this is the age of taxation and little men, we are fallen on evil days.'

High Moor How

In 1781, William Robinson died suddenly, when on a trip to Bowness. He was 48 and his youngest son Isaac was only three. His widow Margaret continued to live at Moor How until she died in 1823. John Robinson, born in 1759 and the oldest son, had a good education at Kendal Grammar School and eventually became master at Town Bank School in Ulverston. As his father had died intestate, John became the heir to Moor How, and this caused a bitter rift between him and his siblings. Eventually, they clubbed together and bought the holding from their brother, vowing he should never return, but as fate would have it, John's descendants did inherit the farm ultimately, when Ann, his youngest sister died in 1856. John of Ulverston, William of Hollins and Thomas of Hare Hill were the three older brothers and the only ones to marry, though bachelor James of Moor How had two daughters and strangely, their husbands were both called John Atkinson. We know from the Mannex Directory of 1851 that James had owned the whole hamlet of Moor How, but he had died the year before the directory was published.

Robert, the next to youngest brother, died at Satterhow, Sawrey, in 1849 and left that estate to his housekeeper, Margaret Robinson Holme, with his share of Moor How to his sister Ann and elder brother James, who died the following year. Letters from those two years from the sons of John, show how their uncles' two wills had split the family into factions, and the wills show the extent of the family holdings. These included the Tower Wood estate, Blakeholme Intack, Satterhow at Sawrey, Moor How (moieties), premises at Claife and Sanderhill in Crook. In a letter from James Robinson (son of John, the original heir to Moor How) to his unnamed brother, he describes uncle Robert's funeral at Cartmel Fell early in February 1849. He was followed to his grave by large numbers of friends and family and close on 100 people dined afterwards at Mrs Tyson's, Strawberry Bank, but how they all crammed in is hard to imagine.

By 1851, the acreages are included in the census. High Moor How had 100 acres and Low Moor How only 56, but there was a third household in which 76-year-old Ann Strickland was the head. No acreage was recorded for the third house, so it seems to have been a cottage, but Ann Strickland had her grand-daughter Elizabeth Dickinson living in as a house servant. Ann died in 1856, aged 82. The higher farm was run by the Kellett family, three unmarried brothers, two spinster sisters and their grandfather of 93. This family had originated in Hawkshead, and the parish register shows that they had suffered the loss of three of their younger members within eighteen months. John died in 1847, aged 49, and 7-year-old Martha died in 1848, in the same year as 48-year-old Annas, who was presumably her mother. Then, in 1852 and 1853, John and Thomas Kellett died. John was the grandfather of 94, so whatever disease carried off the younger generations, he must have been immune. One usually suspects tuberculosis when whole families die in quick succession, but the parish registers give no diagnoses.

Ann Robinson, then 79, was the 'landed proprietor' at the lower property. She employed two relations as servants, Mary Ann Elam and James Holme, a nephew of thirteen. James Holme later became the agent for woodlands at Thorphinsty Hall and Blakeholme, but made a brief appearance in the parish register as 'tea-dealer' of Moor How in 1863 when his daughter Mary was baptised, and two years later he was living at Blakeholme.

By the time the next census was taken in 1861, James Holme's widowed father was ensconced at Low Moor How with his son. He must have inherited the farm through his wife Mary, née Robinson, who had died at Moor How in 1857, and he was her second husband. James, the younger son was at Moor How in 1861 aged 23, was described as a schoolmaster at a grammar school, so probably he was on holiday when the census was taken, though he is not described as 'visitor'. A letter from him, dated 1849, is headed 'Stott Park', so it seems likely that Hawkshead was where he taught.

As the nineteenth century progressed, the Robinson line gradually petered out on the fell. William of the Hollins (1760-1850) had a son James who had gone to work as a land agent in Brindle, and when he died in 1883, he left money in his will for book prizes at Cartmel Fell school. This branch of William's family still live in that area of

Lancashire Their place was taken by newcomers at Moor How, the local family of Edmund Crow at High Moor How, and in 1871, by William Burns from Colton and his family at Low Moor How. At this date, there was also an uninhabited house in the hamlet, still uninhabited at the next census, but its whereabouts is not known.

The Crows (or Crowes as they later became) were at High Moor How until 1893, when Edmund died, aged 73. His son Jacob married soon after and his wife Agnes had two children, Ellen, born at Moor How in 1895 and Edmund Jacob, born the following year at Ludderburn. Sadly, Jacob had died before his son was born, so that is probably why Agnes moved away.

At the turn of the century all the households had changed again. Thirteen people were living at one of the Moor Hows under the roof of Thomas Middlebrough. He had eight children and three farm workers, but next door were a family of only three Rowlandsons. The Rowlandsons were still there in 1909/10, but they did not own their farm; it still belonged to John Robinson, so was presumably Low Moor How. The other farm was owned by Myles Higgin Birket, who by slow degrees was acquiring more and more properties on the fell.

From the entries in the baptismal register of the fell for the twentieth century, one can assume that the Moor Hows were starting places for young tenant farmers. There are many surnames which change every few years, but very few burials. The description of the land in the 1910 Finance Act survey for High Moor How says it all: 'This land is very rocky, no subsoil - about 80 acres of allotment.' Today the houses have been greatly improved, but nothing can alter the land.

Low Moor How

When the photographs of each farmstead were taken in 1993, a small building at High Moor How was a puzzle to its owner, Ted Foster. The end which faced the prevailing wind had a series of small square holes over its surface. This was the most exposed of all the buildings in the group and the highest. The holes were only a few inches deep and did not go through to the inside as pigeon holes would. Many suggestions were put forward, but Mike Davies-Shiel eventually cracked the riddle. They were post holes for battens on which to hang vertical slates; these would protect the wall from the worst of the weather, but the slates must have been needed elsewhere and the timber either rotted or was removed.

The Wood

THIS title needs little explanation even today, for the landscape cannot have altered much since it was named. The steeply sloping land behind the farm is all mixed woodland, and unsuitable for much else because of its rocky nature. The farmstead is sheltered from the prevailing westerly winds and gets the sun for most of the day, so the site was well chosen. Like so many other farms in the district, ancient yews are at the corners of the farmstead.

The house is difficult to date, because like almost all the others it has had alterations and additions over the centuries. We know that it was there in 1679 when it was bought by Myles Birket of Birket Houses for £240. This sum was for the estate, not just the house. Myles, born in 1640, was the heir to his father James but it seems that he had already had to purchase his inheritance of Birket Houses, probably in order to pay out two siblings. This he had done in the previous year, so he must already have had capital.

Myles was married in 1666 to Elizabeth Birket of Crook, and they may have been related, but the pedigree does not show this. They brought up a son and daughter at The Wood - James and Mary - but another child, Esther, died in infancy. In 1717, the year that he died, Myles purchased the manor of Winster. James was given The Wood by his father in 1692, the year before his marriage to Elizabeth Goad. The couple were married at Swarthmoor at a ceremony of the Friends, for this branch of the Birkets had a strong Quaker commitment, and connections with Height Meeting House on Cartmel Fell.

Unfortunately, Elizabeth was soon dead, and James was remarried in 1696 to Elizabeth Hinde of Littledale, the ceremony this time being at Lancaster. His children however seem to have been born at The Wood, as their Quaker birth records show, but James bought Hebblethwaite Hall near Sedbergh in 1712, and this subsequently went to his heir, whilst the Lancashire estate of The Wood went to Thomas, the second son. He died in 1759, and his widow Deborah was bought out by the next brother, James, a West Indies merchant in Lancaster, and a partner with his brother Myles in the Halton Furnace Company. In the mid-eighteenth century James was many times constable and grave for Cartmel Fell for his various estates, which

The Wood

included The Wood and Birket Houses, but as with so many generations of the Birkets, the succession was by no means certain. The pedigree does not show a marriage for James and both his younger brothers, John and Richard, died unmarried, so the Wood eventually passed to a great nephew, Robert Foster, in 1783.

Robert was born in 1754 at Lancaster and was articled to his Rawlinson relatives who were also West Indian merchants. When he was twenty, his grandfather Myles, and his great-uncle James sent him to Antigua as their storekeeper. This must have been an exciting period for the more adventurous young men of the area, as there were so many farmers' sons who sought their fortunes on the other side of the world at this time. Some of them succeeded, but Winster churchyard shows the evidence of many who died young in Demerara, Ceylon and Jamaica.

Young Robert Foster seems to have become bored with store-keeping, and by 1776, his log shows that he was 'mate and midshipman' on the brig *Endeavour,* commanded by Lieutenant Francis Tilsley. She was fitted out with fourteen guns to cruise against American privateers which were wreaking havoc amongst British merchant shipping. Tension between the two countries was great at this period because of the War of Independence, so a British naval ship would be policing the West Indian waters in effect.

After this introduction to the sea in a brig, Robert

Robert Foster at Brigflatts.

was promoted to the 64-gun vessel *Defiance*, and then in 1778 he transferred to the *Jupiter,* commanded by Francis Reynolds, later Lord Ducie. This was a 50-gun ship and saw serious action in October of that year. Several of the crew were killed when engaged with the American *Triton*, and when the master was killed, Robert was promoted to the post aged only 24. The next year, on 17 April 1779, he wrote in his log: '*Pelican,* River Tagus, received Captain Reynolds' acting orders as his lieutenant of this ship.' It seems that he could have made a good career for himself in the navy, having the confidence of people in high places, but he was a dutiful son as well, and resigned his commission at his family's request.

Of course there was a certain element of disgrace in a Quaker family for one of their members to be involved in the armed services, even if basically, it was in a protective role. The Society of Friends disowned him, but we do not know how much this affected him. An engraving in the Briggflatts Meeting House shows Robert at a meeting there, wearing full naval uniform, sword and all. The girls thought him very dashing according to a story, but the elders were deeply shocked. Despite straying from some of the Quaker tenets, Robert was evidently opposed to the slave trade, and in 1791 at Wilberforce's request, he gave evidence before a select committee of the House of Commons on slavery.

On his return to England, he was sent to Hebblethwaite by his grandfather Myles Birket, and he later inherited that estate too. He married twice, both wives being called Mary and both from the Hill, Sedbergh. The first marriage was in 1784 and produced four children, but their mother died in 1799 when the oldest was only fourteen and the second marriage had no issue.

Robert Foster was accomplished in many ways and was friendly with Wordsworth who stayed with him at Hebblethwaite for a week. He also knew Coleridge and Southey, and Professor Sedgwick praised his high mental capacity and genial disposition in the *'Supplement to the Memorial of the Trustees of Cowgill Chapel'* published in 1868.

After a full life, Robert died in 1827 aged 74, and then owned four estates, three of which he had inherited, but the pedigree does not show what happened to The Wood. His children were settled in Northumberland, Kent and Yorkshire, so it may have been sold by this stage. Although it has no direct bearing on this farmstead, it is of interest that one of Robert Foster's grandsons was Myles Birket Foster, the eminent Victorian watercolourist.

The land tax survey of the early nineteenth century reveals that the new owner of The Wood was John Wakefield Esq, and the occupier John Westgarth. This family originated in Troutbeck, but several members seem to have lived at The Wood as Cartmel Fell and Winster chapel registers show. Robert Westgarth, farmer of The Wood, died in 1817 aged only 22. Nothing is known of his short life, but his niece Sarah has a claim to fame in clock-making circles. The Barber/Philipson firm of Cartmel Fell and Winster eventually became Philipsons, clockmakers of Ulverston. Sarah (born in Underbarrow in 1825) married Benjamin Barnett of Winster in 1864, but she must have met Henry Philipson junior soon after and fallen in love. She left her husband and had nine children with Henry Philipson, dying in Kendal in 1910. It is tempting to speculate on Sarah's romantic temperament as four of her children had unusual names, not found in the parish registers locally. These were Aquilla, Priscilla, Phyllis and Hiram.

During the 1830s, a family of Carrs were at the Wood. Robert and Agnes christened three children between 1831 and 1834; their father is described as farmer in the parish register at this time. There were also Carrs at Old House Beck, and they were probably related as the Christian names echo.

The 1851 census shows a family of Askews of the Wood. Father and head of the family is 54-year-old William, a farmer of 60 acres. He and his wife and family of four children were all born in Cartmel Fell and they were still there in the next three census returns, the old man and his wife Betty being 84 and 82 in 1881. Their son Matthew had married and was still living with them, described as

Wedding of William Kellett and Edith Jane Phizacklea at The Wood, 1912.

'farmer's son', aged 41, but there was also a hired hand Samuel Taylor living in, a bachelor of 37. A glance at the Cartmel Fell register shows that the Askews previously farmed The Oaks, which is less than a kilometre away. Two of their children were christened from the Oaks in 1833 and 1836.

An extract from the *Westmorland Gazette* of 3 May 1851 relates an incident at The Wood Farm:

An extraordinary Fox Hunt took place last week at the Wood farm, on the margin of the river Winster, near those noted harbours of foxes and their cubs. Since the days of late James Machell Esquire, the famous Fox Hunter, those creatures, from the degeneracy of want or enterprise of the sportsman, have become unusually troublesome in this locality to the husbandman.

On Thursday last at 10 o'clock in the forenoon, an impudent Fox made its appearance in the farmyard of Mr Askew, the Wood farm. Mrs Askew and her daughter seeing a bold Reynard approach, thought at first sight it was a strange dog paying them a visit, but they were soon undeceived by Reynard seizing one of the poultry and dashing off on his way to Birks Fell. Mr Askew and his servants with their cur dog, set off, full speed in pursuit of the robber. After a run of four and-a-half miles, Reynard finding himself embarrassed with his burden and closely pursued, dropped his prey. The hen was secured alive, and is now safe with her feathered companions.

Following the Askews in the latter part of the nineteenth and into the twentieth century, the Phizacklea family farmed The Wood. John came from the Cartmel area and married Elizabeth Denny from Hale near Milnthorpe. They had a family of two boys and three girls, and Elizabeth's brother Robert lived in with them as a farm labourer. A photograph in the Cartmel Fell archive shows the family having a tea-break outside an army type of bell tent. This may have been the accommodation for summer visitors, as several farms in the district had their regular 'Wakes Week' families to stay, a useful source of a little extra income. Matthew Phizacklea, the elder son, later went on to be a tenant at Burblethwaite Hall and as a sideline was the local gravedigger. He thought he made a good job of this secondary calling because, as he put it,

CARTMEL FELL

'None of 'em ivver got out.'

Mrs Gladys Dunn, who was born at the very beginning of the 20th century, remembers The Wood from her childhood. In the parlour was a huge oak table which was used for special occasions such as a marriage feast or funerals, but its everyday use was for an apple store, the harvest being laid out in many rows for cold-keeping in a little-used room. There must have been many such tables in the old farms and one very well-known one is that at Townend in Troutbeck, now in the care of the National Trust, but there was also one at Oaks and another at Thorphinsty Hall, which because of its size was deemed to be a fixture. Before the present owner bought the property however, the table was removed, presumably having been sawn up or disjointed since it could not have been taken out of the house in one piece. These massive pieces of furniture must have been constructed within the houses for which they were intended. Sadly, the great table has also gone from The Wood.

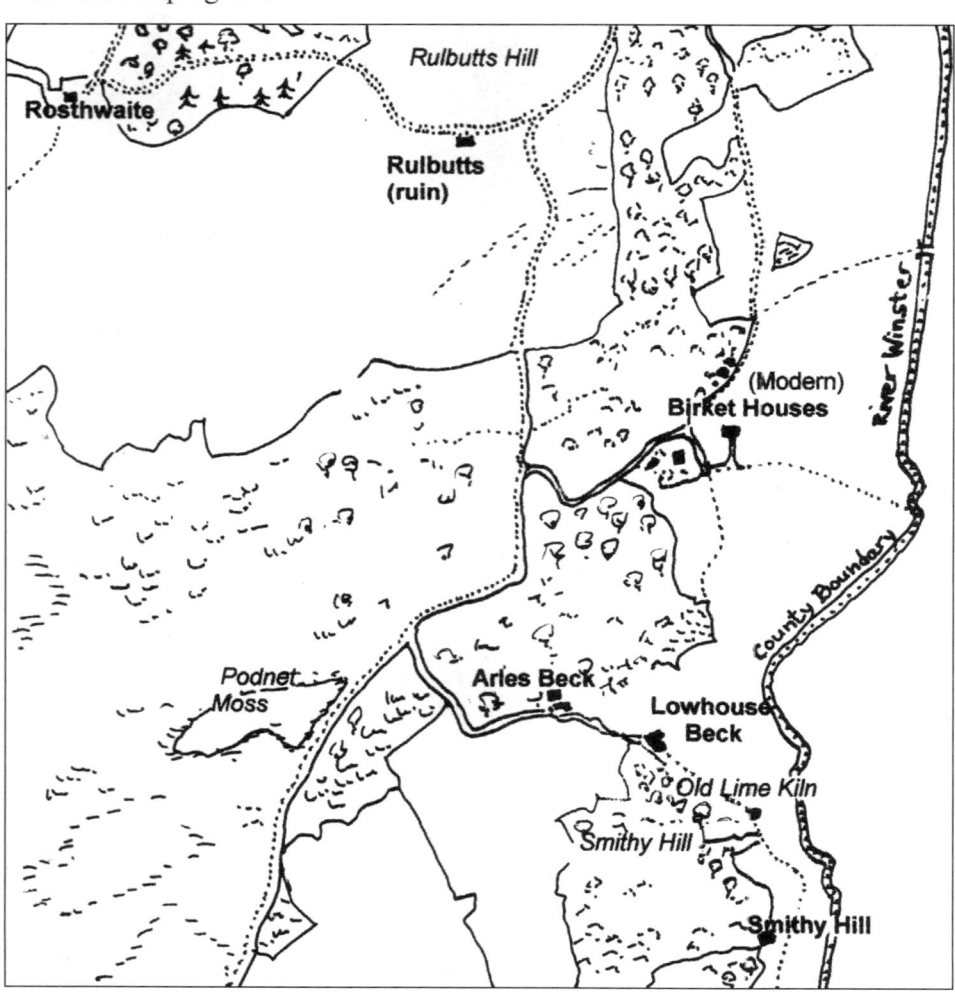

Old House Beck or Low House Beck

(sometimes Lawless Beck)

THE name is self-explanatory as far as the beck is concerned, as a little beck runs above the present house and plunges to the valley below. Today, there is only one house on the site, but formerly there was a High and a Low Old House Beck, frequently corrupted to Arles Beck in documents, and Lawless Beck in speech. The remaining Low Old House has the appearance of a seventeenth century farm house, so this may have been a replacement for an even older house, as the term 'old' was in use in the 1600s. By the time that the 1888-1893 Ordnance Survey maps were drawn, Arles Beck was the higher house, and the lower one was simply Low House Beck.

Until the turn of the twentieth century, a substantial and very old barn remained on the site of High Old House, but this has now been converted into a shooting lodge. This had the area's characteristic massive relieving arch and stepped foundations, which seem to be sixteenth century in origin. The associated buildings are now just foundations and rubble.

There is slight evidence that there may have been a mill dam on this small beck just above Low Old House. Certainly there is an artificial leat leading to where the ground falls sharply away, but no documentary evidence is known. There are fairly extensive buildings attached to what now seems an isolated farm, and within living memory, the track up from the valley was paved, covering a large drain in the steeper parts, but this is now disintegrating. There was a forge at Smithy Hill and a huge lime kiln, and just across the valley there is a potash kiln. This semi-industrial area would have needed good access from north and south, and the occupants of these two farms would have had regular passing traffic.

There is little mention of the two properties in parish records, but they are on the boundary with Winster, so maybe the occupants were more involved with village life there. Quaker records are among the earliest for Old House Beck, when Robert and Jennett Dixon registered the births of their daughters Ann and Mary, in 1654 and 1663 respectively. Robert's burial at Height was in 1683.

The slurring of the name can be traced in several forms over the centuries. In 1700, Michael Harrison of Arles Beck made his will, and in 1720 the family still pronounced it the same way when Thomas, son of John and Isabell Harrison, was christened. In 1754, Agnes, the daughter of John and Hannah Dixon, was recorded as of Alhous Beck. If these Dixons were the descendants of the earlier Quakers, they had returned to the Church of England by the eighteenth century.

There is a date of 1678 with the initials TS, carved above one of the bedroom doors, but the timber of the lintel may have been taken from elsewhere, as it seems a strange place to display one's ownership, and no matching surname can be identified.

Although these two farms were in the centre of Birket lands, one seems to have remained independent from that family. The 1785 land tax register records James Birket as being the owner of one property taxed at three shillings. This farm had work done to it in 1803, as the Birket Houses accounts show, and in May 1816 James Cousen of Old House Beck was paid for stone-getting. At this period, it seems that Old House Beck was the name given to one farm, and Low House to the other. There are court records however, which may have given rise to the local name of 'Lawless Beck.' In the Westmorland Quarter Sessions, date 5 February 1813, a number of near neighbours were summoned and bound over to keep the peace.

There appears to have been a state of tribal warfare in this corner of the parish. The employer at High Lawless Beck (as it was termed in the court) was Robert Martin. Bound over to keep the peace was one of the Westgarth family, the labourer for James Holme who lived at Low Lawless Beck. Yet another Westgarth, Emmanuel was 'of Cartmel Fell', probably of the Wood, and he too was to keep the peace. It seems that the object of this lawless state was the occupant of Roper Ford, a swill-maker called John Park, and he too was bound over. All these territories have common boundaries, so one imagines that the disputes arose over some real or imagined incursions.

Maybe the culprits all decided to move, because a year later in the 1814 land tax book, the owner of Low House was the Rev. Robert Dickinson, and the occupier George Bennett who rented sixteen and a half acres adjoining the homestead. A little later, the censuses help to identify the farms by the acreages, though they do not differentiate them by name. The Dickinson family must have retained ownership of the sixteen acre farm, because in 1851 and 1861, Henry Dickinson, a master mason from Lowick, was farming the land combining it with his trade. He had three unmarried sons at home, all following the same calling and they seem to have worked as a firm. The other farm was much bigger at this period, having 61 acres, but there is no way of telling which was which.

In 1841, Thomas Carr was farming the larger acreage, but ten years later he had gone and Leonard Cragg from Dent was there. He was 39 and had seven children ranging from eleven years to twenty days. He must have been a tenant farmer as his older children were born at Longsleddale and Undermillbeck, but the last five were born in Cartmel Fell. By deduction, he must have taken over Old House in about 1844.

William Gass, an agricultural labourer followed the Craggs, with a family of three sons and a daughter. The parish register shows two baptisms, just days apart in May and June 1855, of Jane Slater and Eleanor Carr, both of Old House Beck. It would seem that the Carrs had retained a foothold even though they were absent in the 1851 census.

Without knowing the actual land that went with each property, it is hard to judge the farming prospects for these two holdings, but for whatever reason, both were empty by the time the 1881 census was taken. The properties verge onto moorland above with woodland around, so another trade would have been essential for the smaller farm. There is only one uninhabited house in the 1891 census, and this is probably when the higher house became derelict. After a period of being uninhabited, the Inland Revenue survey of 1910/11 shows that Low House, as it was then called, was in reasonable condition. Myles Higgin Birket of Birket Houses was the owner, and the land was only two roods, this seeming to be orchard. The next item in sequence is 100 acres of land at Arles Beck, and this includes ruined buildings and a barn, the remains of the old house.

From the diaries of William Pearson, we learn that there were trout in the little beck in the 1840s, and he tells us that the porridge pan was left in the beck for the fish to cleanse. Maybe fat trout were on the menu now and again.

A glimpse of life in the nineteenth century, and the care that was needed to eke out every penny, comes from Gladys Dunn's memories. She was born in 1901, and her family used to come up to Summer Hill from Liverpool for their holidays. Whilst they were there, they had domestic help from the daughter of an old man with a huge white beard who lived at 'Lawless Beck.' Far from being drudgery, this brief employment was a release for the woman whose father would not allow candles to be lit, so their lives were governed by daylight hours, except in dire emergency. The firelight was all that illuminated the house at night, and a peat fire gives only a dull glow. When the fire was too dim to work by, they both went to bed. The coming of spring must have meant so much more in those days, and one wonders if the daughter bought an oil lamp when her father died.

Today, it is possible to trace some of the additions and alterations to Low House. There is an internal window with wooden mullions, once giving on to the land behind the house. The floor level has been excavated to give more head-room and the chimney designed for peat-burning needed rebuilding to produce a draught, but otherwise this is still a substantial yeoman's dwelling. The farm buildings are now fairly ruinous, but the area around has become a beautiful garden, crammed with unusual flowering plants. The only road into the property today is from the north, but once there was a continuing track which came out at Roper Ford on the Winster road, passing the ancient lime-kiln. This route is still negotiable as a public foot-path, but some people might be intimidated by the Highland cattle which graze the open pasture.

Birket Houses

THIS location is quite simply the settlement of the Birket family. It is a surname found all over Cumbria and the earlier spelling is often Birkhead or something like it, birk being the birch tree and head meaning the higher ground or a hill.

The present-day mansion of this name was built at the beginning of the twentieth century by descendants of the first Birkets, but it is not in the same place as the earlier homestead. That was higher up the hill, towards Winster House, and was said to have been of timber-frame construction. There is alleged to be a Victorian postcard on which the old house appeared, but I have been unable to trace one, or even a photograph of the dwelling, though there is a photograph of a door with two little unknown girls and a pony. This came from a descendant of the Cockertons, and is said to be the old house door. Timber-framed houses are now very rare in the Lake District, owing to the surge of re-building that went on in the seventeenth century, so it is hard to guess at the appearance of old Birket Houses, noting that it is plural, but the O.S. map of 1888/93 gives an idea of the plan. The only example of a Lakeland timber-framed house that I know of is the oldest part of Coat How in Rydal.

The earliest spelling of the surname, Birket, was Birkehede, with variations such as Byrkhed, and it appears in the Windermere and Crosthwaite parish registers from their first pages. The very earliest record of the name so far located, is in a rental for Cartmel Fell of 1508, when a Robert Byrkhed senior took a tenement rated at eleven pence a year. Unfortunately, this tenement is not named, so it cannot be proved to be Birket Houses, but in the sixteenth century, this tribe of Birkets were clustered towards the northern end of Cartmel Fell and into Winster, so one can only suggest a possibility that Birket Houses was in existence in the fifteenth century, if not earlier.

A book published in 1873, *Pedigrees of the County Families* by J. Footes, has a large spread for the Birkets of Birket Houses, beginning with James who died in 1596. It states that his son John was admitted tenant of the lands in the manor of Cartmel Fell on his father's death, but probably this should read 'in the manor of Cartmel,' for that was where the manor courts were held, and as stated elsewhere, Cartmel Fell was one of the seven divisions of Cartmel. The parish boundaries would seem to have altered slightly since the turn of the sixteenth century, for whereas Winster was in Westmorland, in the will of Bryan Birket of 1609, he states that he is of Winster in Cartmel Fell. From the wills and the Birket pedigree, it seems that the inheritance of Birket Houses was purchased, maybe in the form of ingressum, but this is not clear. For instance, the will of James Birket of 1676 lays out his bequest thus: 'I doe give all that my messuage tenement or freehold land wth the appurtenances wch I bought and purchased of Nicholas Birket, situate at Birket Houses wch is in Cartmellfell aforesaid of the annual rent of iiis.'

This will tells us quite a lot about the Birket family and its way of life. James described himself as 'yeoman', meaning that he owned the houses and land, described as freehold. There was an orchard on the south side of the 'mansion', so Birket Houses was no cottage, and although the family were quite well off by the standards of the day, they were not living in idle luxury. James had three sons; Miles or Myles was the oldest, James the second and William the youngest. Miles of course was the heir and was already in possession of the messuage at the time the will was made, all except for half of the orchard 'according to a bargain twixt him and me.' It seems that James was the farmer of the estate. To him was left 'all my Plowes and plowegear and husbandrie gear, my hay, bigge, oats, one Cowe called Brody and her calf, and the Geldinge I bought of Mr. Wells, and all my sheep,' and the other half of the orchard.

The youngest son, William, evidently carried on some kind of trade from home, and his father did not want this to change on his death. He stipulated that William 'should have the lower end of the now kitchinge wch is now made into a shoppe, as longe as he likes to stay and work there.' Parcels of land are mentioned, some adjoining the Birket Houses land, such as Bracken Beds at Rosthwaite and Smithy Hill, which was towards Roper Ford, but there was also a farm at Firbank called Birkefield (Birketfield?) which is still in existence, or a mortgage for it on which James had lent money, and this was to be William's portion. As it happened, William followed his father to the grave only two years later, having been the executor of his father's will. William must have had intimations of his early demise, for he made his will in 1678, and from this we learn that he was a cordwainer, that is a shoemaker. The tenement left to him by his father at Smithy Hill was to be charged with producing six shillings a year, to benefit the poor of Cartmel Fell, and we assume that William was a bachelor, as most of his bequests are to cousins. The household items in the inventory are quite unremarkable except for 'bookes', which are a rare item on farms at this period and William's were worth twelve shillings. His work tools and leather were worth £6.10s., and he had a horse, together with hay, straw and oats. This was probably the equivalent of his delivery van, since Birket Houses is not on a main thoroughfare. The profits of his trade were not lying idle, as one can see at the end of the inventory. Owing to William were various sums of money lent on bond, totalling £62.0s.3d.

Returning to his father's will, items of household furniture are mentioned as bequests, and money. Miles received £6, with a bed and a chest that had been his grandfather's. James

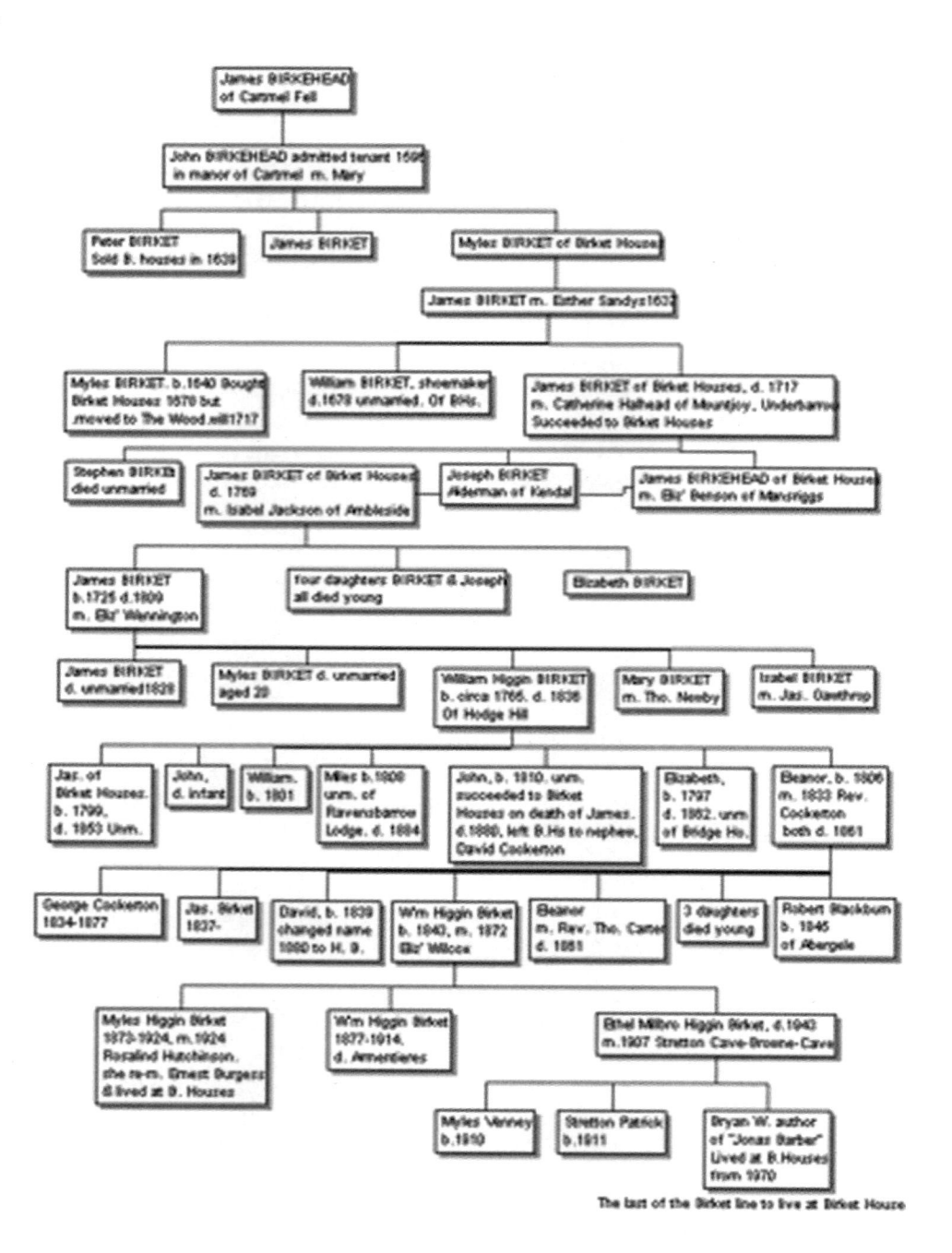

Cartmel Fell

```
James BIRKEHEAD of Cartmel Fell
 │
John BIRKEHEAD admitted tenant 1595 in manor of Cartmel  m. Mary
 ├── Peter BIRKET, Sold B. houses in 1639
 ├── James BIRKET
 └── Myles BIRKET of Birket Houses
      │
      James BIRKET m. Esther Sandys 1632
       ├── Myles BIRKET, b. 1640. Bought Birket Houses 1670 but moved to The Wood. d.1717
       ├── William BIRKET, shoemaker, d. 1679 unmarried. Of BHs.
       └── James BIRKET of Birket Houses, d. 1717 m. Catherine Halhead of Mountjoy, Underbarrow. Succeeded to Birket Houses
            ├── Stephen BIRKEt, died unmarried
            ├── James BIRKET of Birket Houses, d. 1769 m. Isabel Jackson of Ambleside
            │    ├── James BIRKET b. 1725 d. 1809 m. Eliz' Wennington
            │    │    ├── James BIRKET d. unmarried 1829
            │    │    ├── Myles BIRKET d. unmarried aged 29
            │    │    ├── William Higgin BIRKET b. circa 1765, d. 1838. Of Hodge Hill
            │    │    │    ├── Jas. of Birket Houses, b. 1799, d. 1853 Unm.
            │    │    │    ├── John, d. infant
            │    │    │    ├── William, b. 1801
            │    │    │    ├── Miles b.1808 unm. of Ravensbarrow Lodge, d. 1884
            │    │    │    ├── John, b. 1810, unm. succeeded to Birket Houses on death of James, d. 1880, left B.Hs to nephew, David Cockerton
            │    │    │    ├── Elizabeth, b. 1797 d. 1852, unm. of Bridge Ho.
            │    │    │    └── Beanor, b. 1806 m. 1833 Rev. Cockerton both d. 1861
            │    │    │         ├── George Cockerton 1834-1877
            │    │    │         ├── Jas. Birket 1837-
            │    │    │         ├── David, b. 1839 changed name 1880 to H. B.
            │    │    │         ├── Wm Higgin Birket b. 1843, m. 1872 Eliz' Wilcox
            │    │    │         │    ├── Myles Higgin Birket 1873-1924, m.1924 Rosalind Hutchinson. she re-m. Ernest Burgess & lived at B. Houses
            │    │    │         │    ├── Wm Higgin Birket 1877-1914, d. Armentieres
            │    │    │         │    └── Ethel Milbro Higgin Birket, d.1943 m.1907 Stretton Cave-Broene-Cave
            │    │    │         │         ├── Myles Venney b.1910
            │    │    │         │         ├── Stretton Patrick b.1911
            │    │    │         │         └── Bryan W. author of "Jonas Barber" Lived at B.Houses from 1970
            │    │    │         ├── Beanor m. Rev. Tho. Carter d. 1881
            │    │    │         ├── 3 daughters died young
            │    │    │         └── Robert Blackburn b. 1845 of Abergele
            │    │    ├── Mary BIRKET m. Tho. Nesby
            │    │    └── Isabel BIRKET m. Jas. Gawthrop
            │    ├── Four daughters BIRKET & Joseph all died young
            │    └── Elizabeth BIRKET
            ├── Joseph BIRKET Alderman of Kendal
            └── James BIRKEHEAD of Birket House m. Eliz' Benson of Mindriggs
```

The last of the Birket line to live at Birket House

250

had a bed together with bedclothes, and William had the furniture in the house at Smithy Hill. These were a table, bedstocks and a chest, together with the 'louse boardes'.

In his will of 1717, Miles left ten shillings to the poor of Cartmel Fell and another ten shillings 'to poor Friends frequenting the meeting at Height meeting house.' The Birket's Quaker link was firmly established by the eighteenth century, and Miles' son and daughter made Quaker marriages, his grandsons Miles and James becoming prominent merchants in Lancaster. James was instrumental in spreading Quakerism in the West Indies as he spent some years in business in Antigua.

The inheritance of Birket Houses was never a foregone conclusion. Maybe the eldest son was unmarried, or maybe he chose to live elsewhere, but for the best part of 400 years, descendants of the Birkets clung on to their inheritance, though many of its members seemed disinclined to marry. Miles and James died about the same time, in 1717, but two more generations of Jameses followed at Birket Houses, taking their turn as constable or grave as the parish records show. Because of their standing in the local community, the Birkets were called upon to be trustees of the Bryan Beck charity, and because some of the family developed Quaker leanings, they were trustees of Height Meeting also, and designated to supervise Quaker bequests in other parishes. Whereas in the seventeenth century they were described as 'yeomen', by the eighteenth century they had progressed to being 'gentlemen', a distinction which one comes across in other families and which would now be called 'upwardly mobile'.

One of the Birket Houses seems to have been used for either servants or artisans during the eighteenth century. Henry Philipson the clockmaker lived there the year after his first marriage in 1775. Henry worked with Jonas Barber and eventually had his own business, numbering his clocks in the Barber tradition. He was twice bereaved, his second wife dying in 1790, but his third wife, Jane Godmond, was also of Birket Houses when they married. The parish registers and Quaker registers show numerous occupants, some of whom must have farmed the Birket estate once the Birkets became gentrified.

Some household account books survive from around the turn of the eighteenth century and are now in Kendal Record Office. The dairy produce from the farms is reflected in the 440lbs of butter sold in 1802, between May and December, and about half the quantity between January and April the following year when the cows would be eating mostly hay. Regular sums were paid into the Kendal bank of Messrs Wilson, Crewdson & Bateman, and the rents alone for James Birket in 1815 totalled £298.6s.6d. At that period, the top rate of pay for a farm worker in harvest time might be 2s.6d. a day. Agnes Crowe, the housekeeper, was paid £6.6s. for her year's wages, but she had invested her own money with her employer and from the sum of £65.3s, she received the interest of £2.18s.6d. in 1816.

Amongst the household accounts are the funeral expenses for John Birket who died in July 1809. The items are too numerous to list, but included 70 pounds of beef and 55 pounds of veal, eighteen pounds of butter, two gallons of port, two gallons of Lisbon ale and four dozen of bread, and rather surprisingly, cabbage. Silk hoods and hatbands amounted to £6.17s.11½d.

There were considerable draper's bills to Richard Holmes of Kendal and an example is in 1817 when the Birkets purchased Holland cloth, olive superior cloth at 26 shillings a yard, flannel, calico, Welsh flannel and silk. To turn the Lakeland rain, five shillings was paid for oilcloth to make a hat.

The woodlands produced a large proportion of the Birket income. In November 1825, John Hird of Moorhow bought for £290 many parcels of woodland for coppicing. 'If the price of bobbin-wood continue as it does, if it lessens, £10 abated.' The nearest bobbin-mill was at Gill Head and would need constant supplies, but only the timber was sold and not the land it grew on. Times were prosperous for the Birkets at the beginning of the nineteenth century, and in 1812, it was decided to build a new barn. This splendid edifice now adjoins Winster House.

The family name of James was used in almost every generation of Birkets and the sixth generation James Birket, shown on Footes' pedigree, lived at Garnett House, Winster, now called the Old Vicarage. He died in 1809, aged 84 and his first two sons died unmarried, but the third son, William Higgin Birket had moved several miles away to the family holding of Hodge Hill, for which he paid £52.10s. in rent for the year 1805. William's descendants eventually moved back to their roots and rebuilt the ancient holding. He had married Ellen Cartmel of Broad Oak in Crosthwaite, their sons, James and John eventually living at Birket Houses, but both died unmarried in the second half of the nineteenth century. Another son, Isaac, inherited a half-share of Hodge Hill together with his brother John, but whereas John stayed in his native part of the country, Isaac went into the tanning trade in Bermondsey, and there he died of bronchitis in 1847, aged only 34. Their sister Eleanor was the only member of the family of seven children to marry, and she became the wife of the Rev. Robert Cockerton, the curate of Cartmel Fell for many years. It was their son David who was to inherit Birket Houses, but by the terms of his uncle's will, only if he, Birket Cockerton, changed his name to Birket also. Had the Cockertons realised what would ensue when they incorporated the family name at their children's christenings, they might have thought twice, but in 1880, in order to inherit the estate, David assumed the name Higgin Birket but died in 1894, so in 1895, William also changed his name and became W. Higgin Birket Higgin Birket.

John Birkett circa 1850, courtesy of Robert James Cockerton.

In his diary, the Rev. Thomas Price notes a meeting on 28 August 1914: 'Met Myles Birket who told us he was going to join at Hull where his brother (William) is next week. They are guarding the entrances to the Humber.'

Myles survived the war as a captain (later, major) in the 3rd Lancs. Fusiliers and after the war was a J.P. His brother William was not so lucky. Later that year of 1914, on 11 December, Thomas Price wrote: 'Went in the afternoon to see Mrs. Higgin Birkett and enquire about Willie. He was wounded near Armentières on October 26th and has not been heard of since. He was wounded in the head by shrapnel while re-taking a trench, refused to leave but finally consented to go and have his wound dressed. Took a soldier with him, but sent him back again and went on alone.' On the war memorial in Cartmel Fell churchyard is the inscription: 'W. M. H. B. HIGGIN BIRKET.'

In the earliest wills available, it can be seen that the Birket clan was beginning to amass various parcels of land, farmsteads and woodland. Surplus monies were lent at interest as mortgages or bonds, and in this way supplied a very real need in the community. Banks and building societies were a long way into the future, and probably, the wealthier members of the parish knew the client risk extremely well. Together with their merchant enterprises in the West Indies (see The Wood) the Birkets became very affluent by the end of the eighteenth century. The 1814 Land Tax book was copied out in 1867 by John Birket of Birket Houses, Eleanor Cockerton's brother. This lists all the owners of land in the parish, who occupied the houses and land, the names of the fields and woodlands and all the individual acreages. Amongst the farmsteads owned by the family in the

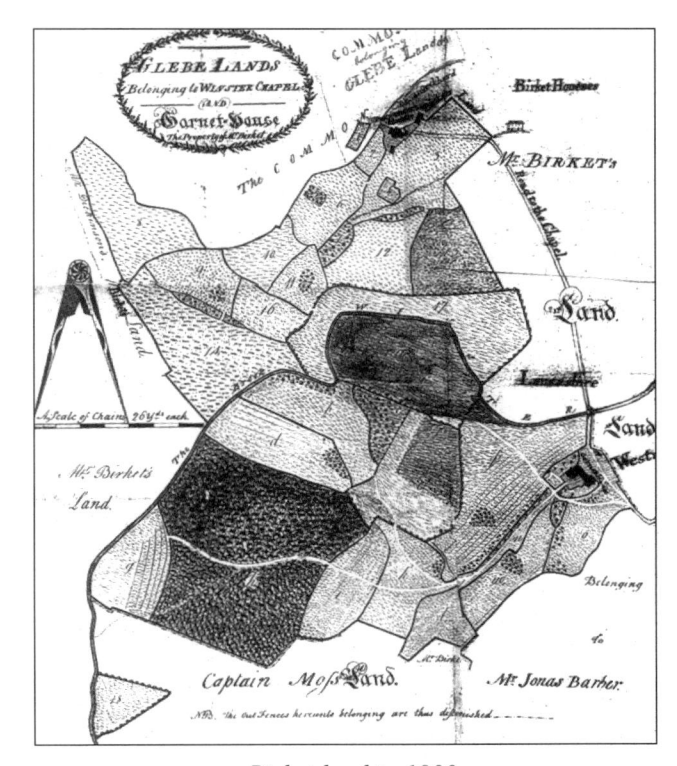

Birket land in 1800.

parish at this time were: Birket Houses, High House, Smithy Hill, Hodge Hill, Bridge House and Hartbarrow. We know from other deeds, such as those for Low Ludderburn, that in the nineteenth century Myles Birket paid off mortgages and settled bequests in 1872, and thus became the owner of Oaks, Great and Little Ludderburn, (High and Low Ludderburn) Swallowmire and Sow How. The Cockerton branch of the family owned Ashes and Little Thorphinsty at the beginning of the twentieth century, and Myles Birket was then living at Ravensbarrow Lodge. In short, the Birkets were the unofficial squires of Cartmel Fell, and because of

Birket Houses 1912.

their large holdings, they were allotted large areas of common land at the time of the enclosures in 1797.

Myles Higgin Birket was living alone in the old house in 1881, though with six servants in his household. He was farming 300 acres, employing five men. The present-day house was built in the Victorian-Tudor style, and finished at the beginning of the twentieth century. The architect was Dan Gibson, and the gardens were designed by the Kendal firm of Thomas Mawson. Dan Gibson died in 1907, aged 41, and the plans for Birket Houses were his last work. Better known to the general public is Brockhole, the National Park Centre between Windermere and Ambleside, being another of Gibson's undertakings.

In 1912, *Country Life* magazine published a long article which featured Birket Houses in the series 'Lesser Country Houses of Today'. It was illustrated by plans and photographs of the newly-completed house, but makes no mention of the owner who was Myles Higgin Birkett. The windows are mullioned with dressed stone, and this was the only material which was not produced locally, since slate does not lend itself to dressing in this way. The roofing slates came from the Tilberthwaite quarries, and the stone came partly 'from a demolished farm-house,' maybe the original Birket Houses. The doorways and some fireplaces have the flat Tudor arch, harking back to a bygone age. The massive chimneys echo the style so much praised by Wordsworth. Some of the panelling inside the house is said to have come from Hodge Hill, and some from the old Tudor house, so maybe the whole style is an echo of the ancient homestead. An Elizabethan cradle from Hodge Hill was said to have been taken to the new Birket Houses, but was last heard of in a sale advertisement in *Country Life* in the mid-twentieth century, when it was termed 'the Winster cradle.' The garden design followed the rather formal pattern of Edwardian fashion, and the plans can be seen at Kendal Record Office. In one of the photographs of 1912 taken by *Country Life*, at the turn of the staircase is a long case clock. This may be the one referred to in the Birket account book for 1817, when Henry Philipson junior of Ulverston was paid three shillings for 'Dressing my clock'. When the Barbers and Philipsons were making clocks in Winster, they were but a five minute walk from Birket Houses, so they probably returned to service their handiwork.

When Major Myles Higgin Birket died in 1946, his obituary mentioned that he succeeded to Birket

Houses on the death of his father when he was twenty-years-old. He was 'a follower of nature rather than games and steeped in the folklore and traditions of the countryside.' The article lists the Major's wartime career, first being commissioned in the South African War, when he had enlisted in the Lancashire Fusiliers. Mentioned in despatches three times, he was awarded the O.B.E. Later, he served in France in the First World War, but his post-war activities revealed his local interests. He was a local magistrate, chairman of Grasmere Sports, served on the committee of fishery protection on the local rivers and was a keen follower of hound-trailing. He bred flat-coated retrievers and pointers and his dogs won prizes at Crufts. Myles did not marry until 1924, when he was over 50 and the couple were childless. After his cremation, the Major's ashes were scattered on Rulbutts hill, with its commanding views above Birket Houses.

His widow re-married the following year, but upon her death in 1969, Birket Houses became the property of her husband's nephew, Bryan Cave-Browne-Cave. In a sense, this was the return of the native, because Ethel Millbro Higgin Birket, Bryan's mother, had been brought up in Birket Houses and he had often been there to stay with the family. When he inherited the house and its furniture, he became interested in long-case clocks and was already familiar with the name of Barber, indeed, Bryan Houses where the Barbers had their workshop was part of the Birket estate and probably took its name from Bryan Birket who died in 1609. Most of Cave-Browne-Cave's working life had been with the B.B.C. and he had worked all over the world in their service, but on moving to Birket Houses in 1970 he began a new project, writing the history of the Barber clocks and their makers. This has become a standard text-book on the subject and a source of reference for others who continue the quest for lost Barber clocks.

In the 1980s, Birket Houses enjoyed a brief period as a hotel and restaurant, but amidst much local opposition. The road to it is narrow, and the people living nearby did not relish the prospect of continual evening traffic. Now it has returned to private ownership, and the sparkling white facade shown in the post card view of about 1910 has mellowed to blend with the local stone.

Postcard of the new Birket Houses, circa 1912.

Rosthwaite

AS it is spelt today, the name means an enclosure or clearing for the horses, from the old Norse *hross tveit*, or possibly the clearing with the cairn, *ros* being derived from raise.

This holding is at the extreme northern end of Cartmel Fell parish, and the most remote from Cartmel. For some odd reason, which is hard to guess, the name of Rosthwaite does not crop up in the parish documents. The yeomen farmers had to do their turns as parish officers and these are well recorded, but the list ends at Birket Houses. Landlords of several holdings could nominate an alternative or deputy, but none occur for Rosthwaite. According to the *Victoria County History*, Rosthwaite is mentioned in 1508, when it was held by William Bellingham, together with Rulbutts, at a rental of 26s. This information was taken from the Lay Subsidy Rolls, and later, in a Cartmel Priory Rental of 1590, Rosthwaite is again mentioned. In 1588 Michael Pull of Tower Wood died and his appraisers made a list of his debts and debtors. There were two men from Rosthwaite who owed him money, Thomas Jackson and William Hall. One wonders if there was more than one dwelling at Rosthwaite all that time ago. So many other farms seem to have been hamlets, the houses all sharing a common name, so that it is quite likely that Rosthwaite had satellite houses too.

There is a hamlet called Rosthwaite in Cartmel parish as well, which makes for some confusion when Cartmel was the mother church for all seven parishes in the division of Cartmel. Throughout the seventeenth century there are entries in the Cartmel register with many different surnames and many spellings for Rosthwaite, but most must be for the Allithwaite dwellings.

One of the earliest entries was for Robert, son of Roger Duckett, who was christened in 1625. There were two generations of Wainhouses baptising their children later in the century, and Waynhouse (sic) wills are in Kendal Record Office. for the 1590s, but Wainhouse was a Cartmel and Flookburgh area surname. In 1667, Austine Fell of Rosthwaite christened his daughter Issabel at Cartmel. Nicholas Carlton was living at Rosthwaite in 1688 and was still there in 1690 as his sons made the journey to Cartmel for baptism. None of the above are likely to have been from this Cartmel Fell farm though, as it is almost at the northern limit of the parish, so it was actually nearer for parishioners to travel to Bowness for their sacraments, and indeed, some chose this option as the registers show. Intermingled generations of the Greenwood family occur in the Cartmel parish registers of the eighteenth and nineteenth century, many of them mariners of 'Rostead.' Almost certainly these are *not* of Cartmel Fell as they can later be checked in the censuses.

Perusal of the Winster church registers shows that this was where many Rosthwaite farmers had their ceremonies performed. Catheren Swainson married Nicholas Long in 1728 at Winster, and they moved from Smiddy Hill (near Roper Ford) to Rosthwaite, where their son John was born and baptised in 1733.

At the beginning of the eighteenth century, Thomas Braithwaite was the owner and occupier of

Rosthwaite in Cartmel Fell. Thomas was a Quaker and a man who put his trust in property, and various bits of evidence remain which show how he amassed land and houses. In 1719 he bought three messuages called Lindeth from Frances Hutton, widow, the eldest daughter of Sir Christopher Philipson. Her father was dead, so it would seem that these farms were her inheritance, and as she was living in London by then, she probably preferred the cash. Thomas Braithwaite refers in his will to his properties at Lindeth 'that were my father's', so his father may have been a customary tenant of the Philipsons.

From Thomas Braithwaite's will, we discover that he was of Rosthwaite and Hollin Hall, which is on the border of Crook and Staveley, and that he was quite a property baron. He owned fishing rights in the lake, the mill and kiln at Michaelland, (Crook), the island of Longholme, Briery Close, lands and tenements at Blakethwaite and much else besides. The total value of his inventory was £994.3s.4d, but his expenses and debts owing on bond came to £969.10s.0d. It would seem that he had borrowed to acquire his many and various estates, but being a good Quaker, was not in debt overall.

Later in the eighteenth century, John and Elizabeth Barrow buried their son Robert in 1753 and later, Rowland Long had two sons baptised from Rosthwaite, but these were of different mothers. In 1763, Thomas was christened, son of Rowland Long and Grace Atkinson, and then in 1777 Rowland and Bridget Long named their baby for his father.

In 1829, the Parson and White directory lists John Airey, farmer of Rostead. He is not defined in any way as yeomen were, so he must have been a tenant farmer. The Aireys had several children baptised at Cartmel during the 1820s, but when their daughter Mary was baptised, they had moved a little further west, to farm at Gill Head.

When the 1841 census was drawn up, the name had become further contracted to Rosted, and was now occupied by the young Clark family. Robert and Agnes had two children and two farm servants, only children themselves. Robert Brown was fifteen, and little Eleanor Mackereth was only eleven. Later censuses give us more detail about the Clarks. Robert had come from further down in Lancashire, having been born at Cockerham, and his wife Agnes came from Kirkby Ireleth. We might speculate on how these two came to meet, and the most likely explanation would be when they themselves were in farm service, having been hired in the same area, perhaps at Ulverston. Robert could have come 'over sands' to the hiring fair. In 1846, the couple had their son Matthew christened at Winster.

This was a farm with plenty of land in the mid-nineteenth century; the 1861 census tells us that there were 60 acres of old land and 75 of heath. The heathland is still much the same today, unenclosed and unimproved, with an unmade road crossing the fell. The Clarks had four children at home in 1861, the two elder ones being employed on the farm, and the two younger at school. From this remote corner of the fell, Winster School would be much nearer than Cartmel Fell, but it would still be a long trudge home on a dark wet winter afternoon.

Families tended to move in and out of Rosthwaite. For fifty years after the Clarks departed, there is a different household in each of the ten-year censuses. In 1871, the James family were bringing up their seven children, and Mary Ann's widowed father, William Pearson lived with them.

In 1881 the Griggs family were working for someone else, as the head of the household is described as 'farm labourer.' They had five children between ten and two years, but they had moved on by 1891, to be replaced by the Becks. This family had six children, two of them scholars, but the four youngest still at home. At the time of the census, a young gamekeeper was staying with them, Joseph Brennan from Beetham, and his descendants still live locally, only their name is now spelt Brennand.

At the beginning of the twentieth century, John Taylor had taken on the farm and called himself 'employer', his employee Herbert Longmire then living in with the family. Two grown up children were still at home, they and their mother all having been born in Crook.

A few years later in the twentieth century the occupier of Rosthwaite was William Armistead, a tenant of Edward Holt at the newly built Blackwell. There were 138 acres altogether with two arable plots and good grazing towards Bellman Ground, but most was rough fell land. In 1909, the Inland Revenue reported that the buildings were in fair condition, (stone and slate,) and the four bedroomed house had plenty of outbuildings with ties for 26 cows altogether and a three stall stable.

Today, the farm is hardly recognisable as its former self. It has been enlarged and modernised and the farm buildings are now rebuilt and used as a horse-training centre with all the latest equipment, so the farmstead is still 'The clearing with the horses', after 1,000 years or more. The unmade road over the fell would be the only feature that former occupants would recognise.

Rulbutts

UP on the open heath above Birket Houses is the ruin of a fairly substantial farmstead. The hill on which this stands is marked on the first O.S. map of 1848 as Rulbuts, and was one of the triangulation points at 569.9 feet. Today, the O.S. have added an extra T to the name of the hill, but in the past it was spelt Rulbouth (booth) in many cases. This holding was on the extreme northern edge of Lancashire on the eastern side of the lake, on an ancient trackway which crosses this craggy, boggy area which was once common land. The name disappeared from documents in the late seventeenth century, implying disuse, and beside it is one of the biggest yew trees in the district, with a girth of nineteen feet, which maybe much older than the foundations of the house.

The first documented evidence of this very ancient farm comes from the *Victoria County History*. In 1508, it was held by William Bellingham, (presumably of Burneside Hall) together with the neighbouring farm of Rosthwaite, for the rental of 26 shillings, the equivalent of about £500 today. The farms were already in existence at that date, and must have been well established to command this amount of rent.

In a will of James Birket of Birket houses, dated 14 September 1676, he leaves the rent of Rulbutt to his middle son, James, in lieu of his child's portion. From the solid stepped foundations, one can guess which building was the house, but there are ruins of outbuildings around about, and some say that this was reputed to be a drover's inn. Certainly, it is on a very ancient trackway linking the isolated farm of Rosthwaite to the Winster valley route. If this was a drove road, it must have been designed to keep cattle away from the villages and more populated areas, for even today it is mostly open heathland, but a new plantation is growing up to the north of Rulbutts Hill. In the boggy areas, one may be lucky enough to find the increasingly rare Grass of Parnassus with its dazzling white flower.

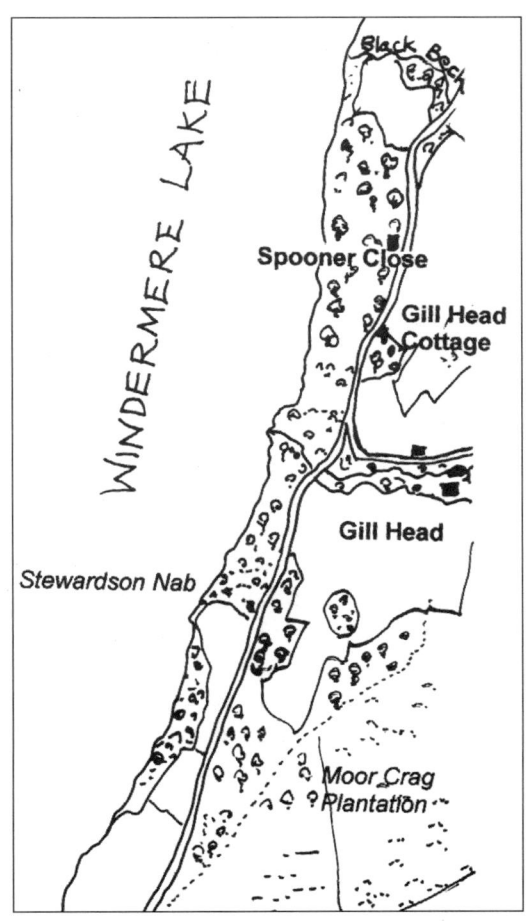

Gill Head

VICTORIAN in appearance, this large country house is now, like so many former gentlemen's residences, an outdoor pursuits centre. The gill tumbles past from the reservoir above, and once turned the mill wheels associated with the area, thus giving the property its name. Sometimes the word 'Gill' is spelled 'Ghyll', and this was the case at Gill Head. The water power was used for the flax and bobbin industries, and also for an associated saw-mill on the lower reach.

This was once the seat of the Poole family, who in all probability built the first house on the site. The surname, also spelt Pull in former times, was well established on the fell by the sixteenth century, as can be shown by wills, and they also inhabited Tower Wood, Moorhow and Prentices, to name a few of their farmholdings.

John Poole of Gillhead, (1709-1767) was a physician and as such, a rarity on the fell. He married Jane Satterthwaite and they had ten children that have been traced, some of whom died in childhood. The oldest surviving son and heir was another John who was born in 1746, but with the inheritance settled, other sons had to move away to seek their fortunes. William, born in 1751 went to America, as did his younger brother Abraham and they settled in South Carolina where many of their descendants still live. Another brother, Michael, moved to Liverpool.

There are memorial tablets to the Pooles of Gill

Head in Cartmel Fell chapel, one of which is a poem for little Betty Poole who died in 1779, aged three. This touching memorial is close to the altar, and shows the standing of the Pooles in the community at the time. The parish registers show other child and infant deaths at this period as there was an outbreak of smallpox. In July 1766, three other members of the Poole family died of this dread disease, and unusually it was indicated in the burial register. Whether this showed the importance of the Pooles or of the pestilence is hard to say. Thomas, son of William was buried on 5 July, Isaac, son of Dr John on the 25th, and his brother Thomas on the following day.

It is relevant to note here that in the parish accounts of the overseer of the poor, in 1792 an outlay of five shillings was spent on inoculating a bastard child. Considering that this was not a wealthy parish, a decision must have been made that it would be an investment for the whole community, so the question could be asked – did that imply that most other children had already been inoculated? This was still a few years before Edward Jenner was promoting his form of cow-pox immunisation, so Cartmel Fell was well informed on preventative medicine. As a comparison in the relative costs of the day, the mother of this same child was being boarded out at a charge of three shillings a week.

It seems that many of the Gill Head Pooles were lawyers, and their signatures appear on various documents as trustees or witnesses. Many of the Bryan Beck charity papers were signed by a Poole, and in 1838, John Poole was treasurer. The sale of the coppice wood at Bryan Beck, which amounted to thirty pounds, had to be paid at Gill Head by the purchaser on 13 February. A few years earlier, an obituary for a forebear of John Poole appeared in *The Lonsdale Magazine:* 'Mr. (John) Poole of Gill Head Windermere died on 17th April 1822, aged 70. Mr Poole was a gentleman of uncommonly agreeable manners and sociable disposition. His greatest pleasure consisted in keeping up a remnant of that old English hospitality, which has vanished in other parts of the country, and is rapidly declining even here. It has often been remarked that no-one was suffered to depart without both eating and drinking with him. Such characters are an honour to Humanity; but, Alas! They are scarce.'

The 1841 census tells us a little more about the family which succeeded the hospitable Mr Poole. John and his wife Elizabeth were 35 (but this was to the nearest five years, and John was actually 39), and they had two small children, John and Jane who were three and fifteen months respectively. Also in the household were two young women, Mary Guy and Mary Noble, but there were no living-in servants. The adjoining entry lists a John Willcock, attorney's clerk, (presumably John Poole's) but he lived in a nearby household of agricultural labourers.

From the notes of the American branch of the family, A. J. Poole wrote in 1895, that it was believed John Poole sold his estate in 1841 for £17,000, adding that although he was a solicitor, John rarely practised, but spent his time engaged in field sports. Another legend has it that Gill Head estate was lost in a night of reckless gambling, the house itself being the final stake. This story was written for the *Daily Telegraph* by R. W. Poole, a descendant, some years ago, but he knew no more, and had no idea of when this might have happened. It was said that the loser in the gamble left his ancestral home with his only possession, a grandfather clock, on his back. Both the American and English versions agree that there was almost no money left when John died.

Trying to unravel this mystery is not easy. We know that John Poole was still at Gill Head in 1843, as that is the address on his will, in which he leaves his estate to his second wife Elizabeth. Inside the will, George Park, surrogate, acknowledges that the widow performed her role as executrix, the personal estate was valued at under £450, and that John had died in 1857, about 28 January. No children are mentioned although there were three daughters and a son, John, but the burial register shows that little Elizabeth died in 1844.

Following the death of John the elder, it transpired that he met an untimely end, and there had to be an inquest. The verdict was accidental death, he having died of exposure after stumbling into a gravel pit. He was 54-years-old and no longer of Gill Head, but was living across the lake at Colton. *The Kendal Mercury* reported the case at some length, and the following facts emerged: The body was found by Mr James Arnold of the Ferry Hotel, the gravel or sand pit being only a hundred yards from the hotel. Several people gave evidence, all saying that they saw the deceased in Bowness on the previous day. Daniel Holme Bellasis of Bowness, who had known John Poole for many years, testified that he was helplessly tipsy and was lying on his back in the dirt at Bowness waterside. It was dark, being between six and seven o'clock at night, but despite his condition, Mr Poole had insisted on rowing himself across the lake, and refused all offers of help. Mr Bellasis was so concerned, he sent two men to row after the boat, but even though they had a lantern, they could not find Mr Poole. It seems as though instinct guided the lawyer to the Ferry Hotel, for his boat was found with shipped oars, drawn up on the shingle there, but not secured. Footprints led from the boat to the gravel pit. The body of John Poole was taken back to his birthplace, and he was buried at Cartmel Fell on 3 February.

This sad story does not prove that this was the man who gambled away his house at cards, but the inquest showed an impetuous, headstrong man who drank to excess. In a night of gaming and alchohol, such a man might stake all in a reckless bet. At the inquest, his wife seemed unsurprised that there was little money in her husband's pocket when he was found.

The 1851 census for Hawkshead reveals that John Poole, a 49-year-old solicitor, was then living at Field Head with his family. He had been born in Cartmel parish (which was Cartmel Fell) and his wife Elizabeth, son John and three daughters ranging from six to twelve years were all living at home. This is without doubt the same man who died of exposure a few years later.

The inhabitants of the fell at that time must have followed events with intense interest. Life was a round of hard work with little social episodes to enliven it, but suddenly, there were many column inches in the local papers, for the second time, centred on Gill Head and its owners.

The first occasion that Gill Head was splashed across local and national papers happened three years earlier in 1854. This time, the drama centred on the Ward family who were then in residence. Was Frederick Ward the winner of the bet, one wants to know? The Wards had two young daughters, Ann

261

Jane and Caroline. They were sent to a boarding school in Appleby, where the young Ann showed musical ability and took piano lessons from the organist at St Lawrence's, John Atkinson. The head mistress of Ivy House began to suspect that there was more than a mutual interest in music between pupil and teacher, and in some alarm, she dismissed the organist, but gave him a good reference. Unknown to her, the couple continued the liaison by correspondence, with the help of a servant called Bella. By this means, they arranged to elope after a school outing to Ullswater on 24 May 1854. Ann made sure that Bella would leave the front door unlocked, and at about one o'clock in the morning, she slipped out to rendezvous with her lover. He had engaged a young farmer to drive them to Gretna Green, and this accomplice was later found to be his cousin.

Miss Bishop, the headmistress, thought she heard a noise in the night, and on getting up, found the street door open. She closed it, but did not discover that she had a missing pupil until 7am the next morning. Imagine the panic! She consulted the head of Appleby police, Mr Bird, and when they found that John Atkinson was also missing, the hue and cry began. Miss Bishop and Mr Bird set off for Penrith, and when they got there, telegraphed Ann's parents and then caught the mail train to Gretna. When they finally arrived, it was to find that the lovers had been married between 7 and 8 o'clock in the morning and had spent some time alone in the lodging house which the blacksmith obligingly kept, but the birds had flown. Intelligence gathered at Gretna pointed to Carlisle as the newly-weds' destination, so away sped Miss Bishop and Mr Bird. They caught up with the runaways at the Coffee House Hotel, their coachman still in tow.

Miss Bishop demanded that Ann should accompany her to another room, but Ann would not leave her husband, so her headmistress went to find a magistrate to make a deposition. Eventually, she and Ann returned to Kendal, and the case came up at the Assizes the following August.

The reason for this case hitting the national headlines in papers such as *The Times*, was that Ann was a considerable heiress in her own right, being worth £10,000 at the time of the 'abduction', but she was only twelve years and one month. Much was made of her older appearance in court, and there was a great deal of mirth. John Atkinson was sent to prison for nine months rather than the two years he might have expected, because the judge decided he had not acted 'from base motives of lucre.'

Ann waited for him to be released, but around this time, her mother left the household, the publicity perhaps being too much to bear. In the 1861 census, Frederick Ward was head of the household at Gill Head, and also living there were Mr and Mrs John Atkinson, he still being described as 'organist', and their seven-month old daughter. This sounds like a happy ending, but it was not so. John Atkinson fell victim to the smallpox outbreak in 1871, and Ann Jane subsequently had two more husbands. She died at St Asaph in North Wales in 1932, but the source of her inheritance is so far unknown.

There were further mysteries at Gill Head. In the 1871 census, Frederick Ward was still head of the household, and was then 51. This in itself is slightly odd, as he ages only nine years in each census, beginning at 42 in 1861, and ending at 69 in 1891, but plenty of others did the same, and the transcripts of the Assizes show how very vague people were about their ages. Ann Jane's own mother was not sure how old she was when she married, guessing about seventeen.

The interesting item in the household of 1871 is that the surname Pool (or Poole) has re-appeared, though who she is cannot be deduced. She is Elizabeth Ann, a boarder of 23 years, unmarried and a scholar. A scholar of what, one wants to ask. It seems a little odd that this young woman is unchaperoned, but she has three children, all with the middle name of Ward. There is Margaret Ward Poole, aged five and born in Liverpool, Alfred Ward Poole, born in Cartmel Fell, and little Sarah Maria Ward Poole, under a year old. This household remains unaltered until 1891, though the details change. Elizabeth's role becomes 'housekeeper', and her birthplace becomes Hawkshead not Coniston, but Coniston was part of Hawkshead parish.

Probably the first Mrs. Ward was still alive for most of the second half of the nineteenth century, so her husband and Elizabeth could not marry, but when he died in 1901, a tombstone was erected to his memory at Cartmel Fell. When Elizabeth Ann died in 1929, her name was added to the stone and she is described as 'wife', so perhaps they married after Jane died. Alfred Ward Poole died in 1940. His sister Margaret never married and is buried with her parents, being 88 when she died in 1954. Ann Jane's full brother, Frederick, was only eight at the time of the scandal. He later joined the army and settled in the south of England from whence his father came.

The nature of the area began a process of gentrification after the Wards' arrival. The 1851 census shows the occupations of the neighbouring householders and out of the five houses which were inhabited, most men were engaged in physical work. There were wallers in two separate dwellings, Joseph Lancaster aged 67 was a master waller and nearby was John Lancaster, a journeyman waller of 30, but he lodged with the Garnett family who were agricultural labourers, as were the Lishmans and Robinsons in the neighbouring properties. All the houses are listed under Gill Head, so it is hard to differentiate, but the last property before Rosthwaite was occupied by John Taylor who was a farmer and master blacksmith. One of his sons was a master shipwright and the other a carpenter. They had a blacksmith apprentice living with them, and a servant described as 'mariner'. Ten years later, that is after the Wards took over 'the big house', there were sweeping changes. Two of the cottages were unoccupied and another had a gardener as head of household. The fourth had a labourer as head and another gardener as a lodger, but the Wards had aggrandised Gill Head by changing the name to Gill Head Hall, and Frederick Ward's occupation was listed as landed proprietor. This must have been when the house acquired its Victorian appearance and the gardens were laid out. In the following century, a number of architect-designed houses sprang up around Gill Head, and it is now a hamlet of Cartmel Fell.

In the first half of the twentieth century, Robert Matthews was doing some decorating at Gill Head. He found a lump in the wallpaper, and on investigating, found a golden guinea concealed there. He took it to Mrs Ward who told him he could keep it. Was this an insurance for a rainy day, hidden by Mrs John Poole? Had she removed others when her husband had gambled with the housekeeping money? We shall never know.

Soon after the Second World War, Gill Head became a children's hotel. It was run by Mrs O'Flynn, a trained children's nurse, and part of the establishment was run as a nursery school for locals and boarders alike. Most of the children were there because their parents were abroad, so some went daily to local schools, and others went there during their boarding school holidays. Gill Head's prospectus boasted central heating in cold weather, with the additional luxury of having the bathrooms heated all the year round. Mrs O'Flynn had one of the early telephone numbers, Windermere 751. Today the estate is an outdoor pursuits centre.

Spooner Close

THERE has been a dwelling or dwellings of this name, down by the lake since 1587, and probably long before that. Today, all traces of past lives have been swept away, but the name survives, and the split-level, timber-clad house which overlooks the lake now, can bear little resemblance to its namesake. The gardens are beautifully landscaped and there are no farm buildings or any signs of industry or of commercial fishing.

The name Spooner may have come from a family, though it does not occur in Cartmel Fell parish records, or it may have been a trade which was carried on at the site. There are a dozen or so Spooners in the Cumbria telephone directory today, so an enclosure made by the Spooner family would seem a feasible explanation, probably after the dissolution of the monasteries.

An early mention of this holding comes from a will of a Miles Wright in 1587, and although his testament reveals little of his lifestyle, his trade is named as smith. This just might be a clue to the name of the holding, for although Miles does not appear to have a surviving inventory, his widow Jenet, who died the following year, did leave one. In itself, this was not a remarkable list of belongings. The usual household goods and equipment, a little hay and straw for the cow and the whye (heifer) and a few poultry. The only unusual item in a very modest homestead was a number of spoons. One was silver, some were of tin and others were horn. Miles was not described as 'blacksmith', so perhaps he had been a whitesmith, and specialised in making spoons. There might even have been several such craftsmen within the close, but unless other wills and inventories can be found, there is no real proof.

When Jenet Wright, widow, died in 1588, at that time her address was Waterside. This property, now also obliterated, adjoined Spooner Close, so perhaps the Wrights owned quite a long strip of lake shore. In those days of poor roads, the lake would have been a very useful highway, and a source of income too, if they had fishing rights.

In 1590, the Duchy of Lancaster rental has an entry under Spooner Close in which a number of the Gurnall family feature: Myles, Richard, Christopher, another Myles and Anthony. Under the same heading are members of the Poole or Pull clan including John, Jacob, James and Robert, but also Richard Ward, William Moore, Edward Bradley and R. Philipson. This seems to be a sizeable gathering of two or three households.

John Gurnall of Spooner Close christened his daughter Agnes at Windermere on 21 December 1621. Three years later, he christened two more daughters, Margaret and Allice on 30 August. Within the following year, three families had burials or baptisms from this address, the Ellises, the Halls and notably the Gurnalls, whose family name peppers the Windermere parish registers throughout the seventeenth century. Cartmel was actually their parish church, but Bowness was far more convenient. The households may have had masters and unrelated servants, but over the centuries the records seem to point to more than one house in the close, with many surnames. Within three years, both John Gurnall and Edward Harrison had children baptised at Cartmel. The Gurnalls had a son and heir, namesake of his father John, christened on 21 December 1673, and the Harrisons chose Anne for their daughter's name on 16 July 1676. On 6 December of that year, Thomas Gurnall was taken to Cartmel to be baptised.

The holding was still in Gurnall hands at the end of the seventeenth century, but by this time their children were not being baptised in the parish church or at Cartmel Fell chapel. After the religious upheaval of the Dissolution, and then in the following century the Puritan-Presbyterian domination, people were beginning to question the edicts from on high, and a wave of new religions was breaking over the remote areas of Cumbria. The Gurnalls had become members of the Religious Society of Friends or Quakers, and in 1683 a John Gurnall of Spooner Close was fined four shillings for non-payment of tithes. This was a year when Thomas Preston of Holker, the tithe farmer, was pursuing the Friends with furious vigour and several other members of the parish of Cartmel Fell were fined or imprisoned in that same year. If they could not pay, their goods were removed for sale, and if this did not raise enough money, prison followed. Most likely, the Gurnalls would attend the meetings at Height, on Cartmel Fell, which had been built six years earlier. Their burials would have taken place at Height, and in the Cartmel Priory registers there are unusual entries for the Friends. Baptisms are not recorded since they did not take place, but births are entered instead. Under the burial columns for 1706, the following entry occurs: 'John Gurnall of Spooner Close, Quaker, buried at ye Sepulcher,' the Quaker burial ground. We know that the Gurnalls held Quaker meetings in their own house as well, as this is noted in Bishop Gastrell's *Notitia* of 1714-1725. In the Quaker registers, the births of the children of John and Agatha Gurnall were entered, Tabitha in 1679 and Jonathan in 1684.

A document dated 1747 was drawn up for Elizabeth Gurnall, widow of Thomas of Spooner Close. This was for a lease and release of two messuages with orchards and gardens. The closes are named: Damm Meadow, the Lang Dyke and Tenture Close, but unfortunately it does not say whether these messuages are actually part of Spooner Close, though they did have three peat mosses on Cartmel Fell to go with them, Thorn Moss Hows, Lingy Hows and Back of Lingy Hows. Perhaps these fields or the mosses will be identified one day.

A family of Stewardsons lived in one of the properties at Spooner Close for much of the eighteenth century, that is in parallel with the Gurnalls, so it seems yet another pointer to this being a little hamlet rather than a single farm. In the previous century, there are several entries for Thomas and Isabell Stewardson in the Cartmel registers. They were married in 1677 when Thomas was described as fisherman, and they had at least five children in subsequent years, but by then they were of Waterside. A stretch of foreshore on the eastern side of the lake is still marked on O.S. maps as Stewardson Nab, projecting from Waterside Wood. The Stewardsons have descendants in the area still.

Fishing was organised on strictly commercial lines at this period. The lake was divided into three parts which were known as cubbles. The High Cubble stretched down the lake from Ambleside to Ecclerigg Crag on the east shore, and Pinstones point on the west. The Middle Cubble went south of Belle Isle to a line from Ash Landing in the west, to Short Nab in the east, and all the rest of the lake to the south was known as the Low Cubble. The word is variously spelt over the centuries, but seems to derive from the type of fishing boat, known on the east coast of England as a coble. The commercial fishing was done with what is now called a seine net, and apparently, up to ten hauls could be accomplished in a day. The net might contain trout, char, pike or perch, and sometimes eels. The nets were very light, and made of cow and horse hair. Unlike those of vegetable fibres, this type of net did not become saturated and heavy when immersed.

A century passed before Spooner Close appeared again in a parish register, this time in that of Crosthwaite, Westmorland. An entry for 1792 gives a good deal of family detail: Mary, daughter of John Long of Spooner Close, and wife of Wilson Martin, shoemaker of Town Yeat, Crosthwaite, christened her son Wilson on 12 February. The clerk also helpfully adds that Wilson was born on 15 January.

The 1799 land tax document shows that John Poole of Gill Head was then the owner, and the occupier was John Robinson, his son-in-law. The Pooles, or a branch of them, also owned Tower Wood, so maybe their lands adjoined. The Robinsons were in occupation of one of the properties at least from 1788 when John and (Isa)Bella christened their daughter Esther, and in 1817 another generation, this time John and Ann Robinson, had their daughter Esther christened, an echo of the previous century. Although the property is not named in the 1814 land tax papers, John Robinson is still in residence, and since the next item on the list is the bobbin mill below Gill Head, this is likely to be the same man and the same house, now described as cottage, which has the implication of being without land.

Almost the last evidence of the old dwelling is in the 1829 Parson & White directory, when George Robinson, bobbin turner, had an entry. No doubt he was related to John, the last tenant, but by the time the 1841 census was taken, Spooner Close has no mention. On the O.S. map of 1846, which has the large scale of six inches to the mile, no trace can be seen of a house by that part of the lake. It could have been cleared when the saw-mills and bobbin mills were swept away, and the whole area underwent a process of gentrification, so it is something of a surprise therefore to find that Spooner Close appears in the Cartmel Fell census of 1891, and seems to be a farm, though the acreage is not given. This was then the home of the Stricklands and their two daughters. Ruth, the elder girl of fourteen was entered as farmer's daughter, which implied a working role on the farm. The holding must have been big enough to support the family and with a little to spare, because the fifth member of the household was Hannah Ramsden, a servant girl of seventeen from Kendal. Seven years later, there is a baptismal entry for Cartmel Fell in 1898: Frances Mary, daughter of Henry and Ada Frances Bowness of Spooner Close, the father's occupation being entered as farmer.

Because of its position down by the lake, Spooner Close was always a little apart from the body of the parish, and the absence of names from parish registers and documents may just mean that it was out of sight and out of mind. As far as church registers can be used as a check on the population at any given time, geography is very important. St Anthony's in Cartmel Fell seems to have been far too difficult to reach from the lake shore, and as mentioned earlier, Bowness or Cartmel were used by the Church of England adherents, and for a while at least, the Gurnalls held Quaker Meetings in their own home. Staveley Church would have been as easy to reach as Bowness, and a search of their records might prove useful. What seems so odd, is the missing census years. Was the close really forgotten, or was it an appendix to some other parish? Victorian bureaucracy was so thorough that it seems likely that this area must be on another schedule, but there is evidence in other areas of omissions of isolated households. Maybe the enumerator could not find the place at the end of a long day, or a page was lost in 1851, and thus omitted from the 1861 census and subsequent ones.

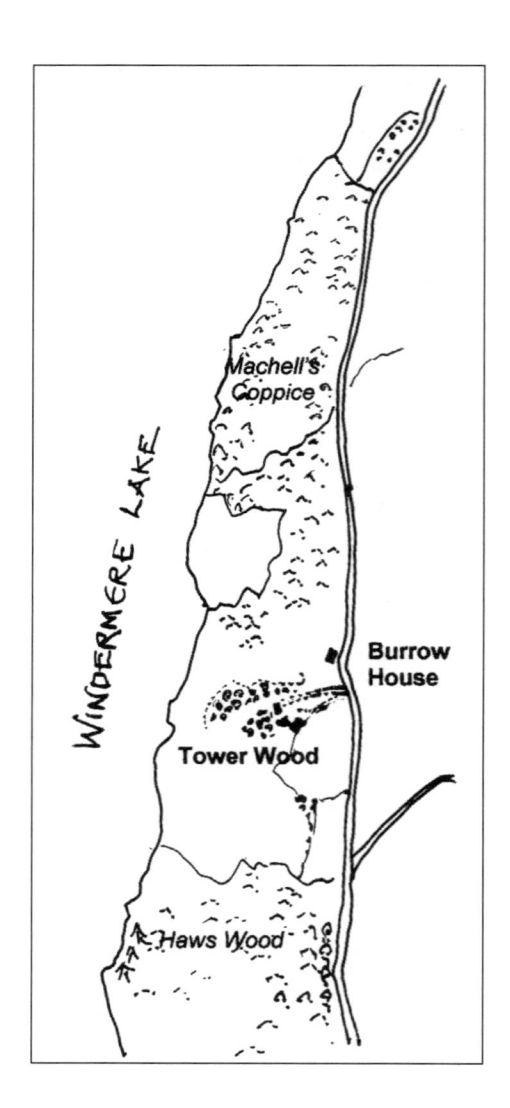

Tower Wood

THERE are hundreds of acres of woodland on this western side of Cartmel Fell, two areas of which were anciently known as Great and Little Tower Woods. Perhaps at some distant era, a watch or pele tower might have been constructed on high ground, but no positive theories seem to have been suggested as to where the tower might have been. Whether the wood gave its name to the house of that name, or whether it was the other way round is open to conjecture, but the most likely answer is the latter. An owner of an estate would be identified to his neighbours by his title to the land, such as Addyson's wood or Addyson's farm (which was Tower Wood) so the lands belonging to the holding assumed the name of the homestead. Many other such woods are so named on the fell, such as Ashes Wood, Little Thorphinsty Wood or Addyfield Wood. This answer of course still begs the queston 'what tower?' The site of the house is on low land by the lake and as such is not easily defensible, so an early pele tower on this site seems a bit unlikely, though it could be argued that a convenient but vulnerable site needed a refuge, and hence the tower. Archaeologists of the future may unearth some clues.

There are several dwellings on the Tower Wood site, and references in wills or parish registers seldom clarify the location. There is a farm with associated buildings and to the north is the little group of Burrow House and Burrow Cottage which are right on the road. To the south is the 'Big House', which like other large dwellings in the area is now an outdoor pursuits centre.

It may be supposed that the earliest dwelling of the group is the largest, and the other dwellings grew up as satellites. To all intents and purposes Tower Wood outdoor pursuits centre looks Edwardian with later additions, but this is not the whole truth. The entrance hall is typical of the Arts and Crafts movement at the beginning of the twentieth century, with oak panelling and an open fireplace, the surround of which has the date 1911 carved on it, and the initials T. H. M., in which the middle letter is probably for the surname, Hall. Arthur Simpson, the contemporary designer and executer of carved artefacts may well have made the over-mantel, as he had workshops and a summer school just up the road at Ghyll Head Cottage. As we move further into the core of the house, its antiquity is revealed. A room in the centre has walls which are far thicker than the later ones, and a fairly high ceiling has huge oak beams supporting riven oak joists. This was always an important house, built for someone of status.

The earliest owner to be traced so far is Michael Pull or Pool, who made his will in 1588. From this document it seems that this was the 'missing' house called Waterside. It disappeared from parish records at about this time, but Michael Pull's inventory declares him to be 'of Waterside,' whilst the attached letters of administration name him 'Michael Pull of Tower Wood.' His widow Alice was his executrix and the document mentions property at Moor How. It seems that these two estates were linked for centuries, as will be seen later. We know from other wills that the Pooles were still at Moor How over a century later and the family were widespread in the north and west of the parish in the sixteenth and seventeenth centuries, and survived at Gill Head until the middle of the nineteenth century.

Michael Pull and Alicia or Alice had three daughters, Isabel, Agnes and Anne, and possibly a fourth, Elizabeth Wallas of 'Morehow', as the farm was then spelt. Michael Pull, Roland and Elizabeth Wallas were witnesses to the will. By the next century, the names had changed at Tower Wood, but the Pooles seem to have had mostly daughters, so inheritance may have been through the female line.

When William Addyson of Tower Wood made his will in 1674, he was facing a similar predicament, but he had no less than seven daughters - Margaret, Agnes, Elizabeth, Anne, Jane, Isabelle and Mabel, each of whom were to receive £11. There seems to have been no son and heir but Anthony Addyson who succeeded him may have been a brother or a nephew.

Anthony made his will in 1686, and we see from this that he too had only two daughters and two grand-daughters. The daughters were Anne and Mabel and the grand-daughters were Agnes Addyson and Margaret Mitchell. Statistically, the odds must have been very much against a run of fifteen girls born to three successive yeomen families, but if there were any boys, none survived. Anthony's executors were men of local standing; James Birket of Birket Houses, John Gurnall of Spooner Close and Thomas Dixon of Orrest Head. They were charged with selling the estate and it was bought by William Robinson who lived there until he died in May 1723. His widow Mary died at Tower Wood in 1730.

Very confusingly, another Addyson will, also of Tower Wood, was made in 1687, that of William, a yeoman, who seems to have been a farmer from the evidence of his inventory, but whether he lived at the neighbouring farm or elsewhere is hard to say. There were the usual everyday items together with wool, yarn, spinning wheels and hemp, growing crops of apples, oats and bigg and livestock amounting to £16.6s. A little money was owing to him for bark and wood and his son Anthony was to have £52 from the estate. The document mentions that Tower Wood was of the annual rent of 5s.4d, payable to William Robinson, James Jackson and Thomas Dixon. If William Robinson was the same man who had just bought Tower Wood House (to differentiate it from the farm) then it seems highly probable that this William Addyson was at Tower Wood farm, and had just acquired new landlords.

The new owners, William and Mary Robinson, had a son Jonathan who married twice. His first wife was Margaret Briggs who gave him a daughter. After Margaret's death Jonathan married the widow of Abraham Poole, Jane, née Cowperthwaite. Possibly, this second marriage brought Moor How back into the loop, as Jane and Jonathan's son William was living at Moor How when he married in 1758. As mentioned earlier, the Pooles had once owned both Tower Wood and Moor How.

Apart from William, there is no evidence of other Robinson siblings, so it may be that grandsons were the successors to Tower Wood. In the 1814 land tax valuation, the owners and occupiers of Tower Wood were James Robinson and brothers. They had over 32 acres of woodland and two acres of plantation, with about six acres of arable land. James Robinson was in the middle of a large family which spanned nineteen years and he died a bachelor at Moorhow in 1850, aged 83.

An article in the *Cumbria Family History Newsletter* in February 1994 describes the strained relations in the Robinson family when the oldest son, John, succeeded to Moorhow when his father suddenly died intestate. The younger members of the family eventually bought him out, but they may have chosen to live at Tower Wood, for a while at least, whilst they raised the money.

The 1851 census does nothing to help clarify the different houses and families dwelling at Tower Wood. There are four holdings listed, all called by the same name, seemingly equating to the area once known as Waterside, so this was actually an area, not just a house, as Height was in former times.

Some of the names are very familiar, and in the largest holding of 100 acres, John Poole, a 70-year-old landed proprietor and a bachelor, was boarding with the Barrows who were farmers. Ten years previously though, John had been the farmer at this holding. Joshua and John Robinson lived in two of the other properties, Joshua being a farmer of sixteen acres and John being an agricultural labourer. Joshua was a great grandson of William Robinson who bought Tower Wood from the trustees of Anthony Addyson.

At the fourth Tower Wood property in 1851 was the family of William Preston. He had no idea, or did not say, where he was born, except that it was in England, and he farmed eight acres. He was a widower with three sons and a daughter still at home and all born on the fell.

Ten years later, the census enumerator helpfully described the Tower Wood properties as High, Low,

Middle and Cottage, in that order from Beech Hill. At High Tower Wood were Edward and Margaret Matthews, farming eight acres. This must have been the same holding previously farmed by the Prestons, and if the acreages are a reliable guide, this is the little farm which is identified as Burrow House in the 1881 census. At that time, Ferdinand Muncaster was the occupant, but he seems to have moved along a peg by 1901, because Burrow House was home to John Airey and his family. Burrow(s) House is further identified in the 1909 Inland Revenue survey. It still had just eight acres and by that time Jane Taylor was the owner/occupier. The farmhouse was in poor condition then, and another 'old house' is surveyed in the same piece. That had two rooms downstairs and two above and must have been the house now called Burrow Cottage. The buildings included a shippon for eight cows, a two-stall stable, calf hull and a hen-house with a barn over all. Jane Taylor had previously occupied the 103 acres that went with 'the Big House', but vacated them in May 1909.

No doubt, the Inland Revenue were about as popular in 1909 as they are today. They surveyed every house and every plot of land with its associated buildings and reported on the state of the nation's assets together with excellent coloured maps. Today, their thoroughness is a blessing to every kind of historian. From this account, we learn that Tower Wood Farm, with its 103 acres, no longer existed by 1909, and that the present-day outdoor pursuits centre, known as Tower Wood, was built on the site. However, as mentioned at the beginning of this section, the core of the old house does still remain. The description of this gentleman's house in 1909 is as follows: 'Porch, hall, billiard room (for full sized table), drawing room, boots and lav. Dining room, smoking room, butler's pantry, kitchen and scullery. First floor; 3 spare bedrooms, bathroom, box room, 2 servants bedrooms, 1 small bedroom, dressing room, bathroom, main bedroom, linen closet. 2 nurseries, (day & night). Stone, slate, rough-cast. Very good condition. Outside; Motor house with store room adjoining, hay store, boat house for 2, landing. Balcony with store above (wood). Large building used as dry dock, stone, slated. Fair condition.'

At this time the owner and occupier was T. Inglis Hall, who must have commissioned the over-mantel in 1911, the letter M being his wife's initial.

As the muddy waters of the many Tower Woods begin to clear, we can see that this was the farm of over 100 acres run by the Flemings, so this was where John Poole had farmed and then retired to as a boarder in 1851. In 1861 Daniel Fleming was the farmer, a widower with a four-year-old son and two step-daughters of eleven and nine, Annas and Martha Kellett.

Middle Tower Wood was Joshua Robinson's home for over 40 years. His wife was Mary in 1841, but from 1851 onwards her name was recorded as Isabella. No burial is recorded at St Anthony's for Mary, but perhaps she was buried elsewhere and Joshua married again. Whereas their original acreage was only sixteen, by 1861 they had 25 though by 1881 it had shrunk back to fourteen.

A new name appears in the 1861 census, that of Tower Wood Cottage. Here lived Margaret Poole, the head of the household and a widow. She was a landed proprietor of 61 years and was born in Windermere parish. The Pooles seemed to circulate continually around Tower Wood, but in so many permutations that they tend to blur. Margaret was buried at St Anthony's in 1868.

Ferdinand Muncaster was born on Colton across the lake and was named after his father, but the younger man was head of the household when they lived at Burrow House in 1881. An opportunity must have arisen to enlarge their farming activities and the family of Ferdinand, his wife Abigail and his father moved to Tower Wood farm somewhere between 1881 and 1891. Although this holding only had just over twenty acres, by 1901, Ferdinand was employing three servants.

Some of the population of the Tower Wood complex must have been forever on the move. The names in the censuses and those in the parish registers of burials and baptisms do not accord, and it seems that Beech Hill was also called Tower Wood from time to time. James and Elizabeth Catherine Wright had children christened at Cartmel Fell in the 1860s and so did the Dewhursts, but they are not in the censuses, having moved on and in the next decade Thomas and Nancy Ellis did likewise. In 1888, Thomas Medcalf, a woodcutter, had his son Frederick baptised at St Anthony's. This pattern of young couples moving continuously was typical of tenants who sought to improve their lot and had few possessions. By the turn of the twentieth century, the tenanted houses at Tower Wood were in poor condition and two were uninhabited.

Blakeholme

THERE is more than one possibility for the derivation of this name, and two of them relate to colour. In some instances it has been spelt Blackholme, which is clear enough, black maybe referring to its appearance from afar. There may have been dark fir trees there at some period, or it may just have been creative spelling. In dialect, blake meant pale yellow, as in 'blake as May butter.' Perhaps there were fields of buttercups or dandelions which shone out to viewers across the lake. Another possibility is that blake is a variant of bleak, but this is unlikely when the site is low down and facing west.

It has been difficult to find much documentary evidence for this farm, but it occupies a site which was dwelt on long before the present house was built. A datestone over the front door proclaims the year 1870, but this must have been a re-building or a re-furbishment. The Cartmel Fell parish church documents have a record of a Myles Harrison of Blakeholme in 1696, when he held £10 of the chapel's money, for which he paid annual interest of £1. He also held money which was ear-marked for the poor of the parish, and in that same year paid 6s.8d. as interest on £3.6s.8d. It would be interesting to know how Myles Harrison made the money 'work,' but such details are not included here. We know from account books found at Height that much invested money went into land and property there, as nothing was more worthwhile to a farmer. In this year of 1696, there are many references to a

Myles Harrison in relation to parish accounts, but more often than not, no address is given. It seems likely that they are all the same man, or one would expect further clarification to be needed, indicating the farm or district he inhabited. The family must have had enough money to live, with some to spare for the good of the parish, as Myles Harrison's mother, wife of Edward, gave £5 to her son for investment, and he was also entrusted with a further £6.13s from James Harrison of Chapel House. Myles must have had a local reputation for growing money.

After this period, there is a large gap in the parish records before there is any further mention of Blakeholme. In 1769, William Harriman was overseer of the poor for his holding of Blakeholme, and the following year he was constable. At the same period, Martin Harriman and Isabel were farming Lightwood, so the two families were probably related. The name Harriman occurs frequently in the mid-eighteenth century on the fell, and then disappears again. After another long gap, we find that John Martin was at Blakeholme in 1829, according to the Parson and White directory, but there are no further details. The same family are there in the 1841 census, but probably the next generation. These are Josh and Hannah, both aged 30, and they have a child, John. Also living with them is Agnes Martin aged 65, probably Josh's mother. Ten years on, the next census is more explicit. Josh is actually called Joseph, and he is a farmer and land agent. This last occupation is interesting, because we know that his successor in the farm was land agent for Thorphinsty Hall and for the Wakefield family, so maybe Mr Martin was too. By 1851 the Martins have five children, the youngest daughter being nameless and only sixteen-days-old on the day of the census. They have a house servant, Agnes Lishman of Winster, and a monthly nurse for the baby, so they are clearly prospering, although the farm has only twenty acres plus ten of heath, as we see in the 1861 returns. The land agent's salary must have supplemented the farming considerably.

Soon after the 1861 census, the occupier of Blakeholme was James Holme, farmer and land agent to the Rev. William Uthwatt of Maids Moreton in Buckingham for the Thorphinsty Hall estate. After Mr Uthwatt's death, his widow relied on James to continue in his post. A portrait of this lady has been preserved by the Holme family. Many of the estate records have been deposited in

James Holme.

Barrow and Kendal Record Offices and these show the day to day business of James Holme, and later of his son who succeeded him in the post.

As mentioned in the Thorphinsty section, James Holme was sometimes in conflict with his employer for being too liberal with his payments to casual workers. The Uthwatts found it hard to grasp the completely different nature of attitudes between the employer and the employed in the north. A story, still related in the Holme family 150 years later, recalls a visit from the Uthwatts' home-counties lawyer. Together, he and James Holme walked up to the plantation near Gummers How. The expedition was to inspect some walling, but when they got there, the waller had just arrived at 10.30am. The solicitor was highly critical; such a late start would not be allowed to happen in Maids Moreton. James Holme quietly pointed out that the waller was paid by the yard, he had walked from Underbarrow and furthermore, he was 82-years-old.

From James Holme's letter book, it seems that he was land agent for the Wakefield family too. He mentions in 1865 that Mr. Wakefield had always taken an active part in the woodland management, and indeed the 1814 land tax copy shows that John Wakefield was both owner and occupier of Blakeholme at that date. At some stage, the Wakefield family must have decided to use the house as a base for their agents, and it still belongs to the family today.

James Holme's son John followed in his father's footsteps as land agent, but by the twentieth century he had moved to Seatle, though he was still at Blakeholme in 1891 as a farm servant. Today, the farmhouse is the home of the manager of the Hill of Oaks caravan park, which is part of the Wakefield estate. On the site, at the edge of the lake, is an interesting relic of the Wakefields' early passion for planes. A seaplane hangar has doors which face the lake and a little slipway slopes down to the water. On the same site is an old water-mill, now converted into two holiday cottages.

On the 1846 six inch O.S. map, close to Blake Holme Nab, the site of 'Cornelius' Shop' is marked. James Stockdale relates a tale about this in the *Annals of Cartmel*. The legend was that a man by the name of Cornelius was in hiding, and as he had some skill in mending watches, he had eked out a living by repairing the country folk's timepieces, living in a single-storey stone hut. By the 1860s, the building was virtually roofless, but was used by charcoal burners at irregular intervals, the walls still being sound. Branches were laid over the gables and a temporary roof constructed, which lasted for the burning season, but then it too decayed, to be replaced in its turn. A little research showed that the folk memories are worth attention, but the detail had become blurred.

Cornelius was a skilled craftsman, indeed he was a watchmaker, not merely a mender. His name was Cornelius Clarke, and he became a freeman of Lancaster on 17 January 1734 on payment of £1. The low fee suggests that he had some connection with Lancaster, possibly having been apprenticed there, or being the son of a freeman. He was then described then as 'of Cartmel Fell.' He married Agnes Kilner of Ayside, she being 24 when a marriage bond was drawn up in 1734, and Ayside was where Cornelius's will was made in 1759. The Clarkes had at least five children, one of whom, Thomas, was also a clock and watchmaker and who became a freeman of Lancaster in 1759. Later in the century he was working in Ulverston. There seems to be no trace of the workshop by the lake today, but it probably occupied the area that the shop for the caravan site now occupies, this being sheltered by higher rocks to the west. Although it seems an out of the way place today, Susan Stuart, author of *A Biographical List of Clockmakers*, points out that it was once between two busy thoroughfares, the lake and the road from Ambleside to Newby Bridge. There were many woodland industries, and various mills using the watercourses from the fell as power sources. Heavy goods were transported up and down the lake, so Cornelius Clarke was probably hardly ever out of earshot of human voices.

Blakeholme Wray

THIS attractively sited country house does not really belong amongst the farmsteads, but is included because of its proximity to Blakeholme. It was built by Sir John Fisher and he created around the house a beautiful garden which runs down to the lake.

Sir John was born in Barrow-in-Furness in 1892, son of the shipping magnate James Fisher. Although the family business was 'James Fisher and Sons', Sir John trained as a mining engineer in Northern Ireland, but because he had joined the Territorial Army in 1913, he was called up at the outbreak of the First Word War. He was one of the lucky ones who came home again, despite being in the battle of the Somme, and when he was demobilised he took over the family business. At the outbreak of the Second World War, John Fisher's reputation was such that he was called to the Ministry of War Transport and appointed director of The Coastal and Short Sea division. In this capacity, he was the organiser of the evacuation of Dunkirk and also of the D-Day landings in Normandy. In 1942 a knighthood was conferred on him for services to shipping.

It seemed that Sir John was a confirmed bachelor, but he surprised even close friends in 1947 when he secretly married a Viennese opera singer, Maria Elsner, and the couple went to live at Blakeholme Wray. Life in the Lake District must have been very different to the one Maria had previously known, but she loved outdoor life and together they enjoyed hunting, shooting and fishing, and also ski-ing and various sorts of boating. They died in 1983, having seldom been parted, and their name lives on through the many charitable foundations they initiated, many connected with the sea.

Sir John and Lady Fisher's housekeeper for some time was Sarah, the wife of John Kellet. Formerly Sarah had been the young cook at Cartmel Fell parsonage. They wanted to build their own bungalow on the other side of the road and asked Sir John if he would sell them some land. He agreed, providing the site did not overlook his house directly, so the couple set to, and with their own hands completed their home. They called it Beckside and over the years have developed a fellside garden with marvellous views.

Appendices

Ten Year Samples of burials at St. Anthony's Church, Cartmel Fell.

1830	May, F, 64	1881	February F. 9
1831	March F, inf.		February F. 33
	June 17 mo.		February M. 77
	July M. inf.		June M. 82
	August F. 29		July M. 40
	August M. 6 mo.		August F. 12
	October F. 75	1891	January F. 13 mo.
	December M. 8 mo.	1901	February M. 82
1841	January M. 76		February M. 77
	January F. 89		March M. 81
	April F. 3 mo.	1911	April M. 75
	August M. inf.		July M. 67
	Septemer M. 67	1921	June M. 28
	October M. 68		December F. 59
1851	February M. 1 yr.	1931	May M. 69
	March M. 77		August F. 72
	March F. 63		September F. 71
	April M. 61		December F. 7 mo.
	May F. 39	1941	February F. 44
	June F. 10		July M. (no age)
	July F. 16	1951	no burials
1861	February F. 54	1961	November M. 60
	February F. 66	1971	September F. 92
	March F. 57		November F. 91
	May M. 1 yr.	1981	March M. 68
	May F. 11		December M. 78
	July M. 59	1991	February F. 80
	December F. 15		May M. 72
1871	January F. 25		September M. 85
	May M. 35		
	July M. 41		

No infant burials after 1962

277

Table of Wool, Hemp, etc.

Date	Name, abode	Wheel	Cards	Looms/ studdles	Hemp	Wool	Flax, linen
1586	John Herrison, Cartmel Fell	plural	plural			Wool,cloth. Total £5.9.4	
1588	Alice Strickland Cartmel Fell	plural	Pair total 6d.				
1588	Roger Strickland, Cartmel Fell (Hartbarrow? Hole in ms.)	plural	pair	Pair of studdles, looms beween his sons. A walk-mill in property	pulled & unpulled		
1588	Robert Briggs (Cowmire?)	plural	pair	Pair of studdles	Pulled & unpulled	Wool & yarn	
1591	Tho. Burrowe, Witherslack				Hemp of this year & yarn, 10s.& 13s.4d. half stone of hemp:1s.8d	Woollen cloth 12s. wool £1.5.0	
1592	Hugh Barrow, Bryan Beck	plural	pair	Pair of studdles			
1593	Brian Harrison, Hartbarrow			Was owed for 4 'Whittes'(blankets) @ 13s. each		2 stones of woollen yarn	
1594	W'm Swainson, Collinfield					wool	
1602	Marg't Wallas, Moorhow		pair				
1606	Ed'wd Robinson, Sow How				Harden cloth	Woollen yarn	
1611	R'd Harrison, Akes (Oaks)	one	pair	Pair of studdles		Wool, £2.12.0	
1619	Rob't Wallas, Hartbarrow	plural	pair				
1619	Rob't Pull, Prentices				Hemp, 4s.		
1625	James Swainson	two	2 pairs	studdles	Hemp & yarn 10s.6d, cloth 2s. hemp	Wool, 57s	Coverlets, sheets, 44s.
1630	Edw'd Harrison, Cartmel Fell	plural	pair			Wool & yarn, 48s.	
1630	W'm Pull, Moorhow	one	pair			Wool, 3s.	
1638	Jhn. Swainson, Cartmel Fell			Pr old Studdles	Hemp	Wool £9	New coarse canvas, 7s. sheets, lin & canvas, £1.4.0.
1638	Jas. Crosfield, Witherslack	plural	plural		Hemp & yarn £1.2.0. cloth & seed	Wool	
1642	W'm Strickland, Hartbarrow	plural	plural		Hemp	Wool + 7lbs. w. yarn, 5s.	yarn
1645	Jennett Simson, (Simson Ground?)	plural	plural	2 lomes (sic)	Hemp & yarn		
1646	Rowland Steavenson, C. Fell			studdles	Harden	Wol'n. yarn	

278

Date	Name, abode	Wheel	Cards	Looms/studdles	Hemp	Wool	Flax, linen
1658	Ed' Casson, Witherslack	one, 1s.		Pr. of looms 6s.			
1660	John Swainson, Collinfield	plural	plural	Pr. old studdles	Harden sheets	Wool, £1.6.0	New coarse canvas sheets
1662	Isabel Swainson	plural	plural		Hemp, 15s.		Sheets 9s.
1666	Miles Birkett, Kitt Cragg	plural	plural			Cloth & yarn, £2.10s	
1667	Ed' Chamley, Meathop	plural	plural		Hemp, summer & winter, 10s.	Wool & yarn, 6s.	2 pieces new cloth/sheet 5s.
1676	Miles Birket, Birket Houses				Hemp & sadle 1s.	Wool & hooks £1.8.0.	
1678	Lawrence Harrison, Greenthorn	one			Hemp	wool	linen
1683	John Gibson, Height	plural	plural		Hemp	wool	linen & yarn
					These 3 items were totalled together £1.12s		
1686	Robert Kilner				Hemp, 10s.		
1697	Edmund Gibson, Height	one	pair		Growing, 1s.6d		
1702	Rowland Hodgson. Oaks					Cloth, 8s.	
1704	Rowland Rowlandson, Simpson Ground						Sheets & table linen, £1.4.0
1715	John Strickland, Collinfield				Hemp	Wool	
1718	Nathan Kilner, Backbarrow,				Hemp & cloth £14.5.0.		Linen yarns 4s.4d.
1723	Jas. Rowlandson, Foxfield					1 stone broken wool	
1727	Francis Turner, Ashes Beck					Wool, 15s.6d	
1743	Thomas Kilner, Poolgarth					Wool, £2.5.0.	

This table was constructed from the scores of wills and inventories I have collected over the years. Some were collected by the late professor G. P. Jones and very kindly passed on to me by Dr. John Marshall, who worked with him. Others I have copied at Preston and Kendal Record Offices.

The purpose of compiling this dossier was to see which products were being used in textile production in this particular area. The system of taking an inventory within a few days of a death is of variable use. Sometimes, especially in earlier times, every item is separately listed, but all too often 'Goods' are lumped together, or a whole loft or chamber is assessed, so quantities cannot be clarified. Where items can be separated, values have been included.

As can be seen, very little flax or linen was recorded, but hempen cloth seems to have been universal and could resemble linen. Some well-to-do families had table and bed-linen, but this must have been bought in.

Lancaster was the port for Irish flax and linen and it supported many flax-dressers and importers, many of whom were Quakers. The raw materials were sold on to be worked in cottage industries or on a larger scale. The account books of Elizabeth Fell of Swarthmoor Hall show how well she organised her flax workers, but also the variety of cloths they could produce. The names have changed over the centuries, but 'Hogaback' was more descriptive of texture than the current 'Huckaback'.

INDEX OF SURNAMES

Adam, T, Bur, X,
Addison, SM, ChH, TW
Alle(o)nby, T, SH, MA,
Argles, Cf, Bur, Sch,
Armistead, R,
Ashburner, PH,
Askew, W
Atkinson, HTG, As, PG, Cf, BB, R, ThH, GH, SG, Bur, QMH, Sch, X,
Airey, Hod H, R, ThH,
Backhouse, SG,
Barber, B.Br,
Barker, Lw, Ff,
Barratt, CoH,
Barrow, As, PG, Cf, BB, R, ThH, Gos, Bur,
Barwick, Lw,
Bathgate, Lb,
Batty, Hod.H, Lw, HH, PH, Bur, Sch,
Beck(s), Ch,H, R,
Bellingham, Rb
Bennett, Lw, Hol, PH,
Bentley, RL, Lw, Ff,
Berry, PG,
Bibby, HH,
Bigland, B.Br, Bbt, H,
Birket(t), Br.Ho, HTG, SM, W, Hod. H, Ch.H, Cf, O, Rb, BkHo, SH, SG, QMH, Sch,
Blades, HodH, MH,
Blewet, Bth,
Bowes, PH,
Bowness, PG, Hc, H, SC, Gos,
Bradley, Sc
Braithwaite, Hol, R,
Bramwell, A
Brennand, R,
Brigg(s), Bho, SM, CoH, Lw, A, X,
Brittain, Sm, Gos,
Broadbridge, Sch,
Brockbank, Sch,

Brooke, X
Burrow, CoH,
Burton, O,
Caldwell, Bbt,
Carr, As, W, Ff, OHB,
Carruthers, CoH, SG,
Carter, D,
Cartwright, HTG,
Casson, SG,
Cervetti, Lw
Chadwick, Sch,
Chambers, Bth,
Churchman, Bur,
Clarke. As, HodH, R, Blk,
Clayton, D,
Cleasby, Bur,
Cloudsdale, Cf,
Cockerton, As, LTh, RL, Sch, X,
Copplethwaite, A
Cousen, OHB,
Coward, H, ThH,
Cowperthwaite, Lw
Crackelt, Gos,
Crag, OHB,
Craghill, Sch H, Sch,
Cranage, Bur,
Craven, Bbt,
Crewdson, Gt , X
Crosfield, SH,
Crosthwaite, PG, JD , Sch,
Crow(e), LTh, Bth, T, Gt, Cf, ThH, Hol, A, L, MH, PH, Sch,
Curwen, X,
Dargue, MA,
Davison, H
Dawson, Cf,
Dicconson, PH,
Dickinson, Lw, A, BB, Lb, ThH, OHB,
Dixon, O, MH, Bbt, OHB,
Dobson, H.
Dod(g)son, SM, PG, Gt, SH, O, PH,
Dodding, QMH,
Downham, SH, X,
Duckett, R,
Elam, HH,
Elleray, SG,
Ellis, TW,

Ellwood, SG,
Fawcett, HodH
Fell, HTG, HH,
Field, X,
Fisher, Blk,
Fleming, SM, ChH, CoH, T, Hc, TW, Ff, QMH, Sch,
Fletcher, Sch, X,
Foster, SH, MH, W,
Fox, As,
Frankland, H,
Garnet(t), BBr, Lw, Hol, As, MH, Bbt, PH, GH,
Gass, OHB,
Gibson, HTG, ChH, Lw, Hol,
Goodman, Ff,
Gordon, CoH,
Graham, CoH,
Graves, JD
Greenwood, ChH , PGN
Griggs, R,
Gurnall, SC, X,
Halhead, ChH
Hall, HTG, GS,TW, QMH,
Hargreaves,
Harriman, Gos,
Harrison, OHB, H, Gos, QMH, Sch , X,
Hayton, Bur,
Herd, Hird, Cf, Hc, Sch,
Hodgson, Sm, HodH, JD, Bth, BBr, Hol, A, O, BB, Lb, Hts,
Hoggarth, Cf, PH,
Holme, Blk, L, ThH, Ff, SG,
Hotblack, Sch, X,
Huck, Gt,
Hudson,
Hutton, HTG, ThH, Sch, X,
Inman, X,
Jackson, Ff,
James, R,
Jenkinson, Bur,
J(G)erman, HTG, MH
Johnson, HodH,
Kidd, Br. Ho, Bth,
Kirkbride, Ff, SG,
Kitchen, ChH, Cf,
Kellett, D, A, L, Blk, Sch,
Kelsall, D, Bbt,
Kelty, Bur,

Kendal. PGN, Bbt,
Kilner, PG, Bth, Hol,
Knipe, CoH, Bth, Hol, PH, Bur, QMH, X,
Lancaster, GH,
Last, D,
Lawrence, A,
Leak, As, Ff,
Lesh, SG,
Lightburn, Hts
Lindow, PGN, Bth
Lishman, BrHo, BB, GH, Sch,
Long, HTG, PG, O, R, SC, ThH, Ff,
Longmire, R,
Lowd, PH,
Lucas, Hc,
Lupton, X,
Lydell, ThH
Mallinson, LTh
Manby. PG,
Mansergh. ChH,
Martin, Blk, Hts
Mason, L, Gos, Bur,
Marshall, Lb,
Matson, BB,
Matthews, PG, MA, Hol, A, BB, L, Hc, Bbt, TW, H, X,
Mattinson, BBr, SG,
Middleborough, MH,
Milburn, Hc,
Mitchell, Ff,
Moon, H,
Moore, SC,
Mounsey, Bur,
Muckelt, Ff,
Muncaster, TW,
Myers, Ff,
Myles, Lb, QMH, Sch, X,
Newby, A
Newcombe, X,
Newton, Lw, QMH,
Nicholson, As, Gt, Cf, BBr, Hc, SG,
Offley, HTG,
O'Flynn, GH
Ormandy, Bth
Otley, Hc,
Park, Lb,
Parkin. HTG,

Parkinson, BBr
Pattinson, SM,
Pearson, HTG, Sm, Hod.H, JD, Bth, B.Br, A, O, Bsd, Ff, QMH, Sch,
Pennington, Lw,
Philipson, As, Hod.H, Bbt, W, SC, Bur, Sch, X,
Phizacklea, PG, W,
Poole, O, MH, SC, TW, GH, Sch, X,
Preston, Hod.H, TW, Sg, QMH
Price, D, X,
Uthwatt, ThH,
Railton, BB,
Ransome, Lb,
Rawlinson, As, MA, PH,
Reveley, T,
Rigg, QMH,
Robinson, Sm, As, LTh, Cf, BBr, SH, Lw, Hol, L, MH, SC, TW, HH, Ff, GH, Bur, Sch,
Rockcliff, JD,
Routledge, Gt, ThH,
Rowlandson, Ff, SG,
Russell, LTh,
Sandys, Hol, Bur, X,
Scales, LTh,
Scott, Hol,
Sewart(d), Lw, Ff,
Shaw, Bur, X,
Shenton, Gt
Simpson, PH, SG, X,
Slater, OHB,
Smith, O,
Stables, ChH, Bth,
Stewardson, Lb, SC,
Stockdale, X,
Stone(s), PH, QMH,
Storey, As, HH,
Stott, T, Cf, X,
Strickland, HTG, ChH, Cf, A, Bbt, H, SC,
Suert, Bbt,
Summers, D, X,
Swainson, Sm, As, LTh, Gt, Cf, MA, Hol, Hc,R, PH, Gos, X,
Taylor, HTG, Gs, As, HodH, HH, Bth, Lb, R, TW, ThH, Ff,

GH, Bur, Sch,
Theckston, Hc, Gos,
Thompson, D, Cf, BBr,
Thornborough, As, LTh, Gt, BB, H, PH,
Tomlinson, HodH,
Tugman, H
Turner, As, Gos, Sch,
Thwaites, Gos,
Tyson, T, Ff,
Uthwatt. HTG, ThH,
Wakefield, D, Bur, QMH, X,
Walker, SM, LTh, Cf, BBr, Gos. Sch, X,
Wallas, Lb, MH,
Ward, GH,
Watson, SH , ThH,
Wayles, A,
Webber, Hts
Webster, HTG, SH, Sch,
Westgarth, W,
Whaley, HH,
White, SchH, Sch,
Wildman, HH, PH,
Wilkinson, Lb, HH, Sch, X,
Wilson, As, CoH, Bth, Bbt, QMH, HH, Sch,
Winder, Gt,
Woof, Sch,
Wright Cf, SC, TW, ThH, Gos,

KEY:

Addyfield, Ad,
Ashes, As,
Barkbooth, Bbth
Barrow Hollin, B. H
Barrow Wife, BW
Birket Houses, Bk.Ho
Blakeholme, Blk
Blewthwaite, Bth
Borderside, Bsd.
Bowland Bridge, B Br.
Bryan Beck, B.B.
Bridge House, Br Ho
Burblethwaite . Bur.
Burrow House, Brow. H.
Church, X
Cowmire Hall Co. H.
Corner Cottage, C.C.
Chapel House Ch. H.,
Danescourt, D.
Foxfield, FF.
Gateside, Gs
Gill Head, GH
Goswick Hall, Gos
Hartbarrow H
Haycote, Hc
Hare Hill, HH
Hare & Hounds H,& H
Height. Ht
Height Meeting Ho, QMH

Heightside, Hts.
Hodge Hill, Hod. H
Hollins, Hol
Joiners Shop, JS
Jumping down, JD
Little Thorphinsty, LTh
The Lound, L.
Low House Beck, LHB
Ludderburn, L.
Masons Arms, MA
Moor how, MH
Oaks, O,
Pattison How, PH
Poolgarth, PG.
Poolgarth Nook PGN.
Ravensbarrow Lodge, RL.
School, Sch.
School House, Sch H.
Silver Birch, SB
Simpson Ground. SG
Sow How. SH
Spooner Close, SC
High Tarn Green, HTG
Low Tarn Green, LTG
Thorphinsty Hall ThH
Thorneythwaite, T
Tower Wood, TW.
Wood, W